MUSSOLINI'S GHOST

MUSSOLINI'S GHOST

THE AFTERLIFE OF A DICTATOR

STEPHEN GUNDLE

OXFORD
UNIVERSITY PRESS

OXFORD
UNIVERSITY PRESS

Great Clarendon Street, Oxford, OX2 6DP,
United Kingdom

Oxford University Press is a department of the University of Oxford.
It furthers the University's objective of excellence in research, scholarship,
and education by publishing worldwide. Oxford is a registered trade mark of
Oxford University Press in the UK and in certain other countries.

Published in the United States of America by Oxford University Press
198 Madison Avenue, New York, NY 10016, United States of America

British Library Cataloguing in Publication Data
Data available

Library of Congress Control Number: 2025946164

ISBN 9780198805908

DOI: 10.1093/oso/9780198805908.001.0001

Printed and bound by
CPI Group (UK) Ltd., Croydon, CR0 4YY

MIX
Paper | Supporting
responsible forestry
FSC® C013604
FSC
www.fsc.org

The manufacturer's authorized representative in the EU for product safety is
Oxford University Press España S.A. of Parque Empresarial San Fernando de Henares,
Avenida de Castilla, 2 – 28830 Madrid (www.oup.es/en or product.safety@oup.com).
OUP España S.A. also acts as importer into Spain of products made by the manufacturer.

Preface

'Mussolini ultimo atto' (Mussolini's Final Act), a painting by the Tuscan-based artist Luciano Boccardini, evokes the final public appearance by the Fascist dictator Benito Mussolini. This was as a dead body hanging upside down from the metal roof of a petrol station in central Milan. The macabre scene occurred on 29 April 1945, when the corpse of the defeated dictator, that of his lover Claretta Petacci and those of several henchmen, all of whom had been executed the previous day, were dumped on the ground in a public square named Piazzale Loreto, where they were exposed for several hours to the general contempt of a baying crowd. As the gathering grew in size, they were appended above the petrol station so that everyone could get a view. There they remained for most of the day until they were cut down and carried to the mortuary. Although photographs of the bodies being abused on the ground and then raised high would not feature widely in the press, and film images shot by the Americans would not be seen in Italy for many years, the event was seared on public consciousness as symbolic of the final end of the man who had ruled over the country for more than twenty years. Once he had been admired abroad and adored at home but, by April 1945, he had not been popular for a long time. Finally, at the conclusion of a bloody civil war, the world was rid of the man universally known as 'Il Duce'.

The figure in Boccardini's painting (see Figure 1) only vaguely resembles Mussolini, but the knee-length riding boots and jodhpurs recall one of the dictator's preferred costumes, and the lifeless upside-down position of the corpse puts its identity beyond question. Other elements of the painting allude to aspects of Il Duce's long rule: the balcony refers to the famous one on Rome's Palazzo Venezia from which he was accustomed to harangue crowds; the water glimpsed beyond the balcony is a reference to the northern Italian lakes where the government of the puppet regime of the Italian Social Republic was based from 1943 to 1945; the red theatre curtain, a common framing device in Renaissance art, alludes to the allegedly theatrical nature of Fascism in power. The painting's title suggests that the tragedy has reached its culmination, and the show is about to end for good. The red balloon, a recurrent motif in Boccardini's oeuvre, adds a touch of playfulness to the broader picture, its clownish associations off-setting the predominantly sombre tone. It perhaps

Figure 1. 'Mussolini ultimo atto' (Mussolini's Final Act) by Luciano Boccardini (2011). By kind permission of the Fondazione Culturale 'L. Boccardini'. Photograph by Heinz Schmidt.

communicates the sense of liberation, of relief, that marked the end of the war in Italy, of which Mussolini's execution and exhibition was the epilogue. A symbol of levity and celebration, the balloon rises from an unseen crowd; its red colour indicates the role of the left-wing Resistance in bringing about the dictator's end.

The painting evokes a critical moment of national significance. Yet it is not a product of the particularly intense emotions that come with the end of a war or a civil war. Created in 2011, decades after the event, it does not capture the end of a dictator; rather, it testifies to the refusal of Mussolini to disappear into the background. The depiction of the posthumous display of the dictator's cadaver, albeit in a style that is far from realistic, suggests that this macabre event still resonates, that it is somehow a matter that has not been put to rest in the Italian national consciousness. The fact that Mussolini appears alone, without his lover or final associates, shows that the specific context of the exhibition of bodies is not the artist's concern; rather he is interested in Mussolini himself and the way the nation continues to struggle to come to terms with the legacy of his personal dictatorship. The dead dictator continues to haunt the nation that, in life, he held for so long in his charismatic thrall.

This persistence should not be surprising. Dictators have a habit of sticking around, of long outstaying their welcome. They embed themselves into the consciousness of the countries they tyrannise, attracting expressions of love and adoration that, no matter how perverse or artificial they may seem, and no matter how brutal and appalling their rule, rarely dissolve into nothing. From Napoleon onwards, many modern dictators have had long and complex afterlives; they have been evoked and their legacies mobilised for political ends. They not only occupy a place in national history, they embody their periods and determine to some degree how those periods are viewed by posterity. Yet most countries find a way to move beyond a dictator, to free themselves of the enslavement—mental and cultural even if no longer political—to which people have been subjected. Consigning a tyrant to the past is rarely an easy process. Lies diffused as truths may prove difficult to dislodge. People may be reluctant to reappraise or own up to their own devotion. Facing up to complicity and responsibility and taking a clear-sighted view may take many years and sometimes may not properly begin until a new generation appears on the scene. Even then the legacy of obfuscations and self-justifications may continue to exercise an influence. The problem in the Italian case is that, despite a postwar political system founded on anti-fascism and an official narrative that removed any aura of greatness from Mussolini, accounts with the past were not settled. A series of omissions, comforting but false assumptions and refusals to face up to home truths about Fascism held sway. To a striking and quite shocking degree, the stories that Fascism itself told about its achievements continued to circulate, with the result that the dictatorship was in some quarters given a positive gloss and, in some of its aspects at least, compared favourably to the fragmented society and crisis-ridden democratic polity of the late twentieth and early twenty-first centuries.

More than seventy years after the end of Fascism in Italy, and only a little less after the end of a war which brought devastation to the peninsula and which pitted Italians against each other in a brutal civil war, Mussolini remains a presence as memory, as image, as historical figure, as a template for strong leadership, and as an example of masculine power. He is a subject of history but also of any number of press stories, local and national controversies, and pseudo-historical polemics. Neither the creation of a democratic political system and adoption of a republican constitution nor the process of European integration and several decades of prosperity have served to eradicate the dictator from the collective consciousness or to have allowed his countrymen—even those who do not view him with any sympathy—to definitively step out of his long shadow. Indeed, in the twenty-first century, there has been a revival of Mussolini as a multifaceted signifier and icon.

This book is about how Mussolini continues to haunt Italy as the subject of innumerable evocations, memories, discussions, stories and representations. As a cultural phenomenon, Mussolini is a commercial resource, an ever-ready topic of fascination whose prominence is both perpetuated and exploited by the press, publishers and the broadcast media. Scarcely a week goes by without there being some new evocation of Mussolini, a proposal to restore some artefact of the regime or to honour the memory of one of its servants. At times, he has also been something more troubling: a reference point for supporters of authoritarian rule and of Italian racial superiority, an idol for those who, for political or other reasons, identify with the aggression and violence of the Fascist movement, and a template for vain male politicians seeking to win attention by self-promotion and aggrandisement. All this suggests that the return of Mussolini as ghost is the fruit of different dynamics and does not correspond to one design or logic. Consequently, the interpretation of the phenomenon must be capable of grasping its complexity.

Memories of Mussolini and his regime filter into the present in a variety of ways. Boccardini was born in Rome in 1937. Men and women of his generation had just begun school when the dictator was deposed. First as children, and then as adults living through the entire postwar period, they repeatedly encountered evocations of Mussolini in political debate, memoirs and media representations, not to mention reminders in the built environment and artistic works. Other generations of Italians experienced the aftermath of the Fascist regime in different ways. Those who reached adulthood between the wars had been indoctrinated with the cult of personality, while those who were small children when the regime fell had barely encountered it. Those born later experienced Fascism more clearly as a fact of the past, albeit one that still cast a shadow. All Italians, regardless of their political views or circumstances, were subjected to reminders and evocations of Mussolini by the press and the audiovisual media as well as various other material and immaterial influences. It is this layering of experience, the interplay between memory, received memory and cultural memory, that makes it difficult to pin down the place he occupies in the collective imagination. He is a fluid presence, at times a figure of the past, a black-and-white personality from history or, even vaguer, a poorly grasped strongman humanised through anecdotes and legend, while at others an intensely vivid protagonist of recent history kept at the forefront of the popular mind by the discovery or release of new documents and letters, long-running controversies, artefacts and images of one sort or another, and evocations and re-enactments in different media. Mussolini's ghost has at times monopolised the news in the way that he did when he was alive. This is not to say that the public is necessarily well informed about who Mussolini was. When the film director Damiano Damiani made a documentary for television about the bodies of Piazzale Loreto in 1980, he did a vox pop in that very square in Milan to test the degree of factual knowledge of what had taken place in April 1945. Among the young, he found that there was very widespread ignorance about the square's significance in recent Italian history.

Cultural memory works in various ways. It can be seen as a receptacle of notions and ideas about the past that form part of a received collective understanding. Although it tends to level out disputes and divisions, it can bear witness to them in a flexible narrative. It may coincide with official memories that are expressed in public rituals, commemorations and ceremonies, but it may also cut through these and form a sort of unofficial, unacknowledged counter to official versions of history. Cultural memory is receptive to impulses hailing from new sources and can, to some degree, be shaped by these. In recent times, the phenomenon of 'multidirectional' memory has complicated this picture, allowing space to a multiplicity of narratives, including some that were previously suppressed. The end of the Cold War and the demise of the dominant ways of conceiving Italian political history opened a Pandora's box and brought into view a series of previously taboo views about the past. These fed into currents of right-wing populism that were sharply critical of most of the political forces that occupied the centre and centre-left of the party system. They also impacted on the way certain practical questions were addressed. One of these is that of heritage and specifically the issue of what should be done about the many aspects of the built environment that date from, and often bear the hallmarks of, the Fascist regime. Although many symbols and representations of Fascist power were removed or concealed in the 1940s, many other monuments to Mussolini's power, ranging from the Mussolini Forum (renamed Italic Forum) in Rome to the horizontal and vertical arches of the Palace of Civilisation in the EUR district, which matched the number of letters in the dictator's first name and surname, were left intact. Throughout the peninsula, train stations, police stations, government offices and schools stood as visible reminders of the investment of the regime in infrastructures.

Mussolini sought to embed his regime in the urban fabric of Italy, as well as the hearts and minds of the people. While some of the regime's proudest buildings lay empty and disused after 1945, eventually falling into disrepair and decay, others were repurposed. In Rome, more than most places, the dictator's presence continued to be felt long after his removal from power. His balcony, stripped of Fascist decorative symbols, stood empty as a reminder of his glory days. The impression that the dictator left on the built environment was not for many years a matter of much concern. In general, a pragmatic approach prevailed with municipal authorities and government departments treating buildings as buildings rather than ideological vehicles. Beyond the odd tourist and the few who indulged in nostalgia for the regime, no one much cared if places had once been harnessed to the purposes of the dictatorship. Decorations and inscriptions were as good as invisible as far as most people were concerned. There were just a few exceptions to this. Villa Torlonia, the neoclassical villa which housed the whole Mussolini family from 1929, was for many years closed to visitors and allowed to fall into disrepair. The huge Fascist Party building in Mussolini's birthplace of Predappio, a town in the Romagna region that was the turned into a site of pilgrimage in the 1930s and filled with the sort of imposing architecture that it was deemed to deserve, was also more or less abandoned to itself.

Only when the buildings and monuments came to be seen as part of national heritage and questions were raised about their preservation did matters of ideology and history to some extent clash with pure pragmatism. To maintain or restore a building was one thing, but what if that building featured exterior decorations of an ideological nature or symbols of the regime. Should they too be restored? To maintain that they should was not necessarily a declaration of political allegiance. It also reflected a view that the material legacy of Fascism, which by general acknowledgement was not without considerable architectural—and sometimes artistic—merit, was part of a common patrimony that did not present any current threat to democracy or social order. This sort of ostensibly reasonable view was a product of a non-conflictual cultural memory of Fascism: Mussolini's regime may have been bad, but it was not evil and it was a part of contemporary Italian history. Thus, while it would have been inconceivable to restore Nazi swastikas, there was little or no harm in maintaining the pastiche Roman motifs that were Fascism's iconographic bread and butter. Such a view could only emerge from an understanding of Fascism that downplayed or wilfully ignored the death and destruction caused by its wars in Europe and Africa, the violence that marked its rise to power and the repression to which it subjected the Italian population.

This is not to say that, once the political context of Fascism was removed, all the various examples of the material culture of the regime continued to provide the sort of persuasive influence they were supposed to have in its heyday. But neither would it be entirely convincing to say that they did not conserve any of their political meaning. The neo-fascist party, the Italian Social Movement (MSI), which regularly won the support of between 5 and 8 per cent of voters between the 1950s and the 1980s, acted as the chief guardian and defender of Fascism's historical role. It regularly defended this or that monument, criticised reconfigurations of others and intervened in debates about Fascist heritage. After that party's transformation into the National Alliance in the early 1990s, its role in government in the mid-1990s, and its subsequent fragmentation and the scattering of its exponents and followers across various formations of the right, what had once been an isolated extremist voice infiltrated mainstream discourse and became indistinguishable from a more diffuse, and less historically inflected, right-wing public opinion. Contemporary Italian populists promote the restoration of Fascist street names and honour prominent figures from the period—like the aviator, minister and one-time organiser of Fascist thuggery Italo Balbo and the war criminal General Rodolfo Graziani—because to challenge the democratic consensus in this way is functional to the assertion of a new way of understanding past and present.[1]

Observers have noted a significant and steady increase over the last twenty years in the quantity not only of political references to Mussolini's personal dictatorship, but also of insidious echoes and evocations of Mussolini which are not obviously political and which relate to society's more general relationship with the past. The sheer multiplicity of the forms in which this posthumous fascination is expressed and perpetuated suggests that the dictatorship is not universally viewed in a negative way. If this is so, it can only be because there was no real reckoning with dictatorship, or working through of society's complicity with it, in the postwar years or indeed later. The phenomenon has been widely commented on in recent anti-fascist historiography. One of the most prominent critics of the failure to come to terms with the legacies of Fascism, the historian Filippo Focardi, has noted sadly that no matter how much historical work is done to overturn popular myths about the regime's merits and achievements, those myths are still widely current and seem impossible to displace.[2] This suggests that a different sort of interpretation is needed of the processes of entanglement and disentanglement of the Italians with Fascism.

It has been observed that no regime ever really ends, since traces of it can be rediscovered and reinvigorated even many decades after its demise.[3] While this is certainly true, there are ways of mitigating this and containing the potential for reinvigoration. One way is via a collective reflection and the adoption of measures to modify or eradicate the factors that contributed to the onset of dictatorship and which sustained it in power. Another way is by means of systematic education about the realities of national history. In Italy, numerous commentators in recent years have underlined the failure of critical self-examination and the connection between this and the lack of any sustained judicial ascertainment of responsibility for Fascism's crimes.[4] Instead of facing the past and accepting a proper apportionment of guilt, many social and political forces as well as individuals preferred to draw a veil over an inconvenient recent past, put the blame elsewhere, and move on. Understandable though such a reaction was, it has had consequences, some of which became fully apparent only with the rise to power in the country of right-wing populism.

In this book there will be a focus on collective psychology as a tool of explanation. The importance of this has been acknowledged by few historians of Italy. However, there was brief recourse to it after the war and it enjoyed special prominence in Germany in the first two postwar decades. The analysis I present will make repeated reference to the way the legacy of Nazism was handled in the German Federal Republic. Though the examination is not truly comparative, since the focus will remain firmly on Italy, I believe that the understanding of what did—and did not—occur after Fascism can be greatly enhanced by looking at the aftermath of Hitler's regime. Setting up a comparison inevitably raises the controversial question of whether Fascism and Nazism can be considered as variants of the same phenomenon. Many historians, including the most prominent Italian historian of Fascism Renzo De Felice, preferred to stress the differences between the two regimes. It is not among my aims to enter fully into this controversy, but it should not be overlooked that marking the distinction between Italy and Germany was one of the prime ways in which Italian commentators, even before the end of the war, sought to spare the country from the broad brush of blame with which the Allies sought to tar the belligerent Axis powers.[5] As Focardi has shown, highlighting the evils of Nazism and the fanatical devotion Hitler aroused in the Germans facilitated the spread of the idea of the 'good Italian'.[6] The Italians, in this view, were never truly Fascist or guilty of the same crimes as the Nazis. The people were not so much supporters of Fascism as victims of it.

Interpretations of this sort entail a significant dose of minimisation as far as the criminal acts of Fascism at home and abroad are concerned. They also tend to underplay the impact of Fascism on the Italian state and society and the extraordinary place that Mussolini occupied in the collective imagination for over two decades. The fascination with Fascism's figurehead spread well beyond the country's borders and found many acolytes abroad. The cult of Mussolini was the first modern personality cult. The Italian dictator forged a style of rule and established a pattern of cultish devotion that would be widely imitated by others, from Hitler, one of his first great admirers, to Peron and Ceaușescu. Under their regimes, the leaders were praised to the skies, hailed as geniuses and elevated to the status of demi-gods. Their words were treated as sacred and their images used so widely as to give a simultaneous impression of ubiquity and omniscience. Their cults shaped the education of the young and the understanding that many had of the nature of politics and of the identity of their countries. Thus the process of disentanglement was complex and challenging.

In Germany, there were also strategies of denial and avoidance of guilt. A diffuse sense of victimhood was fuelled by the suffering inflicted in the final stage of the war by the invading Russian Red Army, the experience of Allied occupation and the expulsion of ethnic Germans from Eastern Europe. However, there was a strong sense among the victorious powers not only that the Nazi leadership needed to be held to account for war crimes, but that German culture needed to change and that the people, who had been devotees of an evil tyrant, required re-education. Many German intellectuals, some of them returned exiles, took the same view. In the case of Italy, the Allies did not take the same approach. There was no Italian equivalent of the Nuremberg trials and there was no sustained commitment to re-education beyond the initial propaganda-based efforts. The trials that did take place were fragmented and not, for the most part, high profile. While a handful of Anglophone journalists, including the American Herbert Matthews, felt it would take a long time for Hitler and Mussolini to truly disappear from the consciousness of the nations they had led, most were inclined to think that the Italians, who had overthrown Mussolini on their own and had taken part in their own liberation, had rid themselves during the war of any enthusiasm that they had felt in the past for their dictator. By war's end, the much-ridiculed and belittled 'Duce' was thought to count for less than nothing. Italy was ready to return to democracy.

Despite much evidence to the contrary, the idea that the influence of dictators quickly fades after they lose power is one that is still widely held. It is doubtful if this has ever been true in the modern age, but the dictators of the first half of the twentieth century were products of the mass age, and the mass media were a crucial tool in their armoury. Thus their images continued to circulate and to serve as triggers of memory even long after their deaths. This fact required particular forms of management. The essential difference between the way the dictator's personal legacy was managed in Germany and in Italy lay at least in part in the degree to which it was acknowledged that the Führer or the Duce had cast a 'spell' that was difficult to break. In Germany, recognition of bewitchment was not universal by any means, but it formed an important way in which the Nazi era was 'worked through' in the following decades. There was an understanding of Hitler as a figment of the mass age, a leader who owed much to cinema and whose representation was central to his magic. In Italy, there was little recognition of this aspect of Fascism even many years after the fall of the regime.

Nevertheless, the Mussolini example illustrates just how complex and problematic aftermaths can be. By rights, the events of Piazzale Loreto should have passed into public memory with just one meaning, namely that the desecration of the dictator's corpse was payback for the violence that had been perpetrated in his name and with his knowledge and often encouragement. Mussolini had used his body as an instrument and as a symbol of power, subjecting Italians to endless images of his physical endeavours. It was somehow fitting that the end of his power should be marked by the gruesome exhibition of his corpse. No matter how grotesque the display, it was a cathartic moment of great significance, a primitive rite of disassociation. In fact, ever since April 1945, and despite the ignorance revealed by Damiani's documentary film, the name of Piazzale Loreto has conjured up ideas of summary justice and popular revulsion for dictatorship in Italy and beyond. On 10 December 2013, the Piazzale was invaded by over two hundred angry protestors belonging to the anti-political and arguably semi-fascistic 'Forconi' movement. Mostly composed of artisans and the self-employed, this loosely organised group staged protests throughout Italy against excessive taxation, austerity measures and the state. In this square, as in other locations, its members blocked the traffic, causing immense disruption and attracting huge publicity. The *Forconi* knew that Piazzale Loreto was a place whose very name sent shivers down the spine in a way that no other square or traffic artery did. By gathering there, they expressed their utter rejection of the political establishment that they were convinced had abandoned them and by whom they did not feel represented. Painted pictures of an upside-down corpse were agitated by Scottish supporters at an international football match between Celtic and Lazio to taunt the latter club's notoriously pro-fascist fans. An extraordinary Twitter spat took shape in 2019 after the Hollywood star Jim Carrey posted a sketch of two inverted bodies that was captioned: 'If you're wondering what fascism leads to, just ask Benito Mussolini and his mistress Claretta.' Merely publicising a photograph of the autobiography of the rightist political leader Giorgia Meloni upside down on the display shelf of a bookshop was enough to unleash an unseemly controversy around the historian Simon Levis Sullam.[7]

However, the very violence of the act of repudiation that occurred on 29 April 1945 somehow changed the perception of Mussolini from tyrant to a sort of victim. Some commentators at the time deplored the actions of the crowd in defiling and abusing the body of a man they had for many years acclaimed. The right-wing journalists Leo Longanesi and Indro Montanelli, who had once been supporters of Fascism and its leader, were so appalled that they reversed the detachment they had expressed and cast themselves in the role of posthumous defenders of the discarded Duce. Montanelli would even claim, to infuse his interventions with an authentic moral charge, that he had personally witnessed the spectacle in Piazzale Loreto, though his biographers contend that in fact he had been in Switzerland at the time.[8] He repeatedly asserted over the years that the treatment meted out by people who had in all probability once taken part in the adoring chorus was a mark of shame that did the Italians no credit. Even for anti-fascists, the event was an embarrassment; indeed, it was never turned into an acknowledged founding moment of the new democratic political system.

In this way, Piazzale Loreto played a part in the peculiar process whereby Italians, after the public repudiation of one personality cult, became subject to another, insidious and unacknowledged, posthumous one. As failed warrior and fallen demi-god, Mussolini became a figure of broken legend, a flawed human being who, despite having led his country to disaster, was deserving of sympathy and forgiveness. After once being worshipped like a deity, he was turned back into an ordinary man. As such, he was someone people could relate to, and in whom they showed curiosity as the veil of propaganda was steadily drawn back and virtually every aspect of his family life, domestic habits and personal quirks was brought into the public realm. New narratives and story lines were created revolving around his active sex life, as his long affair with Petacci (which became universal public knowledge only after his fall from power) and the testimonies of his attendants took centre stage. Mussolini had always been a celebrity of sorts and he remained so after his death.

The strange and complex process whereby Mussolini passed from being acclaimed to being reviled, before undergoing some sort of acceptance back into the national community, was not without precedents in Italian history. In the early modern period there were a number of examples of popular tribunes who seized power on the back of mob support only to lose popularity and be killed. After their deaths, they were rehabilitated and honoured. Normally, these processes lasted a few weeks or years, whereas Mussolini's was drawn out over much of the twentieth century and beyond. From the moment he was deposed in 1943, processes of denigration and re-evaluation (though not, in his case, rehabilitation in any meaningful sense) were initiated which never entirely ended and which persist.

By seeking to understand the extraordinary posthumous vitality of Mussolini, my aim is to shed light on how extremely complicated it can be to work through the legacies of dictatorship and overcome them. In countries like Britain, which have a long uninterrupted history of democratic government, it is not easy to appreciate the extent to which a dictator, even one whose popularity had declined and whose end was ignominious, can remain embedded in a national psyche. Often ridiculed and dismissed as superficial aberrations in national histories, dictators persist for decades as repositories of ideas about politics, culture and leadership. Undoing their multifaceted influence is one of the biggest challenges a democratic nation can face.

Mussolini's fall from power and the subsequent epilogue to his career as Hitler's puppet ruler of the northern-based Italian Social Republic have received extended treatment from historians. More than any other phase of his career, the final part, which was played out in the context of a deadly civil war, has been the object of obsessive interest. Until recently, relatively little attention, however, has been paid to the posthumous part of his story, to his ghostly afterlife as a figure who has haunted the republic as a fount of memory and controversy and as an imaginary presence. While his biography has been written many times and the events of his life written up in scrupulous detail, there have been very few attempts to explain why Mussolini continued to fascinate his countrymen or, indeed, why they remained obsessed with him many years after his fall from power and squalid end. This book is a biography of sorts, but not a conventional one that recounts a life and stops with the death of the subject. It is concerned with a dead person who, despite everything, continues to exercise a long-range influence as posthumous presence and as a powerful figment of memory and of the imagination.

Acknowledgements

I would first of all like to thank the members of the team with whom I worked on the AHRC project 'The Cult of the Duce: Mussolini and the Italians 1918–2005' in the early 2000s: the late Christopher Duggan, Giuliana Pieri, Simona Storchi, Vanessa Roghi, Eugene Pooley, Alessandra Antola Swan and Paola Bernasconi. The director of the Estorick Collection of Modern Italian Art, Roberta Cremoncini, was instrumental in helping us stage the project exhibition 'Against Mussolini: Art and the Fall of a Dictator' in 2006. The project produced a book and a set of three documentaries (directed by Roghi) as well as an exhibition and some spin-offs, which included Duggan's prize-winning study *Fascist Voices: An Intimate History of Mussolini's Italy*. It was a privilege to collaborate with such dedicated and committed colleagues on a project that was the first systematically to study the personality cult of Benito Mussolini.

One of my chapters in the book which took its title from our project was dedicated to the theme of the posthumous cult. That was the starting point for the present volume, which has taken a long time to complete. In the intervening years I have benefited from exchanges and conversations with many friends and scholars, including Robert Gordon, Phil Cooke, John Foot, the late Paul Ginsborg, the late Denis Mack Smith, Richard Bosworth, Albertina Vittoria, Patrizia Gabrielli, Paolo Heywood and Christian Goeschel. Many people have helped me access materials, find traces of the Mussolini cult, locate references or expand through their expertise the range of issues I was considering. It would be impossible to name everyone, but I would like to record special thanks to Dante Bolognesi (former director of the Oriani library in Ravenna), Giorgio Frassineti (former mayor of Predappio), Enrico Sturani, Sonia and Massimo Cirulli, Anna Villari, Michela De Giorgio, Patrizia Gabrielli, Sonia Orlandi, Laura Rorato, Charles Burdett, David Ward, Barbara Montesi, Samuele Animali, Giovanni Scirocco, Susanna Zinato, Alessia Zampini and Thom Winterburn. Fabrizio D'Alessio once again conducted archival research for me in Rome when I was unable to do so myself. I pay tribute here, a few months after his sudden and untimely death, not just to a precious collaboration but also to his ideas and suggestions, his conversation and his disenchanted humour, all of which I miss. Mention must be made of Lucy Riall, with whom I organised in 1997 the annual conference of the Association for the Study of Modern Italy on the theme of 'Charisma and the Cult of Personality in Modern Italy'. That conference, and the special issue we jointly edited of the journal *Modern Italy* that it gave rise to (issue 3:2, 1998), was the real starting point of my interest in this issue. One of the contributors was Marzia Marsili, who gave a paper on De Gasperi and Togliatti and went on to write a PhD on the Mussolini cult's resonances in postwar literature and film at Reading University.

It has been a privilege to be a member of the scientific committee of ATRIUM (Architecture of Totalitarian Regimes in Urban Memory), one of many cultural routes initially created under the auspices of the South-East Europe programme of the EU. For two periods of several years, I have been able to have close experience of towns and cities in and beyond Italy that have to deal on a daily basis with the legacy of Fascism or Communism in their built environments. Ulisse Tramonti, Patrick Leech and Claudia Castellucci have played an extraordinary role in bringing the issue of difficult heritage into the realms of urban policy, education and tourism. Through them and other colleagues and members of the scientific committee, my knowledge of the places of Fascism and their meanings has been greatly enriched.

A book like this cannot be written without drawing on a wide range of work by other historians, as my extensive bibliography testifies. Fascism is an immense and ever-expanding field and Mussolini is one of the great biographical subjects of the twentieth century. I hope I have done justice to the work of other scholars and researchers, or at last been respectful to them. Of all the many books and articles I have read, one of the most suggestive and useful has been Luisa Passerini's *Mussolini immaginario*, a remarkable work that was the first to explore, via the many biographies of the dictator produced up to 1939, the figure of the leader not as man and politician but as figment, idea, representation and myth. I have read that book several times and often turned to it for inspiration.

I did not present the work contained in the book to many audiences before completing it, not least due to the restrictions of the Covid pandemic. But I did deliver two guest lectures, to the British Library's Italian Studies Group and to the Oxford University History Society. These encounters provided me with opportunities to test out my ideas and receive useful feedback on them.

It is difficult to work on a long-running book without a stable physical space and a supportive affective environment. I toiled for years at home in a study that progressively became fuller and fuller, to the point that, towards the end, it was even difficult to move from door to desk without tripping over some piles of books or folders of notes. Simona Storchi was a source of critical suggestions and advice over that period, as well as a provider of emotional support. Through her own research I was able to experience some of the locations and learn about some of the artefacts that are discussed in the book. Our son Alessandro grew from child to teenager as I slowly made progress, and thanks to him I was frequently and delightfully distracted from my grim topic, though over the years Mussolini inevitably became a small part of his world too. I doubt he will forget his visits to the various Mussolini locations in Predappio and Forlì, places where it is hard to imagine many other British-raised boys have ever set foot. I owe much to them both and, if I did not demonstrate my gratitude to them as consistently and lovingly as they deserved, then I would like to state here that I could not have finished the book without them.

Leicester, June 2025

Contents

Other Books by Stephen Gundle xxiii
List of Figures xxv

Introduction: Mourning dictators 1

PART I. DECLINE AND FALL

1. The dictator and the people 19
2. Mussolini's dismissal 32
3. Divided nation 43
4. Death and damnation 56

PART II. 'OUR' MUSSOLINI

5. Getting over dictatorship 69
6. Family and nation 81
7. Anxieties of masculinity 96
8. Imaginary trials 109

PART III. MATERIAL LEGACIES

9. The fate of Duce statues 127
10. Mussolini's places 141
11. Fascist art and kitsch 156
12. Political ghost signs 171

PART IV. HISTORY AND MEMORY

13. Biography as monument 187
14. Performing the Duce 199

15. Pop culture and cultural memory 212
16. The shadow of M 226

Conclusion 240

Endnotes 245
Bibliography 291
Index 309

Other Books by Stephen Gundle

Between Hollywood and Moscow: The Italian Communists and the Challenge of Mass Culture, 1943–1991
The Glamour System (with Clino Castelli)
Bellissima: Feminine Beauty and the Idea of Italy
Mass Culture and Italian Society from Fascism to the Cold War (with David Forgacs)
Glamour: A History (OUP)
Death and the Dolce Vita: The Dark Side of Rome in the 1950s
Mussolini's Dream Factory: Film Stardom in Fascist Italy
The Cult of the Duce: Mussolini and the Italians (with Christopher Duggan, Giuliana Pieri, Simona Storchi and others)
Fame amid the Ruins: Italian Film Stardom in the Age of Neorealism

List of Figures

1. 'Mussolini ultimo atto' (Mussolini's Final Act) by Luciano Boccardini (2011). By kind permission of the Fondazione Culturale 'L. Boccardini'. Photograph by Heinz Schmidt. vi
2. Mussolini as paternal presence and as an expression of the crowd on the cover of *Gente Nostra*, magazine of the Fascist leisure organisation, October 1934. Author's own collection. 28
3. Tono Zancanaro 'W Gibbo' (Long Live Gibbo, 1943). Zancanaro drew his Gibbo figure hundreds of times between 1937 and 1943. In this example, his semi-human (note the hoof) Mussolini-style figure sits on a throne wearing only a G-String that holds several miniature female bodies. Behind him, the deformed heads looking each way allude to the dictator's omniscience. In the background can be seen the echoes of a crowd. By kind permission of the Archivio Storico Tono Zancanaro. 51
4. British soldiers inspect evidence of Mussolini's cult of personality on reaching Forlì-Predappio in October 1944. Image courtesy of the Imperial War Museums (NA 19987). 54
5. On a magazine cover of 1950 Mussolini's widow Rachele prays for her deceased husband to be 'left in peace'. Author's own collection. 89
6. Rachele Mussolini cultivated an image of simple domesticity in the postwar years. This photograph appeared in the original French edition of her volume of memoirs *Ma vie avec Benito* (1947). Author's own collection. 92
7. A postwar satirical magazine features the Christian Democrat leader De Gasperi on the right, Communist leader Togliatti in the centre and a faint shadow of Mussolini on the left. Each is deemed to have or have had a type of salute to impose on the Italians. Author's own collection. 102
8. The equestrian statue of Mussolini brandishing the sword of Islam at the moment of its inauguration in Piazza del Castello, Tripoli 1938. Courtesy of Alamy. 131
9. The boots from the Tripoli statue of Mussolini, now displayed in the museum of the Royal Electrical and Mechanical Engineers in Wiltshire. From the collection of the REME Museum. 132
10. The head of the equestrian statue of Mussolini that stood in the Littoriale sports stadium in Bologna from 1926 to 1943. The head was appropriated by loyal Fascists after the statue was attacked in July 1943 and kept by them long after the rest of the monument was turned into statues of a female and a male partisan. It was last seen at the one-time headquarters of the Historical Institute of the Italian Social Republic. Author's own photograph. 134

11. The Ponte Gardena statue (dubbed 'Mussolini on horseback' by locals) at the moment of its completion at the Battaglia Foundry. The statue, by sculptor Giorgio Gori, was originally commissioned for the Italian pavilion at the 1937 Universal Exposition in Paris. Courtesy of Archive of Fonderia Artistica Battaglia, Milan. 137

12. Mayor Giorgio Frassineti inside the abandoned Casa del Fascio in Mussolini's home town of Predappio. The mayor sought support to turn the building into a museum of Fascism, but his proposal ran into objections and did not come to fruition. Screenshot from the documentary directed by Vanessa Roghi for the AHRC project 'The Cult of the Duce: Mussolini and the Italians' that was led by the author from 2006 to 2011. Author's own image. 152

13. The so-called 'chamber of horrors' at the Rocca delle Caminate castle where Mussolini was accustomed to store craft items and artistic works of dubious merit that were sent to him as personal homages. Courtesy of the Fondi Antichi della Biblioteca Aurelio Saffi di Forlì, Sezione Mussoliniana (G L 01 917). 158

14. 'Oscuramento—il Gran Consiglio' (Darkening: The Grand Council, 1975). Detail of Fabio Mauri's art installation of the Great Council of Fascism of 1943 at which a motion critical of Mussolini was passed. Author's own photograph. 166

15. Extract from Thom Winterburn's exhibition-book *Redux: The Exhibition of Mussolini*, which revisits the display of Mussolini's cadaver in Milan in 1945. The composition inverts images of the live dictator, while keeping busts upright, to allude to the posthumous upside-down hanging that would be his final public appearance. Courtesy of Thom Winterburn. 169

16. The wall slogan that was uncovered during restoration work in the municipal register office of the town of Jesi in the Marche region in 2021. Barely legible, the slogan gave rise to controversy over what should be done about it. Author's own photograph. 172

17. A wall slogan in Piedmont in 2000, in a reasonable state of preservation. Author's own photograph. 180

18. A wall slogan in Jesi in 2023, in such a poor state of repair that it is virtually illegible. The passing of time has turned such examples of Fascist propaganda into the political equivalent of ghost signs. Author's own photograph. 181

19. Historian of Fascism Renzo De Felice debates with his British counterpart Denis Mack Smith (on television screen) in the course of their 1976 television debate. Screenshot by the author. 187

20. Rod Steiger as Mussolini and Lisa Gastoni as Claretta Petacci in Carlo Lizzani's film *Mussolini ultimo atto* (The Last Days of Mussolini, 1974). 200

21. Wax figure of Mussolini in the Rome waxworks museum. Author's own photograph. 214

22. Mussolini returns to life, thanks to the marvels of science, '...but he is black!' From the comic book fantasy *Quando c'era lui* by Stefano Antonucci, Daniele Fabbri and Mario Perrotta (Brescia: Shockdom, 2017). Illustration courtesy of Stefano Antonucci. 223

Introduction
Mourning dictators

At the end of World War II, there seemed to be little prospect of Mussolini continuing to cast his spell over the Italians. The enchantment had long since been broken and the man himself deprived of the aura of greatness with which for over two decades he had been endowed by devoted supporters. The idea that there might need to be some form of reflection on how and why large parts of society had been in thrall to him was shared by few. It was not widely felt that there needed to be a working through of an experience that was considered an unfortunate parenthesis in an otherwise positive pattern of national history. The Italians were fairly rapidly forgiven by the leading Western countries for their complicity in a regime that had deprived them of their liberty in return for a promise of order at home and enhanced power on the world stage. Despite the fact that Fascism set a template for dictatorships across Europe, there was no widespread sense that they bore any guilt for having fallen prey to the delusions of grandeur and the posturing of a megalomaniac. They had at worst been duped. A new chapter had been opened in 1945 and the people had played a part in their own liberation. For this reason, there has been little analysis of the ways in which Italians did—and did not—detach from one of the most extensive and long-lasting personality cults of the twentieth century.

This lack of interest contrasts starkly with the great attention that was shown by world opinion to the question of Germany's emergence from Nazism and the cult of Hitler. In that country it was widely assumed that there was work to do to uproot dictatorship from the fabric of society and from the mentality of the people. Germans needed to be forced to confront their guilt and face up to the evil that had been perpetrated in their name as part of their conversion to democratic values and practices. Thus, the German recovery was carefully monitored as the country emerged from the shadow of Nazism and established itself as a stable and peaceful polity, a member of the Atlantic alliance and a founder of the European Economic Community. Its economic recovery formed the basis for a drive to prosperity that was without equal in Western Europe. However, in spite of the great degree of scrutiny to which the Federal Republic was subjected and regular proclamations from German leaders, it would transpire in the 1960s that issues concerning the Nazi past had been elided rather than faced and that the cult of Hitler had been consigned too swiftly to the past rather than properly worked through and overcome.[1] Over the next three and more decades, this would become a central theme in German politics and culture, one that would engage many forces in re-examining some of the ways in which the transition from dictatorship to democracy after the war had been managed.[2]

The fact that international interest in the way Italy dealt with its past was far smaller testifies to the different view that was widely held of the two dictatorships. While Italian Fascism had been the first to achieve power, it was seen as a mild affair headed by a blusterer whose military endeavours, apart from the Ethiopian war of 1935–36, had largely been failures, Nazism was seen as an utterly evil regime that had given rise to a war machine of devastating efficiency. In exterminating the Jews, it had enacted the worst crime against humanity of the modern age. The differences between the two regimes and between the two peoples and their national characters were deliberately emphasised in the final years of the war and afterwards. Italian Catholic critics of Fascism were among the first to stress this difference, which was taken up by many others in the years that followed.[3] Nazism was seen as being in keeping with the German character while Fascism was deemed to have been out of step with the good nature of the Italians. It was largely overlooked that Mussolini had been the idol and model of Hitler, that the two countries had been allies in the Axis war, that war crimes on an industrial scale had been committed in Africa and in the Balkans by Italian Fascist soldiers, and that there had been widespread support for Mussolini and his regime. Italy was among several countries that sought to exculpate themselves by placing sole blame on the Germans for all the evils perpetrated by right-wing totalitarianism.[4]

Italian historians have recently given attention to the ways in which the legacy of Fascism was debated and negotiated in postwar Italy.[5] Several decades after the German historians' debate over the impact of the Nazi past and the singularity of the Holocaust, the delusions and self-deceptions of the transition to democracy, the alibis and processes of exculpation, the forgetting of some experiences and the selective memory of others have begun to be investigated.[6] The emphasis has fallen on the memories fostered by either side in the civil war, the lack of an Italian equivalent of the Nuremberg trials or the Tokyo war crimes trial, the rose-tinting of the Italian colonial experience, the failures of the postwar purge, and the wide application of an amnesty that was adopted as part of a hasty process of national pacification.[7] Perhaps because of the long-standing conviction, sustained by the Allies during the war for propaganda reasons, that Mussolini was responsible for everything, recent historiography has not focused on the dictator himself or on his personality cult. Instead, it has sought to explore the way wider groups—ex-Fascists, the military, the state elite or the Italians as a whole—escaped being held to account for their roles during the regime.[8] The fixation with the dictator's biography—that began soon after Fascism came to power and which persisted in postwar publishing—also contributed to this reaction against what was perceived to be an over-concentration on the person of Mussolini. But by shifting the focus from the dictator there is a risk of not fully grasping the complex processes by which people became entangled in the cult of personality and therefore the extent of the challenge posed by disentanglement.

This book seeks to bring Mussolini back into the centre of the picture. It is concerned with the ways in which the dictator's cult resonated in the decades after the war, with the manner in which Mussolini's image continued to carry meaning and to give rise to debates, discussions and revisitations. It will argue that overcoming 'Il Duce' was challenging at a number of levels. Not only had he ruled the country for more than twenty years, but he had also shaped national identity and been identified with many of the innovations of the twentieth century including aviation and the mass media. For these and other reasons the process of untangling from Mussolini was far more complex than Italy's postwar leaders ever imagined and in some respects more complex that the detachment from Fascism itself.

The analysis presented here follows a course of inquiry begun in Germany in the 1960s and 1970s which sought to expose the mechanisms by which Germans had failed to properly overcome Hitler or to acknowledge the importance he had held for them. It will employ tools of analysis developed in that context which, with certain adjustments, may also be applied to Italy to illuminate some unacknowledged aspects of the reconstruction and the political and cultural life of the republic. In 1967, two psychoanalysts, Alexander and Marguerite Mitscherlich, published a psychological study of Germany after Nazism that was entitled *Die Unfähigkeit zu trauern* (The Inability to Mourn). The book examined the way Germans dealt with the detachment from the Hitler regime following war defeat and Allied occupation.[9] The authors concluded that patients who were suffering from neuroses of various sorts had problems that were caused by the psychological ramifications of the manner in which the country had transitioned from dictatorship to the postwar democratic order. The Germans, they argued, had not undergone any process of self-examination or reflection. The question of how people fell under the spell of the Nazis had not been faced and there had been no assumption of responsibility for the barbarous acts in which many had been complicit and even actively participated. Therefore, the return to democracy had been passive. The Allies were embraced as the new authority in 1945 and in the following years the reconstructed economy quickly became the focus of collective life. Economic success blanketed over the nation's wounds and ostensibly made it unnecessary to look back or face up to guilt for the horrendous crimes of the Nazis. The whole period—which had seen the German people embrace 'a dream, the dream of belonging to a master race unhampered by conscience'—was in this process 'de-realised', that is to say an era that had been 'exalted and deified' came to be perceived as something remote and unreal.[10] This, the Mitscherlichs argued, was a dissociative mechanism, a means whereby people separated themselves from a regime that was tainted with evil. The Germans adopted a series of defence mechanisms in order to avoid falling into a state of mass melancholy after learning that their idolised leader was an evil monster.[11] This meant that certain issues were not faced, that the 'work of mourning' was never undertaken and that distortions in the collective consciousness led to a diffuse apathy in civic life. In Freudian theory, which provided the framework for the Mitscherlichs' analysis, the loss of a love object (which may be personal or abstract) provokes feelings that can only be overcome if they are acknowledged and worked through.[12] Without this process, there can be no return to normality via acceptance of the reality of an absence and there can be no new meaningful attachment.

In the Mitscherlichs' interpretation, Hitler was the embodiment the Germans' ego-ideal.[13] He was a narcissistic love object who was not loved for himself but for the enrichment and imaginative fulfilment that he offered every German through the Nazi vision of grandeur and racial purity. The loss of a leader whose authority had never been doubted and in whom much libidinal energy had been invested was a massive blow. Only a minority sought, against the main current of public opinion, to discuss issues of guilt and repentance, to raise their fellow citizens from their 'sub-moral state'. Instead of facing up to crimes, much effort went into elaborating accounts of the suffering of the German people, the sacrifice of German soldiers, the sadism of the Allies in bombing German cities and so on, as a self-serving means of side-stepping blame.[14] 'Hitler has not yet been beheaded, either literally or figuratively', the Mitscherlichs asserted provocatively.[15] As a rejected object of narcissistic love, he had simply disappeared 'almost without trace'. The Hitler era, to express it another way, did not end in 1945, and it had still not ended in 1967, when *The Inability to Mourn* was published, because there had not yet been full cognisance of it. It was a past that refused to go away because it had not been dealt with and this meant that 'old ideals...[continued] to operate within the unconscious' with the inevitable risk of resurgence.[16]

In the decades that followed, the Germans attempted to work through the past. The situation of the 1960s would soon change as members of the successor generation began to pose questions to their parents and public opinion became more receptive to debate. The matter was of intense interest to international public opinion, which remained as sensitive to Germany's treatment of its Nazi past as it was when the Mitscherlichs were writing. Over time, the way the country faced up to its guilt won praise and even came to be seen by some observers as a model for other countries that had to deal with difficult legacies even from the distant past.[17] However, studies of official German treatments of the memory of the Nazi era and the Holocaust suggest that these remained highly sensitive matters.[18]

Italy's 'working through' or otherwise of its Fascist past commanded less attention abroad, but it was nonetheless a matter that was fraught with challenges and which in many respects still remains open. Despite having contributed to their own liberation and not being subject to the moral isolation of postwar Germany, the Italians' reaction to the heritage of dictatorship was partial and problematic. Just as with Germany, denial and de-realisation came into play. When foreign historians challenged the country, as Christopher Duggan did in 2013 when he argued that Italy still needed to reckon with its Fascist past, or when Ruth Ben-Ghiat asked in 2017 why so many Fascist monuments were still standing, they were met with hostile responses.[19] In some ways, the Italian trajectory has been the opposite of the German one. In Germany, across fields ranging from official declarations and symbolic acts of remembrance to the visual arts and education, there has been an extensive facing up to the crimes of the Nazi era. In Italy, with the exception of critical minorities, there has been little of the same self-reflexive engagement with the responsibilities of ordinary Italians, with the evils of the regime and the violence it inflicted on its many domestic and foreign victims, or its long-term impact on political culture and social relations. If anything, over the years Fascism has come to occupy a more diffuse and less controversial place in many views of the national past. The moral and political discriminant of anti-fascism began to lose force in the 1980s and was significantly undermined by the inclusion of the transformed neo-fascist party in government in 1994. Gradually and across several spheres, artefacts, people and memories that had once been covered in ignominy underwent a measure of rehabilitation, albeit never without some contestation.

This book begins from the premise that the analytical framework of the Mitscherlichs might help explain the persistence of Mussolini in Italian discourse and cultural memory.[20] Inevitably, some will immediately object that the differences between Italy and Germany are too great to permit such a transfer of analytical tools, even with appropriate modification. It may be argued that the Italians did not remain tied to their dictator until the very end and indeed perhaps never had been as devoted followers as the Germans. This was a view that was widely held after the war. It was a dogma in a significant part of public opinion that the Italians had never really been Fascist; they had not believed in Mussolini, who had achieved and maintained power through violence and repression. At the first opportunity they had risen up and had contributed to the restoration of democracy. They had no need therefore to work through the sense of a loss or to elaborate their mourning for a love-object that never was in order to be able fully to embrace democratic political culture.

The collective psychological approach has not been widely adopted in historical studies.[21] While some prominent historians have explored the possible contribution of psychoanalysis to cultural history, the encounter has never gained universal acceptance.[22] Even in the period of psychoanalysis's greatest popularity in the humanities, it was embraced more readily by literary and film scholars than by historians. Freud's own theories have in the meantime been critically reviewed and widely debunked within the field of psychology.[23] Despite this, over the years a few historians have sought to explore the collective state of mind of the Italians in the aftermath of Fascism.[24] Problems of the collective psychology of the post-fascist period were brought into the clearest focus by Filippo Focardi's influential study of the tropes of the 'evil German' and the 'good Italian' which explored a diffuse mechanism of collective exculpation.[25] Taking a cue from this study, two special issues of the psychoanalytical journal *Educazione sentimentale*, published consecutively in 2017, raised the question of whether the Italians had come to terms with a historical experience 'whose traces, legacies and inheritance continue to weigh on our present on account of their not having been properly recognised and elaborated'.[26] Among the articles was a reprint of a significant article from 1961 by the eminent psychoanalyst Cesare Musatti entitled 'The individual super-ego and the collective super-ego' which addressed some of the very issues with which the Mitscherlichs had engaged.

The Mitscherlichs' method takes us back to Mussolini and to the relationship of the Italians with the dictator. To what extent was there any meaningful mourning of the Duce? Are recent controversies in any way traceable to a failure to mourn? For Freud, mourning was a process that followed either the loss of a loved one or of an idea, examples of which he gave as 'the fatherland, liberty, an ideal, and so forth'.[27] Leaders like Hitler and Mussolini were at once men and symbols; they had a human dimension, but they were also closely bound up with ideologies. Their deaths coincided with the defeat of a set of political ideas, with the end of the concept of fatherland that they had championed, and with the dissolution of the imagined community into which they had drawn their fellow citizens. Precisely for this reason, the processes of working through and the transition to a new order were complex and problematic, so much so that shortcuts, deviations and repressions were perhaps inevitable. It is legitimate to place Mussolini at the centre of any analysis of transitional practices because of the pivotal place he occupied in the power system of the regime and the pattern of consensus it forged. The cult of the Duce was arguably the most potent tool in the Fascist armoury because of the popularity of Mussolini and success with which intense adulation was orchestrated and maintained. Indeed, so successful was it for a period that it gave rise to what prominent historian Emilio Gentile has termed 'totalitarian Caesarism'.[28] A distortion within Fascism, this entailed the sucking up of all power and energy into one figure who ceased to be a rational leader and instead became a demigod who was seen as infallible.

If we are to assess the practices that follow the loss of a modern dictator like Mussolini, we need to have in mind some idea of what the mourning of a prominent and highly symbolic political figure might look like.[29] Studies of the mourning of leaders are few, but there is a major one of Abraham Lincoln.[30] President Lincoln is universally seen as a good leader rather than a toxic one but, at the time of his assassination in 1865, he was divisive figure who, despite his efforts to heal a nation ravaged by a recent civil war, was widely despised by opponents.[31] Nonetheless, there was an extensive emotional response to Lincoln's sudden and unexpected death that impinged on everyday life and which was articulated in rituals, beginning with his highly choreographed Washington funeral and many local funeral services. He was widely, if inaccurately, regarded as the last casualty of the civil war. At a time when many were still suffering from personal bereavements, mourning the lost president was a way of working through different losses. The highly sentimentalised forms of a public grief were sustained by religious practices and cultural ideals.

There are some aspects of the Lincoln mourning that can be applied to Mussolini. Among these are the division of opinion around him and the connection to a very recent civil war. Significant too is the role of the surviving family and a grieving widow who would suffer lifelong trauma. The appeal of relics and the desire somehow to fashion a continued existence in people's hearts—albeit on a much smaller and sectoral scale in Mussolini's case—can also be seen as shared. People had felt a strong attachment to Lincoln and this blurred the boundaries between leader and loved one.[32] His sudden removal from the scene created a gap, a symbolic hole, that necessitated thinking out the aftermath. In Italy, the process of rethinking and rebuilding the nation without Fascism was already underway, and indeed had been since Mussolini's overthrow in 1943, but while the political process had begun, the more complex cultural and psychological challenge of moving beyond dictatorship had not. The removal of a dictator who had systematically muddied boundaries and widely been the object of love was challenging because he had held power outside of a democratic institutional context. Democratic leaders, who would always be succeeded by another, did not customarily command such a level of affective involvement.[33]

Mussolini of course was on the losing side in Italy's civil war and public opinion had already turned decisively against him by the time of his death. He was not assassinated like Lincoln but executed on the orders of the National Liberation Committee, an authority whose legitimacy was solid if not universally accepted. Because his death coincided with the end of the war and the final defeat of dictatorship, the prevailing narrative was not one of grief but of inevitability and of justice done. Mussolini's political demise in 1943 had not provoked widespread expressions of dismay; the response to his physical death was even more muted. Such mourning as there was, was elaborated in ways that were not general, public or official. To speak of an 'inability to mourn', or of a failure to undertake the sort of mourning work that would have allowed for the former adoration of the dictator to be processed and constructively overcome may, for these reasons, seem provocative.

The murder of Lincoln occurred in a context in which few people had seen him with their own eyes and even his photographic image was not widely known.[34] Only several decades later would commemorative statues and biographical films make his features generally recognisable. Twentieth-century political leaders operated in a completely different media environment. They featured widely illustrated magazines and newsreels. In some cases a vast stock of moving and still images would turn them into the best-known and most recognisable people in the world. Thus for them death entailed a removal, a loss, but not necessarily the risk of disappearance from the visual realm. Death curtailed the production of new photographic images but not the circulation of old ones.

The question of how images, and other media evocations and re-enactments of Mussolini, would trigger, interact with, or impede acts of mourning, or simply perpetuate a media presence that was well-established, while transforming (or not) its meaning, is a complex one. Precisely because he was the prototype modern dictator, Mussolini was a personality as well as a political leader: a star of the political scene.[35] Unlike many democratic politicians, he was the object of intense interest and identification on the part of followers. For this reason, any discussion of his posthumous existence needs to take account of the sort of responses that the death of a star occasions and of the way some stars linger in the collective consciousness.

Studies of the mourning of figures from the entertainment world are no more common than those of political leaders, but an interesting analysis by Anthony Elliott of responses to the murder of John Lennon in 1980 may offer some useful insights. In contrast to Lincoln, whose supporters made great efforts to ensure that he was remembered, there was no risk of Lennon disappearing. On account of his various facets and roles, from musician to poet, peace activist to avantgarde artist, he was both championed and denigrated, idealised and dismissed. His murder provoked an outpouring of grief on a grand scale that extended across the globe. The media fuelled this and fed off it, supplying endless photographs, features, interviews, and tributes. Lennon's sudden and barely comprehensible removal posed an issue of negotiation, a 'difficult problem that would not go away', Elliott asserts.[36] His death was a media event that gave rise to a renewed demand for his music from different periods of his artistic life. In this sense he continued to inhabit the universe of contemporary culture, even participating posthumously, via unreleased recorded songs and the manipulation of archive footage, in a long-desired but frequently deferred Beatles reunion.

Despite the semblance of a working-through process, Elliott argues that Lennon was not properly mourned. This was due in part to the far-reaching cultural changes of the 1960s of which he was such a central part. The rise of mass consumption undermined tradition and social hierarchies leading to a new understanding of the connection between personal and community life.[37] 'The sense of loss provoked by his death was exacerbated', Elliott argues, 'by the repression of death in contemporary culture'.[38] Thus public mourning did not so much signal a coming to terms with the pain of loss but a denial of it, a desperate, impossible bid to retain Lennon among the living instead of letting go. Basing himself on French historian Philippe Ariès' insight into the concealment of death and the treatment of it as scandalous and abhorrent in modern society, he argues that Lennon's death was trivialised and turned into an object of mass consumption. Denial and rationalisation were the key psychological mechanisms at work here, as they were in earlier deaths of prominent popular cultural figures including Marilyn Monroe and Elvis Presley. The difficult emotional labour involved in mourning, in coming to terms with the void left by his sudden and violent removal, was frustrated at a cultural level by the perpetuation of his presence in the media, by the denial of loss through commodification.

Mussolini—whose life ended in 1945—would seem to have little to do with this, but it may be argued that, in a national rather than an international ambit, his death, having been unmourned in the postwar years, was followed by trivialisation and exploitation in subsequent decades. The lack of mourning reflected a refusal to acknowledge and work through the deep attachment to him, while trivialisation came about because he had not passed culturally into the realm of the dead. The place he occupied in the collective imaginary derived not from the persistence of the political culture which had spawned and sustained him, but from the formative place he occupied in the nation's mass consciousness. In this respect, he can be likened to one of the 'strange angels' that cultural commentator Andy Bull discusses in his exploration of the posthumous place occupied in the Western imagination by Monroe, Presley, James Dean and John F. Kennedy.[39]

Mussolini, the Fascist dictator, does not sit easily in the company of contemporary cultural icons. However, after Garibaldi, he was the first Italian political leader to register in international and national consciousness as a presence with a recognisable physiognomy and persona that had an impact beyond politics. He was seen and heard by millions of people, both in person and through mass communications. To some extent therefore it can be said that he became a permanent feature of the mediatic repertoire of the nation and was undoubtedly a political icon.[40] He was a protagonist on the world stage in a way that postwar leaders were not. Although, unlike Bull's strange angels, he did not die at the peak of his career or as a young man, his life was abruptly curtailed. Moreover, his memory was coloured by that fact that the collective enthusiasms of his times were more universally shared than almost any political moment in the polarised polity of the postwar republic. In later years, the Fascist period came to be seen by some as a simpler, happier time than the postwar decades, despite the prosperity that came in the 1960s. Such an image may be false, but the fact of its existence helps explain how a dictator who led his country to catastrophe still preserves a residual capacity to cast a spell over seventy years after his demise.

This observation points to the need to review the approach taken by the historian Sergio Luzzatto in his 1997 book *Il corpo del duce* (published in the USA under the title *The Body of Il Duce: Mussolini's Corpse and the Fortunes of Italy*), which constitutes the only important treatment to date of Mussolini's posthumous existence.[41] Luzzatto explores the relationship Italians had with Mussolini's much-displayed body while he was alive and the complex trajectory of his corpse before it was finally buried in his birthplace of Predappio in 1957.[42] The book was the first to tackle the issue of the particular resonance and legacy of the Fascist leader, although it did so from a very specific, if unquestionably important, point of view, that of the dictator's body. My concern is less with the physical Mussolini, whether alive or dead, than with his ghost, that is to say a series of disembodied echoes, resonances, memories and shadows. These reverberations were present in the postwar years, though they were often contained by a strong sense that the dictator belonged firmly to the past. They became more diffuse and insidious as the generations with historical memory of Fascism and its leader aged and died. More than direct knowledge, it is received information, fantasies, impressions and figments of collective memory that have shaped debates and understandings of Mussolini. These are interwoven with, and stimulated by, material and visual culture.

To establish a basis for analysing this phenomenon, a sense of the body different to that which Luzzatto employed is required. Some modifications to Polish-born German historian Ernst Kantorowicz's famous idea of the king's two bodies can be of assistance in achieving this. In his interpretation, medieval kings had, like everyone else, a 'body natural' but at the same time they stood for the 'body politic'.[43] This idea has been revised by Burkhard Schnepel, a historical anthropologist who has studied royal effigies in Renaissance France. He has argued that the effigy acted as a third body that bridged the other two bodies, particularly in the period between a king's death and the enthronement of a successor.[44] Its purpose was to suggest continuity at a time when the perishability of the monarch's natural body was prominent in the collective mind. It rested on the idea that a representation could contain elements of both the physical and the political. This third, represented, body was developed greatly by Louis XIV, the first monarch of the modern era to construct a cultish presence by projecting himself as an infallible sun king and demanding that triumphal arches, statues, busts, paintings and medals were distributed throughout his realm to ensure he was glorified by his subjects.[45]

It may be argued that modern dictators (of the 'totalitarian' rather than the 'tin pot' variety) also had three bodies.[46] They possessed a corporeal being and they had a personal political authority that blended them with the body politic of the state. But they also had a complex representational system that extended the presence of their likeness far and wide. Modern media, including cinema, radio and the mass production of printed materials and objects, permitted an exponential increase in the quantity of these representations and artefacts.[47] The third body of the dictator consisted of all these instances as well as the rituals of the personality cult. In most contexts, the images, whether unique or mass produced, were taken to possess something of the dictator himself and any offence against them was severely punished. However, we can go further. To the third body may be added a fourth, consisting of metaphorical rather than literal images of the person of the dictator. Mussolini was written about widely, for example in school textbooks and the exercise books of schoolchildren, his sayings were transformed into wall writings and his ways of speaking and gesticulating were so widely known that the merest hint was sufficient to evoke him. The capital letter M referred to no one else. These were all manifestations of strong encouragements to think of the dictator and his ideas as a constant dynamic presence.[48] The fourth body was—to different degrees—an effect of the other bodies and was largely a figment of collective psychology. It consisted of a mixture of triggers and responses that together testified to the strength of the personal identification with Mussolini that obtained during the heyday of the regime.

The first three bodies are conventionally seen in the contemporary age as time-bound: the physical body decays and dies, the authority wanes or collapses, and the images for the most part end up on the scrapheap, in the hands of collectors or in media archives. The fourth is essentially temporary anyway, having little sense beyond the rule of the dictator. But each may also have an afterlife. The dead body, the physical remains, may retain political value though embalmment or, more commonly, burial sites and funerary monuments. The body politic persists in imprints on the state, that is, in institutions created or moulded by dictatorships which continue to exist even in the context of regime change. The third body, however, which may be termed the mediatic or mediated body, is not marked as posthumous or 'post' in the same way.[49] It continues to exist and evolve even long after the death of a ruler or the end of a regime. Though it may contain nagging reminders of the past-ness of a physical existence, it is a rich corpus which can persist, be re-proposed or reinvented in new contexts, or through new media, and which can be added to in multiple ways. As long as there is an imaginary charge, which derives its initial impulse from the role and the achievements in life of the dictator, devotees and denigrators alike will continue to revisit and rework his representational legacy. Life and afterlife, which may be easy to distinguish in the case of the first two bodies, are not so easy to separate in the case of the mediatic body. The third body is transhistorical and may also be transnational. The fourth body persists insofar as there is a psychological tie to the dictator. Such a tie may be denied or even publicly severed but, unless there is a process of detachment involving a working through of the previous identification, it cannot be said to have been overcome. In the absence of a working through, the dictator will continue to figure in unacknowledged ways in collective or cultural memory.

In recent years, there has been growing interest in the ways in which the past inhabits the present. The idea of linear historical progression has been queried from different viewpoints, leading to a more complex view of temporality. In their discussion of time, French theorists Michel Serres and Bruno Latour have suggested that time filters, that is to say its flow is better thought of in vertical rather than horizontal terms.[50] According to Serres, 'time can be schematised by a crumpling, a multiple, foldable diversity', giving it some of the qualities of a 'crumpled handkerchief'.[51] As a spatially foldable phenomenon, time loses its conventional specificity: what is near and what is far is subject to change, and the past can never be scythed off from present and future. The notion of the past trickling into the present has been taken up by the historian of theatre, Joseph Roach, who has argued for what he terms 'the deep eighteenth century', that is to say an eighteenth century that is still with us, that 'isn't over yet'.[52] By this, he means that many of the phenomena that were central in that century, including slavery, colonialism and modern celebrity, persist in our time as themselves and as their consequences.

The idea of 'deep fascism' is not new. In the decades following the end of the war, the view was often advanced, especially on the left, that Fascism had not been expunged from the Italian state or society. The Communists talked of Christian Democratic rule as a 'new fascism' and, in the 1960s and 1970s, protestors targeted institutions including schools and universities which were deemed to operate in ways that had not changed since the time of Mussolini.

Such views appeared to find confirmation in the complicity between the intelligence services and neo-fascist terrorists during the period of the so-called 'strategy of tension' that was aimed at de-stabilising democracy. This book considers the way in which fantasies and memories of Mussolini informed these concerns as well as the actions of those who retained some sort of declared or undeclared attachment to the man and his regime. It also takes the discussion well beyond the first postwar decades to examine the ways in which figments of collective memory shape debates and understandings of Mussolini. The political and cultural landscape of Italy today bears little resemblance to that of the postwar years. Following the end of the Cold War, the media-mogul-turned-politician Silvio Berlusconi served long terms as prime minister, during which the anti-fascist consensus of earlier years was significantly eroded. Forces and individuals with an investment in the memory of Fascism moved from the margins to the centre of the political stage.[53] Populist politicians, moreover, have understood that cultural battles over the legacies of Fascism have contemporary value. To rehabilitate a figure from the 1930s, to restore a building with Fascist associations and inscriptions, to replace the name of a park or a road with the one it was given under the regime, to laud an achievement from that time, all stir up controversy and create a climate in which authoritarianism gains currency and democratic political culture is weakened.[54]

Despite the suffering that Mussolini inflicted on his people, and those of the lands that the Fascists invaded and brutalised, attitudes flourish that are appreciative of the dictator's achievements in bringing the national community together, promoting public health, imposing order, developing sport and leisure, and introducing what for many was their first taste of prosperity. These convictions, entirely divorced from historical reality, derive from fascist propaganda and persist because of the lack of any serious national reckoning with Fascism after the war or any sustained effort to purge its consequences and re-educate the population.[55] Berlusconi was just the most prominent figure to voice the entirely erroneous opinion that 'Mussolini never killed anyone'.[56] He also dubbed the internal exile to which dissenters were sentenced a holiday and even argued that the man who overthrew democracy was in fact a believer in it. Against this background, it is scarcely surprising that Mussolini has continued to work his influence on later generations, cropping up not only in the pages of history books but in the representations of popular culture, the chants of football supporters and decontextualised evocations of his trademark gestures and attitudes.

Various factors need to be considered in seeking to explain all this. A key element of the cult of personality was the belief that the dictator could do no wrong—a belief that dated back to his rule and which was reinforced by propaganda.[57] Many did not blame him for the failings of Fascism and instead made his collaborators and underlings the object of their disapproval. No matter how improbable it may seem, the tendency continued in the postwar years and fed directly into a barely disguised current of nostalgia. The Mussolini family was significant in shaping public perceptions. The Duce's widow Rachele became a public figure and, with time, so did his surviving four children and a handful of his grandchildren. In their own way, they testified to the normality of Mussolini, a man and an Italian who was in the final analysis like all others, a husband and father to living people rather than just the son of dead ones. In addition, it should not be overlooked that Mussolini remains the best-known Italian of the twentieth century. He is a figure who, in both life and afterlife, has taken on representative or 'typical' qualities. The circulation of his image has only served to enhance this. It is inevitable therefore that certain discourses, such as those revolving around the question of national character, which came to the fore once more in the early twenty-first century, always seem to return to him.[58]

* * *

This book is divided into four parts. The first part is concerned with the establishment and impact of the personality cult, with its decline and transformation between 1943 and 1945, and with the death of the dictator. The second part explores the way in which Italians dealt with the aftermath of the cult of the dictator and responded to its various legacies. The third part addresses the fate of monuments and places that were associated with the dictator, residues of dictatorship in material culture and wall writings. The final part explores the way the dictator has been and continues to be discussed, depicted, transfigured and memorialised in contemporary culture.

PART I

Decline and fall

I

The dictator and the people

Reflecting in 1983 on the impact that Mussolini had had on him as a boy and young man, the novelist Italo Calvino recalled that 'you might say that the first twenty years of my life were spent looking at Mussolini's face, since his portrait was hung in every classroom, as it was in every office and public establishment'.[1] Born in 1923, Calvino was just old enough remember the clean-shaven Mussolini dressed in formal civilian wear whose image communicated 'modernity, efficiency, tranquilizing continuity—all of it with an authoritarian severity'. He recalled the pensive attitude of official portraits and the turning point that saw the dictator mainly present himself in uniform. He could remember that young children used to be asked to 'make a Mussolini face' and that, in response to this invitation, a child would 'adopt a stern look and stick out his lips aggressively'. 'In short', he observed, 'Italians of my generation were starting to carry around the portrait of Mussolini inside themselves, even before they knew enough to identify it from the walls'.

What Calvino was evoking was the process whereby Mussolini became a part of the imaginative world of every Italian and of the mental make-up of the young. The dictator was an unavoidable, continuous presence for most of the twenty years of the Fascist regime. His image was almost inescapable, his special qualities were constantly highlighted, every success was attributed to him, and his authority was hailed as unimpeachable. As a consequence, the population was made to feel not only that its destiny was bound up with the leader, and that its fortune was dependent upon his unique genius, but that each individual was somehow only completed and fulfilled by identification with the shared idol.

Historians of Italian Fascism have not generally pursued a psychological or psychoanalytical approach to the study of the popular worship of the Duce. When the most important historian of Fascism, Renzo De Felice, refers to the psychological, as he often does, he is almost always talking about Mussolini's individual psychology.[2] There are just a few hints of interest in social psychology.

In his volume *Mussolini il fascista* (Mussolini the fascist), he refers to an ability to inspire faith in a wide variety of people as being important in laying 'the psychological bases of that myth of Mussolini that would be one of the most typical components of the future fascist regime'.[3] He also highlights his hypnotic and emotive impact and the 'psychological subordination' of his close collaborators.[4] Despite the rarity, at least until recently, of psychological interpretations of the leader–mass relationship in Italy, there has long been an awareness that Mussolini was not simply a remote figure who inhabited the mysterious chambers of power but a man who was widely felt to be familiar, who people thought they could address with their problems and concerns and who they wanted to draw as much as possible into their lives.[5]

Mussolini was a new type of leader. He was the prototype of the modern dictator, a politician who responded to the challenges of the era of democracy in a way that conventional leaders could not. The widening of the political sphere unsettled elites who were searching desperately for ways of keeping control in an unfamiliar context. The crowd theorists Gustave Le Bon and Gabriel Tarde highlighted the need for charismatic statesmen capable of dominating the mass of people. The crowd, they separately argued, was a passive entity, with a psychology of its own, that was rarely rational and that was subject to easy manipulation ('crowds are as incapable of willing as of thinking for any length of time', Le Bon stated).[6] Impressed by powerful images and legends, it was forever in search of a master.[7] Those who exercised a fascination over others—men who, through their actions, acquired prestige (a factor that Tarde especially considered to be important)—were particularly able to take on this role. The model leader, it was thought, should be a modern version of Caesar, a figure of authority external to institutionalised power capable of instilling fear as well as admiration.[8]

Charismatic leaders did not appear routinely. They only emerged in moments of crisis and disruption in which large numbers of people, especially of a conservative disposition, were drawn unconsciously to seek out someone with the capacity to shape events, someone who could bring an end to disorder and guide a whole society back towards what was regarded as its proper purpose.[9] They came to the fore, in other words, at moments in which there was a break in the existing order of society and older forms of leadership had failed. Mussolini conformed to this type. He was a left-wing firebrand who had cut his political teeth in the central Romagna region and who had been propelled by the extraordinary circumstances of Italy's entry into World War I and the social conflicts of its aftermath into a position of national leadership. Unlike

Hitler or Lenin, whose charisma emerged within a single political movement, he possessed a personal charisma that was a powerful force of attraction across the political divide. The fact that this rose and declined several times and in different contexts alone shows that it had a foundational force. In Freud's view, the crowd did not bow—as Tarde and Le Bon argued—to any dominating figure. Rather it was a fixture or structure that filled the gap in its centre 'with the founding figure of the leader', a sort of substitute father whose character had to sit well with that of the group.[10]

Italy's democratic institutions were a product of the liberal tradition of the Risorgimento. But Italian culture had also demonstrated a susceptibility to the appeals of strong leadership.[11] Garibaldi had captured the imagination of wide swathes of the country, and one of his early followers, Francesco Crispi, had as prime minister in the late 1880s and early 1890s constructed an image of forceful leadership that had been linked to a bid to turn Italy into a colonial power. By World War I, nationalist intellectuals had for years been urging the regeneration of the nation and cultivating yearnings for a chief who was at one with the spirit and destiny of the nation. For a period, the warrior poet Gabriele D'Annunzio was seen as the most credible bearer of this project.[12] However, by 1922, it was Mussolini who was endowed with the aura of a messiah by right-wing groups. As a politician who had migrated from the far left to the right, he offered the hope that the threat of left-wing revolution could be quashed once and for all following a period of social turbulence in which Fascist violence and intimidation had all but crushed the workers' and peasants' movements of northern and central Italy.

When Mussolini became prime minister in 1922, he perhaps did not at first seem all that different. He presented himself in full institutional mode and even donned the traditional ceremonial uniform of president of the council of ministers. But he distanced himself from the elitist practices of Italy's liberal leaders in key ways as he reached out to the mass of Italians.[13] He immediately made more of a connection with the population of the peninsula than any previous head of government by visiting the country's various regions.[14] Over time, the tours became an important institution of his ever more personalised rule. They were carefully organised and planned to include a wide variety of meetings with officials and the people, visits to institutions and workplaces, speeches to mass rallies, and inaugurations of buildings. The encounters of the chief or Duce with the masses were important rituals, occasions when the leader blended emotionally with the crowd and became the interpreter of the collective will. Journeys were lengthy and articulated, sometimes lasting over a week and involving short stops in numerous towns and cities where Mussolini bestowed personal largesse. Preparation for them was meticulous. Mussolini usually spoke in town squares which had long traditions as centres of civic sociability, taking up a custom favoured by Garibaldi, by the Socialists and by the Church.[15] This community-building exercise, which connected the local to the national, was part of the broader Fascist aim of reinforcing and extending patriotic feeling and a sense of belonging to a newly invigorated nation.

Mussolini's uniqueness was demonstrated by the spate of biographies that appeared from the early 1920s. These were an active part of the process whereby he was built up as a figure of unusual significance. One of the earliest biographies, by Alberto Beltramelli, was published in 1923 and significantly was entitled *L'uomo nuovo* (The new man). It stressed the fact that the subject originated from the Romagna region, which was described as a 'unique land of effort and of battle, of joy and of violence, of dramatic loves and hatreds, of formidable apathies and activities'.[16] Among the qualities the author—who himself hailed from Romagna—identified with the 'robust race' of the region were simplicity, goodness and spirit of sacrifice. Another biography, authored by Mussolini's advisor, confidante and lover Margherita Sarfatti, was especially important. Entitled *Dux*, it had the precise aim of turning him into a figure of legend. According to the cultural historian Simona Storchi, in order to achieve her aim, Sarfatti drew on a variety of discourses deriving from religion, literature, her own field of art, and popular culture, to present Mussolini in three distinct but interlocking ways: as a 'Roman' of the modern era; as a man of superhuman qualities who, from childhood, was destined to lead; and as an 'aristocratic plebeian', that is to say a man who was at once superior and deeply connected to the experiences and vicissitudes of the people.[17] Sarfatti followed in the steps of right-wing intellectuals in founding legitimacy for his power on a concept of the state in which the head of government was the embodiment of supreme authority.[18] This was important in the aftermath of the crisis that followed the assassination of opposition deputy Giacomo Matteotti in 1924, a crisis which threatened Mussolini's position as prime minister and which ended with opposition parties being outlawed.[19]

The Mussolini government quickly consolidated its support after the establishment of one-party rule. The speed with which many people rushed to applaud the dictator was especially galling for anti-fascists, who had thought that Mussolini's rule would be short-lived. 'The circle of people who you can respect becomes ever smaller... day by day', wrote Nello Rosselli; 'you have to conduct a proud internal struggle to continue to believe, and to place hope in, ideal values on which the great majority, even of intelligent people, has turned its back'.[20] It needed a conscious effort, and a certain moral sternness, to resist the siren call of conformity. The idealist philosopher and historian Benedetto Croce saw that there must be something wrong with a society that proved to be so vulnerable to tyranny. He argued that the rise of Fascism should be seen as an illness that fed off biological impulses and which had infected the realm of psychology.[21] Initially, Croce saw Fascism as a solution to the sick nation, a form of strong medicine. By 1924, he saw that it was part of the problem and urged a return to constitutional methods. The philosopher lacked the profound psychological insight of Freud, but he saw that there was a background of obscure desires and impulsive currents to the rise of Fascism and that the libido was a factor in the way Fascism was embraced.[22] This line of argument was later developed in more explicitly Freudian, as well as literary, terms by Carlo Emilio Gadda, who denounced the way 'Eros in its unconscious and animalesque forms...dominated the tragic and depraved scene'.[23] Croce detected a decline within Italian nationalism after World War I; a healthy patriotic sentiment became contaminated by a way of understanding and behaving that was increasingly marked by a brutal, atavistic aspect.[24] Many fell prey to the pressure of collective humours and convictions, all the while believing that they were behaving in a particular way because they wanted to.[25] Writing in 1938, Croce observed that once the individual lost faith in himself he looked for something to latch on to—a party, a church, a state or a race—'not with the aim of establishing a collaboration that is also always opposition, but in order to conform or to dissolve himself as an individual into it'.[26] 'More than once', he continued, 'I have had occasion to ask someone who declared to me their adherence to one of the above-mentioned things: Why? Do you believe in it?—Only to receive the response: Well! It's a matter of feeling at one with others—with others who prevail at the present time or who one thinks will prevail in the near future'.

Liberals had always known that liberal-democratic culture was not well rooted in the country. The Catholic counter-revolution of the sixteenth and seventeenth centuries informed an undercurrent of hostility to liberalism, democracy and socialism that was taken up by Fascism.[27] The effect of Catholicism on the Italian people and on its way of engaging with public affairs had, arguably, undermined the development of individual responsibility.[28] The Communist Gramsci, the liberal Gobetti and other anti-fascists believed that Fascism fed off a barbarism and a savagery that were deep-rooted.[29] Mussolini made little or no effort to distance himself from the culture of violence and coercion, whether linguistic or physical, that was a defining feature of Fascism's attitude towards its domestic enemies. Recognising that the social and political unease that produced Fascism was not purely conjunctural, some commentators felt that the dictator played on the worst aspects of the Italian character. He boasted and threatened, performing with a swagger and employing a set of poses that drew heavily on Italian stereotypes and popular cultural motifs.[30] By means of his exhibitionism, he set himself up as a type who Italians could recognise and find familiar, a fact that triggered identification. Some Fascists also believed this, though they did not see it as negative. The writer Curzio Malaparte argued that Fascism had a basis 'that was not institutional or social, strictly speaking, but ethical and, sometimes, even biological; that is to say something that on the one hand concerned collective morality and, on the other, took on a naturalistic connotation'.[31]

The mere sight of Mussolini could be emotionally uplifting and even intoxicating. The dictator underscored this by adapting his mode of address to suit different audiences on his tours. He flattered crowds with local references and promises of his attention. His simple, sculpted phrases were not difficult to follow and resonated on an emotional level. 'His way of speaking is of an extraordinary simplicity, combined with a magical effect', remarked one observer.[32] 'He does not define, he does not reason, he strikes home directly. He does not mince his words; he gathers together the feeling of events or of people in a phrase, even in a word.... He treats all situations with violence, he describes their various phases with sharpness, pushing them to their extremes: the pathetic becomes tragic, the comical satirical, a random fact or two are transformed into history'. In a context in which popular culture was infused with religious beliefs and superstitions,[33] crowds were drawn by means of his hypnotic oratory into the euphoric illusion that together with their leader they were true protagonists of a special phase in human history.[34]

There was a psychological aspect to the impulse to conformism that went beyond cultural factors. Any change of regime, the prominent psychoanalyst Cesare Musatti, who was born in 1897, argued in a 1961 essay, leads to changes in the way people think and feel.[35] While, in normal circumstances, each person develops a personal ego-ideal—understood as a moral compass—under dictatorship another dynamic is at play: 'alongside the nucleus of the individual super-ego, an accessory parasitical super-ego [is] constituted that [is] collective and social in origin'.[36] In other words, a 'collective ego ideal' takes shape that is 'assimilated to the surrounding environment'. The projection by the masses of their ego-ideal on to the leader entails a form of psychic collectivisation that makes the leader into a receptacle for the primitive narcissism of every member of a nation.[37] For this reason, Musatti asserted, 'no-one who lived in Italy and in Germany in that period was able to subtract themselves' from the prevailing new social situation or avoid the impoverishment or regression of individual conscience and identity that inevitably occurred.[38] The ready spread of group think was widely attributed in the case of Nazi Germany to a strong social and cultural predisposition towards the acceptance of authority. Hitler was the 'saviour' of the nation, the redeemer leading Germany to its historical destiny after a humiliating military defeat, more than a decade of political turmoil, and a far-reaching economic crisis. The Italian crisis was not so deep, but it was deep enough for there to be a widespread hope that one man could sort out the country's problems.

The personality cult was fuelled by a spontaneous movement of public opinion. Yet it could only be sustained and developed through organisation. It took shape in a context of mass politics in which political parties were instrumental in building and maintaining popular feeling. The Italian National Fascist Party (PNF) took over practices pioneered by the Italian Socialist Party and added a great number of new ones. Not just in the big cities, but in every provincial town in the country, a new pattern of civic life was formed in which citizens were organised by the party in a set of new collective rituals, drawn into a suggestive symbolic world and subjected to systematic propaganda, all in a manner that recalled the liturgy of the Church.[39] This sort of appropriation was a product of the secularising tendencies of the modern era and is the reason why Fascism has been described as a political religion. A highly centralised force that was both a complement and a supplement to state power, the PNF was a tool of political integration on a massive scale, an example of the sort of 'artificial' or manufactured social group that Freud saw as more structured and long-lasting than a crowd.[40] A part of the state, a sort of militia, a form of church, a tool of acclamation and a provider of goods and services, the party became a key feature of community life. Discussion and debate were actively discouraged, however; instead orders were received from on high, with the inevitable result that a certain repetitiveness and stagnation, and even depoliticisation, would eventually set in. With a membership of over four million at its peak, the party inevitably included many who were not particularly interested in politics and who joined because they had to. In the ascendant phase of the regime, these problems were not widely felt. A forward-moving impulse of initiative and activity that Mussolini and the regime keenly cultivated acted as a stimulus to enthusiasm and participation.

Celebrating the party's achievements was a central and constant feature of Fascist propaganda. A new calendar of commemorations and anniversaries was adopted to drill the Duce and his political mission into the imagination of the young and the population more widely. One of the most significant examples of self-celebration was the Exhibition of the Fascist Revolution that opened in Rome in 1932, on the tenth anniversary of Mussolini coming to power. This event was designed to cement the synthesis of the history of Italy and the history of Fascism. It also demonstrated the extent to which the party had come to be dominated by a leader cult. The regime's accomplishments were funnelled into glorification of the leader, who was represented in a myriad of ways. Not only were there pictures and photographs; there was a reconstruction of Mussolini's office in the so-called Fascist 'den' of Via Paolo da Cannobio in Milan and also indirect evocations, allusions and atmospheres, all of which were designed for maximum impact on the visitor. It was one of the most significant moments in the elaboration of the Fascists' image policy.[41] The exhibition remained open for years and it inspired the practice, which was intended to drive home the perception of a collective mission, of painting Mussolini's turns of phrase and slogans on the walls of private and public buildings throughout the peninsula (see Chapter 12). These were more ephemeral than the many monumental public buildings that bore the regime's imprint, but they communicated their messages with undeniable clarity.

Italy was economically backward in many respects and Fascism promoted certain anti-modern themes in its efforts re-mould the national character. The image of Mussolini as a conventional strongman type seemed to spring from a template of firm, physical leadership dating back to Roman times. But it would not be accurate to see him in stark contrast to Hitler, a dictator whose highly mediated image arose in the context of a more advanced society in which mass communications played a crucial role. Mussolini's career took shape in the modern city of Milan and he had an acute understanding of the press. He actively sought to dominate the headlines, to grab attention, to convey meaning through images and slogans. In the 1910s, cinema became a popular form of leisure in urban areas and Mussolini coexisted for a while in the popular imagination with Maciste, the Herculean screen muscleman known for his patriotic endeavours and brusque righting of wrongs.[42] In other words, the Mussolini image, although it initiated in the political realm, and played on long-established stereotypes, was shaped by modern popular culture and the world of cinema stardom. When the film industry collapsed in the early 1920s and the stars suddenly disappeared, Mussolini filled their place, becoming a focus of interest on a scale that was unprecedented for a political leader.[43] According to the anarchist Camillo Berneri—who would die in the Spanish civil war—he was a great actor who performed in ways that the modern public expected of its idols.[44]

With the development of radio and sound cinema, public rallies, like other events, came to be conceived more in terms of the sounds and screen images that could be widely transmitted than the needs of a given occasion. Mussolini was increasingly drawn into the world of the media, which were harnessed to the task of fostering a sense of common purpose and collective identification.[45] Newspapers, magazines, posters, photographs and postcards, newsreels and radio provided a regular renewable complement to ceremonies and rituals.[46] They helped the dictator to take hold of the popular psyche and assisted the process of interiorisation. Indeed, in his memoirs, the one-time party secretary Giovanni Giuriati described him as 'a one-man cinema', by which he meant that he had become an omnipresent ever-changing image.[47] In this phase, he acquired a presence that was less tangible and immediate in line with the policy of the 1932 exhibition.[48] In place of the previous identification of self and crowd, he became a superhuman manifestation of the essence of the crowd, a development that was given powerful expression in photomontage and the graphic arts (see Figure 2). The quality of imitation that had always been so important for the popular success of the Mussolini character (even with children, as Calvino testified) prospered further in this context. Local officials and some senior Fascists modelled their speech, posture and appearance on those of the chief.

There is no shortage of evidence that many people felt a strong sense of identification with Mussolini as a figure with whom they could communicate directly and confide their sufferings, as well as declare their devotion. Private diaries written at the time record the boundless faith that many had in the dictator.[49] Some of this was of course induced. Letters from school children were often prompted by teachers and were a reflection of the fact that the young were systematically encouraged to respect, love and obey the Duce. Even in the war years, groups and individuals pledged their devotion.[50] A group of five schoolgirls animated by quasi-erotic fervour wrote: 'We want to feel you inside us and for us; we want to warm ourselves always by the ardent fire of your passion. We want this direct communion of spirits, that increases our capacity for resistance, our belief in a great conquest and our certainty in a radiant future'.[51] 'I am very close to You because You are the "Father" of the Italians. I am an orphan and I feel worthy of being your adoptive daughter', wrote one young

Figure 2. Mussolini as paternal presence and as an expression of the crowd on the cover of *Gente Nostra*, magazine of the Fascist leisure organisation, October 1934. Author's own collection.

woman.[52] This paternal perception was quite typical, though the dictator was also configured as maternal since his persona incorporated feminine as well as masculine aspects.[53] Any form of personal experience of the dictator could be intensely memorable. 'Recalling the happy day a year ago when I had the great joy of hearing Your strong, rousing and persuasive voice, I feel within me such a wave of fascist faith that I cannot stop myself from conveying to you all my fervent admiration and devotion', wrote a married woman from Brescia.[54]

Mussolini even became a part of the dream life of the Italians. People who were diffident about Fascism still found him inescapable. Musatti claimed that the power of suggestion extended to opponents, who could not exclude Mussolini from their minds. 'During the regime, I gathered some dreams of firm anti-fascists, some of whom had been persecuted for their opposition to the regime, dreams in which Mussolini himself appeared', he wrote in his 1961 essay.[55] Surprisingly, 'in their dreams these antifascists were on excellent terms with Mussolini, they were treated by him affably and they formed a cordial friendship with him'; 'the figure of Mussolini in these dreams is a paternal figure, a bad father figure if you like, but still a father, with whom, in spite of everything, one aspires to live in harmony'.[56] In a book published in 1933, the journalist Franco Ciarlantini wrote about the way the imaginary Mussolini operated in the minds and the hearts of the people.[57] The Duce had become a part of their lives and his image had projected itself into their spirits. 'What this real or fantastic image achieves is of incalculable power', he noted. Everywhere the name of Mussolini evoked 'internal impulses within individuals and external impulses within the masses'.[58] The fact that anti-fascists were having such dreams showed that Mussolini was felt to be not only an external authority; he had been interiorised as an 'internal authority'.

The cult had a strong top-down aspect to it, in keeping with the anti-democratic character of Fascism. Successive secretaries of the Fascist Party worked to elaborate and orchestrate the cult of Mussolini as a tool of subordination and control within the party and as a means of building and maintaining the allegiance of the mass of Italians beyond it. However, it was never solely a coercive tool. There was a widespread sense that the cult was a shared phenomenon to which people made their own contributions. It was not purely something that was lived as imposed; rather it was personal and treasured. People projected their own thoughts and desires on to the dictator; they attributed to him qualities that were imagined and aims that were in line with their own hopes.[59] The author and Fascist deputy Carlo Delcroix perceived that Mussolini became a part of people's sense of themselves: 'Peoples, like men, when they are taken by great passions, do not know to what extent they love their idol and to what extent they love themselves, seeing in the idol a projection of their own image'.[60] Everyone acclaimed Mussolini, praising him and acknowledging him as their leader, he asserted, 'but perhaps everyone wants to depict him and interpret him in their own way...perhaps like all idols who people want to make their own'. Many people sent Mussolini gifts and homages that were often the result of the sender's craftwork and might be a painting, sculpture or embroidery. Beyond individual acts of devotion and the collective ones promoted by the party and the state, there was an entire realm of commercial activity around the Duce, with companies and individuals seeking permission to market products that made use of the Mussolini image or name.

Despite the existence of the monarchy and the influence of the Church and economic interests, Mussolini's personal power was extensive. Many of the supposed achievements of the regime were personally attributed to him, including the Concordat with the Vatican of 1929, which eliminated long-standing disagreements between Church and state, a fact that brought the Catholic masses fully into the system of Fascist rule. The historian De Felice, in his discussion of the years that marked the apex of Mussolini's popularity, suggests that the climate of enthusiasm that was generated following the invasion of Ethiopia was either the result of sincere alignment with the political and patriotic aims of the war or 'the fruit of a mixture of suggestions and influences, some of a cultural type, others of an emotional type, partly autonomous and to a greater degree determined by the environment and especially by the massive, uninterrupted and in a way astute hammering effect of the regime propaganda'.[61] Others, including British historian Paul Corner, have questioned the extent to which there could really have been consent, highlighting both the various forms of coercion that were a permanent feature of Fascist rule and the failure of the regime to integrate recalcitrant parts of the population.[62] Fatalistic peasants and northern factory workers remained in significant measure external to its pattern of values and beliefs. In the sphere of everyday life, moreover, the regime did not truly succeed in shaping the domestic realm or forming a holistic people's community in the same way as Nazi Germany.[63] But the pattern of consent under the regime and engagement with the personality of Mussolini were not quite the same thing. Mussolini's standing owed a great deal to a much-trumpeted, if not always real, record of achievement. The conviction that he was a political genius was widespread. Risky and dangerous undertakings, such as the invasion of Ethiopia in 1935, when they were successful, only served to enhance the sense that his judgement could be trusted. The decision to go to war in 1940, which was taken by Mussolini personally, regardless of a lack of adequate preparation, caused this to waver. But the decision seemed to be vindicated by the successes of Italy's Nazi ally. Siding with the likely winner looked like it would bring substantial rewards. The setbacks in Italy's military campaigns, therefore, were an unexpected development. The widespread hardships and dislocations that the war and the aerial bombardment of the peninsula brought had a significant impact on public opinion.[64] The pattern of consent revealed fragilities that few had suspected; self-interest and private reservations simmered beneath public deference. Some started to wonder if they had been tricked or if they had made a big mistake in placing their faith in Mussolini.[65] Others, however, blamed incompetent or corrupt underlings, who were supposed to be enacting the Duce's will, for inadequacies and failures. Even as the situation went from bad to worse, he was still a leader whose imaginative reach was even greater than his not inconsiderable power; he was a projection of the nation's ambitions and destiny, for twenty years the man to whom everyone looked. One of the reasons why it took so long to oust him was the difficulty top Fascists and even the king had in overcoming a mental and political attachment to him. Events would show that, despite the immense difficulty of doing so, it was easier to remove the dictator from power than it was to dislodge him from the realms of the imagination and collective psychology.

2

Mussolini's dismissal

Eighteen-year-old student Luce Mangione heard about the fall of Mussolini when her friend Graziella knocked urgently at her door at 23.30 on 25 July 1943.[1] 'Fascism has fallen! Long live liberty!' the friend shouted before embracing her and swinging her round. 'Have you gone crazy?',[2] Mangione responded, seeking to quieten her visitor before she woke up everyone in the house. Raised in a Fascist household, she could not immediately make sense of the fact that Mussolini had been replaced as head of government, despite the ever more difficult war situation. She soon learned that not everyone fully shared her devotion to Mussolini. When they heard of his arrest and imprisonment, even some relatives did not hesitate to air critical opinions. 'Have they killed that scoundrel of a tyrant at last?' asked her widowed aunt when, wanting to know what was going on, she came down from the upper floor. Mangione had been evacuated for safety from Rome at the time of intense Allied bombardments to her grandmother's house in Alatri, 72 km away, while her father remained at his post in the Air Ministry. However, against parental advice, she had returned to Rome to help the injured and homeless after the bombing of the San Lorenzo quarter on 19 July. She carried out this work, always proudly dressed in her Fascist uniform, despite the heat. For Mangione, Fascism was not a remote authority but a way of life. She had for as long as she could remember been enrolled in party organisations; she had been awarded certificates and diplomas for her voluntary work and she had pledged, when she joined the Fascist University Organisation (GUF), to 'carry out the orders of the DUCE and to serve the cause of the Fascist Revolution with all my strength and, if necessary, with my blood'.[3]

The disastrous pursuit of Italy's war fuelled the widespread disaffection that the aerial bombardment of cities including Rome exacerbated.[4] However, young enthusiasts who had embraced their Fascist education were not so easily shaken. Mangione reacted to the wholly unexpected news of the arrest of

Mussolini with incomprehension and indignation. After two days of reflection, she formulated a plan: she would go to Rome and report to the offices of the GUF, hoping that she would not be too late to join other young Fascists in restoring order. Unbeknown to her parents, on the morning of 27 July, she put on a dress over her uniform, prepared a sandwich and made her way to the station, catching the dawn train to the capital. Aboard the train, she heard people curse Mussolini, complain about poverty and hunger, and express the hope that the war would now end. At one point on the journey, the train came to a sudden halt beside a Campo Dux training facility where some young Fascists belonging to the M Battalion were sitting on a wall singing political songs at the tops of their voices. It was when she saw the police officers trying to silence the youngsters that Mangione realised that the regime had really fallen.[5] In Rome, she found that the Fascist Party headquarters had been surrounded and was occupied by Carabinieri. One officer, who was given the task of accompanying her to the police station where she was to be detained, instead decided to let her go, telling her to get rid of her uniform and to wake up. From a bar where she took refuge, she telephoned the secretary of the GUF, who refused to take her call. Other young Fascists that she contacted were all cowering at home in fear. Disarray and disorientation seemed to affect everyone. Only a Romanian anti-fascist of her acquaintance came to help her with some civilian clothes. By 17.00, she was on the train back to Alatri, her 'heroic odyssey' having come to an end.[6]

The removal of Mussolini was an astonishing event, a watershed, for many of those who had been educated to think of him as infallible and the regime as permanent. News that the king had replaced Mussolini as head of the government with the chief of the armed forces, Marshal Badoglio, was broadcast on the radio shortly before 11.00 p.m. As the startling news spread, the streets of major cities filled with those eager to savour an unfamiliar liberty and vent their anger against Fascism. Groups of people, some still dressed in pyjamas, gathered to rejoice at the end of the regime and, it was widely hoped, the imminent end of Italian involvement in the war. In Rome, crowds headed to the Quirinale Palace waving tricolour flags to hail the king and Badoglio. Some converged on Palazzo Venezia, where Mussolini's office was located.[7] Though 'fists and kicks achieved nothing against the age-old walls and iron doors', it was reported in the *New York Times* that 'electric torches illuminated the world-famous balcony while the people, especially the women, literally intoxicated themselves by shouting all the invectives in the Roman vocabulary against the former dictator'.[8] The party headquarters at Palazzo Braschi, where Mangione had headed, was sacked. Across the city Fascist posters and portraits of the Duce were torn down and thrown on to small bonfires which blazed on the pavements.[9] The shouts and noise even penetrated the Villa Torlonia, the Mussolini family's residence, where they were heard by the dictator's wife and children.[10] Fascist buildings and newspapers were stormed and *fasci littoriali* hacked off the exteriors of the buildings that bore them.[11] In Milan, the demonstrations lasted all night.[12] There too Fascist Party offices were broken into and bonfires of printed material, membership files and portraits started. It was the same story in other major cities.[13]

Through most of day on 26 July, the attack on the symbols and images of Fascism continued in an atmosphere of joy and exaltation. Busts and portraits of Mussolini were particular targets. In the city sports stadium in Bologna, a large equestrian statue of Mussolini was battered and the horseman dislodged.[14] The head was detached from the body, tied with a rope and dragged through the streets. The jurist Piero Calamandrei wrote in his diary: 'All over the country people were pulling down fascist symbols and destroying them. Stone and ceramic *fasci* were torn off buildings and thrown to the ground, while in some public buildings the lictors, the symbols of Roman authority which had been adopted by fascism, were covered with flags or cloths or hurriedly painted over'.[15] Vituperation was heaped on those believed to have profited illegitimately from the regime. The houses of Fascist officials who had visibly enriched themselves were daubed with graffiti announcing that 'The easy life is over'.

Calamandrei noted that 'the vendettas have been marked in these first days by a tone of happiness'.[16] An atmosphere of shared effervescence and intense joy reigned in which strangers embraced each other and people seemed to rediscover themselves.[17] In general, the targets were more symbolic than personal. There were no accounts of serious violence against individuals. In Lucca, Calamandrei recounted, the local party chief or *federale*—'a violent man who was always going round in uniform'—came out on to the street dressed in his customary way, his chest covered with medals and badges. He walked around with a challenging air but no one confronted him. Instead, women and children followed him, teasing him and making fun of his 'nice costume'; 'he is dressed like a clown, we are in carnival' they taunted. Finally, he was forced to go home and exchange his uniform for civilian clothes. His car was seized and he was ordered to walk round on foot like any ordinary citizen.[18] 'Fascism is dead!', was the cry, and with it many pulled Fascist buttonhole badges off jackets screaming, 'Away with these bedbugs!'[19] Those who failed to cast off these visible signs of Fascist allegiance found themselves suddenly out of step. One man who was in a requisitioned school in a Bologna suburb where doctors were working following the bombing of the hospital recalled that a military officer came to the door and announced 'Bighead has gone; bighead has fallen! Anyone wearing a party badge should remove it.'[20] He remembered that a sergeant-major of the blackshirts standing close to him refused to do so. He was assaulted by a former soldier, who removed it by force. In Florence, a low-ranking official was reportedly forced to swallow his party badge.[21]

Fascism had long preached the merits of war and seen it as a necessary rite of passage if the nation was to assert itself on the world stage. An aggressive foreign policy was developed not only to establish Italy's status but to bring a new impulse to the regime and maintain the climate of enthusiasm it privileged.[22] Mussolini launched an unprepared Italy into war alongside Germany in 1940 in the hope that, by doing so, he would secure benefits and influence but also in the expectation that, after twenty years of Fascism, the Italians would be ready to bear personal hardship and sacrifice for the greater ambitions of the nation.[23] However, the conflict had been marked from the start by setbacks and, in a few months in 1942, the Italian army in Russia had been all but destroyed, and the Allies had landed in Africa with the result that the Italian empire that had been loudly proclaimed in 1936 ended. By 1943 even Libya, which had been a colony since 1912, was lost. Many families had suffered the loss of fathers or sons abroad, and material hardships increased by the week. The aerial bombing of Italian cities came as a huge shock. The events of the war were the key factor explaining the relish with which people divested themselves of a sense of belonging which had been widely, if not universally, shared. As historian Lucio Villari has written, the bombardments, above all, had a 'psychological and political impact', alerting the Italians to the imminent danger to the country and to themselves.[24]

Most Italians knew nothing of the plots to oust Mussolini that culminated on 25 July. For weeks some senior Fascists had been growing alarmed that the war situation was putting the very existence of the nation in peril.[25] The leader's sole response was to try to shift blame on to his closest collaborators by dismissing nine out of twelve cabinet ministers on one day in February 1943. Crisis became inevitable following the defeats that the Axis powers suffered in Africa and by the trauma that was caused by the landing of the Allies in Sicily on 10 July.[26] The approval by the Fascist Grand Council of a motion, presented by former foreign minister Dino Grandi, urging Mussolini to restore command of the armed forces to King Vittorio Emanuele, provided the monarch with the excuse he had needed to accede to demands in the military and among his own officials that Mussolini be dismissed as a premise to Italy's exit from the war.[27] In fact, the feeling that Mussolini had begun to lose his grip and that the regime was no longer so dynamic set in not long after the proclamation of the empire in May 1936, which many saw as the highest moment in the history of Fascism.[28] The historian De Felice talks of a season of 'super mussolinismo' that was inaugurated in those days.[29] This affected the dictator personally, as success seemed to go to his head.[30] Mussolini, De Felice says, 'always had a great estimation of himself and extreme faith in his political sensibility and ability'; after the victory in Ethiopia this turned into a sense of predestination for lasting greatness.[31] The Fascist Party as a tool of mobilisation proved to be ever less effective as, following its greatest triumph, complacency and habit set in. Politically, it was insignificant, with not a single party congress being held after 1925. In effect, it became a gigantic chorus, as intermediaries between the great leader on the one hand and the mass of Italians on the other were largely abolished.[32] The mass rallies that had been so important in establishing the regime as one commanding a significant degree of consent, and which had once provided evidence of the genuine enthusiasm that it could mobilise, turned into ritualistic displays that required a high degree of orchestration and indeed conscription.[33]

Mussolini often spoke of the ways in which Fascism was changing the Italian spirit, while also denouncing those within the party who lacked discipline and 'our psychology', that is to say a fervent quasi-religious commitment to ever-more ambitious goals.[34] The alliance with Germany was supposed to have a galvanising effect, but the Axis was not popular with practising Catholics or many others who remembered the enemy of World War I.[35] The entry into the war was seen by the dictator as a test for the Italians' capacity for hardship. In fact, military setbacks and worsening material conditions only exacerbated the situation of stasis at home.[36] It was not just among the mass of the population that a decline in the Duce's standing occurred. There was also a reduction in the charismatic hold that he exercised over senior Fascists.[37] In order to rouse the party and revitalise faith in the Fascist cause, Mussolini turned to a new generation of men whose entire political formation had occurred under the regime. After several of them failed in the role of party secretary, he resorted to a long-standing official and one-time *squadrista*, Carlo Scorza. However, not even he was able to correct the conviction that what mattered to the regime was façades and exterior impressions more than substance. Fascism had ceased to promote faith and courage and turned into 'a school of exhibitionism', journalist Paolo Monelli commented.[38] A remote unapproachable Duce who seemed to have embraced his own myth was a concern for those who had trusted in his political genius. He had never cultivated close relations with even long-standing associates, but now distances were more marked than ever. Within the upper echelons of the regime, various explanations were advanced for the erratic decisions and imperviousness of the Duce. One of them was that the ageing leader had lost his grip and fallen under the influence of his young lover Claretta Petacci and her manipulative family.[39]

In May 1942, Mussolini visited Sardinia. The purpose was to organise a display of unflagging support in deepest Italy that, it was hoped, would provide a boost to a demoralised mainland public opinion. Mussolini felt a special bond with Sardinia, which he had visited on three previous occasions, to the extent even of stating that he wished he had been born there.[40] He praised the Sardinians as 'a race that has remained in a state of superb primitiveness... Poor people who, however, are enthusiastic and devoted to the regime'.[41] Sardinia was the region least affected by the war and it was not unduly affected by food shortages. The images that appeared in official newsreels, after his return to Rome, showed that the Duce everywhere encountered cheering, excited crowds. One journalist who covered the visit confessed years later that, contrary to what he wrote at the time, 'Mussolini on that occasion did not have the look or the determination of the past. He seemed a bit sad, maybe even tired'.[42] But another, who saw him in Sassari, recalled that his eyes were 'really magnetic but also (it is a strange vision that I remember) vaguely smiling';[43] he had a capacity 'to force people to stop thinking, to obscure doubts and anxieties, to continue believing in the demiurge'. It is possible that between the first and the second observation, he had re-charged his batteries by feeding off communion with the crowds. Certainly, when he was back in Rome, Giuseppe Bottai noted that he 'has returned from his journey plainly intoxicated'.[44] 'He refers to the crowds who flocked to see him "without—he says with pleasure—too much police intervention."'

Any effect was short-lived. With the war being lost on all fronts and Italy the target of aerial bombardment, by the end of 1942 morale collapsed.[45] In his last radio speech in December 1942, Mussolini offered no hope or real solution to an increasingly desperate situation. It seemed as though he had run out of steam. Regime spies reported that disaffection was being expressed openly.[46] With the war going badly, Mussolini and other high-ranking Fascists had been denounced for months. 'The chorus of popular hatred does not even exempt the Duce', another spy stated. After the loss of Italy's African colonies, spies reported that the one-time 'founder of the empire' was being dismissed as 'the destroyer of the empire'. Mussolini's prestige and popularity had been declining since the loss of Italian East Africa and the establishment of complete German control of Libya. Some looked back and blamed his lack of foresight, his ill-conceived and ill-managed attack on Greece and his idiosyncratic view that wars were won not on the field of battle but by the peoples with the greatest determination. Reliance on the Germans and the declaration of war on the United States did nothing to restore his prestige.

Mussolini spoke from the balcony of Palazzo Venezia for the last time on 6 May 1943. As Italian and German troops were about to surrender in Tunisia, he recalled former triumphs in Africa and launched the watchword 'Torneremo (We will return)!' No matter how badly things were going, he always proclaimed certainty in ultimate victory. But, despite the conventional acclamation of the mass crowd that punctuated the speech with cries of encouragement, the 'warmth' it transmitted was 'many tones below that of other occasions', Mussolini himself admitted; 'it was—if it can be expressed like this—a rather concerned enthusiasm'.[47] 'The Duce's hold on the Italian people diminished almost to zero and stories began to get around that he was failing mentally', wrote the Rome-based American journalists Reynolds and Eleanor Packard; 'we ourselves felt, on the rare occasions when he made public speeches, that he did not have his old fire, and the Italians took this as an indication that his control of affairs was slipping'.[48]

Even high-level Fascists who had passionately believed in Mussolini's genius grew desperate: 'What use is faith when you have no idea what you are having faith in? Faith to a man, in politics, can only be faith in the ideas that he incarnates. Take away the ideas, and all you have left is corporeal, physical faith', wrote Bottai in his diary in May 1943.[49] But there were also signs of physical decline. When former party secretary Giovanni Giurati was received at Palazzo Venezia, along with other senior officials, on 16 July 1943, he found that the dictator 'looked tired and depressed; even the occasional fillip during our dramatic encounter no longer resembled the flash of his old polemical attitude; rather it seemed the result of a nervous reaction produced by over-work or worries, or perhaps by a genuine illness'.[50]

When Mussolini was removed from power, many celebrated, but there was an odd lack of reaction on the part of Fascists. After all, even in a situation of public apathy, there were many who shared the 'faith'. In fact, he was deposed with little fuss and with very limited reaction by the mass of party officials and members, the Fascist militia or even by the M battalions that were stationed in the capital.[51] Fascism 'dispersed like fog', Paolo Monelli judged.[52] Mussolini himself wrote of his astonishment that the fall of the regime 'was provoked by fascists and carried out by people who wore the party badge'.[53] In the notes he jotted down while he was kept in captivity after his arrest, he could not believe that everything had collapsed. 'When I think back now to the tasks, the achievements, the work and the hopes of these twenty years, I ask myself: maybe I dreamed it all? Was it all an illusion? Was everything superficial? Was there nothing that was profound?'

In fact, the situation was complex. The lack of reaction was due to a number of factors. Many Fascists were caught completely off-guard by the speed of events and were unclear precisely what had happened.[54] No word went out at any stage that the action of the king should be resisted. Indeed, Party Secretary Scorza gave the order to avoid provocations and collaborate with the new authorities. Badoglio's announcement that the war would continue alongside Germany convinced some Fascists that they would find a role for themselves in the new government. Others simply accepted that the war situation and the change in popular sentiment meant that the Fascist era could not go on. Panic gripped those who were in some way compromised. For many people, the overriding aim became to shrug off any personal affiliation or evidence of responsibility.[55] Papers, questionnaires, party cards and lists of party members were torn up, piled in stacks and torched in assaults on Fascist Party offices. Antonio Santovito, a messenger boy for the party office on Via Bartolo da Sassoferrato in Rome, watched in amazement as long-time Fascists took great care to throw membership rolls containing their names into the fire.[56] Shopkeepers and householders also moved to remove marks of devotion from their property: portraits were taken down, slogans scraped off walls and emblems knocked off with hammers and chisels.[57] The most pressing task was to cancel evidence of now embarrassing proclamations of support.

Images of Mussolini were among the most striking and obvious targets of the crowds who vented their anger at the symbols of the regime. The toppling of statues, busts dragged through the streets, photographs and portraits being burned gave the impression of the leader being lynched in absentia. In fact, what was going on was different. The universality of Mussolini's presence as the symbol of the regime—in the press and the media, in wall writings and slogans, school textbooks, official communications and so on—meant that it was unavoidable that anger at the regime should find expression in attacks on this widespread iconography. The carnivalesque atmosphere of delight in desacralisation was the mirror image of the exaltation and enthusiasm that had once surrounded the Duce.[58] In effigy, Mussolini was cast down and trampled underfoot, in a proof that an excess of communication, a too extensive diffusion of a ruler's image, can act as an invitation to ridicule and disrespect.[59]

Nonetheless these acts were tied into a mentality in which he was still central and still filled the popular imagination. Despite being 'the most hated man in Italy', as he himself wrote that the king had told him, and his being taken, following his dismissal, in an ambulance to a safe location 'for his own protection',[60] there were reserves of identification with Mussolini, both conscious and unconscious. The second, political, body of the leader had been destroyed and the third, representational, body was the object of iconoclastic attack, but the fourth—the imagined figure—persisted. Even at the moment when disaffection was widespread, he remained lodged in the collective imagination, even if his public appearances had diminished.[61] Many did not blame the Duce for problems or military reverses.[62]

In the capital and a few large cities, anti-fascist activists emerged on 26 July 1943 to play a key role in identifying targets and giving a political thrust to the reaction to his fall. Outside of the larger centres, however, in smaller towns and the provinces, there was little in the way of public rejoicing or active participation in destruction. Cities like L'Aquila, Bari, Campobasso and Pavia were quiet, while there was limited evidence of indignation in Varese, Bolzano and other centres.[63] In private diaries, disorientation was the prevalent emotion, even in the big cities that saw widely reported acts of iconoclasm.[64] Authors were numbed or perhaps traumatised; certainly, some young people were at a loss to understand what had happened.[65] The critic Mario Praz, who had kept his head down and adapted to the reality of Fascism, referred to 'a confused crowd' that behaved like 'an animal freed from a cage that does not know which way to go'.[66] There was no popular insurrection but rather astonishment, followed by feverish rejoicing in which many felt obliged to join as a sort of after-effect of mass conformism. In psychoanalytical terms, what had occurred was a break in the collective super-ego. The Italians may tendentially have been individualists, as some have argued, but Fascism's propaganda and promises whipped them into a state of enthusiasm in which there was a widespread shared internalisation of the dictator.[67] Now what was happening was the dissolution of a group identity. Writing about group psychology, Freud argued that 'the loss of the leader in some sense or other, the birth of misgivings about him, brings on the outbreak of panic...the mutual ties between the members of the group disappear, as a rule, at the same time as the tie with their leader'.[68] The conformist mentality, already weakened by disaffection, collapsed with the fall of Mussolini.

But this does not mean that Mussolini was somehow instantly dislodged from the collective consciousness. It was easy to destroy miniscule objects like party badges; it was more difficult to dismantle the structures that Fascism left behind, whether these were institutional, social or mental.[69] Those who had grown up under Fascism, and who had absorbed wave after wave of propaganda, were completely disoriented.[70] It was if the meaning of their whole life was cast into doubt. When Luce Mangione (who would later become well-known as writer Luce D'Eramo) tried to make some sense of what had occurred, she pulled from a drawer an envelope that contained documents she had accumulated over several years of activity in the service of Fascism:

> In that envelope were all my fascist membership cards from when I was a Piccola Italiana, my merit diploma, certificates from the Littoriali competitions I had won—the regional one at fourteen, the national one at eighteen—awarded at the end of June, less than a month before...various certificates for work I had done for this or that fascist group of war orphans, unmarried mothers and so on, two diplomas for colonial education and culture, a Red Cross one for first aid. I pulled out my GUF membership card and read the oath: 'In the name of God and of Italy, I swear to carry out the orders of the DUCE and to serve the cause of the Fascist Revolution with all my strength and, if necessary, with my blood'.[71]

Never having properly taken in these words, she felt that now they resonated within her and demanded that she rise to them. 'They had become part of me through my youthful distraction and habit and now the hour had come for me to confirm my pledge'.[72] Those who had sincerely internalised the Duce cult were bereft. If they had had doubts, these were pushed aside by the enormity of what had happened. Even in the province of Reggio Emilia, where there had been a strong socialist presence before Fascism, and a significant number of people had experienced internal exile, prison and torture, there were loyalists.[73] One Fascist woman recalled with horror seeing people attacking Fascist symbols and throwing out portraits of 'the great prisoner': 'Crying, I took refuge in the Saint Nicholas church. In the quiet of the church, I closed my eyes and saw, as if I were watching a screen, the beautiful mass rallies in Piazza Venezia in Rome. Outside in Via Roma, I saw a parade of people waving banners and portraits of the king, of Badoglio and, strangely, a woman raised up a portrait of [the aviator and Arctic explorer] Umberto Nobile'.[74] Aldo Carugati, a young artillery corporal from Lombardy wondered who could fill the void left by Mussolini, a man who, for many, had been 'a supreme, infallible leader, almost a God'.[75] They had trusted and believed in him above everything.[76] Convinced supporters were 'dumbfounded' and 'bewildered' that such a great figure, who had been a part of everyone's lives, had suddenly become worthless.

The Badoglio government moved swiftly to repress those manifestations of anti-fascism that risked escalating into uncontrollable disorder. A radio appeal was broadcast on the afternoon of 26 July ordering everyone back to work. Demonstrations that occurred after that were repressed, sometimes violently, as in Bari and at the Reggiane factory in Reggio Emilia on 28 July.[77] The announcement that Italy would continue to wage war alongside Germany rapidly dampened spirits and fuelled an impression that the military government was little better than the regime. Some even wondered why Mussolini had been deposed. No discussion of the responsibilities for Fascism or of society's deep complicity with the regime was initiated or encouraged. Instead, in the days following 25 July a series of actions were undertaken to discredit Mussolini and senior Fascists, to dismantle key parts of the regime and tackle corruption. While censorship was swiftly restored, the government encouraged a campaign of denigration that was intended to demolish what remained of the Duce cult.[78] Newspapers including Milan's *Corriere della sera* revealed, to many for the first time, details of Mussolini's affair with Claretta Petacci that undermined his heroic image. On 29 July it was announced that the Fascist Party was dissolved and in the following days Fascist laws were revoked. Action was taken to recover fortunes that had been accumulated illicitly by senior political figures.[79] As far as Mussolini himself was concerned, complete silence soon fell. From being a constant presence in the press, his name abruptly ceased to be mentioned. He simply vanished, as if into thin air in an act of removal and wilful forgetting that left many wondering even if he was still alive.[80]

3

Divided nation

On 12 September 1943, four days after it was announced that the Badoglio government had signed the armistice with the Allies, officially sanctioning the end of the Axis alliance, German paratroopers dramatically freed Mussolini from the mountain fortress of the Gran Sasso in the Abruzzo region where he was being held. Photographs of the event show a clearly worn-down former leader in civilian clothes and a brimmed hat surrounded by his liberators. While some of the men around him smile broadly, his own smile is forced. Six days later, on 18 September 1943, his voice was heard once more by those who had tuned their radio sets to an Italian language station ostensibly broadcasting from the German city of Munich.[1] 'Italian men and women, after a long silence, once more a voice reaches you that I am sure you will recognise', the former dictator began. 'It is the voice that gathered you together in difficult moments, that celebrated with you the triumphant days of the fatherland. I have waited a few days before addressing you because, after a period of moral isolation, I first needed to renew contact with the world'. The fact that Mussolini was not only alive but ready once more to play a leading role was welcomed by those who felt a personal and political tie to him. It was greeted positively by those who were appalled or disorientated by his overthrow and especially by the circumstances of an armistice that lacked honour and felt like a capitulation. But some listeners understood that it heralded a phase in which not only would the Germans and the Allies do battle in the peninsula but the Italians would be plunged into civil war.

Mussolini was seen in this period in a series of both unfamiliar and unprecedented ways. He described himself following his dismissal and arrest—in a diary he published the following year—as 'politically defunct' and expressed the view that he would soon be forgotten.[2] For Italians who moved towards anti-fascism, he was an enemy, a political opponent whose aura, in so far as it still existed, was wholly negative. In his time, he had commanded respect and even admiration abroad but now he was an object of derision fit only for denunciation. Allied propaganda depicted him as Hitler's lapdog, a once powerful dictator who had lost all credibility. In what has been called the 'grey zone', that is to say among the majority of the population who did not actively commit either to the return of Fascism or to the cause of anti-fascism, disenchantment manifested itself in a certain new sense of realism about the man and his capabilities. Resentment against Mussolini was far more diffuse in relation to the war—the poor conduct of it, the terrible outcome, the misjudgements, all of which had led to ruination, bombing and death—than in relation to the twenty years of his dictatorship. A certain nostalgia for the vigorous Duce of old, who was bound up in memory with the ascendant phase of the regime, conflicted and sometimes combined with negative feelings about the present. By contrast, for those who rallied to his side in the newly constituted republican government that was established in the north with Hitler's backing, he was still the Duce, the leader of Fascism who had been betrayed by men less worthy than him and by those Italians who had turned their backs on him. With the birth of the Italian Social Republic (RSI), which was proclaimed on the radio on 24 September 1943, the day after his return from Germany, Mussolini became for the first time a head of state, albeit one who was no less subordinate a figure than when he had had to share authority with—and concede precedence to—the king. Indeed, ever since the formation of the Axis, he had been secondary to Hitler, a status that had been emphasised by the course of the war. Once a source of inspiration to the German dictator, he had been an ally before turning into a dependent and then, finally, with the German-backed RSI, a vassal. As Renzo De Felice later wrote, he was a man who from 8 September 'until his physical death was no more than the shadow, the ghost of the man who had died politically on 25 July'.[3] He was a political corpse who had risen. He himself had taken this view and he repeated in his diary that he considered himself 'a dead man whose death has not been announced'.[4] The resurrected Mussolini was a polarising figure who proposed himself to the country as a rallying point for those who had deplored his betrayal by the elite and the abandonment of the alliance with Germany.

Mussolini may have succumbed to Hitler's pressure to head the RSI, which set up government in and around Salò, near the northern lakes, out of a desire to 'finish on a high note' with a return to his republican, socialist origins.[5] However, it seems probable that the question of national honour was more at the centre of his thoughts. The republic had a powerful appeal for the many, especially young, Italians who still nurtured fidelity to the Duce and to the symbols and values of Fascism. To the population of the territories governed by the RSI, Mussolini was depicted as a man of honour and service who was counterposed to those who had betrayed him and come to an agreement with the nation's enemies. Among the soldiers of the RSI were hundreds of thousands of Italians, some of whom had been conscripted and others who chose to throw in their lot with 'the last incarnation of fascism'.[6] The argument, advanced by those who sought to separate the Fascist regime from the nation, that Fascism was an exterior imposition, a distortion or a temporary infatuation, led to the view that the RSI was a further exterior imposition, a Hitler-backed order that had no following among Italians outside of the thuggish minority of extreme Fascists and those who had not yet freed themselves of the spell that the dictatorship had cast. However, though the puppet state that was set up under the rescued Mussolini would gradually see its territory reduced and its ability to offer a plausible vision of an Italian future weaken, it proved capable, for a short time, of winning a not insignificant level of support. For the many Italians who had been enthused by Fascism and who still nurtured fidelity to the Duce, the republic was a powerful symbol.[7] Some were astonished to hear Mussolini's voice on the radio. 'Could it really be Him?', some young Fascists asked themselves.[8] Surprised by his unexpected return, young people who had grown up in families of strong Fascist convictions were motivated to renew their commitment to the fatherland. Many still sent letters to Mussolini. One young man who left Rome in June 1944 to join the RSI wrote to Mussolini that 'I have a wish, a wish for the future, to see you once more at the balcony of Palazzo Venezia'.[9] Thirty girls from the 'Honour and Combat' youth group in Rome, headed by their twenty-three-year-old commander, left their families to travel to Milan in June 1944, declaring 'our faith lies solely in Mussolini'.[10] For them, Mussolini represented both fatherland and family. Asking for an audience with their hero, they proclaimed, 'you have been dearer to us even than our mother'.[11] They threw themselves into the cauldron thinking that Italy and Mussolini were inseparable.

The Mussolini who reappeared in the Autumn of 1943 was not the same as the leader who had been toppled and arrested. For the Fascist diplomat Giuseppe Bastianini, he appeared 'not as a dominator, but only as an old chief who had much suffered'.[12] There was a sense of him among some loyalists as a flawed human being deserving compassion. Though politically not as visible or as active as before in a situation in which the re-founded Fascist party was more significant tool of public policy, the leader could count on perhaps surprising reserves of affection.[13] The female 'auxiliaries' who flanked the military forces of the RSI, and who were interviewed by historian Maria Fraddosio fifty years later, could recall a 'mythical image of Mussolini' that persisted not only beyond 1943 but for decades afterwards.[14] 'Many women volunteers', Fraddosio observed, 'felt the same affection for their Chief that had imbued the vast majority of the Italian people in the years of their adolescence and youth'. A deputy commander of the women's division of the elite naval unit the Decima Mas, named Luciana Cera, who was born 1921, recalled the well-being she felt while growing up, 'and over this feeling of well-being there reigned a mythical, reassuring figure: Benito Mussolini. He was there and everything was fine'.[15] 'I often wonder what my relationship to Mussolini was', she mused; 'not that I ever had anything to do with him or even saw him at close quarters. But he ruled my life. Later on, in the shameful tragedy of 8 September 1943, I was not surprised to see that it was He who withstood the enemy and picked up the remnants of Italian honour. And, as always, I was behind Him'. The volunteers saw Mussolini in an even more paternal light than had been the case before. Though evidently weaker physically and visibly older, and lacking political vitality, he was putting himself on the line.[16] Curiously, Fraddosio argues, at the time when the myth of Mussolini was entering into crisis and fading in the eyes of a demoralised public, it was re-born among these women who could not resign themselves to his disappearance from public life.[17] No longer infallible, he was a loving father, a 'constant ideal', who was both familiar and authoritative, with the aura of the risen Christ.[18]

The cult of Mussolini was understated during the life of the RSI, in stark contrast to the heyday of the regime. Newsreels had once fuelled the cult, presenting the Duce constantly and flatteringly; now he only appeared occasionally, when inspecting troops, marking an anniversary or, on rare occasions, meeting Hitler.[19] The cult was less insistent and pervasive, more a pale residue than a mechanism of integration for the country.[20] On just one occasion was Mussolini at the centre of a serious attempt to rouse support, and that was for the speech that he delivered at the Lirico Theatre in Milan on 16 December 1944. Held to commemorate a party official who had been killed in a partisan ambush a year previously, the event was carefully prepared with the precise aim, at a time of reversals, of relaunching Mussolini and the political system that he embodied.[21] The theatre, located not far from the Duomo of Milan, was packed full of loyalists, while a huge crowd had been mobilised to fill the surrounding streets. The hour-long speech, broadcast to the crowd by loudspeakers, contained a passionate defence of the achievements of the RSI that was charged with memories and references to Mussolini's long-standing political ties to the city.[22] Powerful and effective, the speaker repeatedly evoked the theme of betrayal of the fatherland on the part of the monarchy, the military and anti-fascist groups. National honour was at stake, and Mussolini presented himself and the RSI as the catalysts of national redemption.[23] Despite everything, final victory was still being promised.

Newspapers gave the event blanket coverage while other media were deployed to enhance its propaganda impact. Newsreel footage of the speech was intercut with scenes designed to confirm the popularity of Mussolini and the enthusiastic reception he received in the streets, most especially when he stood atop a tank to address supporters. Of course, images of applauding crowds do not necessarily show spontaneous enthusiasm but, thanks to careful manipulation, they did give the impression that people could still be mobilised in large numbers. Tens of letters intercepted following this event also testified to the regenerating effect that sight of the Duce could still have. One woman wrote of feeling 'the same faith that I have always had in our great DUCE who yesterday my eyes saw again with great joy. I heard the people of Milan shout in chorus with me "Viva il DUCE"',[24] while a man wrote to a female friend: 'With great joy, I saw once more our great DUCE, a bit older and still the same masculine figure as ever. He passed through an immense adoring crowd; he was firm, unbending and smiling as he stood on top of a vehicle. He seemed almost moved to see once more after so much time the city that first gave an impulse to his original ideals'.[25]

The Lirico Theatre speech and Mussolini's days in Milan were a desperate bid to raise morale that may have inspired those who were present. According to Mussolini's wife, the dictator himself was thoroughly charged up after the event: 'In twenty years of fascism, not even once have I had such a reception', he told her.[26] There was, however, no wider impact. Even a week or two afterwards, further military reverses cancelled any serious effect. A few months later, all hope had been lost. The writer Carlo Mazzantini had a different impression of Mussolini to those enthusiastic supporters when, many years later, he remembered a visit the Duce had made to his loyal troops in the Spring of 1945. For him and his comrades, who had not seen him in Milan and were familiar mainly with the media image, he was by this time a remote figure who had little relevance for their struggle; 'in our eyes, he stood as a kind of distant hermit, a shadow of his former self, lacking any kind of real substance'.[27] When he appeared before them, 'there he was in the flesh—as close as could be—and yet even then he didn't seem to be real'.[28] Surprising themselves, they wondered who he really was. 'Who was that shrunken man in a bare uniform...surrounded by foreign soldiers: head of a defeated army? Of the country he's bewitched, and which now, deluded and disillusioned, refused him and didn't acknowledge him anymore as its leader [nothing was left]. It was like being part a postscript, a useless apocryphal afterthought.'[29]

The faded Mussolini revealed an acutely vengeful spirit.[30] This manifested itself in the trial and execution in January 1944 of those—including his son-in-law Galeazzo Ciano—who had voted against him in the Fascist Grand Council and failed to escape. More prosaically, individuals who had switched allegiance after 25 July were tracked down and dragged before the courts. As the tentative support that had been offered by the northern population evaporated, the Fascists turned on a people from whom they were ever more detached. Reprisals were carried out by the Fascist soldiers of the RSI against their enemies, resulting in acts of barbarity including public shootings and displays of executed bodies.[31] Those who preferred to keep their heads down and avoid any involvement were presented with a series of choices and obligations. Protecting oneself and one's family in a period of conflict and violence became the priority in a climate in which all trust dissolved into thin air. As the journalist Gian Franco Venè later observed,

> Fascism, which in the years of the regime made its entry into lower middle-class homes to deposit there good-humouredly the uniform of the Balilla [Fascist youth organization] and to transmit to couples the blessings of a large family by listing the economic benefits established by the Duce, now beat down the doors of family homes, rummaged at gunpoint under beds and in attics, broke open trunks, threw around innocent trousseaux, grabbed by the collar the grandad left behind in the city with his memories.[32]

The attitude of hostility was fuelled by a sense among the Germans that the Italians had betrayed their leader. The Nazi propaganda minister Goebbels asserted, 'Mussolini will go down in history as the last Roman but behind his powerful figure a gypsy people will end up rotting...with their infidelity and betrayal, the Italians have lost any right to a national state of a modern type. They must be punished very severely, as the laws of history demand'.[33] The retaliatory intent could not have been clearer. However, in some novels written after the war by men and women who had been members of the Resistance, it was acknowledged that it was not only the fascists and the Germans who were blamed for these for reprisals against the people. It was also the partisans who provoked them by their guerilla raids and acts of sabotage.[34]

While the Germans were imposing their domination on central Italy, including Rome, and the RSI was being established in the north, at the opposite end of the country the Allies were rapidly occupying territory.[35] After landing in Sicily in July 1943, they had reached Naples by October before their progress slowed. Since the proclamation of war against Italy in 1940, the British had made Mussolini a target. On Christmas Eve 1940, Churchill gave a speech in which the dictator was accorded sole responsibility for Italian involvement in the conflict against Britain, a view that he would later repeat in his memoirs.[36] In the propaganda broadcasts by the Italian language station Radio Londra, there were two Italies, which were represented respectively by convinced Fascists on the one hand and the majority of the population on the other.[37] Most Italians were exonerated of responsibility for Fascism and war. However, in reality, in 1941–42 it was unclear to the British how far Mussolini was still admired and supported, and for this reason he was not attacked directly. Only from the end of 1942 did this change. As the war in the peninsula progressed, it was seen as a priority to discredit Mussolini and to crush the loyalty to him that remained.

For the Allies, the Mussolini issue was awkward because, in the 1920s, he had acquired great popularity abroad. Even consolidated democracies seemed to find him suggestive. Between 1923 and 1943, he appeared on the cover of *Time* no fewer than eight times (Hitler managed one cover, Stalin two).[38] Mussolini was seen as having saved Italy from revolution and disorder and having rapidly overcome long-standing vices of inefficiency and indolence.[39] His dynamic approach won him many admirers in Westminster, the press and more widely in Britain.[40] Even in the cautious Foreign Office, there was some sympathy. The French journalist Maurice Bedel, was one of many foreigners who saw Mussolini as a personality; he likened his smile to that of the singer and entertainer Maurice Chevalier.[41] Another French observer, Henri Béraud, was impressed with the fact that his image was everywhere, on postcards, in magazines, even on shop counters and at stations.[42] Mussolini's most famous encounter was with the celebrity interviewer Emil Ludwig, whose book-length interview was translated into several languages.[43] The two men shared a fascination with Napoleon and the conversation covered history and ideas as well as politics.

However, admiration was not the only sentiment. Americans related to Mussolini's forcefulness and determination, but they found a contradiction between the Fascist aim to create a dynamic and monolithic state and the prevailing stereotype of the Italian character which the dictator seemed to embody. Despite the good press that Mussolini received, there was always the matter of what American historian John Diggins calls 'the comical image'.[44] It was difficult sometimes to take seriously a man who could so easily be portrayed as a buffoon or showman.[45] Thanks largely to the work of cartoonists, his jut-jawed posture and arrogant swagger were transformed into the comical traits of a man who was even once dubbed 'the Falstaff of the *Fascisti*'.[46]

The positive aspects of his image began to turn in the mid-1930s and were in sharp decline before the declaration of war in 1940. The once-dynamic leader was turned into a dangerous warmonger, a blusterer, and then into a lackey of Hitler. In a typical satirical strategy of belittlement, he was depicted in feminine guise, as a petulant child or as animals such as a rhinoceros, toad, dog or fish. The most powerful of all the foreign parodies of Mussolini was Charlie Chaplin's 1940 film *The Great Dictator*. Remembered mainly for Chaplin's double-playing of a Jewish barber and the Hitler-esque dictator of the fictional state of Tomania, Adenoid Hynkel, it also featured comic actor Jack Oakie in the role of Benzino Napaloni, rival dictator of the allied state of Bacteria. A swaggering buffoon, Napaloni speaks with an Italian accent not unlike that of Chico Marx and is used mainly in moments of pure farce.[47] The film was included in a package of twenty films that were distributed in liberated areas by the Psychological Warfare Branch of the Allied forces with the aim of persuading Italians of the merits of their military campaign.

The power of satirical art was familiar to some one-time Fascists who turned their artistry from regime-approved targets like the ultra-thin modern woman or the foppish dandy, to Mussolini himself. The artist Mino Maccari, who had made his name as leader of the ruralist *Strapaese* movement, had often featured satirical engravings of personalities in his magazine, *Il Selvaggio*. Like the journalist Leo Longanesi, he had been allowed to poke fun at contemporary foibles on account of his fundamental alignment with the Fascist regime. Now he turned his talents against the fallen Duce. The paintings he exhibited at his house in the Tuscan village of Cinquale on 6–7 September 1943 were strikingly derisive.[48] The 'Dux' series was perhaps not strictly satirical since there was little need to deflate a man who had recently lost power, but some of the techniques of satire, notably physical distortion and reduction, were deployed by the artist. Maccari's deliberately small-scale, cartoonish pictures did not rob Mussolini of all dignity (his features were distorted and blubbery but he was neither feminised nor turned into an animal) and, in one or two of them, he was even drawn sympathetically to some degree. Nevertheless, the artist scoffed openly at his large head and mocked his total identification with power.[49] The bloated and lecherous figure of the dictator was also the inspiration behind the hundreds of drawings and sketches of a character called 'Gibbo' that the

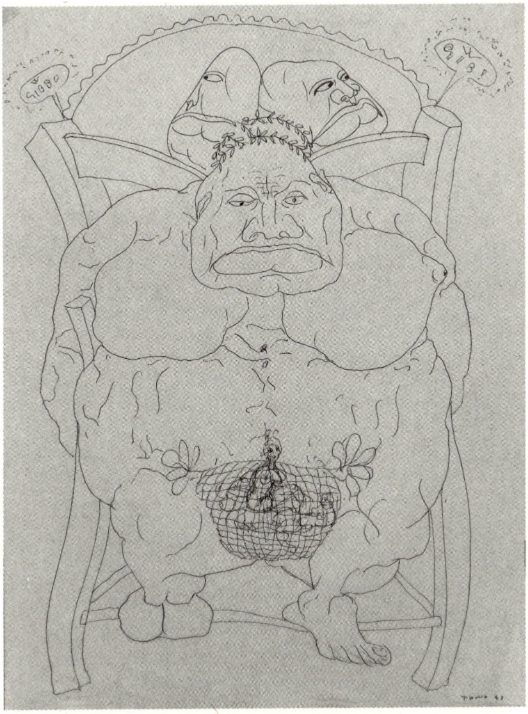

Figure 3. Tono Zancanaro 'W Gibbo' (Long Live Gibbo, 1943). Zancanaro drew his Gibbo figure hundreds of times between 1937 and 1943. In this example, his semi-human (note the hoof) Mussolini-style figure sits on a throne wearing only a G-String that holds several miniature female bodies. Behind him, the deformed heads looking each way allude to the dictator's omniscience. In the background can be seen the echoes of a crowd. By kind permission of the Archivio Storico Tono Zancanaro.

anti-fascist Paduan artist Tono Zancanaro produced between 1937 and 1943 and which he circulated after Mussolini's fall (see Figure 3).[50] Though inspired by an eclectic range of sources including a circus wrestler who resembled the Duce and a deformed woman well known on the streets of Padua, Gibbo was a repulsive version of Mussolini. In turn horrible, absurd or amusing, Zancanaro's imaginative creation served as a vehicle to attack the pomposities and vanities of a highly personal dictatorship. The writer Carlo Emilio Gadda would follow a similar line in the vitriolic text he began to work on in 1941 and which would see the light of day only in 1967, and even then in abridged form.[51] Drawing on classical caricatures of figures of power as well Tuscan and Roman popular expressions, he fashioned a sarcastic denunciation of the 'parvenu prince'—the 'priapic imago of the podium'—who had for twenty years postured and performed for an Italian people who had regressed to a pre-ethical state of quasi-erotic enslavement.[52]

Despite some caution, the Allies were convinced that the Italians could be won over. 'In Italy we have no doubt that the downfall of Mussolini will be heralded with joy by the common man', Radio Londra announced.[53] Fascism had turned the armed forces into political instruments with disastrous consequences, starting with the Greek campaign. The invasion of Sicily was the final straw. According to the London *Daily Mail*, the landing was greeted with celebrations on the part of a population that had been demoralised by the ineptitude of Italy's military command and the emptiness of promises of victory. Jaded and war-weary, the population embraced the troops as liberators. The journalists who accompanied the Allied forces left accounts of their experience of war and peace in the peninsula. One of the first books arising from the Allied campaign was John Hershey's 1944 novel *A Bell for Adano*, which focused on the efforts of an Italian-American officer named Major Joppolo to help the local people in the town of Adano, who are keenly mourning the loss of a 700-year-old town bell that had been removed by Fascists and taken away to be melted down for weapons. Using all his influence as the town's interim administrator, he provides the town with a bell that is offered to him by the commander of an American warship.[54] The novel was swiftly turned into a film. *A Bell for Adano* (Henry King, 1945) displays a serious effort to capture something of what the soldiers encountered as they began their eighteen-month-long campaign in Italy.[55] When Joppolo first reaches the town, his eyes fall on the Fascist slogans painted on the walls. A large silhouette of Mussolini's head adorns the side of one building. When the American walks through the empty rooms of a large municipal building, he notices a large rectangular dust mark on a wall where a painting once hung; Mussolini's portrait had been removed, but the trace of its having been there remained.

As they gradually took control of the territories of the Italian empire and then fought their way up the peninsula, the troops were repeatedly faced with monuments, images and inscriptions that testified to recent subordination to a dictator. When the British Eighth Army under General Montgomery entered Tripoli in January 1943, bringing the Italian empire in North Africa to an end, they came face to face with an equestrian statue of Mussolini holding aloft the sword of Islam, which had been presented to him in a lavish ceremony in March 1937.[56] The statue was commandeered by soldiers belonging to the regiment of Royal Electrical and Mechanical Engineers and taken down in order that the metal could be used for the manufacture of spare parts during preparation of the assault on Sicily that would take place in July.[57] In Rome, Allied soldiers were fascinated by the places of Fascist power like Palazzo Venezia and its balcony, from which Mussolini had harangued the crowds. According to the dictator's son Romano, visiting Palazzo Venezia and entering the Sala del Mappamondo, where the dictator's office had been, was the ambition of Allied soldiers newly arrived in Rome. He further recalled a soldier named Sergeant Finn who later told him that he had gone into 'Il Duce's empty office in Piazza Venezia together with my fellow soldiers from the Black Devils Brigade. I sat in Mussolini's chair and put my feet up on his desk. Then I went out and looked from the balcony. There was a mass of people yelling outside. I didn't speak Italian but I felt I had to say something to them. I raised my arms and yelled, "Viva l'Italia"'.[58] The Duce's son, with this anecdote, painted a picture of the Allied soldiers' derisive attitude towards the Italians. Certainly, at all levels, there was a degree of suspicion towards a population that had rapidly changed allegiances. The status of co-belligerent against Germany that was conferred on Italy and its royal government showed that the country was not regarded as an ally.[59] Indeed, in many respects it was treated as a defeated enemy. 'Co-belligerancy', the British Foreign Office said, 'means trying to treat the Italians as friends and foes at the same time'.

The Allied army made steady progress in its battle to conquer territories north of Rome, at least until the Winter of 1944, when German mountain defences seriously slowed the advance. Florence was liberated in August 1944 and in October 1944 the towns of the Romagna region fell. When Allied soldiers entered Mussolini's birthplace of Predappio and the nearby town of Forlì in October 1944, they found evidence of a pervasive cult of personality. Although by that time, some items had been looted, enough remained for troops to be photographed holding portraits of the Duce and other objects that appeared to have been sent to dictator as personal homages (see Figure 4).[60] These sorts of artefacts aroused curiosity, but they were also a source of concern to the Allied command because they demonstrated that the cult was not just imposed and orchestrated.[61] There had been significant engagement and a nuanced interplay between the official and unofficial, the high and low, the private and public. The attachment to Mussolini, in other words, had not been quite as superficial as some had supposed but was as deep as others had feared.

In occupied areas of the peninsula, which by October 1944 included Naples and the whole of southern Italy, supreme authority remained with the Allies. The question of using the occupation to impress on Italians the consequences of Fascist imperialism was prominent in British minds, while both they and the

Figure 4. British soldiers inspect evidence of Mussolini's cult of personality on reaching Forlì-Predappio in October 1944. Image courtesy of the Imperial War Museums (NA 19987).

Americans were keen to ensure that de-fascistisation took place in the country's institutions without it going too far. The Badoglio government was supported, while the Resistance was encouraged only within strict limits for fear that it might escalate into a force for social revolution. The management of the occupation, however, left a great deal to be desired and in Naples it was disastrous.[62] Severe bombing had damaged the social fabric and led to homelessness, a lack of water and sanitation problems which together contributed to give the city the air of returning to a plague-ridden past.[63] People were reduced to a basic struggle for survival, something that the writer Curzio Malaparte described as 'humiliating, horrible, a shameful necessity'.[64] Prostitution, the black market, food shortages, displaced children living on the street, and crime were indicators of a complete social breakdown.

The American journalist Herbert Matthews, who covered the Allied invasion and the final months of Mussolini's rule at the head of the Nazi-backed RSI, was acutely alert to the hostility that much of the Italian population felt towards the Americans and especially the British.[65] 'Throughout the war, well-meaning Americans and Britishers really believed that Italians and others should have been thankful for having their countries used as battlefields and turned into shambles', he later reflected.[66] 'Had we looked upon this as punishment and retribution for shameful policies, it would have made sense, but to go into Italy, destroy it, and then tell people they ought to be grateful, was hypocrisy'. He was not surprised when the bitterness of Romans, reduced to a wretched state by the consequences of war, was crystallised in a slogan that was painted one night on a wall in the Trastevere district: *Arrivolemo er puzzone* (We want the big stinker back).[67] The stinker was Mussolini and the graffito became the most characteristic expression of the discouragement and resentment of the common people.[68] It was all the more striking because the Trastevere district had only a few months before been the scene of women's protests against the German occupation and giant red writings had appeared on the walls, reading 'Bread, death to the fascists and the Germans. Long live Stalin'.[69]

To suggest that there was widespread nostalgia for Mussolini in cities like Naples and Rome would be a serious overstatement. But nor was public opinion fully aligned with the Allies. While peace was widely welcomed, contemporary diaries convey a sense that the Italians did not so much deprecate the war as regret the fact of having lost it.[70] The regime's fault was not to have launched an unnecessary war but to have failed to turn its dreams of greatness into reality after it had whipped up enthusiasm for a project of military expansion. The armistice was a humiliating outcome and, even in the South, there was shame at a dishonourable surrender. Despite censorship, jibes against the Allies multiplied in the satirical press and the theatre revues. This was striking, because by 1944 all the certainties that Fascism had sought to inculcate in the population as it aimed to project the country towards a future of conquest had been shaken to the core.[71] The brutal expansion wished for and enacted by the Fascist regime had been forced back upon itself. Bombardment, famine and the sounds of foreign invaders replaced the orderly choreography and paternalistic reassurances of the mid-1930s.[72] Yet the man who, more than anyone, was responsible for reducing the country to this state, thanks to Hitler's backing, had not yet been finally swept way. He was still hanging on at the head of an ever smaller and more fragile RSI. Furthermore, if his words were to be believed, he was still convinced that final victory and redemption were somehow possible.

4

Death and damnation

Early on the morning of Sunday 29 April, several trucks manned by partisans rolled into the centre of Milan. When they reached the Piazzale Loreto, a short walk from the central station, the men unloaded their macabre cargo. The bodies of Mussolini, Claretta Petacci and twelve senior Fascists were dumped on the ground without ceremony. The Allies had not yet reached the northern city, though they would do so in a matter of hours. It was in the hands of partisans who had seen off the last Germans in an uprising that also occurred in the other big cities of the North, the last in the country to be liberated. It was a spring morning and soon people began to gather to view the spectacle. Following broadcast of the news on the radio, many more arrived to verify for themselves that the man who had ruled them for more than two decades was dead. Loudspeaker vans called on people to come and see. Many came out of curiosity, in celebratory mood, but the attitude of the crowd turned from happy to angry as it gave voice to hatred for Mussolini.[1] For anti-fascists, the dictator had signed his own death warrant long before; for others, antipathy was more recent.[2] Mussolini's dead body was turned into a spectacle in retribution for the blood that Fascism had spilled or caused to be spilled by taking the country into war. More acutely pressing though were intense resentments arising from the brutality of the last few months of the RSI.

The scenes were captured by a photographer, Fedele Toscani, using both a still camera and a movie camera, and they were witnessed by journalists including some foreign correspondents. People gathered round to deliver blows and kicks to the bodies; some spat on Mussolini's corpse, while bullets were also fired. Insults were shouted and abuse heaped on the once powerful dictator. Even in death Mussolini was unmistakable; bashed and beaten out of shape, the head was still the shaved round one with the prominent jaw that everyone knew. By late morning, the bodies had been hoisted high and hung by their feet from the metal roof of a petrol station to allow the ever-growing crowd to get a view. The one-time Duce drew most attention, as he always had. 'Beside him, also head downwards, hangs the body of Claretta Petacci, his mistress', wrote Challinor James, the Swiss-based correspondent of the *Daily Mail*:

> her dark hair tumbled about her face; her white lace blouse curiously clean against the hideous thing that was the Duce. On either side of them hang 15 other Fascists, mostly members of the Duce's 'Republican Fascist' Cabinet. All day the people of Milan have been milling round these hated men. They have fired bullets into the body of the man who once claimed to lead them. They have kicked it, and they have spat on it. To-night it seems that they will not be satisfied until they have torn it to pieces.[3]

A picture of Mussolini's corpse lying on the ground while armed partisans regard it with a mixture of triumph and contempt was published on the front page of the *New York Times* under the title 'The inglorious end of a dictator'. The paper's correspondent wrote: 'The story of his final downfall, his flight, his capture and his execution is not pretty, and its epilogue in the Piazza Loretto [*sic*] here this morning was its ugliest part. It will go down in history as a finish to tyranny as horrible as any ever visited on a tyrant'.[4]

Mussolini had been captured by partisans as he was seeking to flee to Switzerland under German protection. Once news of his detention was received, the order to execute him was imparted by the Committee of National Liberation (CLN). A Communist partisan, known by the battle name of Colonel Valerio, was despatched to Como to take charge and carry out the order.[5] Despite some resistance from the local partisans holding the fallen dictator, he fulfilled his mission on the afternoon of 28 April. Exactly how Mussolini died has long been disputed. In the following days, news sources reported that that he had been shot in the back or he had been tricked into thinking he was being saved, only to find himself face-to-face with his executioner.[6] The nature of his end would be discussed in minute detail for decades afterwards by those with an axe of one sort or another to grind and would become a side chapter of the story of war's end in Italy.

Mussolini's death was the last decisive moment in the civil war that saw Italians wanting to give shape to a new Italy fight against fellow countrymen who, by choice or by compulsion, were enrolled in the forces of the RSI. For some time before he met his final end, Mussolini had been compared to Napoleon. The dictator sometimes saw himself in the guise of the former emperor on St Helena and consoled himself with the thought that, after a period of repudiation and denigration, he had gradually come to be recognised as a great Frenchman.[7] The parallel also occurred to others, especially after

Mussolini was rescued and reinstalled to power. The contemporary historian Luigi Salvatorelli re-examined the Napoleonic legend in a book published in 1944, in which he aimed to show its relationship to contemporary Caesarism or 'ducismo'.[8] Like many, the historian conserved a modicum of admiration for Napoleon, the 'creator of a new order', who he considered 'the most important personality of the nineteenth century, perhaps also the precursor... of the twentieth'.[9] But he also saw Napoleon as the source of the modern, irrational activism of the dictators because his dynamism was an end in itself, independently of what it produced or any moral value.[10] Napoleon, he argued, was the founder of 'ducismo' or 'Führertum', first because the intimate connection between the system of personal rule and war was established by him and, second, because in all of these permutations 'the nation is conceived and treated like an army that obeys without question or, better, like a flock that gathers, leaves and returns to the pen at the command of the shepherd, who milks and shears it and takes it to slaughter as and when he likes'.[11]

By the final days of the conflict, many of Mussolini's once committed backers had gone to ground. By the time his dead body was brought to Milan and subjected to the abuse of the baying crowd, public discourse was already shaped in such a way as to suggest that all sympathy had evaporated. The macabre spectacle of repudiation that took place in Piazzale Loreto provided dramatic visible evidence that the Italians were ready to embark on a new path. In simple terms, it communicated to the world the message that they no longer cultivated any residual attachment to their dictator. His death was required, wrote the Socialist Pietro Nenni, to placate the memory of martyrs from Matteotti on, and the memory of 'all the sons of Italy who have left their youth in the Libyan desert, on the steppes of the Don, in the Greek mountains'.[12] It was seen to be necessary for the resurrection of the country. Mussolini had to die, Nenni continued, 'by the hand of the people so that tomorrow it becomes possible to forget the past, to forgive minor guilts and to proceed to the national reconciliation that is necessary to face the tasks of the reconstruction'.[13]

Under the terms of the Armistice of September 1943, Mussolini was to be handed over to the Allies. The dictator himself was convinced this was the intention of the Badoglio government.[14] But, in the confusion of the desperate scramble to leave Rome, the matter was allegedly overlooked—with dire consequences. It was the opinion of the Americans that the leaders of Fascism should be captured and put on trial before an international court, as would occur with the surviving members of the Nazi and Japanese leaderships.[15] By contrast, the Resistance was keen to avoid a trial, and above all an international one, because it would inevitably have turned into a trial of twenty years of Fascist rule. This would have shed unwelcome light on numerous complicities, on the extensive backing Mussolini had received from within the state and the social and economic elites, not to mention the support he had been given by the wider population. As anti-fascist General Raffaele Cadorna, who joined the Resistance in 1944, would write in his memoirs, published in 1975, it was important to impose silence over 'facts and circumstances where it was very difficult to separate the responsibilities of a people from those of a leader'.[16] To grant a platform to the ex-dictator would have cast a shadow over the narrative of a nation unified in its opposition to Fascism that was being constructed as a basis for a new democratic order. Also, and by no means secondarily, it was important that Mussolini was dealt with by Italians, that they oversaw the end of Fascism themselves. Even some foreign observers thought this was important.[17]

Piazzale Loreto was chosen as the location because in August 1944, fifteen anti-fascist prisoners had been shot there by the Republican National Guard in retaliation for partisan attacks and Allied bombing raids, and their bodies had then been left on display for a whole day. This gesture caused huge offence to the whole city, including to some still sympathetic to Fascism.[18] The piazza therefore had a symbolic importance, and dumping the corpse of the dictator and his associates there set up an equivalence that satisfied a demand for revenge. In fact the square had been popularly if briefly renamed 'Piazza 15 Martyrs'.[19] However, the decision was not approved by the top command of the Resistance, and it was felt by some to have profaned a place that had been bathed with the blood of martyrs. The use of a different location in the square for the display of Fascist bodies made little difference.[20] The Resistance leader and soon-to-be prime minister Ferruccio Parri deplored the spectacle as 'a Mexican butchery', referring to the violence of the revolution of 1910 and the civil conflict that followed. Other Resistance figures battled vainly in the years that followed to promote the memory of the fifteen martyrs over that of the dead dictator.[21]

The crowd's behaviour was deemed by the CLN to have degenerated into excess. It was seen as a product of the degeneration of civic life under Fascism, being regarded as 'understandable solely in relation to the climate sought and created by Mussolini' and so Fascism itself was 'the sole culprit'.[22] The exhibition had the benefit of providing incontrovertible proof that Mussolini was dead, and that fact could only be achieved by some sort of public display of his body. Had he been hastily buried without ceremony following his execution, questions would have been asked and his death might well have been doubted.

He had returned once from the political grave, and it needed to be made clear he could not return a second time. The Socialist Party paper *l'Avantì* declared that the spectacle of Piazzale Loreto was 'horrible' but 'necessary':[23] 'The people were forced to execute their tyrant to free themselves of the nightmare of an irreparable offence', it declared.[24]

Some commentators agreed. Writer Carlo Emilio Gadda was pleased and expressed great relief.[25] Luigi Meneghello, who was a partisan belonging to the liberal Justice and Liberty group later wrote that 'it was necessary to get rid of fascism in a way that was perceptible to the senses, shrug it off in a showy and exemplary way'.[26] From this point of view, what occurred in the square was, symbolically, 'a modern ritual of dethronement that preserved some aspects of the ancient rite.[27] The writer Aldo Palazzeschi affirmed that 'justice has been done in the most exhaustive way. In such circumstances you cannot take limited measures; justice has been as abundant as was the evil'.[28] These views were endorsed by public opinion in the Allied countries.[29] Images of the dictator's battered body were published prominently in the press in the USA and Britain.[30] However, did the repudiation contain an element of opportunism? The journalist Antal Mazzotti was not alone in reaching the conclusion that the huge crowd of Piazzale Loreto was a crowd 'that in the past would have rushed to any piazza in Italy to scream deliriously for Mussolini'.[31] 'Who amongst this composite crowd had not at some time—three, five or ten years earlier—been moved by the triumphalist speeches of the dictator?' French historian Pierre Milza later wondered.[32] 'Before becoming the most hated man in Italy, had he not been the most loved?', Milza reflected, recalling that, for about fifteen years, Mussolini had been an 'object of cult and adoration in all sectors of society'. If true, this was a devastating criticism of the supposed opportunism and base conformism of the Italians. It echoed some remarks that had been advanced about the casting off of exterior signs of Fascist allegiances in July 1943 and also about the change in war-time alliances heralded by the armistice.

In fact, there is no evidence that the people gathered in the square on 29 April were the same as those who had acclaimed Mussolini, especially if the reference is to his speech of December 1944. On that occasion, 20,000 Fascists were brought to Milan from the surrounding provinces to fill out the streets, while 1,600 ultra-faithful loyalists in uniform occupied the Lirico Theatre.[33] This time the crowd was neither conscripted nor orchestrated, although it has been suggested that the noisy roar and shouts of invective that emanated from it were not consistent and fell away when not periodically stimulated.[34] Many of those who were identified in accounts of the day as examples of the people's rage—like the woman who is said to have fired bullets into Mussolini's body in revenge for the deaths of her children—were motivated by genuine grievances.[35] Despite the efforts of anti-fascists to portray the ferocity displayed towards the bodies as payback for the whole experience of Fascism, more specifically it was a product of the anger that the brutal conduct of the Fascist armed forces and the Germans had stoked with the tactics of reprisal and massacres, a key example of which was the mass execution that had taken place in that very same square in August 1944.

Public opinion is never a unified phenomenon and even in Piazzale Loreto, as well as genuine anti-fascist anger, there was evidence of idle curiosity. The spectacle was for some simply that, a spectacle. The prospect of seeing Claretta Petacci, the woman who had been the dictator's lover, was itself a draw. Away from the square where the macabre events unfolded, the atmosphere was quite different. The journalist Emilio Radius found as he moved around the city that some people were ready to deplore the exposure of the bodies: 'In Corso Buenos Aires, for example, near the intersection with Via Vetruvio, people sought to remove their eyes from the sight of the corpses hung up by their feet and only had words of disapproval for the authors of the outrage. However, these words were few and were weighed carefully, with a concern not to overdo it and not to be taken for leftovers of the side that was so abhorred'.[36] He found people at the corner of Via Gregorio who had seen the bodies advising others not to do so. In churches and outside of them, women were reciting the requiem for the dead and making the sign of the cross.

The death of Mussolini was followed by public acts of retribution in other cities against Fascist officials who had been guilty of causing death and destruction during the RSI. These included some executions, such as the botched hanging of the provincial secretary of the Fascist Party in Turin, Giuseppe Solaro. Across the north and centre of the country, the bloody settling of accounts would continue for months. However, in much of the country, as well as in certain strands of opinion, the death of Mussolini was experienced in silence. This mute strand of opinion that was to a large degree contained in private thoughts, would not in that moment find any form of expression, though it would be articulated in the years that followed by right-wing journalists, including Indro Montanelli. Montanelli voiced the feeling that the posthumous lynching left him with 'a vague sense of shame'.[37]

For some observers, the whole affair seemed like a macabre parody of Fascist culture. All eyes, in other words, remained trained on the man who—whether adored or reviled, worshipped or abused—had occupied the Italian imagination for over twenty years.[38] The imagery of his battered corpse was a product of what young RSI volunteer Carlo Mazzantini later called 'our iconographic vision of the world'.[39] Standards of civil coexistence had dropped dramatically in a context in which people were brutalised by Fascism and war.[40] The conduct of the crowd bore witness to the specific experience of civil war in the northern cities and Milan in particular. One historian even judges that the whole spectacle seemed to rest on a peculiar unconscious assumption that the Duce was still alive.[41] Piazzale Loreto never became an event to be celebrated and remembered in official commemorations. Nor did the place itself become a site of lasting remembrance, either for the fifteen martyrs (a somewhat nondescript monument was erected in their memory to one side of the square) or for the spectacle of 29 April 1945. The petrol station was demolished in 1948 and subsequent urban innovations turned the square into an anonymous non-place.[42] Mazzantini was struck by the fact that the corpses strung up with Mussolini—who was 'just a shadow of his old self anyway'—were mostly non-entities. There were none of the bigwigs of Fascism, some of whom—the traitors of 25 July—had been shot months before, while others had disappeared into hiding. Mazzantini observed: 'How many of the leaders were there, the ones who had been on the front pages of the newspapers until then? The ministers, the academics, the scientists, all the ones who gave lectures and speeches? What about the writers and journalists, the ones who went around smiling and shaking hands, or who were simply there?'[43] These were people who in some cases would never appear in public again, while others would find ready ways to insert themselves quietly into the new order of things.

For some dedicated Fascists who had thrown in their lot with the RSI, the news of Mussolini's death came as a total shock.[44] People like Zelmira Marazio, who had been a volunteer auxiliary, feared for their own skin as they were at risk of anti-fascist reprisals. Between 1945 and 1947 some five thousand auxiliaries were targeted. For her and for many others, the path from Fascism to democracy was far from simple, also because, in her case, Fascist and religious beliefs were intertwined. Mussolini's death left her with a deep psychological wound: 'for us he remained beautiful, great, luminous, as we had loved him', she wrote years later. But doubts inevitably entered her mind. 'How could God have let this happen?', she wondered. A priest helped her by telling her that the best did not always triumph and that she was suffering like Christ, who had also been misunderstood and betrayed. She left her native Turin and went to rebuild her life as a teacher in Sicily. She had no regrets and felt no guilt about her past, and she never spoke about her youthful political engagement during thirty years as a teacher. Only towards the end of her life did she write a memoir. Another believer, Carlo Ciseri, was less dramatically affected, but he still found adjustment to postwar life difficult; Mussolini's regime had encapsulated everything he cared for deeply, his very idea of Italy and its glories.[45] He returned in 1946 after five years in prison camps in Africa to a humiliated and divided nation. He had vowed after World War I never to get involved in politics. Mussolini had caused him to overcome his disenchantment. For twenty years, he had participated fully in the collective passion for the Duce, keeping press cuttings and tributes. After 1945, he immersed himself in the private sphere and never indulged in reflection on the past.

Inevitably the end of Mussolini would be compared to that of Hitler, the collective love-object of the Germans. The Führer avoided capture and execution by taking his own life in his Berlin bunker on 30 April. He made sure there would be no public desecration of his body by leaving orders that it should be burned immediately after his death. In his case too, there was shock among loyalists, to the extent that some even committed suicide rather than live on after him.[46] However, as historian Volker Ullrich writes, ordinary Germans 'greeted the news of Hitler's death not with sadness but with apathy, even relief. The Führer myth had lost nearly all its power in the final months of the war, and with that, National Socialism was robbed of its major appeal. The spell had indeed been broken'.[47] What the loss of a love-object meant was barely perceived in a context in which the relationship with the hero of past years was abruptly truncated. But this is not to say that there was not a deep trauma. With Hitler, Alexander and Margerete Mitscherlich asserted, 'identifications that had filled a central function in the lives of his followers were attached to his person .... He had become the embodiment of their ego-ideal'.[48] 'The loss of an object so highly cathected with libidinal energy—one about whom nobody had any doubts, nor dared to have any, even when the country was being reduced to rubble—was indeed reason for melancholia', they wrote, 'Through the catastrophe, not only was the German ego-ideal robbed of the support of reality, but in addition the Führer himself was exposed by the victors as a criminal of truly monstrous proportions. With this sudden reversal of his qualities, the ego of every single German individual suffered a central devaluation and impoverishment'.[49]

Some historians have argued that the profound symbiosis between leader and led that existed in Germany was not to be found in Italy, where the relationship was more pragmatic, even utilitarian. What is surely true is that Mussolini's position as ego-ideal had been weakened in stages and had been undermined by the presentation of alternatives to Fascism far earlier than had been so in Germany. The transformation of Mussolini from love-object to a focus of collective hatred was to some degree a consequence of the replacement of a media system of insistent exaltation with a more heterogeneous one in which opposition and denigration were repetitive motifs.[50] The process had begun immediately after Badoglio replaced the dictator as prime minister in 1943. Moreover, Allied propaganda had stoked hatred and contempt for Mussolini personally. Radio Londra had blamed him for the sufferings of the Italians in a deliberate strategy to shatter the image of the superman among a population that, despite the war and atrocities, had not yet embraced active anti-fascism.[51] After the liberation of Rome, left-wing newspapers joined in. But the feelings of melancholy over the removal and ignominious end of a figure in whom much energy had been invested were widespread in a part of public opinion, though this was not for sure the most prominent or vocal part. The repudiation and damnation that in Germany was decided and communicated by the Allies was in Italy embraced and promoted by Italian anti-fascists. Mussolini was expelled from the community and indicted for all the crimes of Fascism by fellow countrymen who spoke for another Italy. Those who felt differently, who had identified with and interiorised the cult of the dictator, and who did not feel that everything about Fascism and about their own pasts was worthless, were excluded, though they found spokesmen willing to give expression to their views. These were barely legitimate in the context of the return to democracy, but the very violence of the act of repudiation that occurred on 29 April 1945 somehow changed the perception of Mussolini from tyrant to a sort of victim. As the historian Giovanni Scirocco has observed, 'Right from the start, Piazzale Loreto represented a dramatic caesura between victors and vanquished, between fascism and Liberation; it was the symbol of a memory that marked the end of an epoch and the beginning of a new one and that, as such, could not be unanimous and not even shared or reconciled. At best it was in common'.[52] Right-wing journalists and commentators adopted an indignant stance and, at first cautiously, cast themselves in the role of posthumous defenders of the discarded Duce. The appalling end of his career somehow not only sanctioned the opening of a new political season but legitimated a memory of the regime in which personal investments in consent were not a source of shame.[53] In this way, the spectacle of Piazzale Loreto played a part in the peculiar process whereby a failed leader and fallen idol became a figure of some sympathy, an imperfect individual who was deserving of understanding and indulgence. No longer a demi-god, Mussolini became once more a common man marked by human flaws. The unspoken implication of this was that he could perhaps be pardoned for having carried his country to catastrophe. As the veil of propaganda was steadily drawn back, virtually every aspect of his family life and domestic and personal habits was brought into the public realm. New narratives and story lines were created revolving around his foibles and vanities, his long affair with Petacci and the tales his family members and staff peddled about him. Mussolini had always been a celebrity of sorts and he remained difficult to ignore as he began a new existence as a ghost.

PART II

'Our' Mussolini

5

Getting over dictatorship

After the bodies were taken down from the petrol station in Piazzale Loreto, they were taken to the morgue of Milan's Musocco cemetery, the most important in the city. Mussolini's disfigured body was subjected to an autopsy by Professor Caio Mario Cattabeni, who took measurements, extracted a portion of the brain and established that seven bullets had killed the dictator. The event was attended by various officials and representatives of the Allies and was photographed. Further autopsies would be conducted over the next days. Several weeks after this, the bodies that had been exposed in the Piazzale were buried without ceremony in unmarked graves (that, in reality, were readily identifiable) in Field 16 of the cemetery. There, it was expected, would end the story of Benito Mussolini, though not everyone believed this. The American journalist Herbert Matthews caused considerable controversy when he argued that, as long as a trace of the Fascist spirit remained, Mussolini would continue to cast a shadow. He offered a prescient warning: 'Mussolini is buried now in a pauper's grave on the edge of Milan, but even if his body lies there it is foolish to think his spirit will'.[1] Mussolini and Hitler 'in death will live to plague us all for generations to come. That ill-assorted pair, those strange political bedfellows are going to haunt this world of ours until we lay their ghosts—if we ever can—by instilling democracy in the hearts and minds of Germans and Italians'.[2] As he saw it, the party and the practices were only the 'trappings of Fascism'.[3] The real problem lay with the mentality of the people and the 'spirit of Fascism'.[4] In brief, this consisted of faith in a strong man and admiration for force and violence. 'The young have been deeply engrained with a love of soldiery and its attendant uniforms, medals, pomp and glory, and defeat has not eliminated that feeling', he warned. Already in 1943, in the immediate aftermath of Mussolini's downfall, George Murray of the *Daily Mail* argued that, despite suggestions to the contrary, the one-time Duce would not become a 'forgotten dictator': 'I suspect that it will take history a long time to forget Mussolini, if it ever does', he stated.[5] It did not matter that he was 'a braggart and a poseur'.[6] On account of his evil, rather than despite it, 'he represents in his person a well-defined phase of world history'. He brought 'blood and misery not to a few thousands in Italy but to millions in many countries' and, of course, he was Hitler's mentor. 'Had the Italian lived and died a blacksmith like his father', Murray argued, 'the Austrian might never have been more than a doss-house lounger'.

Exorcising a dictator is a complex matter. Modern dictators have a rare capacity to situate themselves in the imagination of their fellow men and to create forms of emotional and psychological involvement on the part of all but the most hardened opponents. This is something that it is not usually easy to admit after the tyrant has been defeated or swept away. If, by the time of his death, Mussolini had lost entirely the imaginative hold he once commanded and the spell he had cast over the Italians was truly broken, then there would be no need to inquire into the mechanisms of psychological dependency that had tied people to the man. But this was not the case, despite what many wished to think. The clumsy actions that were taken in relation to Mussolini's mortal remains are proof of that. The dictator had once been seen by many as a father figure; he had been the personification of Fascism but also of the nation. There had been an investment in him to the extent that many Italians saw Mussolini's story as their own.[7] By embodying traits including an idea of a past greatness to be reasserted, male sexual power and personal vanity, he became a sort of reflection of a diffuse national self-perception.[8]

All of this was shaken and in some aspects shattered by the complex transitions that Italy underwent between 1943 and 1948. People were thrust into a dramatic and unstable context in which their sense of themselves and of their roles in society were upset and, in some cases, destroyed. The interim period between Fascism and democracy was a time of existential as well as political uncertainty; power as a sense of certainty was replaced by a void.[9] The very matter of how to think about power was at stake: democracy was the new credo, but it did not prove easy to undo the habit of thinking of authority as something that was embodied in one man—or the fact that the 'one man' was always inevitably Mussolini.

In their work on Germany after Hitler, Alexander and Margerete Mitscherlich argued that, for the German people, it was simpler to consign Hitler to oblivion, to deny to oneself and others that the Führer had been a collective love-object and an ego-ideal, than it was to own up to the fact that a loss had been experienced that was the equivalent not so much to the death of a dearly loved relative or friend as of a part of oneself.[10] Wilful forgetting was the shocking opposite of the atonement that the international community demanded of the Germans and in which German governments formally engaged. The silence over Hitler, his repression in psychoanalytical terms, was necessary, the Mitscherlichs explained, to allow people to maintain a sense of self-worth and pick themselves up from a devastating defeat.

In Italy, the historian Luca La Rovere has argued, the same goal of repression was achieved by means of an intensive labour of elaboration and re-elaboration of the past. By these means a type of active de-realisation of Fascism occurred.[11] The way the regime was thought of was fragmentary and contradictory, composed of collective and individual instances that could not be integrated into a coherent account. Efforts to heal the trauma of dictatorship and its end took the form of talking about Fascism, recounting it and mulling it over as a national experience.[12] However, 'active removal' of this sort was a part of the process, one that—it might be suggested—was accompanied by a series of displacements that involved denial, forgetting, repression and negotiation. In addition to the public process that was concentrated in the first instance in the immediate postwar years, and that itself involved blocking out aspects of Fascism and a refusal to accept collective responsibility for its crimes, there were many private acts of reinvention that concealed and repressed past alignments and enthusiasms instead of confessing and confronting them.

In Italy, as in Germany, there was a strong emphasis on the great suffering that had been experienced by common civilians during the war and the foreign occupations. This, it was hoped, might mitigate calls for an acknowledgement of guilt. In general, however, Italians were not inclined to accept that the German and Italian regimes had much in common. A soft or reductive view of Mussolini prevailed according to which he was a histrionic exhibitionist who had captivated the Italians temporarily and misled them before they had returned to their senses and rejected him. They had taken to the streets when he was overthrown, they had detached morally and then practically from the Axis war, and unlike the Germans, they had participated in the liberation and had rejoiced when he was killed.

In a 1946 article, the philosopher Croce elaborated the theory that any nation could have succumbed to dictatorship on account of a vulnerability of modern man towards inhuman values, which he labelled 'a tendency of our spirit'.[13] There was nothing specifically Italian, in other words, in the rise of Fascism. If Mussolini came to play a capital role in the lives of millions, it was not on account of intrinsic individual propensities or nationally specific weaknesses of a political and cultural type. Rather, he argued that the country had been contaminated by a negative modern influence. Borrowing from Jewish apocalyptical writing and the German philosophical tradition, he formulated the idea that 'the Antichrist' was not so much 'among us' as 'within us'.[14] This was 'not simply human sinfulness'; rather 'the true Antichrist lies in the denial, negation, outrage and ridicule of values, which are deemed to be empty words, fabrications or, worse still, hypocritical traps'. It consisted of the nullification of freedom and individualism that was the essence of totalitarianism.[15] However, whereas the Germans had succumbed to authoritarianism because their culture was organically predisposed towards it, those Italians who had fallen under the spell of the dictator had been infected by a 'German ethos'.[16] The writer and convert from Fascism to Communism Massimo Bontempelli warned that it would not be possible to move towards a better future 'if first we have not crushed outside and inside of ourselves the spirit that we call Germany, which manifests itself a bit everywhere, because in the intimate nature of every people there has remained some element of primitive wildness'.[17] He argued that the Germans were evil and the Nazi regime was the embodiment of that evil, while the Italians, who were fundamentally good, had never really betrayed their true character.

To explain the spread in Europe of the totalitarian virus, intellectuals preferred to focus on the German case rather than the more familiar domestic one.[18] The psychologist Guido Lami, who wrote a book entitled *The German Psyche* (subtitle *Observations on the psychogenesis of totalitarianism*) shortly after the war, suggested that a European-wide 'psychopathic epidemic' that was the result of intense collective emotions had led men and women to embrace dictatorial regimes.[19] Around an ideological core that was presumed to be rational, a set of psychic instances were concentrated of an emotional and instinctive nature that were ever more independent of the control of reason.[20] As he saw it, 'the essence of the psychological collectivisation of the masses' (which he termed 'the genetic mechanism of dictatorship') lay in the projection on to the person of the dictator of the psychic instance of the super-ego on the part of the members of the mass, group, class or nation.[21] His argument was that under dictatorship a regression of the inhibitory moral role of the superego occurs, diminishing an individual's powers of logical and moral criticism, which leaves the dictator free to lead people where he wants. 'Psychic collectivisation'—that is, the transformation of individuals into an amalgamated mass—occurs when instinctive currents are harnessed and rational ones pushed aside. It takes the form of a diffuse investment of the libido in a leader or political project that offers protection in a context of fear.[22]

In Lami's opinion, the cult of the Führer found an extraordinarily fertile terrain in German individual and collective psychology on account of 'a very strong Germanic sense of the collective interest embodied in the state'.[23] The situation in Italy was different, in his view. Like others, he was of the opinion that the Fascists were not evil so much as delinquents, thugs, idiots with no past, an ignorant and unrefined rabble, headed by a man Croce now dismissed, with striking condescension, as 'a poor devil, ignorant and short on intelligence'.[24] In *The German Psyche*, Lami cited the cry often heard at Fascist mass rallies 'Duce, tu sei tutti noi' [Duce, you are all of us!]. However, he believed that the influence of Fascism on youth, while not insignificant, was 'much less deep and engaged' than the influence of Nazi ideology on German youth.[25] In his diagnosis, there was no deep symbiosis with the leader. Italians were won over to Fascism on the basis of individualism and self-interest, by means of favouritisms, career opportunities and so on.[26]

This line of argument was not entirely convincing to the victorious powers. After all, at one time, it had been Mussolini who had been the embodiment of strongman rule in Europe, a leader who—with the support of his people—had imposed a new direction on his country. He was a strategic model for would-be dictators including Hitler.[27] Stalin argued that 'the Italian people could not be absolved of guilt. It was the Italian people who had thrown up Mussolini'.[28] The very designation 'co-belligerent' masked an ambivalence. Italy was an ally, but it was also a defeated enemy. The negotiations that led up to the peace treaty of 1947, from which Italy was excluded, and the harsh terms which it was more or less forced to accept, showed that, as far as the international community was concerned, the Italian people and their government had to bear responsibility for Fascism and for the disastrous impact it had had on Europe and the world.

In Germany too there was a reluctance to face up to the issue of national guilt. The debate over this question in fact was conducted by a determined minority in the face of mass indifference or hostility. But the universal condemnation of the evil of Nazism meant that, even if it met with resistance, the guilt question was unavoidable. It soon became an important part of the way Germany returned to the international community.[29] In Italy, this external stimulus was missing. The debate about guilt and responsibility was so brief and so widely unwelcome that it has been referred to as the 'lost debate' about collective guilt.[30] The matter of the moral and political responsibilities of the Italians was not one that was faced readily or willingly. The journalist Andrea Damiano, writing in his diary in early 1943, noticed that many were keen to blame Fascism for the disastrous situation in which the country found itself, forgetting that they had backed the regime and drawn benefit from it.[31] It was not an imported phenomenon and frank discussion and expiation constituted, he reflected, 'the necessary antidote against the resurgence of the totalitarian temptation and the indispensable route to the moral, let alone the political, reconstruction of the nation'.[32] The question emerged in the aftermath the liberation of Rome in June 1944, when the new government formulated measures for sanctions against Fascists. Developments in the North truncated the reflection on the heavy heritage of Fascism that developed mainly in Rome. Defeating the enemy was the priority and this reduced the focus on self-examination. Once the whole country was liberated, it receded further. The discovery of the brutality of the Germans and the RSI, together with the heroism of the Resistance fighters, had the effect of bringing a halt to discussion of the guilt of the Italians, whether moral or political.[33] With respect to those who had fallen in with the conformism of the 1930s, the guilt of those who persevered in the error by joining the RSI seemed far greater.[34] In the narration of the war that would develop in the following years there was little self-interrogation or reflection on wider responsibilities. Indeed, for reasons of national reconciliation and pacification, guilt as an issue seemed to disappear, with the consequence that there was little critical awareness in the public sphere of what Fascism had meant for Italy in terms of political violence, anti-semitism, the repression of dissent, colonial atrocities and the wider sacrifice of lives.[35] Only a few commentators acknowledged that blaming Mussolini was not much of an excuse, since dictators in the modern era were products of collective impulses and needs. The Duce, in other words, was nothing less than an imaginary projection of the Italians and defects in the national character. 'The "Duce" has never existed, but there exists this image that is a faithful mirror into which we should look', the writer Aldo Palazzeschi asserted: 'It is we who day by day gave him those hands and that voice, those eyes and that jawline: the "Duce" is our creation, he is flesh of our flesh, blood of our blood and we created him in a moment of vanity, of distraction and exaltation'.[36]

In the most widely accepted version of recent events the alliance with Germany and the collaborationism of the RSI were downplayed. As historian Tony Judt observes, Italy had difficulty acknowledging its recent brutal history and found ways to 'block the memory or at least re-cast it in a usable way that would not corrode the fragile bonds of postwar society'.[37] For obvious reasons, no political force wanted to put the Italians in the dock, but there were differences over how far officials should be purged or punished. The Communist leader Palmiro Togliatti could not accept Croce's argument that Fascism had no social or economic roots, or that it had been merely superficial, but he nonetheless felt that the poison had not spread as widely as in Germany. He conceptualised the majority of Italians as victims of Fascism who had been deluded by the pursuit of empire and the posturing of its chief.[38] Intellectual reflection on the acquiescence to Fascism was not as far-reaching as some hoped and there would be no widespread *mea*—or *nostra*—*culpa*. Over four decades later, the political philosopher Norberto Bobbio, who was born in 1909, observed that 'the problem of guilt has remained an exclusively German problem'.[39] 'On the guilt of Mussolini, of high officials, of the fascists, an infinite number of volumes has been written. But on the guilt of the Italians, taken one by one, and not as a people?'

The fact that almost everyone had been incorporated into the regime, and most had actively cheered the Duce and his successes, remained a sensitive and difficult matter. The impulse towards amnesia, and through amnesia towards exculpation, was the product of a memory of the recent past that was constructed in such a way as to draw a veil over Mussolini and his regime and to move on.[40] For the Church, religion was the best remedy for what Italy had been through and it called for forgiveness whenever desires for revenge manifested themselves. Atonement was a matter for individuals and their consciences, not a collective process. The Church's position was not an external one. Fascism had effected the absorption of Catholicism into the national culture with a view to stabilising the regime and drawing the religious masses into 'Fascist and Catholic Italy'. Under the regime, the culture of the nation entered the Catholic world and Catholicism entered the culture of the nation.[41] Asserting that any examination of conscience was above all a personal rather than a political matter sidestepped discussion of this nexus. In an article entitled 'The Conspiracy of Silence', the leading Socialist Paolo Treves asserted that not only was there a widespread conviction that Fascism had ended but that it had not really existed.[42] To judge by certain public discourses, Treves argued, it seemed that no one had really believed in it and therefore that the Italians had never really been Fascists, at least in an ideological sense, or in thrall to Mussolini. The assumption that the Fascist book was closed for good was a convenient way of avoiding scrutiny of a series of collective and individual decisions to come to terms with Fascism, support its policies and exult in its triumphs. Many people, the young especially, had experienced Fascism as 'a completely natural dimension' that was not too demanding, as one memorialist later wrote; to demand accountability for what had been a widely shared and unthinking adherence—that was now concluded—provoked resentment.[43]

The notion that Fascism could be made to disappear by collective will, as if at the wave of a magician's wand, was equivalent to the process of repression in Germany analysed by the Mitscherlichs.[44] The collapse of the collectivised super-ego dissolved that part of the self that had been invested in a collective project and led to the de-realisation of the dictator and his regime. Several commentators at the time noted the emergence of a 'divided self' or 'multiple selves', a notion that psychologist R. D. Laing would later reprise in his discussion of the phenomenon of de-personalisation in capitalist society.[45] The Sardinian jurist Salvatore Satta wrote about the forced but ultimately temporary transformation of 'traditional man' into 'new man',[46] while journalist Andrea Damiano too suggested that an identitarian reconfiguration occurred in the wake of the catastrophe of war defeat and civil war.[47] By this means, it was possible to consign that part of the self that joined the collective super-ego to the past and rediscover a regular self for the present and future. Later Cesare Musatti deployed the idea of the double self in his discussion of conformism both as the regime was established and later as it fell apart.

What was actively forgotten and made to disappear was not, for sure, the recent civil war with its divisions between Italians and its brutality, although much effort was put into cancelling the story of those who had given their support to the RSI and elevating the sacrifices of those who had fought for the Resistance.[48] What was de-realised was the slavish devotion to Mussolini of the 1920s and 1930s, the ready abandonment of democracy, the enthusiastic backing that had been given to an aggressive foreign and imperial policy and the acceptance, whether for convenience or from conviction, of the Fascist regime as a mass order. This process was complex and multifaceted. It took different forms to that in Germany because Italy had not stuck to its dictator to the bitter end and because the crimes of which Fascism was guilty, in the peninsula at least, were not seen to be comparable to the monstrous evil manifested by Nazism. This view, however, conveniently left aside colonial atrocities and war crimes in the Balkans, which in official memory and many fictional works were entirely blanked out.[49]

One of the most striking signs of the refusal of the middle classes and especially public sector employees to take any responsibility manifested itself in the resentments that were unleashed by proposals to carry out an extensive purge of one-time fascists from the public administration. Indignation over the real and threatened application of the purge took a political form with the rise of rise of the Uomo Qualunque (Anyman) (UQ) movement in 1944–46. *Qualunquismo* was the heir of moderate and Catholic Fascism.[50] Formed in 1944 to express the view of the common citizen who did not feel any affinity with democratic politics, the UQ was composed of people who felt detached from the emerging official life of postwar Italy.[51] Its appeal was fuelled by a perception that the purge was illegitimately being inflicted the lower middle class while letting bigger fish off the hook. Especially in the South, committees appointed by the parties antagonised public employees by applying anti-fascist criteria where there had been no struggle for liberation. The UQ saw democratic politicians as being no different to Fascist ones and in some respects worse when they exhibited moralistic and 'Jacobin' intentions. It was a movement of people who wanted to live in peace without having their consciences troubled by political zealots. Its followers were respectable middle-class citizens, who had been quite happy to allow an authoritarian dictator to make decisions for them.[52] The Duce's only mistake in their view had been to go to war with Hitler instead of remaining neutral.

Negotiating the question of the adoration that had been conferred on Mussolini was not an easy matter. After all, the dictator had not simply been tolerated. The writer Bontempelli, who had himself been an enthusiastic Fascist, acknowledged that years of adulation needed to be in some way accounted for. 'If it is politically, morally and humanly criminal to adore a man', then the Italians were guilty of crimes, he wrote.[53] Applauding the death of Mussolini, after years in which he had been applauded in life, was not sufficient to overcome the automatic, unreflective subservience to Fascism that lasted for much of the regime.[54] Because this was an uncomfortable issue, there was a strong impulse towards collective amnesia and the de-realisation of that part of the self that had been invested in the Fascist project. Bontempelli would become one of the few to be obliged to pay for his past affiliation when he was barred from taking a seat in the Senate in 1952 on account of his earlier membership of the Fascist Italian Academy.[55]

Mussolini did not disappear in the same way that Hitler did in Germany. The Führer had literally vanished. He disappeared from view and his death was not confirmed by the display of a body. He left no relatives and the political movement which he had founded was destroyed. The situation in Italy was very different. The effort to consign Mussolini to oblivion was not easy. He remained an object of discourse and he had not been expelled from the imaginative realm even if his name was mentioned with less frequency than before.

In the elections to the Constituent Assembly in 1946, the Christian Democrats emerged as the largest party. Founded in 1942 by men who were unimpeachably anti-fascist, the party did not indulge in any open nostalgia for Fascism. Its leader, Alcide De Gasperi denounced in the Constituent Assembly press organs that aimed 'to renew in unsophisticated minds almost regret about the past regime, exploiting the difficulties of the moment that are the result of the dictatorship and fascist systems'.[56] Nonetheless the key to the success of the Christian Democrats lay in the way that they took over and rearticulated some of the key values that had been absorbed by Fascism in its quest to win support and stabilise the regime. The party provided a response to a diffuse desire for order and leadership among the middle classes. Following the expulsion of the parties of the left from government in 1947, the Christian Democrats positioned themselves as the principal force of anti-communism. This attitude informed their anti-left campaign during the first postwar parliamentary elections in 1948, which resulted in a historic victory. Crucially, they managed the transition from a situation in which the Catholic masses, who were left disoriented and without a real identity after the definitive crisis of the regime with which they had for so long identified, were provided with a new set of reference points that were more compatible with the values of the postwar era.[57] 'The Catholic sensibility was superimposed on the nationalist and colonialist legacy of fascism (profoundly sedimented in the collective sensibility of the Italians), as a "natural" bridge of transition to other shores', Catholic historian Renato Moro has observed.[58] By means of a reformulated, and in many respects weaker, national identity, a continuity with the recent past was guaranteed that functioned—in the words of Moro—as 'a sort of thoroughgoing collective "self-absolution", that offered a defence against less consolatory examinations of conscience about collective responsibilities'.[59]

As in West Germany, a new horizon of economic development and prosperity was held out to replace the Fascist imperial dream. In the context of the Cold War, which brought an enormous boost to anti-communism, America offered an ideal of civilisation and an appealing new way of life.[60] It filled a cultural and political void and constituted the model for a new form of patriotism based on consumption that, American propaganda insisted, necessarily combined with freedom and democracy. Popular culture was a propulsive force of Americanisation in Germany, and it was in Italy too. 'Self-colonization' through selective acceptance of external stimuli, set the tone for a cultural shift that would in time be more extensive than Fascism's efforts to transform the Italians into a warrior people.[61]

The past, of course, was always present, and all the more so because, no less than in Germany, it was unmastered. In that country, there was—to borrow the words of philosopher and returned exile Theodor Adorno—a widespread attitude that 'everything should be forgotten and forgiven', closing 'the books on the past and, if possible, even [removing] it from memory'.[62] In Adorno's view, this was the symptom of a present that was still marked by the collective narcissism fostered by dictatorial regimes.[63] The German leader Konrad Adenauer—speaking before the phenomenon of de-realisation had been identified or labelled—warned in 1946 that recent history could not be moulded into something people wanted it to be and it did not go away if you closed your eyes. The development of mass society and the attendant widespread conformity that had facilitated dictatorship still held perils. 'Neither Italian Fascism nor National Socialism in Germany would have been possible', he declared 'without a certain propensity of broad layers of the population to abandoning one's personality'.[64] The new conformisms of the era of Americanism and consumerism installed a powerful present and future orientation that was far from devoid of returns and revivals, ghostly hauntings and phantasms. These phenomena included not only stories and imaginings, watered-down memories and sharp reminders of past errors, but also people whose experiences were not only denied citizenship but were also denied the right to exist. While the UQ and sectors of public opinion refused to accept that Italy had been defeated on the battlefield, De Gasperi, by contrast, acknowledged the truth: 'We had a military defeat that was much more than a military disaster'.[65] There were certainly people, among them one-time supporters of the RSI, who felt utterly left behind. The writer Carlo Mazzantini experienced the very sense of being a walking corpse or non-existent that the Mitscherlichs noted was an extreme manifestation of psychological distress.[66] In an autobiographical novel that was the fruit of many years ruminating over his experiences, he described an encounter in Rome some years after the war with a fellow former soldier from the RSI. As the two men look around at people enjoying themselves in a lively bar, his comrade shares with him a painful realisation: 'Don't be fooled into thinking that you're a man you know, a concrete human being like one of them! You're nothing but a shadow, a ghost. We're the spectres of something which never was—the faded mark on a page which has now been erased!'[67]

Within memory writing, from the Resistance side, there was a strong emphasis on the present and on the very recent past.[68] The pressure to contribute an account of events was felt by protagonists large and small of recent history. These were not necessarily heroic, though there was no doubt over their alignment with postwar values. On the other side, it would sometimes take many years of rumination before authors could put their work in the public realm. The evidence of diaries confirms that the working-through process sometimes took a religious course; in other instances it was channelled into private meditation on life choices and experiences. Fascism became a private torment that individuals had to mull over on their own and in silence.[69] It was not a shared process. In public only a handful of writers gave voice to the ghosts of Fascism, including the adoration of Mussolini, colonial violence and anti-semitism, all of which remained alive in popular memory despite the collective impulse towards amnesia. Ennio Flaiano's prize-winning 1947 novel *Tempo di uccidere* (A Time to Kill), which explored the theme of one man's lingering but unacknowledged guilt for the rape and accidental killing of a woman in the colonies, was a rare example of a meditation on the callous violence that had marked the imperial experience. It ran counter to a dominant colonial memory that recalled Italy's African endeavours with pride in the postwar period, both in public discourse and materially in thousands of decorative objects and images that adorned Italian homes.[70] For his part, the high-profile novelist Alberto Moravia sought to investigate the psychological aspects of mass politics in order to get to the root of the consent that had been accorded to Fascism.[71] In novels, including *The Conformist* (1947), he delved deeply into the reasons why so many found fulfilment through alignment with Mussolini's regime. It has been said that, in his fiction, he reflected on responsibilities, 'to the extent that one could, to a degree, speak of "expiation" or something akin...to a psychoanalytical "working through"'.[72] The fact that this occurred within the realm of fiction, however, suggests that there were limits as to how far it was consciously shared.

6

Family and nation

In the 1930s and the early 1940s, the Mussolini family occupied a position of prominence in Italian life. While the Duce's wife Rachele remained largely in the shadows, even after she moved the family to Villa Torlonia in Rome in 1929, the children Edda, Vittorio and Bruno were well known to the Italian public. Edda became a public figure with her 1930 marriage to the Count Galeazzo Ciano, an event that rivalled the marriage four months earlier of crown prince Umberto to Princess Maria José of Belgium. The younger children Romano and Annamaria, who were still in their teens when their father was deposed, figured less prominently in the public eye. The wider Mussolini clan also played a part. The dictator's brother Arnaldo (until his death in 1931) was a close collaborator, even Benito's right-hand man. His parents, long dead by the time he came to power, were also drawn into the public construction of Mussolini as a man who came from a simple background in the Romagna region. Alessandro, the blacksmith father, perhaps on account of his socialist revolutionary activism, was overshadowed in regime propaganda by his wife Rosa Maltoni, the primary schoolteacher who was mainly responsible for raising Benito and his siblings. While Mussolini resisted allowing his own name to be used in the naming of public places and institutions, he approved many requests for schools to bear the name of his mother, just as he would allow the names of Arnaldo, his nephew Sandro, and later his son Bruno, to be used for such purposes after their deaths.[1]

Following the downfall and death of Mussolini, his family members lost the privileged position they had once occupied. From being, to all intents and purposes, the first family of the country, eclipsing even the royal family in the press, they became awkward survivors, reminders of a period that many were seeking to forget as Italy embarked on the reconstruction and embraced democracy. Taken into custody in turn by partisans, the Americans, the British and the new Italian authorities, Mussolini's widow and her children were moved several times. They were not free to live where they chose and were subjected to a regime of internal exile. Many of their possessions and their property were confiscated and they were provided with no significant economic support. Their surname was covered in ignominy. The names of late members of the family were removed from the places and institutions that had borne them, with only a few elementary schools in remote locations continuing to be named after the ex-Duce's mother.

From their initial degradation and obscuration, the Mussolini family would gradually come to occupy a place in the collective imagination of postwar Italy. The key figure in this re-emergence was Rachele. After being scarcely visible during the regime, in part by her own choice but also because she was a barely literate woman who did little to disguise her peasant origins, she became a public personality. The visibility of the family was an important factor in ensuring that the sort of total disappearance of a once adored dictator from the public realm that occurred in Germany did not happen. The Führer was a man whose whole existence was bound up with politics.[2] As an Austrian, an outsider, he was always a phantasmagorical figure.[3] After his death, it seemed almost as if he had not been real. There was no one to pick up the pieces, to bear witness to the private man or to keep his name alive in the minds of the German people. In Italy, it was largely the family members, with contributions from former associates, who narrated a selective but digestible 'story of Benito' that was the complement to the process of political de-realisation.[4]

Under Fascism, Rachele Mussolini's public image—such as it was—was a propaganda one: that of the exemplary wife and mother. This quality ensured that she was not widely viewed afterwards in a political light. After the war, her point of view on her husband was almost entirely personal and domestic. In interview after interview in the 1950s and 1960s, she spoke with feeling about her husband and her family, sharing many details and episodes that were not previously known. There had of course been a wide awareness that Mussolini had a domestic life. His holidays in Riccione were covered in the media, as were the marriages of his daughter and his sons Vittorio and Bruno. When his young child Annamaria contracted polio in 1936 and Bruno was killed in a test flight of a new military aircraft in August 1941 at the age of twenty-three, there were waves of sympathy. The development of this dimension in the testimony of Rachele and other family members therefore struck a chord and corresponded to a need to think about Mussolini in ways that were not divisive or ideological. It can be said that the dictator's widow played a key part in the postwar humanisation of Mussolini, a process that went together with his normalisation and even his de-fascistisation.[5]

The domestication of the former dictator was problematic and not without contradictions and inconsistencies. It was also in some ways blatantly false. In life, Mussolini seemed to have found his family to be an embarrassment, and he tried to persuade the Fascist press not to write about them.[6] He kept a certain distance from his wife, with whom he rowed violently, and his children who, though some of them would remember his attention to them fondly, were mostly treated with little regard. Festivities like Christmas and Easter were occasions he dreaded.[7] However, the expression of family sentiments came in useful under the regime and the postwar process of domestication had its uses too. Historians have argued that it was facilitated by the lack of any formal trial or reckoning.[8] It was this that led directly to the resurfacing of sentimental, pathetic visions of the ageing dictator and the construction of an aura of family around him. The family memory also had a function in obstructing the formation of a critical assessment of the leader.[9] It brought sympathy, indulgence and identification where judgement and repudiation were called for.

The significance of the family narrative lay not only with the continuing presence of blood relatives, that is to say women and men who not only testified by their mere existence to the fact that Mussolini was a man like any other; it also connected with the wider sense of the dictator as a part of the texture of family ties that linked all Italians to each other and to the nation.[10] Mussolini was configured in many different ways as a relative of everyone under the regime: he was a father figure to young people who were encouraged to think of themselves as his children. To the very young, he was even placed on the same affective plane as their mothers.[11] To women, he was an ideal husband or boyfriend, a man who might father their children.[12] These ideas were communicated in propaganda and in the writings of the regime's many tireless intellectuals. The basic idea was that Mussolini was not only 'in ourselves' thanks to his ability to take hold of men's minds, as Swiss writer and philosopher Max Picard argued about the phantasmagorical Hitler in 1947, but that he was literally 'one of us'.[13] This perception was not specific to Mussolini. The relationship between political leaders and nations in the twentieth century became fused with familial sentiments.[14] Dictators above all, on account of their expansion of the sense of the political sphere to include all aspects of public life and many aspects of private life, were able to achieve this. Even Hitler used the absence of a wife and family to situate himself as the husband of the nation. The extension of the political sphere in this way paradoxically entailed its de-politicisation and what might be called its re-creation in biological terms.[15] Nostalgic Fascists traded on these linkages between man and nation. The magazine *Meridiano d'Italia illustrato* offered readers a compendium of images dating from Mussolini's Socialist days to Piazzale Loreto and beyond, beginning with a programmatic statement: 'For the whole thirty-year period that goes from 1915 to 1945, the destiny of Italy was, for good or ill, linked to that of Benito Mussolini. And, as happens with every country that is subject to a long dictatorship: at a certain point, the history of that country gets confused with, and becomes as one with, the personal history of the dictator'.[16]

Mussolini gave the Italians what they wanted, in a certain sense, by performing for them, hypnotising them with a re-edition of established national stereotypes.[17] The sacrifice of the regular, moral super-ego to a potentially criminal collective super-ego was facilitated by the psychic collectivisation that resulted from the climate of dictatorship.[18] The dictator's exhibitionism could stimulate in spectators a recognition of themselves that was boundless thanks to the collective exaltation that quashed any sense of inferiority and swept aside moral reservations. The abandonment of individual identity manifested itself in a number of ways that included superficial imitation of the dictator's mannerisms and the mechanical repetition of slogans. The fact that Mussolini displayed a limitless vanity encouraged the same behaviour on the part of others who gave in to a leadership style that was overtly narcissistic.[19]

Some of this persisted into the postwar years, especially among those who had been shaped by dictatorship or who continued to feel a bond to Mussolini who, in the minds of loyalists, was in some way a living force, and perhaps even still alive. For several years it was given indirect justification by his wife, who would bear the unenviable fate of a dictator's widow. In 1964, she would sum up her view: 'For a long time, I did not even have any concrete proof of the death of Benito. Even some partisans wrote to me arguing that the man killed at Giulino di Mezzegra was not my husband but someone else. From time to time, I thought perhaps it was a gigantic trick and Benito was alive and safe who knows where. The fact that they hid his remains from me gave me pause for thought'.[20] The pre-political dimension of Mussolini's life had a broad appeal that the *Meridiano d'Italia* was happy to employ alongside its political agenda. In publishing numerous photographs, without offering—it ingenuously asserted—any positive or negative judgement, it claimed to place for the first time at the disposal of the Italians 'a sort of great "family album" that shows everyone that which was, in its multiform aspects, also "their" history'.[21] 'Is all this good? Is it not good?' it asked rhetorically. 'This does not interest us.

The evaluation of the facts, we have stated at the outset, is beyond our scope. But a people that wants to be free cannot be so until it accepts as "its own" all "its" past, whatever has come about as a result of that past'.

The idea of the Italians as one big family of which Mussolini was—and continued to be—a part, like any recently deceased relative, was one that itself was informed by the incorporation of the masses, even of more remote regions, into the nation that occurred under the regime. The compromise with the Catholic Church led to the creation of the notion of Fascist and Catholic Italy that proved so beneficial in stabilising and expanding consent.[22] But it also meant that the regime never dictated the terms of Italian family politics in the period and failed to change the way families saw themselves. It did succeed, however, in drawing men and women, children and even the old, into its mass organisations and activities.[23] It was also effective in the realms of mass culture, harnessing cinema, radio and the press to its purposes. In this way, it functionally nationalised the masses, making them for the first time feel part of a national community.

The Mussolini family was displaced and partially dispersed at the end of the war. In this it suffered a fate that was shared by many families whose members had been killed or taken as prisoners of war or for forced labour, and who had lost their homes and livelihoods. Rachele and her two youngest children were prevented from fleeing to Switzerland and were compelled to surrender to the Resistance, which placed them in prison. They were freed by the Americans who in turn handed them over to the British, who interned them in a prison camp in Terni. When the Italian authorities became responsible for their fate, they were despatched to the island of Ischia where they remained until 1957. Vittorio escaped illegally and travelled by ship from Genoa to Argentina in 1947. Edda was in a different position. Pardoned under the Togliatti amnesty of 1946, she was able to return to Rome where she occupied the large apartment she had once shared with her husband.[24]

Unlike the royal family, the male members of which were constrained to live in exile following the abolition of the monarchy in the referendum of June 1946, the Mussolini family remained, albeit under special conditions, in Italy. Curiosity about them was considerable for several reasons. The peculiarly personal dramas that were interwoven with political events were among these. The family had been torn apart by the execution in 1944 of Edda's husband Galeazzo Ciano, which Mussolini had done nothing to prevent. One of those who voted for Grandi's motion at the Fascist Grand Council of July 1943, the former foreign minister had once been seen as a possible successor to the Duce. Against her mother's advice and indeed despite her personal disapproval of her husband's conduct, Edda had pleaded with her father for his life. The content of these desperate encounters, which led to a break in relations between Edda and her parents, was the subject of speculation that would gradually be filled out with public testimony that, if anything, heightened perceptions of the drama.[25] Though mother and daughter would be reconciled in 1947, Edda proudly insisted on being referred to as Contessa Ciano and publicly defended her husband's memory. There were further tragedies. The twenty-year-old son of Benito's sister Edwige was also executed on 28 April 1945, one of forty-three members of a division of the Republican National Guard who were summarily shot after placing themselves in the hands of the local Committee for National Liberation on hearing news that the RSI had surrendered. Gina Ruberti, the widow of Bruno Mussolini, drowned in Lake Como after falling from a speedboat during a storm in May 1946.[26]

Mussolini's mistress Claretta, who entered history by dying at the side of the fallen dictator, was an inconvenient figure. Though the position of Claretta and her family was widely known, especially in Rome, even in the later 1930s, the relationship only properly entered common knowledge after July 1943, when scurrilous articles were planted in the press with the aim of ridiculing the deposed dictator. With the macabre exhibition of Piazzale Loreto, she acquired the romantic aura of a woman who had given everything for love. The Mussolini family could do nothing about the way history had bound together the names of the one-time Duce and Claretta and, although the issue rankled, Rachele, who had been hostile to her husband's lover in early 1945, was generally magnanimous in her remarks, knowing that the reviled and corrupt Petacci family would have little or no purchase on public opinion.[27]

Rachele took charge of reconfiguring the image of Mussolini in the popular imagination of the postwar years. As the Duce's widow, she had a certain cultural capital that facilitated—while at the same time camouflaging—what was in practice a political operation.[28] She possessed a moral authority that was underscored by the fact that she had not benefited materially from her husband's position. At a time when there was much resentment against the profiteering of senior Fascist officials, many of whom had exploited their position to acquire great wealth, her lack of any trappings or refinement reinforced a questionable belief that Mussolini himself had never profited from power. Ever the simple, down-to-earth woman from the Romagna region, who notoriously had raised chickens and even pigs in the gardens of Villa Torlonia, Rachele became a living testament to the ordinary aspects of the life of a man who had been presented to the Italians as utterly extraordinary and exceptional. She communicated this in the book *Ma vie avec Benito*, published in France in 1947. This appeared in Italian the following year as *La mia vita con Benito* (My life with Benito), published with the subtitle 'Una famiglia per l'Italia' (A family for Italy).[29] Reduced to semi-poverty, she was obliged, despite warnings from her daughter, to enter into a relationship with the press and publishers to obtain funds. By this means she spoke directly to the hearts of the Italians.[30] This cycle reached its climax in 1957, when she granted the weekly *Oggi* the scoop of a series of ghost-written articles entitled 'Benito il mio uomo' (My man Benito) that were promoted by the magazine as a unique, human and moral testimony.[31]

One key aspect of the way Rachele contributed to the development of new narratives around Mussolini was her insistence on suffering. The passage from Fascism to democracy involved the elaboration of new rituals and practices to account for the legacy of those who had given their lives for the cause of liberation.[32] The war dead were a prominent part of public and political discourse to the extent that the postwar republic was founded on loss and mourning. At the same time, practices of commemoration became fragmented and diffuse, as families and others sought to subtract them from the realm of the state and civil society and address their loss in the private realm. From this culture of mourning, former Fascists were anything but excluded, though there was little or no official acknowledgement of their grief. It was the martyrs of anti-fascism and the Resistance whose sacrifices occupied centre stage and provided a moral foundation for the postwar political order. It was only in the Church's acknowledgement of all the war dead without distinction, regardless of ideology or alignment (that was embraced by the Christian Democrats), that those who had died in Fascism's wars found de-politicised citizenship.

The Mussolini family's suffering was divided into two parts. On the one hand, its members shared with many other Italians a profound sense of personal loss. This bereavement they shared with anyone who sought to grieve privately for a son, father or husband, regardless of whether they had been absorbed into collective commemoration or not. However, there was a second, more specific aspect to their suffering that was not compensated by any official mourning ritual. Mussolini had not been given a funeral of any sort and his body had not been returned to the family after it was removed from Piazzale Loreto. The fact that he received no funeral or proper burial offended the sensibilities of moderate and right-wing Catholic opinion. There were many people who did not have a body to bury but the Mussolini family was unique in having the body of their loved one effectively confiscated by the state. The dictator's corpse was buried first in an unmarked grave in Milan's Musocco cemetery before being dug up and hidden by Fascist loyalists who continued to attribute to it political significance.[33] On its return to official hands, it was concealed in an undisclosed location until, eventually, it was returned to Rachele Mussolini for interment in August 1957 at the same time as she was released from internal exile. The dictator's widow articulated the injustice of the situation and campaigned ceaselessly for her husband to be given a Christian burial in his town of origin (see Figure 5). The series of articles based on interviews she gave to the magazine *Oggi* in 1957 marked completion of this mission.

Rachele complained that she received no pension for her husband despite his having been former prime minister, and her accounts of the economic difficulties she faced were woven into the narrative of suffering that was constructed largely through the mass media. It began with newsreel reports on the family's exile on Ischia. The coverage testified to the continuing public interest in Mussolini's heirs, a phenomenon that the illustrated magazines of the post-war years catered to amply. A portrait of Mussolini himself appeared on a mainstream magazine cover—*Oggi* on 28 June 1951—though in uniform, suggesting that he was still viewed less as a man than a dictator. Despite her reputation, Rachele handled the many interviews she gave to the press with notable astuteness. She never gave in to journalists' desires for scandalous secrets or the revelation of significant behind-the-scenes information.[34] Instead, she stuck to a script in which she spoke of herself and the travails of her life during and after the civil war, evoked her early life and romance with Benito, and recounted in a familial, domestic key the experiences of the dictatorship. 'I do not engage in politics, I conserve only my memories', she stated in one magazine article.[35]

'Donna' Rachele—the informal title of honour accorded to her under the regime was still widely accepted—performed with consummate ability the role of the grieving widow. There was nothing false or forced about this. After all, she was indisputably a widow and, as such, had every right to mourn her husband. However, she understood that her widowhood had a number of uses. After all, widows of the fallen had formed a highly manipulated symbolic aspect of Fascist mythology.[36] She dressed regularly in black and talked incessantly about her husband, the places he had inhabited, his interactions with his children and his relationship with the Italian people. Her overriding purpose, she claimed, was to obtain justice for him and for her family, in keeping with the idea of the widow as a self-sacrificing witness to the continued presence of a dead husband in the collective mind. Like many widows, she was invested in

Figure 5. On a magazine cover of 1950 Mussolini's widow Rachele prays for her deceased husband to be 'left in peace'. Author's own collection.

her husband's legacy, though of course the legacy in question was a particularly controversial one. She did her best to defuse controversy by fashioning a memory of the dictator that was as broadly acceptable and as widely shared as possible. She constituted the vehicle whereby the lived reality of Mussolini as a family man rather than a despised dictator became a part of the national imagination. She claimed that he appeared to her in dreams and, in some respects, she acted as though her own comments on postwar politics and culture might have been communicated to her by him from beyond the grave.[37]

Rachele mediated between the Italians and the memory of the dictatorship held by those who had not fallen foul of Fascism or experienced its brutal side. Nothing could alter the negative views of those who had opposed or become ideologically detached from the regime but these, arguably, were a minority. Dignified and resolute, she played into a feminine stereotype by defending and supporting her family in adverse circumstances. When she was finally allowed to return to her home town, which she had never really abandoned except by constraint, she somehow closed the circle.

Rachele claimed not to be a political figure, yet nor was she exactly apolitical. During the regime, she had frequently returned to her home region. Indeed, she had become a local power centre, with her own network of friendly officials and informers and her own channels of influence. It became apparent in published memoirs that she had a much clearer view of the danger Mussolini faced in the aftermath of the Grand Council of 1943 than he did, and she had urged resolute action against the plotters.[38] She was something of a symbol for those Italians who, in spite of everything, remained loyal to the Fascist project and to the cult of the Duce. After returning to her home of Villa Carpena—situated between Predappio and Forlì—which, like the nearby Rocca delle Caminate, was still formally in family possession as it was legally registered in her name (though returned to her only in 1957), she opened a restaurant where visiting diners hoped to catch a glimpse of her. She maintained close relations with leading figures in the neo-fascist Italian Social Movement, including Pino Romualdi (giving the lie thereby to persistent rumours that he was one of Mussolini's several illegitimate children) and Arturo Michelini. She became an icon of sorts, the object of a minor cult consisting of homages as well as the sort of devotional devices, like postcards, that had prospered in relation to the Duce. She was a physical reminder of Mussolini, in some respects his feminine continuation. She was in this sense a vital element in the process whereby the ostensibly hyper-masculine Mussolini became, in memory, a feminised presence endowed with a strong affective dimension.

The family home of Villa Carpena had been sequestered after the war and had been turned into a shelter for displaced persons. Before that, it had been plundered, like the Rocca, and both locals and passing Allied soldiers had freely taken objects of value and souvenirs. Unlike the medieval Rocca castle, which had been acquired and gifted to Mussolini by the local authority following a call for donations, Villa Carpena, which had been bought with Mussolini's earnings as editor of the Socialist newspaper *Avanti*, was dear to her heart. The former was an imposing semi-official residence where Mussolini relocated during the summer and continued the work of government. It was where he speculated that he might have lived had he retired from politics in 1936, as his wife had urged him to, or indeed after his deposition in 1943.[39] When she returned to Predappio, Rachele found Villa Carpena in a dilapidated state. Some displaced families were still there. She later said that she made it her business to find somewhere for them to go—cultivating an image of public spiritedness that she would take care to reinforce when she decided to dispose of the Rocca.[40] Rejecting substantial offers from potential buyers who planned to turn it into a commercial facility, she sold it for a lesser figure in order that it might be turned into a centre for children's welfare. Rachele restored Villa Carpena, recovering some of the objects and furniture that were still in local hands. Her son Romano later recalled it as a place where he spent many happy times.[41]

In the 1960s, the villa had something of the feel of a museum about it. There were numerous portraits and busts of Mussolini as well as other artefacts and souvenirs. But above all it was family home, albeit with some differences. Alongside the normality of her domestic life as it was related in the illustrated press, which connected with the image of the peasant woman (see Figure 6), Rachele Mussolini fashioned an iconography that was geared to maintaining Mussolini in the public eye. For example, she was pictured in magazines praying in the crypt of the Mussolini tomb in the San Cassiano cemetery in Predappio with a large marble bust of the Duce behind her. Such poses may have been requested by the magazines themselves, but she was complicit with these efforts and seemingly understood the symbolism. She was the focus of a new visual repertoire of pardon and memory.

Her book of memoirs, *Ma vie avec Benito*, was, in a sense, the counterpoint to journalist (and Mussolini's mistress) Margherita Sarfatti's biography *Dux*, which had been published in 1925.[42] While the latter was written with the intention of building the myth of the 'plebeian aristocrat', the new man, who had awakened in the Italians an awareness of their historic destiny, Rachele's volume offered a domestic reduction. However, both books presented the man in a favourable light, and where Sarfatti's served a purpose in the mid-1920s, Rachele's memoirs served another in the very different context of the 1950s and 1960s. The use of her husband's first name in the title was significant. In many press interviews, she referred to him in this way, humanising and familiarising him. In contrast, to the younger members of the Mussolini clan, who gathered

Figure 6. Rachele Mussolini cultivated an image of simple domesticity in the postwar years. This photograph appeared in the original French edition of her volume of memoirs *Ma vie avec Benito* (1947). Author's own collection.

regularly at Villa Carpena, she was accustomed to refer to him as 'Il Duce'.[43] It is quite possible that she also did this with journalists, who deemed it opportune to substitute the political title with the first name. Indeed, the editor of *Oggi*, which published in 1957 the series 'Benito il mio uomo' (My Man Benito), told journalist Anita Pensotti, who collected Rachele's memories, that he already had the title of the series in mind and that the portrait that should emerge was that of 'a domestic Mussolini, seen through the eyes of his wife and children, within the intimacy of the domestic walls'.[44] Rachele saw it as her job to ensure that the next generations of the family had knowledge of her husband's role and importance. Years later, Romano's daughter Alessandra, who would enter politics via the neo-fascist Movimento Sociale Italiano (Italian Social Movement), blended the two modes by referring in public to her grandfather, whom she never knew, as 'Nonno Duce' (Grandad Duce). Her father Romano, in his own volume of memoirs, published only in 2004, referred either to 'my father' or 'Il Duce'—the two terms which are combined in the title of *My Father Il Duce*.[45]

Did Rachele think of a political legacy in dynastic terms, in other words, that a descendant of Mussolini might one day return to power? Mussolini himself had shown no dynastic preoccupations and, with the exception of his son-in-law Ciano, had avoided placing family members in strategic positions in the regime. Whereas Napoleon, his frequent reference point, had taken every possible step to insert his siblings and children into the royal families of Europe and establish new potential dynastic families as far afield as Mexico, the unfamilial Mussolini had no such aspirations. In the case of the emperor of the French, it would be almost forty years after the Battle of Waterloo before the title was revived by his nephew, Louis-Napoleon, who seized power in 1852 and proclaimed a Second Empire. Aware that he lacked what has been termed 'the sheer radiant, overpowering brilliance' of his uncle, the self-styled Napoleon III claimed to be the follower rather than the successor of Napoleon.[46] Rachele would hardly have thought in this way. However, she seems to have had an instinctive understanding that the family surname carried weight and possibly even currency, despite the debacle of 1945. At the very least, she wanted her grandchildren and her nephews and nieces to feel pride in the achievements of Mussolini. In this sense, she can be said to have mobilised them in defence of a legacy and ensured that, within the ambit of the far-right, they were equipped, should the need arise, to breathe new life into a potential Mussolini tradition.

If Rachele was a figure of mourning, it must be asked if she could be said to have contributed to a larger process whereby the Italians elaborated a mourning for their dictator, in psychoanalytical terms working through the loss of a love-object who had been widely internalised. This is a complex question for a number of reasons. First of all, Rachele's mourning was primarily private. However, it was also staged and publicised, with the complicity of the press, in order that it might trigger responses from the politicians, to whom she pleaded for the return of Mussolini's mortal remains, and from a wider public. However, mourning was, as the Mitscherlichs argued, a means of acknowledging that a love-object had been lost and detaching from it in order that psychic energies might be directed elsewhere.[47] This was not what neo-fascist leaders or Rachele wanted. Within the Fascist community, there was a shared belief that Mussolini was still 'live', not usually in the way that Hitler was sometimes rumoured to be—in the jungle or in hiding in South America—but in spirit, as a source of inspiration.

Mussolini remained a central figure for Fascists, even in death. On the one hand, there was a conviction that his word still carried validity. 'A new word from Mussolini is like the sound of the sea in a shell; if you are attentive, you can still hear it: imprisoned and distant but not enfeebled', wrote one-time minister Ezio Maria Gray.[48] In his view, the central theme of justice was its core truth. The Fascist journalist Vanni Teodorani also felt that those who had heard his voice remained uplifted:[49] 'It was enough to have heard his voice once' to be inspired and motivated, he claimed. 'Still today, his speeches and writings... move and exalt us'.[50] The question was whether it was all down to the long-range influence of the live Mussolini or whether there was a way in which the dead Mussolini or his extra-corporeal spirit constituted some form of active presence. The Italy of the present, Teodorani argued, had lost all hope.[51] The only serious hope for Italy to raise itself up again lay with Mussolini: 'Like Mazzini "then," Mussolini is today, everywhere one hopes, and the day of his apotheosis the whole world will want to be present, to recognise itself and redeem itself in the glow of the Great Man of the twentieth century'.[52]

Thus political mourning for the dead dictator was not elaborated as a collective rite even after his mortal remains were returned to the family and interred following a highly political funeral in September 1957. At that point, it was beyond all dispute that Mussolini was truly dead, although no less inspiring. From then on, pilgrimages to Predappio resumed as the village became a sacred site for those who indulged in nostalgia for Mussolini and one or both of the regimes he had headed.[53] Precisely the nostalgic factor impeded the configuration of mourning as a process of detachment.[54] Instead, a posthumous cult of Mussolini was fashioned that took several forms. For loyalists it was a political matter that protracted, perpetuated or revived the intense attachment to the man that had been a cornerstone of the regime's system of rule. For others, it was shaped more by religion and a sense of Christian piety. Elements of the Fascist political religion bled into the Catholic template and accorded Mussolini a position that was different from that of any other man or woman whose death was a result of conflict or war.

The way Mussolini was experienced in the postwar years has more to do, I would suggest, with the afterlife of a Hindu guru than a political leader. The guru, who in life is worshipped as a god or goddess, is perceived, after their death, to still be present via their aura.[55] 'Omnipresence' is used to describe a guru's posthumous identity by those who feel it and believe it. The dead guru is perceived by former disciples to be totally merged with everything, to be all-pervading. For this reason there is a wariness of the trivialisation of the guru through trinkets.[56] What was more important was the disembodied influence, that is to say the interiorised conviction of the guru's significance.[57] Yet the impulse to perpetuate charisma after its departure through material and visual reminders was always strong, as these helped perpetuate the memory of a guru and reactivate something of their presence.

The role of Rachele Mussolini, though she did not die until 1979, became exhausted in the 1960s. With the transformation of the country during the economic boom, she, like much of peasant Italy, was sidelined and eclipsed. In this she shared the fate of an iconic figure dear to the other side in the civil war: Alcide Cervi, the dignified peasant father of seven anti-fascist sons who were shot in a retaliatory execution in 1943.[58] Once much present in the pages of weekly magazines like *Oggi* in the 1950s, with a woollen shawl on her shoulders, busy in the kitchen while recounting memories of the husband to whom she remained devoted, she faded from view.[59] That old-fashioned image lost force and began to seem irrelevant in a period in which the role of women was changing and, following legal changes in 1963, new opportunities in the professions and the public sector were opened. Her memories and those of the Fascist period receded from the place they had occupied in public life, despite the curious fact that she was not averse to commenting on the pop cultural personalities of the 1960s, with rock and roll star Adriano Celentano meeting particularly with her approval.[60] Whatever she said, she was by then an older woman in a period that was in thrall to youth. However, the Mussolini family conserved a place of sorts in the public eye and younger family members would help ensure that the family name would continue at one level or another to remain live and topical and have political currency. It was testimony to Rachele's role that most of the Mussolinis of later generations who stepped into the political realm were women.

7

Anxieties of masculinity

The twin images of Mussolini in the postwar years as rapacious sexual predator and as attentive husband and father, for all their contradictoriness (not only in content, but also in intent—the first being mainly an anti-fascist construction, the latter a product of family testimony) highlighted the issue of his masculinity. This was not a new development. In numerous ways, from the moment he left behind his socialist origins, his manliness was either an unspoken aspect of the qualities of youth, vigour, energy and decisiveness that were attributed to him or an evident part of the way he occupied the public stage as a dictator. Mussolini's propaganda image was heavily dependent on conventional masculine traits, including physical strength, sporting prowess, sexual potency, paternal authority and a predilection for war.[1] The Fascist emphasis on action over words, the role of violence in political conflict and nationalism as aggression found in Mussolini an exemplar. Public perception of the dictator was not simply as a man but as a summation of manliness, a model of manly traits that were to serve as an example to the Italian people. Gender historians Barbara Spackman and Sandro Bellassai have both asserted the centrality of the idea of virility to the Fascist view of the world.[2] Indeed, for Spackman, it is the 'master term' which encompasses the varied emphases on youth, sacrifice, heroism, sexual potency and physical strength, as well as authority and obedience.[3] Bellassai argues that character and body were two spheres in which the Fascists sought to effect a re-virilisation of the Italians by means of physical activities, education and war: 'The exaltation of the warrior', he asserts, 'was…tied to a general cultural climate in which problems such as the loss of the virile vigor of "lineage", the demographic problem and therefore the quantitative weakening of the "race", and the exaltation of the thrilling and "dangerous life" as opposed to the debilitating monotony of the petit-bourgeois existence acquired new political value'.[4] Fascists tried to freeze the crisis of masculine identity that they felt was rampant in the 1920s and restore a natural, primitive state that had been undermined by modernity and political divisions.[5] That example was situated within a programme of what Mussolini himself sometimes referred to as Fascism's historic mission to transform by various means and methods the Italians into a virile people capable of turning their country finally into a great power.[6]

In the aftermath of the war the Fascist idea of emphatic and hyperbolic masculinity no longer enjoyed the same currency. It did not disappear; but it persisted as fragments and cultural norms rather than as a political project. Military defeat, the loss of empire, civil war, foreign occupation and the collapse of the regime all served to bring about the end of the Fascist project of male enhancement. The colonial adventure in particular had been cast as an opportunity for masculine regeneration; the Ethiopian war was seen to project national power and virility at the same time.[7] Though the much-vaunted Fascist 'new man' that the empire was expected to create did not come into being, adventure and risk bestowed a masculine accent on the whole enterprise.[8] Bellassai has argued that, with Fascism's fall, 'an entire epoch of gender relations was overcome'.[9] But this did not mean that it left no traces. The end of the war heralded challenges in many fields and change left the way open for alternative forms of paternalism.[10] There was also the problem of addressing the persistent cultural undercurrent left by Fascist education on the consciousness of those who reached adulthood under the regime.[11] Some of this specifically concerned the person of Mussolini; other elements included the bellicose attitudes of Fascism and the cult of war it promoted. Less obvious were the more general ideas of masculine dominance and pre-eminence in the public realm that were shaken but not displaced.

Italy's conversion to democracy and republicanism was accompanied by the return of some of the features of political life before Fascism. Old men who had begun their political careers before World War I initially dominated the scene, while the return of pluralism brought debate and discussion once more to the fore; the exterior signs of military activity disappeared from the political realm. With the extension of the franchise to women and the election of women to the Constituent Assembly and then, in 1948, to Parliament, politics ceased to be an exclusively male prerogative.[12] Even if female deputies were few, male politicians could not ignore half the electorate. Procedures had to adapt, new appeals needed to be formulated and styles of leadership were obliged to change. The gap left by the formal disappearance of a cult of personality that had been so crucial in bringing consent to the regime presented a challenge to the parties. The cult had become a feature of collective psychology and formed a key vehicle whereby people had understood their relationship to the state. Combined with the monarchy, it had been a channel of socialisation of a paternalistic type whose end left some bereft or disorientated. A system that had been based on a cult of authority on the one side, and obedience on the other, gave way to democracy, a plurality of voices and an assertion of equality.[13] However, this did not mean that leaders were not important. Leaders perform a variety of functions as poles of popular attention who can personalise political engagement and invest the political realm with emotional and symbolic value.[14] Even in a democratic system, they invoke broad themes and offer a way of thinking about the political that can be cast in personal terms.

The Catholic Church was the first to understand the nature of this problem. Its promotion of the charismatic cult of Pope Pius XII occurred in response to it. The cult began from 1942 and was reinforced in the emotive contacts between pontiff and populace that followed the bombing of Rome in July 1943. A whole series of initiatives in the following years, many of which took the form of mass happenings, served to anchor the faithful to the Church and discourage them from giving credence to the siren calls of the left.[15] If Mussolini had been hailed by the bourgeoisie after World War I as the saviour of the nation from chaos, then Pius XII filled a similar role from the mid- to late 1940s. Whereas Mussolini posed as the strong man not afraid to resort to violence, the Pope, by contrast, was presented as a defenceless victim, the fragile contemporary embodiment of the suffering Christ.[16] He was an anchor in troubled times that saw a significant reversal of the decline in religious practice that had occurred under Fascism.[17]

The leaders of the postwar political parties that occupied the public stage from 1944 were united in their determination to block any tendency to present themselves as extraordinary individuals. They situated themselves more in relation to the current of humility associated with the Pope than the swaggering Mussolini model. In their own ways, the Christian Democrats, the Communists and the Socialists, as well as smaller parties, exhibited an aversion to strong leadership which manifested itself in a tyrant complex.[18] The two most important party leaders, the Christian Democrat Alcide De Gasperi and the Communist Palmiro Togliatti, both adopted a professorial manner and dressed smartly and conventionally. Although each was engaged in the potentially charismatic task of building a party and founding a new political system, this was not played up. Postwar leaders presented themselves in a serious, reflective way, as men of principle and reason rather than showmen.[19] De Gasperi, who hailed from the mountainous region of Trentino Alto Adige, was quite explicitly contrasted to the 'lowlander' Mussolini—although in his day the dictator had also been associated with mountains.[20] His family image as father and grandfather was stressed and his personal gentleness noted. Togliatti, who was separated from his wife and who formed a new relationship with a young Communist deputy to the Constituent Assembly, Nilde Jotti, could not offer a familial image and so he was presented in a more narrowly political way. However, both De Gasperi and Togliatti were configured as fathers of their respective political families even if each had to take account of a superior presence that absorbed part of the authority that in a different context would have belonged exclusively to them. If, for the Catholics, the Pope occupied a supra-political space, for the Communists it was Stalin in the Kremlin who was a form of ultimate authority.[21]

In peace time, masculinity had to be stripped of Fascistic norms in order to create a model that was more in tune with the times and the new democratic context.[22] It is important not to understate this novelty but also not to minimise the ways in which a male-dominated political culture persisted. The extent to which the political sphere was feminised in the postwar years was checked by a series of practices which, while they did not reverse or explicitly obstruct the entry of women into the national political realm, had the effect of ensuring that their progress did not overstep certain limits.[23] Women were addressed directly at election time but the women who were fielded as candidates were often placed lower down party lists that were dominated by men. In political rallies, a certain type of oratory was customarily expected, which meant that the principal speaker was nearly always a man. When the anarchist-turned-monarchist Maria Rygier addressed a rally in Ancona, she was booed and jeered, though some of this had to do with disapproval of her dramatic change of political position.[24] When women spoke, there was a risk of abuse, even when the orator was experienced. Often the women who managed to overcome the obstacles and win election to parliament found themselves faced not only with subtle forms of marginalisation but with a passive acceptance of norms about gender roles. Within what should have been a process of emancipation, therefore, many conventional ideas and assumptions remained in place. This would continue to be the case for many years, with the result that women politicians even into the 1970s rarely became senior ministers and did not feature strongly in the media's treatment of politics except as anomalies or curiosities.[25] Thus, it is fair to say, that political leadership in the postwar years continued to be generally associated with a male image of power.[26]

Change was limited because, for a variety of reasons, established ideas about gender proved to be extremely persistent. Indeed, so strongly was male domination entrenched in society, and so forcefully was innovation obstructed, that anti-feminism seemed to be almost a national characteristic, a given shared by all the politicians who were laying the foundations of the new state.[27] For the historian Patrizia Gabrielli, even the Resistance was, despite the contribution of women at all operative levels, a 'temple of virility' in which the conventional masculine values of heroism and sacrifice flourished.[28] But offsetting mechanisms were required in a context in which the end of war and demobilisation resulted in a crisis of masculine identity in all the nations that had been involved in the war.[29] The persistence of a highly partial rose-tinted view of a colonial experience which hinged on the invisibility of the colonised and the fantasies of racial superiority that were intrinsic to imperialism in a small way offset the blow of the loss of an empire whose acquisition had been seen as crucial to the reassertion of Italian virility.[30] The great popularity of white musclemen in the genre cinema of the 1950s provided a further imaginary consolation for the loss of imperial prestige.[31]

In the aftermath of the fall of Fascism and foreign occupation, the Church was an important factor in the reassertion of traditional social norms. If social conformism was in part a reflex of a traditional society in which gender divisions and hierarchies had been reinforced and institutionalised under the regime, it was also a response to the disruptions of the war years that had seen families fragmented and dispersed, conventional roles shattered and, during the Allied occupation, widespread prostitution. The Church became the spokesperson for a widespread desire for a return to normality, placing the family at the centre of its social message and promoting a return to traditional values. The Communist left, to better reach its objective of winning wide support in civil society, preferred not to disturb social norms and minimised the gap between its policy positions and tradition.

The sharp divisions of the Cold War period contributed to a reassertion of male political supremacy by shifting the focus of political discourse from reconstruction and reform to larger geo-political matters. Leaders too became more prominent. Togliatti did not encourage any return of the sort of myth-making around leaders that marked the early Italian socialist movement, but he was aware that, as the leader of the Communist Party, he was the bearer of institutional charisma. He allowed a form of personal cult to take shape following the attempt on his life in July 1948. This expanded in the aftermath of the death of Stalin in 1953.[32] De Gasperi too became a cult figure for moderate public opinion. Paternalism flourished in a context marked by the removal of a long-lasting dictatorship, although cultish practices were also related to a need to overcome the lacerations of war through new models of collective identification.[33] Inevitably, leaders were measured to some extent against Mussolini, even though they stressed differences and distanced themselves from the leadership style of the Duce.[34] Those Italians who remained in Ethiopia at the invitation of that country's government found a ready replacement for their devotion. As historian Angelo Del Boca noted in the mid-1960s, 'By a curious transference, the Italians of Addis Ababa have wound up by substituting Haile Selassie for the Duce they had adored'.[35] In the peninsula, potential substitutes tended to be eccentric. With his arrogant bluster and unquestionable propagandistic verve, the founder and leader of the postwar flash party, the *Uomo Qualunque* (Anyman—discussed in Chapter 3), the Neapolitan playwright Guglielmo Giannini, was the first of several postwar politicians whose public persona would recall aspects of the former dictator (in spite of his attacks on 'the buffoon of Predappio').[36] Giannini mobilised a diffuse hostility to the anti-fascist parties (accused of re-creating a Fascism of their own) that betrayed a certain intolerance of democracy itself. Another populist figure who prospered in the South was Achille Lauro, the shipping magnate and president of the Napoli football club who promoted a personal cult of himself as *O' Comandante*. Between 1952 and 1957, he served as mayor of Naples.

On the right, and especially in the satirical press, there were repeated attempts to give the impression that there was little difference of substance between Fascism and the democratic political system. Though they had ostensibly brought the regime to an end, the parties were maliciously portrayed as having taken over practices associated with Fascism: the mass rally, mass membership, the cult of the leader. Cartoons in magazines like *Don Camillo* author Giovannino Guareschi's *Candido*, *Il Travaso* and *Asso di bastoni* drew parallels of this type to mock democracy. One cartoon published in *Il Travaso* in May 1948 (see Figure 7) was particularly eloquent. It showed a faint Mussolini making the Roman salute and providing a template for a more clearly highlighted Togliatti and De Gasperi, who were depicted alongside him, respectively making a clenched fist and the sign of a blessing. The caption implied that the first was the gesture that had been imposed, while the second was the one that the left would like to impose, and the third—with the April 1948 election having recently taken place—was the one that was likely to be imposed. The writer Curzio Malaparte, once a keen Fascist, provocatively claimed that after the Liberation, the tripartite government of Christian Democrats, Socialists and Communists had given rise to three Mussolinis in place of one, and that was

Figure 7. A postwar satirical magazine features the Christian Democrat leader De Gasperi on the right, Communist leader Togliatti in the centre and a faint shadow of Mussolini on the left. Each is deemed to have or have had a type of salute to impose on the Italians. Author's own collection.

without counting the 'hundreds of thousands of little Mussolinis' who made up much of the membership of the anti-fascist parties.[37]

Postwar governments were dominated by the Christian Democrats, but only De Gasperi offered a form of strong leadership. He dominated his party and sought to assert Italy's prerogatives—which included, in the face of stern and irremovable international opposition, the maintenance in some form of its colonies—on the world stage. By his championship of order and tradition and his practical common sense and flexibility, Malaparte argued, De Gasperi gave the Italians a type of leadership that matched their character.[38] After his resignation as prime minister in August 1953, the strong model dissolved and his successors were obliged to enter into extended negotiations with smaller parties and mediate between the factions and currents within their own party. They also deferred wholly to American leadership of the West. In such a context, the Mussolinian model of decisiveness, physical strength, energy, national assertion and media-savviness constituted a resonant memory.[39] For sympathisers, like the one-time Fascist journalist Giovanni Ansaldo, 'the pitiful mediocrity of those who came after him made him seem like a colossus'.[40]

This all may seem odd, given that some historians have argued that Mussolini was a weak rather than a strong dictator.[41] There is also the fact that it is difficult to argue that he was a good leader. His continuing appeal, in this regard, needs to be seen in relation to what has been memorably called 'the allure of the toxic leader'.[42] Toxic leaders are those who engage in destructive behaviours and exhibit dysfunctional characteristics including arrogance, amorality and excessive personal ambition.[43] By means of the deployment of symbols and common beliefs, they trick and enslave people who believe they will protect them. Because such leaders respond to human needs, it is very difficult to break the spell they cast. Among them are the totalitarian leaders who, Hannah Arendt noted, are distinguished from democratic ones by the fact that they have an ability to metabolise themselves into the collective psyche of their peoples.[44]

One of the ways in which Mussolini manipulated cultural symbols and myths drawn from Italian history was by establishing a bridge between himself and strong leaders of the past. This had some striking and unexpected consequences for the way he was viewed. The leader on horseback was a shorthand for charisma. Since Roman times, the horse had been turned to political uses and Mussolini raided a visual repertoire of leadership to position himself in this way. At least two major equestrian statues placed him in a line of warriors dating back to Charlemagne.[45] He turned out to be the last Italian leader to make use of the symbolism of the horse. When satirist Leo Longanesi argued after the war that 'destiny has changed horses', he was not entirely right.[46] Destiny had changed direction for sure, but not from one horse to another. Rather, technology and social change as well as the political transition had left the horse behind.[47] Mussolini, of course, had taken care to associate himself with fast cars and aviation too; he was after all a modern leader, even if he saw himself in the mould of the charismatic leaders of history.[48] But he understood that the horse was the political animal par excellence that had long been bound up with leadership, charisma and military prowess. In the eighteenth century, it had been seen as a vital agent of modernisation. By situating himself in the imagination on horseback, he channelled Napoleon, Garibaldi and other warrior leaders. No postwar leader was associated with any form of transportation, ancient or modern, and so the image of movement, daring and individuality that Mussolini had cultivated fell by the wayside, except insofar as it was imaginatively associated with the one-time dictator himself, albeit not always positively: 'rider of horses and of women's bosoms, in all his glory; big bum on horseback', Gadda dubbed him.[49] This meant that at one level no leader replaced him. His charismatic imagery persisted in the collective imagination as ghostly Other.

The gender aspects of the Mussolini persona were quite complex. An acute early observer of the dictator, Camillo Berneri, argued that he exhibited a psychic dualism: 'feminine sensibility and cruelty, cowardice and courage, sincerity and simulation'.[50] Nevertheless the outwardly projected image was one of hyper-masculinity, to the extent that the Sicilian author Vitaliano Brancati, writing in 1950, noted that ridicule was the 'the only way to cure however much there was of the feminine in the Italian people of the fatal passion for the masculine look, the virile voice, the strong jaw, the strong-willed forehead and the other anatomical pieces of the new idolatry'.[51] This broad line of conduct was adopted by anti-fascists after Mussolini's fall. Piquant details of his affair with Claretta Petacci appeared in a pseudonymous publication of 1944 entitled *Vita segreta di Mussolini* (Mussolini's Secret Life) in which the still-living Duce was variously mocked as 'the erotomaniac tyrant' and 'the Da Verona-style dictator' (a reference to the popular light erotic writer Guido Da Verona) and accused of having behaved towards his young mistress like 'a money-laden old client'.[52] The aim of a text like this was, even more radically than Voltaire had been with his anecdotal reduction of Louis XIV, to illustrate the decadence and immorality of the dictator and his regime.[53] The aim was to turn the leader figure into a 'negative exemplar'.[54] *Vita segreta di Mussolini* referred to Asvero Gravelli and a handful of other senior Fascists as 'pimps and hangers-on of the tyrant', implying that, among other things, they procured women for the Duce.

Anecdotes, titillating or otherwise, were of less interest to anti-fascists after the war. Rather it was former loyalists and close collaborators who supplied numerous anecdotes to convey Mussolini to the Italians in a digestible and rather sympathetic form.[55] One of the first and most enduring compendiums of trivial insights into the everyday customs of the dictator was published in 1946 under the title of *Memorie del cameriere di Mussolini* (Memories of Mussolini's attendant). The volume has remained almost constantly in print since then. The author, Quinto Navarra, had been the chief attendant of the Duce's office in Palazzo Venezia. The volume's insights are only very marginally illuminating as far as the politics of the period are concerned. In relation to the dictator's personality and foibles, however, it offers much. The tone conforms to a perception of Mussolini and his modes and manias that enjoyed a certain currency, and would even be regarded by his own younger children as lying 'somewhere between the serious and the comical'.[56] One anecdote that quickly became the best known, on account of the way it fitted with a common view of the man, to the point of acquiring the status of an *exemplum*, concerned his sexual appetite.

According to Navarra, for a period of twenty years, Mussolini 'received almost regularly a different woman every day'.[57] Allegedly, 'his adventures were interspersed between one official "audience" and another, according to a regular rhythm and at pre-established times'. These were not protracted or leisurely encounters. According to Navarra, 'Mussolini never dedicated to love two or three minutes more than was necessary; he dedicated to the women no more time than he was accustomed to dedicate to the workers of the iron and steel industries or to the peasants'.[58] The women were chosen for him from among the many who sent him admiring letters and were received in his normal working environments, including the Sala del Mappamondo in Palazzo Venezia. They were never offered the hospitality of a cup of tea or any other beverage, even though the meetings always took place late in the afternoon.[59] The women were usually bourgeois but not necessarily young or conventionally attractive; in fact, in this respect Petacci was the exception. Navarra claimed that he only realised that the Duce was having sexual relations with his visitors when he noticed that the carpets and cushions were stained. The dictator always took care that the women exited the rooms 'in perfect order and above all suspicion'.[60]

The Navarra volume, it later transpired, was the work of Leo Longanesi and Indro Montanelli, who had in the 1930s both been prominent journalistic supporters of the regime and who now cultivated what one close colleague termed 'a secret semi-admiration' for the fallen dictator.[61] They took Navarra, who was living in Milan and had fallen on hard times, under their wing and pumped him for stories of his master.[62] Their model was the memoirs of Napoleon's head valet Constant (Louis Constant Wairy), which had been published in Italian by the Milan publisher Rizzoli in 1941, in a series of mostly foreign nineteenth-century classics edited by Longanesi himself.[63] Originally published in several volumes, the 'Memoirs of Constant, first valet of the emperor, on the private life of Napoleon, his family and his courts' was a classic example of anecdotal reduction.[64] The author hugely admired Napoleon while also being fully party to his domestic life and the ways of the court. Despite many references to the 'emperor' and 'his majesty', it was not the great man who emerged from his text. Rather it was the human being and his dealings with servants and family, the man given to childish vanities, seen 'in the simple guise of a private person'.[65] It was a Napoleon without aura, as he was remembered by the servant who attended to his daily needs.

The Navarra book was a publishing success also because of the quasi-comical flourishes of the prose and its concentration on the all-too-human foibles of the dictator. It was sympathetic at one level and denigratory at another.[66] Even the story that Mussolini had sex with a different woman in his office almost every day, which left some contemporary commentators unconvinced, was presented in such a way as to raise a knowing smile rather than repulsion.[67] It was later discovered that Longanesi, aware of the importance of sexual anecdotes in Constant's volume, had badgered Navarra, warning him that, if he did not offer enough gossip on this topic, he would insert the claim that Mussolini was impotent. Historians have been unsure whether to regard this anecdote as actually true or simply 'hearsay' as Renzo De Felice judged.[68] At any rate, it was broadly plausible. One of the dictator's biographers, Pierre Milza, has written that, 'Mussolini's Don Juan tendencies formed part of the panoply of signs that in the eyes of the average Italian contributed to the image of the superman',[69] while Richard Bosworth, author of the most recent important biography in English, asserts that sexual prowess was 'linked to his image and charisma'.[70]

The way in which Mussolini occupied a narrative space in the postwar period certainly had something to do with the limited changes that occurred to the pattern of gender relations.[71] The former dictator was an embodiment of manliness as well as authority in a way that postwar politicians were not. Anecdotes about his sexual adventures normalised the one-time Duce rather than damning him. While few indeed in postwar Italy continued to regard him as an exemplary leader, for even among those who had followed him in the final phase of his political life there was a certain disenchantment, there remained an attachment, a sympathy and even a kind of nostalgia. While Mussolini's sex life might, in the eyes of foreigners, have underlined his abnormality, for male Italians, especially those of a certain generation, this was far less the case. Womanising was an aspect of the anecdotal Mussolini that situated him within the realm of a diffuse normative masculinity.[72] It was not incompatible with the persistent image of the benevolent, if flawed, leader. As a masculine exemplar or, to put it more prosaically, as an ideal type of the Italian *gallo*, Mussolini retained an allure. While his regime may have ended in disaster and he may have personally met an end that was exemplary in an entirely different way, his *style* of leadership, with its masculine swagger and implications of sexual vigour, proved to be a longer-lasting influence. If initially confined to the eccentric fringe of democratic republican politics, it would once more come to the surface and form a template of sorts in the 1990s as the political system of the 'first republic' crumbled and then fell following the end of the Cold War and the eruption of the 'Tangentopoli' corruption scandals.[73]

Through the first postwar decades, Mussolini was a negative model, a figure whose name alone brought to mind the risk of authoritarianism in country in which there was a proven taste for strong leadership.[74] Parallels were drawn or comparisons made by opponents whenever a politician was deemed to be exercising too much authority or benefiting from excessive or unctuous media coverage. But such observations were rarely wholly negative and in some cases the politicians involved revelled in them. In public opinion there was still a favourable disposition towards a type of leadership that did away with mediations and offered the prospect of swift and ambitious decision-making, cloaked in national pride.[75] It had been widely assumed in the postwar years, that peace, prosperity and consumerism would lead men to find outlets different from the conventional, and potential destabilising cults of strength, fitness and fantasies of adventure.[76] However, in the era of mass consumption, these too could be commercialised and packaged. In the 1980s, a certain resurgence of the idea of the man of providence occurred, leading to a revival of the tyrant complex in the political system and the media. The Socialist Party leader Bettino Craxi, who served as prime minister between 1983 and 1987, channelled the idea of strong leadership, mobilising the shadow of his distant predecessor.[77] The Mussolini analogy that was deployed by cartoonists to ridicule this tendency did nothing to hurt Craxi's standing and possibly even enhanced it.[78] Holiday pictures of Craxi wearing a bathing costume on the beach in Tunisia suggested a re-proposition in a contemporary key of Mussolini's physical exhibitionism at the Italian resort of Riccione.[79] After Craxi, other politicians seeking to disrupt the status quo tapped into deeply held sentiments and traditional gender norms. The Northern League championed a type of politics that drew on the masculine idea of the strong rustic leader.[80] A later leader of the League, Matteo Salvini channelled the Duce with few reservations, tweeting the stock phrase 'Molti nemici molto onore' (Many enemies, much honour) on Mussolini's birthday in 2019.[81] Touring the country, he spoke from balconies in the fascist-era new town Sabaudia, Mussolini's local provincial capital of Forlì and elsewhere. Comparisons between media-magnate-turned-prime-minister Silvio Berlusconi and Mussolini were numerous, with one prominent journalist later remarking that his rule was 'a comic farce that however lasted for twenty years, like [that of] his distant predecessor'.[82] These examples give a brief sense of the ways in which Mussolini still ghosted Italian political leadership into the twenty-first century. However, it was not necessarily male right-wing politicians who most effectively articulated populist conservative concerns. Uninterested in defending Mussolini and generally preferring not to even mention him, female right-wing politicians championed conservative nativist positions on the family and gender, placing them within a nationalistic discourse and against second-wave feminism.[83] Promoting the traditional family and a view of women's rights that ignored inequality, women including Brothers of Italy leader Giorgia Meloni, who became prime minister in 2022, moved beyond a template of authoritarian male leadership in terms of style while leaving broadly in place the very hierarchical and gendered view of social relations that had long underpinned it.

8

Imaginary trials

Mussolini was sentenced to death by the National Liberation Committee for Northern Italy. A decree emitted on 25 April 1945 determined the death sentence for all the members of the Fascist government and other senior Fascists who were guilty of having overturned the constitution, destroyed liberty, created the Fascist regime, compromised and betrayed the country and led it to 'the present catastrophe'. The decree was signed by leaders of all the parties that belonged to the committee. The sentence was decided without a trial, so Mussolini was neither able to hear the charges against him nor allowed the opportunity to defend himself. It had been the intention of the Allies, to whom the fallen dictator was expected to be handed over on his arrest, to put him before an international tribunal. Mussolini was aware of this and, although he claimed to want to avoid this outcome at all costs, at the time of his apprehension he was carrying documents that he expected to use in his defence.[1] However, the anti-fascist leadership was convinced that his fate should be decided by Italians and that, as a consequence of Fascist actions during the civil war, he merited one sentence only. Among the population of the areas that had been governed by the RSI, hatred of him was intense. The vengeful crowd in Milan's Piazzale Loreto testified to a satisfaction that retribution had been enacted. But the sense that Mussolini deserved to be tried and judged was widespread. The lack of a proper trial, and the subsequent failure to stage the planned 'Italian Nuremberg', meant that the Italians did not get the chance to reckon with a leader who had inflicted immense damage on the country or with the regime he had headed.[2] He had never been properly held to account. By contrast, among those more sympathetic to Mussolini, there was a sense that, by means of his summary execution, an injustice had been perpetrated. For his keenest supporters, the ex-Duce had been turned into a martyr to the Fascist cause.

Consequently, after the war and at various intervals over the following twenty and more years, there were various imaginary trials, none of which had any legal or political value. All of them were the work of journalists, for whom Mussolini was an endless source of copy. The ex-dictator could be revisited and recounted in many different ways by all manner of commentators and witnesses. His story could be told again and again, and his period of rule could be assessed and reviewed from different points of view.[3] The trial format took various forms, although all of them were framed as quasi-judicial; they were reviews of the conduct of one man staged with a view to reaching a verdict. The authors and creators of these various initiatives all sought to make an impact on public opinion, to stimulate people to think about the impact and legacy of the dictator.

The basic assumption of the trial format was not usually that the absence of a judicial trial had deprived the Italian people of the opportunity to hold a reckoning with their oppressor. Such an approach might have highlighted embarrassing complicities that would have entailed a serious working through of society's relationship with the dictator that, for many years, would prove to be difficult. Rather it was assumed that there was a case to be made in Mussolini's favour, that evidence in support of his actions needed to be presented and weighed before any verdict could be reached. The format of the trial, therefore, arose in a context in which the anti-fascist view of recent history was not universally shared and in which there was a certain sympathy for the fallen tyrant despite the ruin he had brought to the country.[4] In this sense the main impulse to judge Mussolini was located within a pattern of sympathetic memory that was largely anecdotal and which was elaborated mainly by one-time Fascists.

The very first of the fantasy trials, which became a sort of model for others, was, however, not the invention of an Italian at all and nor was it very sympathetic to the accused. But it was not as hostile as might have been expected. It was the work of the left-wing British journalist Michael Foot, who in the 1980s would become leader of the Labour Party (one of the major UK political parties). Using the pseudonym Cassius, in 1943 he published an imaginary 'trial of Mussolini' that had as one of its key elements the indulgence and credit that had been granted to the dictator by foreign admirers and politicians.[5] Acknowledging that 'in the case of Mussolini it is clear that an unforeseen accident might at any moment deprive him of the chance of vindicating himself before a public tribunal', Foot invented—in the interests of 'fair play'—a trial in which a man 'assumed guilty for having assisted in the unleashing of world war has the right to state his case and to speak for himself'.[6] The court that Foot imagined—assuming that save for 'an unfortunate accident' Mussolini would one day probably receive justice from a real tribunal—was instituted by the British government at the request of the Allied powers. Its task was to ensure that justice was meted out to the 'Arch Criminal of Italy', as he was regarded.[7]

Foot recognised the unusual nature of his exercise. With leaders of defeated nations, he argued, judgement, if it was passed at all, was usually achieved by means of the assassin's bullet or public anger. In other instances, the task was left to posterity. But this was risky and unpredictable as even the most evil of rulers had found posthumous admirers and defenders. Napoleon, he said, was still the subject of debate between those who portrayed him as 'the spoilt child of the French revolution' and those who saw him as a 'blood-thirsty tyrant'.[8] It was the task of Mussolini's contemporaries, those who had seen the illusions and tragedies of the present epoch and lived through the period in which the man in the dock was 'a chief figure in the eyes of his fellow human beings' to judge him. They were better qualified than 'the historian of a hundred years hence cloistered in his study'.[9] The indictment accused Mussolini of being 'a prime enemy of the human race and a chief criminal responsible for the greatest war in history'.[10] His offences were numerous. They included establishing a dictatorship, defying international obligations that he had himself undertaken, making war on Abyssinia and in Spain, allying with Nazi Germany and assisting it in its ambitions against the free world by invading France and declaring war on Greece, Britain and Russia, countries with which he had signed pacts of non-aggression.

Foot's Mussolini speaks little. He pleads 'Not Guilty' and intervenes only once after that to justify his ruthless methods and his ambition to turn Italy by any means into a great power.[11] It is left to his nominated counsel to conduct a defence that is largely a forceful act of accusation against the British politicians who had indulged him and turned a blind eye to numerous acts of aggression as well as of those parts of public opinion that had applauded him. Figures living and dead, including Austen Chamberlain (foreign secretary 1924–29) and his half-brother Neville Chamberlain (prime minister 1937–40), the prominent Conservatives Winston Churchill and Samuel Hoare, the proprietor of the *Daily Mail* Lord Rothermere and the journalist Ward Price are called as witnesses to explain their conduct and account for their view of Mussolini as a great figure of the age, the incarnation of a new spirit in the Italian nation. Even if Conservative government ministers had been ready to condone Mussolini of any crime prior to 1940, condemning him only when he made war on England, the Judge warned the jury of twelve British citizens that finding him guilty only of joining with Nazi Germany in its war would be tantamount to an acquittal of any crime committed against the Abyssinians, the Spanish and the Italians over a twenty year period. 'Although Mussolini is condemned, Fascism will leave this court acquitted'.[12] That would hardly act as a deterrent to 'future imitators of Benito Mussolini'. The complicity of British interests in Mussolini's acts up to 1940 is revealed in all its moral bankruptcy by the voices of spokesmen for Abyssinia, Spain, and the Italian people, who detail the suffering that was caused by the aggressions of the dictator.

Foot wrestled with the problem, that he formulated as an argument deployed by the defence, that there was no criminal code in international affairs. In his speech, the defence counsel in fact challenges the moral right of the court to try Mussolini. The former dictator, he claims, could be held to be guilty of errors and blunders but not of criminal acts.[13] In counter, it is argued that there were standards of international conduct and morality in international affairs, and not only brutal realism. These involved honouring treaties and judging internal developments in other countries. The doctrines that informed the establishment of the United Nations in 1945 (two years after Foot was writing) formalised this and crimes against humanity were for the first time treated as offences under international law. In conclusion, Foot's judge invites the jurors to pass verdict not purely on a single man but on a whole epoch and thereby send a message that will have an impact on the future shape of Europe and the world.[14] Their verdict in short was to be a political one since, without that, the trial would be pointless. The judge's summing up points unequivocally towards a guilty verdict, but the author concludes his account before the jury retires to consider the evidence and come to a decision. The matter is thus left open for readers to draw their own conclusions. This was later taken to be tantamount to an absolution. When Foot's book was published in Italy in 1946, it was given the rather misleading title: *Un inglese difende Mussolini* (An Englishman Defends Mussolini).

In the immediate postwar period, the issue of trying those who were responsible for initiating and waging World War II was of widespread concern. For the victorious powers, it was important to establish the illegitimacy of the conduct of the rulers of Germany and Japan and inflict on them a condemnation that was not solely political but also judicial. In 1945–46, the Nuremberg trials put the spotlight firmly on German guilt while the Tokyo trials condemned Japanese crimes. The leading figures of Fascist Italy were not tried in the same way—although there had been plans to hold international trials in Italy—

because the country had ended the war on the Allied side.[15] As he was dead, Mussolini would not have been tried, just as Hitler was not in the dock at Nuremberg. However, before international opinion, Mussolini was at the very least guilty of entering the war at Hitler's side. Within Italy, needless to say, the matter of judging Mussolini remained a complicated question. The parties and the government did not feel obliged to address it directly. In the country, those who wanted to raise the topic of complicity saw it as important and so did those who wished to destroy the remaining psychological and political entanglement of the Italians with their dictator. However, these were the concerns of minorities. While there were some who deplored the way he had been dealt with, few (except for some committed loyalists of past and present) were willing to take up his defence in public.

Over time, the negative judgement on Mussolini that dominated official public opinion came to coexist with other more forgiving views of the one-time dictator that derived in part from popular memory and in part from the anecdotal reconfiguration of the man as an individual with foibles and flaws who had perhaps not been such a bad leader after all. The sense of a need to rethink Mussolini, to formulate some form of shared opinion of him that was not solely conditioned by anti-fascism, was championed by right-wing journalists including Longanesi, Montanelli and others. A notable contribution to this current was a curious text entitled *Il buonuomo Mussolini* (The good fellow Mussolini) in which Montanelli, adopting the voice of the Duce, set out the latter's supposed final will and testament and brought his wishes into the postwar era.[16] Longanesi and Montanelli set themselves up as architects of the re-absorption of Mussolini, re-cast as a faulty but well-meaning human being, into the collective consciousness of middle Italy. Through their efforts an indulgent memory of Mussolini took hold in conservative public opinion.

The first Italian imaginary trial appeared in 1959 under the title *Processo a Benito Mussolini* (Trial of Benito Mussolini).[17] This anonymous pamphlet (the author is indicated as 'Notorius') neither attempted to weigh the evidence nor to imagine a courtroom in any detail. It began with an assumption that the judges were international and that their task was to condemn Mussolini's actions. The dictator is no longer alive in this imagined scenario and therefore does not defend himself and cannot be sentenced. It is left to his defence counsel to speak up for him and tell 'the whole tragic truth of one of the greatest Men in history' in order that future historians might evaluate him favourably.[18] For the author, Mussolini could be likened to Christ, as both were executed prior to trial and sentencing. Like Foot, Notorius points a finger at the foreign politicians, especially the British, who favoured and backed Mussolini as long as he was seen as a bulwark against Bolshevism in Europe. Each of the major crimes of which the dictator is accused is forcefully rebutted. In conclusion, and in the face of a public that, the author thinks, would be ready to lynch Mussolini were he to appear before it alive once more, it is suggested that, far from being condemned by history, he will have a monument erected in his honour one day by a future strongman leader.

A more substantial and less blatantly partial trial was authored by the journalist Mino Caudana. After publishing a series of articles about the one-time foreign minister Galeazzo Ciano, he furnished a blow-by-blow account of Mussolini's life that first appeared over no fewer than 166 instalments in the right-wing Rome daily newspaper *Il Tempo* in 1958–59. These were then republished as a book of great size and weight in 1960 under the title *Il figlio del fabbro* (The Blacksmith's Son).[19] Caudana suggested that, over the period from 1926 until the conquest of Ethiopia and the proclamation of the empire in 1936, Fascism had achieved many positive things, among them the eradication of the Bolshevik threat and the restoration of order. As a result, it enjoyed 'the complete and joyful consent of all Italians'.[20] Over this period, the standing of Mussolini was at its highest. The man in the street, 'saw in Benito Mussolini the dynamic and providential man who, indefatigably, deals with the many problems of Italian life: health care, the campaign against tuberculosis, the aqueducts, the sewers, the country's standing in foreign lands, and the regulation of drug use'. What he did not notice was 'the prisons and the remote islands had been filling up with political prisoners'. Looking around, he 'found that there was nothing to scandalise him'.[21] Only the war in Spain and the alliance with Hitler set alarm bells ringing.[22]

The journalist used a narrow range of references, mostly consisting of memoirs that had either been published under the regime—the reconstruction of the Ethiopian war was based on the memoirs of General Badoglio, published in 1937 with a preface by Mussolini—or in the years after the war.[23] For Mussolini's personality, he relied on Quinto Navarra's heavily re-elaborated memoirs. This led some to see the lengthy book mainly as a compilation, a 'memoir of memoirs', that reconstructed Fascism to some degree from within.[24] But there was a significant degree of creative re-elaboration on the part of the author.[25] Caudana invented dialogue to enliven dramatic moments. He did not ignore unsavoury aspects of the regime. For example, he accorded due attention not only to Giacomo Matteotti but to the liberal Giovanni Amendola and other prominent anti-fascists who died as a result of violent Fascist assaults in the

1920s. He also discussed the racial laws of 1930 in some detail. In this sense, his book was not the work of a Fascist sympathiser but nor was sympathy entirely absent.

If Montanelli's adoption of Mussolini's voice in *Il buonuomo Mussolini* had seemed a provocation, then Caudana's adaptation of this device of the talking dead was stranger still, unless it is considered as an example of the persisting ties between the dictator's story and the nation. In fact, the text opens with an imagined scene in the San Cassiano cemetery in Predappio in which deceased members of the Mussolini family welcome the return among them of Benito.[26] The volume ends on a sentimental note with a scene that is set in the Como prison where Rachele Mussolini is being held at the time when the announcement is made that her husband has been killed. Another prisoner who does not know her identity comments indignantly on her calm state at the news that has just been broadcast on the radio.[27] 'And why aren't you crying?', she inquires accusingly, 'Have you never lost anyone?' This episode was lifted directly from Rachele Mussolini's own memoirs.

With *Il figlio del fabbro*, Caudana established his position, which may be described as sympathetic and moderately judgemental. Another journalist, the former Fascist Giovanni Ansaldo, described him as having adopted 'a very curious sentimental form of Mussolinism'.[28] His next enterprise, which was even more ambitious, reflected this. Inspired by Foot (and perhaps Notorius), he revived the device of an imaginary trial, in this case not looking forwards to a possible real trial but backwards to one that had never happened, he conducted a wide-ranging 'trial of Mussolini' that purported to examine all aspects of the conduct of the regime and its leader in the imaginary framework of a judicial process.[29] The 'trial' was not a loosely conceived device deployed solely to justify another revisitation of Mussolini's career. In the volume *Processo a Mussolini* (The Mussolini trial), he set up an imaginary court of the type that the Allies had planned to establish. However, he specified at the outset that he would end his account with the withdrawal of the judges to consider their verdict. He therefore avoided the temptation to formulate a verdict of his own. Over three volumes amounting to a total of 1,650 pages, Caudana fulfilled his aim to examine the events of period between 1919 and 1945 in what he claimed was a dispassionate way, 'without incense or poison' as he put it.[30]

To start, it was necessary to imagine that Mussolini had not been captured by partisans and killed at Giulino di Mezzegra on 28 April 1945. Unlike Foot, who speculated about what would happen in the future to Mussolini, Caudana offered a form of alternate history in which real events were recast on the basis of a fictional re-imagining.[31] In Caudana's account, Mussolini surrenders to the Americans on 4 May and is handed over to representatives of the United Nations in accordance with the dispositions of the armistice. It is announced that he will be tried for war crimes by the Court of Justice of the United Nations. Caudana took pains to register the indignation of the Italian anti-fascist forces over the fact that the dictator would be judged by foreigners. The question of whether Mussolini should be judged by an international court or an Italian one is imagined to have been brought to a head with the request by Count Carlo Sforza, the High Commissioner for Sanctions against Fascism, that he be tried before a special Italian tribunal. This is supported by Togliatti and the respective leaders of the Socialist and Action parties, Pietro Nenni and Ferruccio Parri. The Allies had already recognised the competence from 1944 of the High Commission. However, this is rejected on the grounds that 'allowing Italian anti-fascists to try Mussolini would grant their government a recognition and a prestige that our governments are not ready to concede'.[32]

The trial, which takes place in Naples, begins in September 1945, a few weeks after the explosion of the second atomic bomb on Nagasaki and the surrender of Japan. The president of the Extraordinary International Court is British, while other judges represent each of the victorious powers. The event is imagined to be—like the 1946 Nuremberg trial, which it is said to follow—an event of global significance, that draws hundreds of journalists to Naples. The acts of which Mussolini stands accused are numerous and include initiating the war and crimes against humanity, war crimes, and overthrowing democratic freedoms.[33]

Caudana's Mussolini is humanised and placed within the familial dimension that his widow constructed after the war. The fallen dictator is described as 'very thin but not pained'.[34] 'The cheeks are hollow and form two bags each side of lips that are a little too tight, the only sign of the moral torture that in this moment cannot not be feeling'. 'The jawbone is marked by the shadows created by the lights, that form a sparkling halo around the profile of the by now completely bald head'. Before the court, he is defiant. Invited to plead, he responds: 'I declare that I acted for the wellbeing, greatness and future of the fatherland'.[35] Unsurprisingly, if only for narrative convenience, Caudana's Mussolini opts to defend himself, all the while insisting that he will not adopt legal argumentation as 'this must be the trial of twenty years of history, not of one man'.[36] His concern is not any immediate verdict but 'that which will take place in the distant future in the heart of the Italians: the trial of Mussolini's Italy'. Nevertheless, the court imposes a public defender whose task is to ensure that the accused remains purely and solely that. This role is filled by Folke Bernadotte, a real-life Swedish diplomat of undisputed integrity who played a key role in negotiating the release of prisoners from concentration camps.[37]

Caudana's trial follows a predictable itinerary, with all the various charges being detailed and Mussolini and his nominated defender offering explanations and justifications in each case. The violence of the Fascist squads, the seizure of power, the murder of opponents, the establishment of the dictatorship, the suppression of freedom of the press, the conquest of Ethiopia, the invasion of Greece and the entry into war alongside Hitler are all reviewed. Caudana has little difficulty imagining Mussolini's argument that he was not personally responsible for Fascist violence and that he operated for the greater good of the nation. Indeed, he even claims that, despite his being supreme commander, responsibility for Italy's disastrous war was down to the generals who were materially directing military operations. A similar self-exculpatory defence is also deployed to justify the reconstitution of the Fascist Party and government at Salò and of having continued the war at the side of Hitler until its bloody end. He claims, as supporters did in reality, that his aim was to prevent Italy from becoming a fully occupied country at the mercy of the Germany's needs. 'We fought for Italy: for the salvation of the Italian population and for our honour'.[38]

As Mussolini comes to his feet to answer the final charge, he assumes once more a familiar guise:

> The duce rises, with a brisk gesture he adjusts the headphones over his ears. He has lost weight, has aged and looks worn out. And yet, instinctively he seems to pick up as he rises to his feet. Even if he is wearing a frayed double-breasted blue suit, perhaps the same one that he wore when he went to see the king for the last time, even if he stands in the dock in the Sala dei Baroni, everyone has the terrible impression of seeing him once more on the balcony of Palazzo Venezia like many times before. Between him and his audience the magical contact that on so many occasions whipped up 'oceanic crowds' into an unforgettable enthusiasm, is magically recreated.[39]

The Italian people who had once been idolised Mussolini are not absent from Caudana's fictionalised trial. He depicts a crowd of ten thousand people who have converged on Naples to follow events. The divisions of the recent civil war are mapped on to them. On the one side, there are 'partisan chiefs and "federali" [the use of a term applied in the past exclusively to local Fascist Party bosses is revealing] of the left-wing parties who want to witness the condemnation of the "puzzone" [big stinker] as Mussolini has officially been designated by the fickle Italian bourgeoise'.[40] On the other, there are the 'fascists of the last hour': 'the many Italians who were proudly anti-fascist under the "sinister regime" and for that reason were not were not brought before the 1,082 "special tribunals for the epuration" [the courts instituted in the wake of the liberation to purge the public sector of Fascists], but who became fascist, with the enthusiasm of the convert, out of indignation over 25 July and 8 September' (that is, the dates of Mussolini's dismissal and of the armistice). The author's sympathies are evident from a description that purports to take no sides, but which dismisses the former as politicos and fickle followers while attributing numbers and honour to the latter. Left out are the average Italians for whom the author elected himself spokesman in his previous work and for whom Mussolini had for so long been a uniquely involving leader. Caudana's refusal to conclude with a verdict leaves the outcome of the trial unresolved, though his open conclusion carries a strong flavour of potential acquittal.

Several years later, Paolo Pavolini, a moderate left-wing journalist who had belonged to the Resistance, revived the scenario of the trial to bring Mussolini once again under scrutiny.[41] His point of view was markedly different to Caudana's. He was indignant that, in the early 1970s, Fascism was still present in the interstices of Italian society; not only had the elites that had collaborated with the Fascist regime resumed their places and power under the republic, but violent, subversive Fascism had not been stamped out. The explosion of a bomb in Milan's Piazza Fontana in 1969, killing seventeen, was, after initial attempts to pin the blame on anarchists, exposed as the work of neo-fascists.[42] The Nuremberg trials had ensured that in Germany everyone knew the truth about the Nazi regime and the responsibility for its crimes that individuals bore. The absence of any grand public trial in Italy ensured that a fascist undercurrent remained intact in public life. The return of democracy allowed many to falsely claim that Fascism had passed into history. In Pavolini's view, putting Mussolini on trial in a fictional court that was imagined as having been established in October 1946 was a way of combatting a fascism that was still live.

He took pains to set up his fictional tribunal in a plausible way. The trial is based on the clauses of the armistice between Italy and the Allied command, which obliged the Badoglio government to deliver Mussolini to the authority of the United Nations in order that he could be judged for war crimes. It was to be international but was to take place on Italian soil. The elected location is Verona, the city that had in January 1944 hosted the show trial and execution of Galeazzo Ciano and other Fascists who had voted against Mussolini in the last meeting of the Fascist Grand Council. As in 1944, there are political reasons for conducting the process far from Rome to reduce any embarrassing comparisons with the present government of Italy, on which the trial had been imposed after a protracted dispute over who should judge the former dictator. The form of presentation is daily newspaper reports for a short-lived Florence-based Resistance paper which Pavolini had himself been involved with, *La Nazione del Popolo*.

Like Caudana, Pavolini accords a central role to Mussolini, whose decision to defend himself transforms the trial into a political platform and vehicle for self-justification. He takes the stand against a background (in this scenario) in which both Claretta and the Fascist officials executed at Dongo are dead and their bodies have been exhibited in Piazzale Loreto. Mussolini alone escaped this fate. By the time the trial starts, he has recovered some of his former vigour. Dressed in civilian clothes and flanked by two military policemen, he is a reduced figure but no longer has the 'deathly pallor and fixed stare' that marked the pained appearance of the 'puppet leader of the puppet republic of Salò'.[43] He has recovered in health and calmness and has gained weight. After the charges are announced by the American president of the tribunal, the ex-Duce, in a three-hour-long initial speech, offers an extended justification for all of Fascism's acts, taking care to distance himself from Hitler, with whom he claimed to have poor relations, and to implicate the western powers in the events of which he was accused. These include undermining the League of Nations and illegally invading Abyssinia. 'In many celebrated trials, and mine will be one of these', he proclaims, 'the accused is sometimes transformed into accuser'.[44] 'In fact, I accuse the Anglo-French governments of 1935 of having unleashed those uncontainable forces that re-awakened the apocalyptic flames of another world conflict'. In a powerfully self-exculpatory speech, he claims that every act was aimed at limiting Hitler and balancing Germany's power. 'The real tribunal whose judgement interests me is that of posterity not that of my contemporaries',[45] he argues, asserting his faith that in time he will be seen as an architect of a Europe of peace who only failed because of the hostility and incomprehension of others.

After this initial peroration, the court offers a platform to representatives of nations attacked or invaded by Fascist Italy, each of whom lists the crimes committed against his country and demands a guilty verdict. These seem to have a galvanising effect on Mussolini, who dismisses efforts to label him as a liar, a criminal, an assassin, and a traitor as motivated by rancour and littered with errors. 'Mussolini', Pavolini writes in his imagined newspaper report, 'uttered these words using, just like in his heyday, the entire apparatus of his iron jaw and his rolling eyes. The attribution of so many crimes, far from demolishing him seem to have inspired a swaggering counter-attack. He is once more the Mussolini of old: the bombastic tribune of Palazzo Venezia and so many other balconies, from one of which he once began a speech proclaiming "Today, I feel in form"'.[46]

It is this very return to form that leads to a brusque change of direction in the trial. The representative of Italy, nominated by the government, intervenes to denounce the procedure as weighted in favour of the accused. Guglielmo Sangiorgi, a figure from the Resistance invented by the author, was not about to let this happen.[47] Mussolini should not be tried as a war criminal, Sangiorgi asserts; rather Fascism itself should be in the dock. Mussolini should be judged as the creator of this evil doctrine that led to war. A change to the procedure is needed, he argues, to denounce Fascism and make sure that it could never rise again.[48]

With this, the focus of the trial shifts to the crimes that had been committed first and foremost against Italians, that is to say those, it is argued, who had suffered most. Sangiorgi's prosecution case is a lengthy and detailed one that takes in large swathes of Italian history. His argument is directed especially at Italy's pre-fascist ruling class that had 'created' Mussolini, the very ruling class, he states, that had returned after the war. His intention is not to absolve Mussolini but rather to demonstrate that he was far from being the only one responsible for Fascism. 'Mussolini should be judged', he argues, 'as the most recent expression, juridically and morally criminal, of a historical process in which others also bear responsibility. For this reason, gentlemen of the international jury, I beg you not to emit a verdict of guilty or innocent but to decide to hold a new trial and to hand over the accused to his natural judges, the Italian people'.[49]

Pavolini focusses on the elites and adopts the view that the mass of Italians had never supported Fascism but rather had been its victims. However, there was acknowledgement that the regime had found backing in the interstices of society and that some needed to atone. The famous graffito that appeared on a wall in Rome in early 1945 apparently calling for the return of Mussolini was, he asserted, the expression of minorities who did not want to be held responsible for the privileges and prejudices they had accumulated under the regime. 'Behind these minorities, there is an apathetic and cynical majority that lacks the courage to put on trial the historical responsibilities of our country and conduct a vigorous and ruthless examination of its conscience'. 'Vogliamo indietro Mussolini' (We want Mussolini back), Sangiorgi concludes, so this process can begin.[50] Against an obstinate refusal to work through the consequences of Fascism, he urges its necessity.

What would Pavolini's imaginary court respond to this irregular if comprehensible and passionately motivated request? The answer would never be known for, before a decision can be taken, Mussolini collapses and dies. Like Caudana, Pavolini thus refrained from concluding with a verdict. However, by curtailing the matter abruptly in this way, he did not adopt the same position as Caudana. His intention was to shift focus and to suggest that, with Mussolini gone, the Italians should finally turn away from the ex-dictator and look more closely at the causes of his regime. They had to examine the structures of society that had allowed him to come to the fore, exercise great power and wreak such damage. This would necessarily entail an acknowledgement of responsibility and some measure of atonement.

Aside from these imagined tribunals, there were various looser attempts by the press to submit the ex-dictator to a posthumous trial. These typically took a slightly different form from the courtroom drama format of Foot, Notorius, Caudana and Pavolini. There was no formal list of indictments or presence of counsel in these treatments from which Mussolini himself was absent. The 'trial' in such exercises was really an assessment that presented itself as dispassionate and fair in a context in which, in reality, polarised partisan views were dominant. It was in this sense more akin to a psychological working through than the mock trials that, whatever the aim, maintained the focus as ever on Mussolini. One of these assessments was published in the magazine *Epoca* under the general title 'The Trial That Never Was' in several instalments in 1965.[51] After an opening article by the prominent journalist Luigi Barzini Jr, there were further articles by other writers including Mario Missiroli, Ignazio Silone, Domenico Bartoli and Giovanni Artieri, most of whom were figures from the centre-right. The premise was that the young needed help to understand how it was that people followed Mussolini for so long through a twenty-year dictatorship and the catastrophe of the war.[52] In many of the articles, the scapegoating of Mussolini as the sole person responsible for the crimes of Fascism was replaced by a view which attributed some of the blame to the Italians. Thus, Barzini sought to explain Mussolini's hold over people by referring to the charisma that he exercised over those who knew him well: 'Many men literally fell in love with him as though he were a woman, irrationally and blindly willing to forgive him everything, the weaknesses, the cowardice, the errors, the lies, the presumption, the stubbornness and the ignorance'.[53] However, it was not only close collaborators who were enchanted: 'Noone who was there will ever forget the spectacle of the piazza bursting with crowds listening to him: heads close together like the stones in a mosaic, with all eyes turned towards the same point, the balcony or the podium from which he was speaking. It was a scene that was both threatening and terrifying'.[54] Mussolini achieved this feat by a mixture of deception and flattery. 'Propaganda, choreography and dramatic twists had drugged the country. Almost all had lost or forgotten the capacity to judge things with a cold independent spirit; they allowed themselves to be dragged along by the wave of emotion'. They were tricked by a man who used deception as a political tool. Albeit with a measure of caution, it may be said that this approach acknowledged the role of the dictator as ego-ideal of the Italians. 'The majority of Italians did not realise that they were extras in an immense inebriating performance in a papier mâché epic which not even he himself, the author, knew how it would finish'.[55] The personality he invented was not purely his choice 'but a character that many Italians were ready to admire, the personification of their secret aspirations, capable of calming their most obscure anxieties'.[56] For Mario Missiroli, a former editor of major newspapers, the reason lay with the man himself, 'his capacity to fascinate collaborators and work crowds into a delirious frenzy'. His abilities as a communicator enabled him to embody a period in national life that lasted up to 1938.[57] After that, however, his popularity declined.

Epoca received many letters intervening in the discussion. After the initial articles, it modified the title of the series to 'Chi era veramente Mussolini' (Who Mussolini was really) without explanation but perhaps to maintain the focus firmly on the man rather than truly to open up the complex and difficult issue of psychological and cultural entanglement. When one young person wrote to assert that the 'trial of Mussolini' should in reality be the trial of two generations of Italians who had adored him, an older reader reproved him for his 'insolent letter', asserting that young people had no right to comment on things that only experts could properly understand.[58] Another reader wrote: 'I do not accept posthumous reprovals for the choices that young people made at that time, whether they opted for the "reds" or the "blacks"'.[59] Only one reader, writing from Genoa, suggested that a lesson could be learned from the former German president Rudolf Heuss, who had said that all Germans needed to ask for forgiveness for what the Nazis had done. 'For twenty years I have been waiting for an Italian personality to say similar words (even if Fascism was not the same as Nazism). I am still waiting. We judge and we condemn but we are always careful to say "I wasn't there" or to confess "I was there but in bad faith". It is our mania for avoiding "getting involved" that renders us incapable of judging, and perhaps unworthy to do so'.[60] These comments showed a shift away from the figure of Mussolini towards a scrutiny of the Italian people that contained the potential to turn, belatedly, into the very process of mourning for the dictator that the Mitscherlichs had identified as necessary but impossible in Germany. But this potential was not realised. Most of the historians who, from the mid-1960s, started to take over the matter of the interpretation of Fascism from journalists would never take it upon themselves to berate or judge the Italian people. Indeed, such an attitude would have been incompatible with their professional identity. Instead they began the serious work of reconsidering and interpreting Fascism as a historical phenomenon, a process that would itself prove controversial.

PART III

Material legacies

9

The fate of Duce statues

On 29 January 1961, a huge figurative monument was blown up by an irredentist group protesting against the failure of the Italian government to grant sufficient autonomy to the Alto Adige region in the far northeast of the country. The six-metre-high statue of a caped near-naked rider on horseback with his right arm raised stood on a two-metre-high plinth at the entrance to the Montecatini hydro-electric plant in Ponte Gardena. Situated twenty kilometres from Bolzano, it had greeted visitors to the plant since its opening in 1938. On the evening of the explosion, fragments of the statue were scattered over a considerable distance, some reaching well beyond the railway station 150 metres away. A handful of workers who had been gathered in the open space in front of the entrance until a few minutes before claimed it was a miracle they had not been killed. Newspaper reports condemned the 'hateful attack' that had destroyed a monument dedicated to the achievements of 'Italian labour'.[1] Photographs were later published of metal pieces including the head of the horseman lying amid the debris at the foot of the plinth. Among the local—mainly German-speaking—population, few regretted the passing of a statue that was known locally as 'Mussolini on horseback' and which was deemed to depict an idealised Duce in the act of giving the Roman salute.[2]

The destruction of this relatively unknown statue raises several questions about the nature of Fascist statues, some of which were destroyed in 1943–45 while others remained in place for many years after the war. Why was a statue of Mussolini erected in such a small and peripheral place (in the 1930s, Ponte Gardena had a population of 230 people)? Why also was approval given for a statue of limited artistic merit made of lightweight aluminium, albeit of considerable size, when the cult of the Duce was at its height? More pertinently, how did such an obviously Fascistic creation come to survive so long into the postwar period, long after the iconoclasm of 1943 and the officially sanctioned removal of Fascist symbols and names in 1945–46? Why did it take a group that was dubbed as terroristic to destroy it and why was this act condemned in the press as an affront to Italian workers?

To seek to answer these questions is to engage in a reflection on the complexity of the processes affecting the material legacy of Fascism. Some of these concern public policies towards the art works and the uses of buildings. Others, however, are less tangible and involve questions of modification, cancellation and removal, which may occur at a psychological level as well as a physical one. In the course of its existence, the Fascist regime transformed the built environment. It invested heavily in infrastructure and prestige projects. Expanding the presence of the state into previously neglected areas of the country, it left a vast network of political buildings, schools, leisure and welfare centres, sports facilities and other structures.[3] Many of these conformed to officially approved rationalist aesthetics and were adorned with Fascist symbols. They bore names that reflected the key events and dates in the Fascist calendar or which were drawn from the Fascist pantheon. Monuments and statues of various sorts, frescoes, mosaics, murals, busts and paintings brought a decorative dimension to this material propaganda.

Representations of Mussolini were extremely varied. While slogans and busts were common, and more elaborate representations—for example in mosaics and murals—were quite numerous, full-size statues were rare. In fact, for many years, the only significant statue of the Duce was an equestrian statue that was situated in the Littoriale sports stadium in Bologna. This bronze equestrian figure was commissioned in 1928 by the Fascist *podestà* of Bologna Leandro Arpinati and created by the prominent sculptor Giuseppe Graziosi.[4] Mussolini had inaugurated the new stadium on 31 October 1926. On that occasion, he had entered the arena on horseback to loud cheers from the assembled crowd of blackshirts, having survived an assassination attempt a few hours earlier. The event commemorated the fourth anniversary of the March on Rome and the Duce, who at that time was still frequently seen in civilian clothing, was attired in the uniform of the honorary corporal of the Fascist Militia. Made from bronze derived from cannons captured from the Austrians during the Risorgimento, the statue placed Mussolini in a long line of hero-leaders; the statue evoked the Renaissance *condottieri* filtered through a classical prism, as was evidenced by the cape (initially the plan had been for the rider to wear a fez and there was no cape).[5] The whole process of the conception, execution and inauguration of the statue was a much-publicised event. At the inauguration, the Fascist minister Giuseppe Bottai delivered a brief speech in which he asserted that the statue incarnated Mussolini's *numen*, that the effigy constituted a tangible manifestation of the Duce's spirit.[6] For fourteen years the statue stood witness to innumerable athletic and sporting events including some matches of the 1934 World Cup.

Mussolini was alert to the iconographic significance of equestrianism, which had long between associated with the politics of conquest.[7] With Roman equestrian statues occupying some monumental sites and popular imagery of Garibaldi frequently depicting him on horseback, he needed little encouragement to appropriate established iconographic formulae and cast himself as a Caesar on horseback.[8] In his long-running competition with the king, he was not going to renounce a key tool in the theatrical show of power that also had associations with terror.[9] For a leader of a new type, dubbed a 'plebeian aristocrat' by his biographer and close associate Margherita Sarfatti, the horse's reputation as a noble, aristocratic animal had elevatory potential. For these reasons, Mussolini worked on his horsemanship, riding frequently in the early morning and appearing on horseback on numerous ceremonial occasions.

The equestrian statue of the leader was not, however, a commonplace feature in Fascist Italy. Nor indeed were full-figure statues of the Duce of any sort. Mussolini was happy to pose for photographs, paintings and busts.[10] After some initial resistance, he allowed himself to be immortalised in any number of ways by admiring artists.[11] He was not keen, however, on statues. This was not due to any diffidence towards the form of the figurative statue as such. Fascism constantly ritualised and monumentalised itself, commemorating events, people and places of significance to its own history.[12] Rather, it was a matter of superstition. Mussolini occasionally made reference to statues and busts and almost always it was in relation to posterity. In his preface to the Italian translation of Sarfatti's biography, *Dux*, he referred to 'the bust that the public man will end up having in the village of his birth', thinking that this would be also his own destiny.[13] Statues, as philosopher Michel Serres has shown, are complex signifiers.[14] They are related to place and stability but also to death. Conceptually, he argues, the statue is 'weak and ghostly... a corpse'.[15]

However, though not keen on intimations of his own mortality, Mussolini succumbed in other ways to the temptation to make statues of himself; grandiose settings and choreography helped turn him into a sort of living statue. Many observers noted the petrification of the Duce's image after he became the founder of the empire. When Bottai returned from the war in Ethiopia and went to meet with Mussolini, he found that 'not the man, but the statue' stood before him; 'a hard, stony statue, from which a cold voice came out' that was devoid of all human warmth.[16] He seemed to adopt martial and sculptural poses in a phase in which he was elevated on to an even higher pedestal and appeared to have more in common with the great figures of history than ordinary men.[17] Like other twentieth-century totalitarian regimes, Fascism elaborated the aspiration to invest the body of the charismatic leader with the durability of the institution that he embodied and encompassed. This turned the leader into a monument, almost an inanimate object.[18] For Serres, leaders have to depersonalise in some way: 'something leaves in order to occupy the place that's exterior to individuals but interior to the collective';[19] 'let no-one give orders who doesn't know how to discorporate', he adds. Mussolini in fact was a highly corporeal leader and the description of his physique was almost a genre of sorts.[20] Clichéd descriptions of the head, the jaw, the eyes and so on abounded. However, there was also a tendency to ritualise and to monumentalise the Duce. Conceptually, he was situated beyond the reach of ordinary mortals. He came to be identified ever less with his human history than with the grander and more permanent parts of the nation, with the sky, the mountains and the landscape.[21] The writer Vitaliano Brancati produced a number of texts—one of which was entitled *Everest*—in which he was turned into a literally gigantic figure towering over humanity.[22] The Duce was seen somehow as superhuman, eternal and unchangeable, a figure of rigid permanence more than movement.[23]

Approval was given for a handful of statues of Mussolini, usually with a special justification. As with all uses of the Mussolini name or image, even the most minor, these required the approval of the Duce himself.[24] In the case of the Bologna equestrian statue, permission was granted for a number of reasons that had to do with the political importance of the city within Fascism, the fact that it represented a real event, and it offered a reminder that Mussolini had not succumbed to the attempt on his life by a petty would-be assassin. Only one other equestrian statue could be said to be of equal political significance, and that was erected beyond Italy's borders. On 20 March 1937, Mussolini entered Tripoli on a white horse, where, in the course of a lavish ceremony, he was presented with the sword of Islam by a Berber chief, Yusef Kerbisc. The golden, highly decorated sword had been made in Florence on the orders of Mussolini himself. This staged event, that was highly symbolic in the iconography of Fascist colonialism, was marked by the inauguration, the following year, of an equestrian statue of Mussolini holding the sword aloft (see Figure 8). The work of sculptor Quirino Ruggeri, it was placed in Piazza del Castello, the main square of Tripoli.[25] The statue was still standing when the British Eighth Army under General Montgomery entered Tripoli in January 1943, bringing the Italian empire in North Africa to an end. However, it did not last long. As they

Figure 8. The equestrian statue of Mussolini brandishing the sword of Islam at the moment of its inauguration in Piazza del Castello, Tripoli 1938. Courtesy of Alamy.

advanced through Italian occupied territory, the British pulled down or destroyed a number of Fascist stone monuments, including, it is widely supposed, a striking gigantic head of Mussolini that had been sculpted in 1935 from rock in the valley of Adua by soldiers belonging to a unit of the motorised artillery under the direction of their artistically inclined commander.[26] The head bore witness to the Fascist idea that the natural environment could effectively be harnessed to the regime's purposes as well as to the belief of many soldiers engaged in the imperial war of conquest that they had gone to Africa 'with Mussolini'. It had even featured in the cover of the prestigious weekly *L'illustrazione italiana* and been the object of a famous desacralising photomontage by the German visual artist John Heartfield that situated a pile of skulls at the base of the head.[27]

The Libyan capital served as the headquarters of the assault on Sicily that would take place in July 1943. The metal of which the equestrian statue of Mussolini was made therefore had a significant use value. The statue was commandeered by one of the five Advance Base Workshops of the Royal

Electrical and Mechanical Engineers (REME), pulled down and taken away to be used for the manufacture of spare parts.[28] Bits of it had different destinies. While the sword was presented to a museum in Tripoli, the horse's testicles were converted into an ashtray. A little later, the boots found a new home in an REME workshop that was established in the Ansaldo works in Naples. They ended up on either side of the fireplace in the sergeants' mess, where they were used to hold the fire irons.[29] The rest of the statue also went along and was in the end used to manufacture ball bearings. When the manufacturing workshop was disbanded in 1946, a quartermaster sergeant packed up the boots and sent them to the REME HQ training establishment in Arborfield. From there, they found their way to the REME museum at the Ministry of Defence site in Lyneham, Wiltshire, where they can still be found today (see Figure 9).

Fascist statues in the peninsula were not attacked or destroyed by Allied soldiers in the way that colonial ones were. Rather it was anti-fascists who vented their fury on monuments, symbols and decorations in the aftermath of Mussolini's fall and later. The equestrian statue of Mussolini in the Bologna sports stadium was symbolically powerful and therefore was as tempting a target as statues had been during other sudden transformations. During the French Revolution, no fewer than five equestrian statues of Bourbon kings were toppled between 11 and 15 August 1792.[30] This was tantamount to denying them their historical status as men of power. In Bologna on 26 July 1943 an angry crowd made its way from the city centre to the sports stadium where the horseman was dislodged and rolled down the steps of the pedestal. The head became separated from the body and was pulled joyously on a rope through

Figure 9. The boots from the Tripoli statue of Mussolini, now displayed in the museum of the Royal Electrical and Mechanical Engineers in Wiltshire. From the collection of the REME Museum.

the streets of the city and was eventually abandoned. After the end of the war, the commission responsible for the conservation of Bologna's artistic heritage was faced with the problem of what to do with the remaining parts of the statue. Initially, it was proposed to remove the horse from its location, detaching the remaining parts of the horseman and making the necessary repairs before relocating the horse in a public place.[31] However, this solution did not satisfy everyone. After local elections were held in 1946, the left-wing city administration ordered the removal of the horse and its transfer to one of the stadium's warehouses, on the grounds that, despite being the work of a recognised artist, the horse, deprived of its horseman, continued 'to tower over the whole stadium' as a ghostly reminder of the recent past.[32] The statue was officially deemed to be of no particular artistic value by the Sindacato Belle Arti (Fine Arts Commission), freeing the way in 1947 for the former partisans' association ANPI (Associazione Nazionale Partigiani d'Italia) to be given permission to use the bronze from the horse to create two figures of partisans—one female and one male—to symbolise the sacrifices of the liberation struggle. The armed figures were created by the sculptor Luciano Minguzzi and placed outside ANPI headquarters in the Montagnola gardens. In 1986, they were moved to Porta Lame, a city gate that was the site of an important battle in November 1944 between partisans and the German and Fascist forces. The two partisans were anonymous embodiments of the thousands who had taken part in the Resistance. The fact of their being male and female was a challenge to the Fascist identification of combat as a masculine prerogative.

For many years the iconoclasm that followed Mussolini's fall and its aftermath was not studied in any detail.[33] Yet the removal, negation or obliteration as well as renovation, re-making and re-appropriation of decorations and monuments can all be found in the period of Fascism's fall and defeat.[34] The Graziosi statue offers an interesting demonstration of the different pressures at work in the postwar years. It was unambiguously a political statue, but only after it had been expelled from city's artistic heritage could it be destroyed. Even then, cost factors jockeyed with proposals for reconfiguration. A sense of the complexity of the stakes involved in this issue is be gained from the story of the rider's head on the statue, which has been told by cultural historian Simona Storchi. For loyal Fascists, the statue remained a sacred object and some of their number succeeded in salvaging the head after it was abandoned following its desecration.[35] It was buried for safe-keeping before it was dug up in the early 1950s and taken to the offices of the neo-fascist Italian Social Movement (MSI). Here there was a small 'devotional space' with the photographs of the fallen and in the middle was situated the head.[36] In 1994, when the MSI was in the process of transforming itself into the post-fascist National Alliance and was disposing of all the symbols that had associated the party with Fascism, Filippo Berselli, a newly elected senator for the Alleanza Nazionale, took custody of the head with the intention of disposing of it. To prevent this, loyalists headed by Arturo Conti, founder of the semi-clandestine Historical Institute of the Italian Social Republic, appropriated it and took it to the institute's office in Via Marconi, where it was held for at least ten years (see Figure 10). For Conti and people of a like mind, the metallic head of Mussolini still contained the dictator's *numen*. It was both a memento and a legacy, which had been handed down through generations and of which he saw himself as the last custodian.[37]

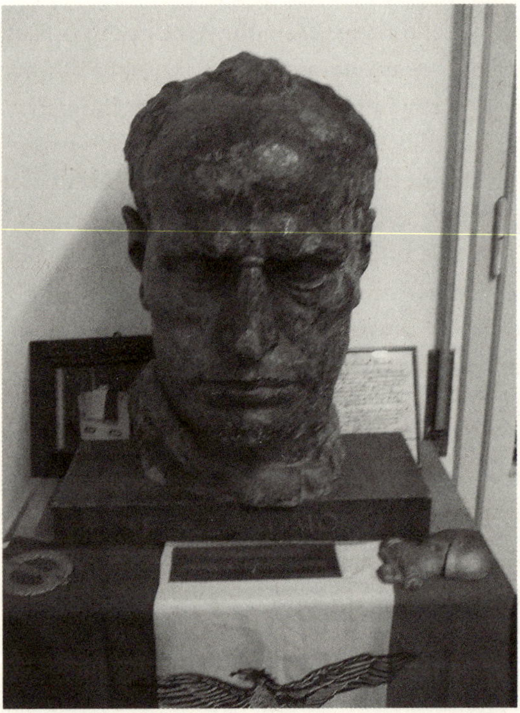

Figure 10. The head of the equestrian statue of Mussolini that stood in the Littoriale sports stadium in Bologna from 1926 to 1943. The head was appropriated by loyal Fascists after the statue was attacked in July 1943 and kept by them long after the rest of the monument was turned into statues of a female and a male partisan. It was last seen at the one-time headquarters of the Historical Institute of the Italian Social Republic. Author's own photograph.

A small number of other statues of Mussolini occupied locations of varying importance. There were not many of them, but their rarity lent them a certain significance. One of them was located in the Gaslini Institute paediatric hospital in Genoa whose new buildings were officially opened in 1938 by Mussolini himself in the course of a three-day visit to the city. Founded by wealthy senator Gerolamo Gaslini in 1931, the institute was created in memory of his daughter Giannina who in 1917, at the age of eleven, had died of peritonitis. It is said that it was suggested to Gaslini that he should establish the institution to make amends for tax irregularities that had come to the attention of the authorities.[38] It was intended to be a model of its kind, located near the sea and with open air facilities, where sick children could be sent to recover. For the main courtyard, following approval, a statue was commissioned depicting a child and Mussolini.

The inauguration of the institute was a thoroughly Fascist occasion. It at once signalled the regime's drive to improve the health and welfare of Italians and Gaslini's personal deference to the Duce's authority. One photograph of the occasion shows Mussolini in the grounds of the hospital inspecting a large bronze statue of himself in uniform bending to caress the head of the figure of a young girl. This benevolent depiction of paternalistic care enjoyed a certain visibility under the regime, featuring in press and publicity regarding the hospital. However, because it lacked any obvious connotation of power or conquest, the statue was not—so far as can be determined—the object of collective wrath in the aftermath of Mussolini's removal from power. Nevertheless, it was clearly an embarrassment to the institute's management and as such it was quietly removed.[39] There is no record or testimony of how or when this happened or of the fate of its constituent parts. The statue simply disappeared without trace in an act that was simultaneously one of physical removal and psychological de-realisation. After 1943, it was never seen again. Today the Gaslini flourishes and is regarded as one of the best children's hospitals in Europe. Photographs of the statue are absent from the historical section of the institute's website.

A further statue of the Duce was situated at the entrance to another institution devoted to the health and welfare of the people. This was the *Colonia 3 gennaio*, or the '3 January' health institute, located in the hills outside Turin, that was a centre for heliotherapy. January 3rd was a highly significant date in the Fascist calendar because it was the day in 1925 when Mussolini asserted his supreme authority in a speech to parliament and effectively became dictator. The large statue depicted the uniformed Duce standing with his right arm raised and was created for the occasion of his visit to Piedmont in May 1939. The centre was visited by Mussolini on the first day of his tour, which was one of the fullest and most extensive regional tours and also one of the last.[40] Like the Gaslini, the history of the treatment centre was bound up with the personal circumstances of a prominent entrepreneur. The modernist villa that housed it was built in 1929 for Riccardo Gualino, a businessman with many domestic and foreign interests, who was forced to vacate it when he ran into financial problems. His speculative activities were deemed to have caused harm to the national economy, and he was arrested on charges of fraudulent bankruptcy in 1931. His property was confiscated and he was sentenced to five years of internal exile, which he spent on the Aeolian island of Lipari. He was allowed to return to Turin in 1932 and he then moved to Rome in 1933. The villa was converted into a sanatorium the year after Gualino's arrest. It was damaged by bombing on 13 July 1943. The statue was probably one of the casualties of the bombing, but there is no record of its fate. Partially restored in 1945, the villa was acquired in the 1980s by the Piedmont region, restructured and turned into a conference centre and hotel.

There were a small number of other statues of Mussolini that were situated in the children's summer camps that were established by the regime on the Adriatic coast. These were all full figure life-size statues on pedestals that served as focal points for daily devotions on the part of the children who benefited from the regime's spartan largesse. As with other buildings associated with the regime, the camp facilities were later stripped of obvious political symbolism and were eventually abandoned. In some cases, the ruins still stand, forgotten and decaying. When artist Dan Dubowitz and architect Patrick Duerden went on a road trip in search of them in 2007, they were astonished to find that the empty spaces—some still with pieces of original furniture—conserved something of their ideological purpose. 'The abandoned summer camp sites appear to me to be a metaphor for the legacy of the regime in the national collective consciousness; a legacy that is complex, difficult and painful to contemplate, but which is too important to be forgotten', Duerden noted.[41]

The only statue of Mussolini that survived the regime was the one located at Ponte Gardena (see Figure 11). Why it survived is a question that has much to do with the nature of the statue itself. It is an interesting case that offers a way in to thinking about the reasons why the cult of Mussolini was not fully extirpated from the material environment after 1945 and why multiple signs of it could still be found much later, despite local controversy and occasional international perplexity. The statue was conceived by the Florence-born but

Figure 11. The Ponte Gardena statue (dubbed 'Mussolini on horseback' by locals) at the moment of its completion at the Battaglia Foundry. The statue, by sculptor Giorgio Gori, was originally commissioned for the Italian pavilion at the 1937 Universal Exposition in Paris. Courtesy of Archive of Fonderia Artistica Battaglia, Milan.

Paris-based sculptor Giorgio Gori, whose scale model won a competition in 1935 for a sculpture symbolising Italian labour to grace the entrance to the Italian pavilion at the forthcoming Universal Exposition in Paris. The title of the competition won by Gori was 'L'Italia in cammino' (Italy on the march). His statue was not originally intended to represent Mussolini, a fact that would be important in determining its survival. However, over time, it came to be associated with Fascist values and the Duce. After being fused in the Battaglia artistic foundry in Milan, it was transported to Paris where it went on show in 1937 at an Exposition that is remembered today for the dramatic architectural confrontation between the Soviet Union and Nazi Germany, whose pavilions were located directly opposite each other in ideological face-off.[42]

Situated at the foot of the Eiffel Tower, the Italian pavilion harnessed the talents of some of the most prominent and most devoted Fascist architects and artists of the time. These included Marcello Piacentini (who designed the exterior), Giuseppe Pagano (who was responsible for the arrangement of the exhibits) and Mario Sironi, who staged the colonial exhibits and whose mosaic entitled 'Corporative Italy', originally shown at the Milan Triennale, was expanded to include figures engaged in various forms of labour that were accompanied by a Roman eagle. The entire pavilion was intended to function as propaganda for the new Italy being forged under Mussolini's leadership.[43] Piacentini used both modern materials, like reinforced concrete, and classical forms such as colonnades and galleries in his design. Italy's contribution to the history of technology was underlined and recent innovations like linoleum and shatter-proof plate glass (known by the name Thermolux) were showcased. The country was depicted as a model society combining the best of both capitalism and communism under a benevolent dictatorship that valued artists and craftsmen as well as workers. The novel waste-mould casting of Gori's statue in an aluminium known as Anticorodal—a permanently modified alloy which had been used in industrial production since the end of the nineteenth century—instead of the much heavier but more conventional bronze, showed how it was possible for classicism and modernity, and art and industry, to combine. The statue was subsequently transported to Milan where it was judged impressive enough to be displayed at the Sample Fair of 1938. It featured in an illustration on a cover of the popular weekly *La Domenica del Corriere* dedicated to the opening of the trade fair, where it was renamed 'Il Genio del Fascismo' (The Spirit of Fascism).[44] Having been acquired by the Montecatini company, the statue was later moved to Ponte Gardena, where it was installed at the entrance to the newly built hydro-electric power station. The title it had now acquired was prominently displayed on the stone plinth.

In the later years of the regime it became the practice to conceive statues that combined general elements of the Fascist purpose with hints and allusions to the Duce and his leadership rather than blatant representations. Often these were conveyed through the sheer size of the works. The most extraordinary and ambitious of these was only ever realised in part and was never displayed in public. This was an enormous bronze colossus, almost twice as tall as the Statue of Liberty in New York, that would have towered over the whole Foro Mussolini sports complex in Rome, but never came to fruition due to the fall of the regime.[45] In the intentions of Renato Ricci, head of the Opera Nazionale Balilla, the Fascist youth organisation, and the sculptor Aroldo Bellini, the giant figure would have represented Hercules, though the face would have born the unmistakable traits of Mussolini. It would have been situated behind the speaker's podium in a new square where it was envisaged that gigantic rallies of up to half a million people would have been held, replacing Piazza Venezia as the main location in which the Duce would address the crowds. Though first conceived by Ricci as early as 1933, the statue was not designed until 1936. Only a foot and the head had been cast before the imposition of sanctions by the League of Nations and the consequent austerity measures forced postponement of work on the colossus and the balconied building.[46]

Where there was no obvious likeness of Mussolini, reconversion was relatively easy. A statue bearing the title 'Genio del Fascismo' (Genius of Fascism), that had been placed before the Palazzo degli Uffici, the first building to be completed in Rome's EUR district, managed to escape the attention of iconoclasts. A work by the sculptor Italo Griselli that avoided both the equestrian form and the bulky muscularity of Gori's creation, it depicted a young male athlete giving the Fascist salute with a long right arm. After the war, Griselli's boy was simply renamed 'Genio dello Sport' (The Spirit of Sport) and it still stands today on its cylindrical base in its original location.

The Ponte Gardena statue underwent a similar renaming. 'Al Genio del Fascismo' (To the Genius of Fascism) was erased from the plinth and replaced with a new legend that read 'Al Genio del Lavoratore Italiano' (To the Genius of the Italian Worker). The aim was clearly to effect a cosmetic change that would rid the statue of the Fascist patina that it had acquired in Paris and Milan and enable it to transition unproblematically into the era of republican democracy. However, this proved not to be quite so simple to achieve. After its destruction, the sculptor Gori explained in an interview that his statue had never been intended to depict Fascism or the Duce.[47] He thus effected a retrospective de-fascistisation to the intended benefit of himself and the now defunct statue. For the horseman's features, he claimed to have used his brother as a model. Moreover, the raised right arm was not even a Roman salute but a gesture pointing the way to the future. The problem was that the form of the statue was imbued with Fascism and the association with Mussolini could not be so easily erased. The idea itself of the modern equestrian statue with its classical and Renaissance associations was a Fascist trope. It had already inspired the prominent monument in Bologna, while the flowing cape, a device that had previously been used to effect by Graziosi, had more to do with the man of destiny than the Italian worker. Moreover, the 'Al' (to the) of the original title seemed like a dedication to an authoritarian force that could scarcely be transferred in a democratic context to workers—now mostly identified with the left—or to their labour. The focus on the nobility and achievements of Italian labour had in any case been a theme of Fascist propaganda used especially insistently in relation to the colonies. For these reasons, the statue remained an object of antipathy. No new dedication could assuage such feelings in a region where the regime had sought forcibly to Italianise the German-speaking population.

A first attack on the statue occurred in 1946 when a group seeking independence for South Tyrol damaged it, leaving a hole where the horse's head was joined to the body. Nine years later, another group stuck dynamite in the gap, though the explosion was not sufficient to do much harm. Only when a much larger quantity of dynamite was used in 1961 was the statue finally destroyed.[48] Despite local perceptions of the statue's identity, the destruction was not interpreted as being anti-fascist so much as anti-Italian. It was timed to coincide with difficult discussions between Italy and Austria over the status of Alto Adige rather than as a reaction to the various neo-fascist attacks that took place in Rome and in Umbria in the same period.[49] It is not known what happened to most of the fragments of the statue, but the horse's head was appropriated by the irredentists as a trophy. Today it is on display in the Tyrol Panorama Museum in Innsbruck. Like the boots of the Tripoli statue and the jealously guarded head of Graziosi's statue, these surviving pieces of Fascist statuary continue to carry some meaning for anti-fascists and nostalgic Fascists alike. They are fragments of an era, testimony to the incomplete removal of a contested heritage that continues to resonate in unexpected ways in the present as a ghostly evocation of a fallen idol who had once been likened to a living statue.

10

Mussolini's places

No place in Italy was more bound up with Mussolini's personal dictatorship than the balcony of Palazzo Venezia in central Rome. When he appeared on it, Mussolini was unequivocally Il Duce, the figurehead and undisputed leader of Fascist Italy. Mussolini harangued the crowds from there on many occasions, most fatefully on 10 June 1940 when he declared war on France and Great Britain. On 11 December 1941, he also briefly appeared to declare war on the United States, an event witnessed by the US journalists Reynolds and Eleanor Packard, who entitled the book about Fascist Italy they wrote the following year *Balcony Empire*.[1] Located just north of the Capitoline Hill, facing Venice Square, the palace from which the balcony protruded was initially a papal residence built in the fifteenth century. After extensive rebuilding, it was in 1564 given by Pope Pius IV to the Republic of Venice for use as its embassy. Later it became the residence of the Austrian ambassador to the Vatican. After World War I, it was seized from Austria and subjected to extensive restoration. Mussolini elected it as the seat of his government in September 1929 when, as prime minister, he moved his office there from the Palazzo Chigi, the more modest building that democratic Italy allocated to its leaders.[2] Positioned a stone's throw from the Roman forum and just metres from the imposing if overblown Victor Emmanuel monument—dedicated to the first monarch of a unified Italy—the splendid Palazzo Venezia was situated perfectly to bring the seat of power into a physical as well as ideal relationship with the grandeur of ancient Rome and the national revival encapsulated in the Risorgimento. 'There is no doubt', historian Renzo De Felice writes, 'that, by moving himself to Palazzo Venezia, Mussolini wanted to make a gesture that marked the beginning of a new phase in his government: Mussolini felt that he was by now the "duce" from every point of view, the "Caesarian individual" who was shaping the history of the new Italy. His official seat therefore had to be historical too—for the past and for the present—isolated and at the same time in touch with the remains of that Rome of the Caesars that Mussolini wanted to emulate'.[3] By making the palace the centre of government, Mussolini shifted the visual focus of the square away from the monument to Italy's first king, which became merely a side backdrop, and created a counter to the present-day royal Quirinal palace.[4] As a result of this redefinition, Palazzo Venezia became the true ceremonial centre of the country.

The balcony became a motif of authoritarian leadership. For many Italians nothing visualised the exercise of power under the regime more than the image of Mussolini on the balcony addressing massive adoring crowds.[5] When he was required to deliver a speech in other public locations, forms of stage or raised platform were adopted to achieve a similar hierarchical relationship between leader and mass and choreograph the Duce–people relationship in a dramatic, imaginative and enduring manner. As Mussolini became ever more the object of cultish adulation, stages were set progressively higher and higher, a fact that provided transparent evidence of the increasing distance, both literal and emotive, that was opening up between the leader and the crowd.[6]

Mussolini's most triumphant appearance on the balcony came on the evening of 9 May 1936 when, two days after the end of fighting in East Africa, he proclaimed the foundation of a new Italian empire to delirious crowds who recalled him to the balcony no fewer than forty-two times.[7] This is remembered as the moment when support for the regime reached its apex. After 1941, he did not appear very often on the balcony of Palazzo Venezia, and his last appearance there was on 5 May 1943 when, despite numerous military reverses and loss of the empire, he proclaimed his certainty in war victory. After his overthrow, the doors to the balcony remained closed and the Fascist symbols that had been affixed either side of them were removed. The square below was placed off-limits during the Nazi occupation with the result that for those months it was strangely deserted.[8] Life returned in 1944 but of course the Duce did not. As the journalist Piero Saporiti wrote, the period between 1943 and 1945 was the period when the absence was most felt: 'in these two years, the ill-omened Venezia Balcony was empty. The Duce had come down from it and no-one was leading the Italian people'.[9] Closing it meant that the spirits associated with it would soon disappear. But the mental image was not so easily banished. To look at or to imagine the balcony was inseparable from picturing the Duce posturing at the helm of the nation. This 'ghosting' process was not confined to Italians. In the countries that were at war with Italy, the comical image of the swaggering, theatrical Mussolini was well established by the time he was deposed. Cartoonists like David Low in Britain deployed a variety of stock images to ridicule the vainglorious Duce and among these there was of course the balcony. It was no accident that more than one American soldier who arrived in Rome in June 1944 took the opportunity to step out on to it and jut out his jaw and place his hands on his hips in the manner of the Duce. Preservation of the image over a long period of time was aided by the fact that for many years after the summer of 1943 the outlines of the Fascist lictors were still visible.[10] Indeed, the faint traces of the symbols on either side of the doors were only finally removed from Palazzo Venezia during preparations for the Jubilee of 2000.

On the political right in the postwar years, the balcony of Palazzo Venezia persisted as a symbol of authoritarian rule, not to critique Fascism of course but to critique the supposed dictatorial tendencies of the postwar parties or to establish an equivalence between Fascism and Communism. It was no longer Mussolini who occupied the balcony and harangued the crowds in satirical cartoons, but rather the Communist Party leader Togliatti.[11] Over time, this polemical device would weaken, but the image would never disappear. To put a political leader on the balcony was for generations of cartoonists a device to underline their arrogance or overweening ambition. Among others, in the 1980s the Socialist prime minister Bettino Craxi was depicted there (see Chapter 7) and in the 2010s the same fate befell another centre-left prime minister, Matteo Renzi. The balcony also retained a currency in everyday culture. For Romans, it served as a meeting place long after it had ceased to be a political stage, though a certain mystique about the room behind the balcony doors remained. Only when the National Museum of Palazzo Venezia was reopened in 2010 as a site of important exhibitions, was it possible for the public to enter the magnificent Sala del Mappamondo where Mussolini had had his office. However, due to its close association with the dictator, the balcony remained closed; no one ever stepped out on to it for any public reason.

Nowhere else in the capital carried the same significance, though the Fascist imprint on the city was extensive and was associated with a variety of locations and buildings, most of which were not historic in nature. Indeed, for some, the whole of Rome was a Fascist place.[12] Direct and indirect references to Mussolini were not at all rare in Fascist building projects, but these were less personal than the very specific associations that were forged with places that the dictator inhabited. The restoration of grandeur to Rome entailed the re-making of the city to open up space around monuments to allow the jewels of the age of Augustus to shine once more. New additions would underline the revival of empire and incorporate this into the reshaping and development of the modern city. One of the most ambitious projects was the Foro Mussolini, a complex of housing, sports arenas and new roads situated in Monte Mario on the north bank of the Tiber.[13] By the 1930s the Foro was a key political showpiece, used as a stage for military and gymnastic displays and as the highlight of visits by foreign dignitaries, notably that of Hitler in May 1938. This 'city within a city' came, more than any other single work or complex, to represent Mussolini's Rome.[14] It was to be matched by an even larger development located to the South which was almost a second city. The EUR (Esposizione Universale Roma) was a huge architectural centre that was to be opened in 1942 with a grandiose exhibition that would mark twenty years of Fascism. Due to war, the exhibition was never held, yet both these developments would survive into the postwar years, the latter even being completed under the republic by the very architects who had worked on the original Fascist project.[15]

In the open spaces of the forum complex, there were no figural representations or statues of Mussolini. Despite being named the 'the Duce's gymnasium', a room in the baths complex of the Foro, designed as both a functional space for, and an idealised space of, Mussolini, which was completed in 1936, featured a series of allegories relating to the Duce rather than any overt representation.[16] An allegorical mosaic by Gino Severini alluded to his power as a leader, while an idealised classical statue by Silvio Canevari evoked his renowned (or supposed) athleticism. The architect Luigi Moretti, who designed the whole complex, opted for an obelisk to stand as the sole overt tribute to his leadership. Erected in 1932, Mussolini's obelisk was intended as a counterpoint to the one that stood in St Peter's square. First employed by the ancient Egyptians before being adopted by the Greeks and then the Romans, obelisks served as symbols of state power and military glory. Shaped as tall, four-sided tapering monuments, they exercised a powerful visual fascination that lasted into the modern era. Moretti believed his obelisk, erected in the Italian capital, would symbolise the glory of empire and civilisation of Rome. With its inscription of 'MVSSOLINI DVX' in vertical sans serif lettering, together with the art-deco aesthetic of the base, the monolith effected a conjunction between the modernist tendency of its design and its historical value as a symbol of Rome. The mosaicked Piazzale dell'Impero in which the obelisk stood also made reference to the formal features of ancient Roman pavements while instancing Mussolini's leadership by means of a series of figures and repetitions of the word 'Duce' as if the often-voiced acclamations of the rallies had been impressed on the built environment.[17] The idea of empire that was bound up with obelisks was consolidated in 1937 with the installation in the square that faced the

Ministry of the Colonies of a 24-metre vertical stone monument dating from the sixth century that had been seized as war booty from the Ethiopian city of Axum. A visible sign of imperial power, the ancient obelisk became a key motif of Fascist propaganda about Africa. It was eventually returned to its original location, after much resistance and many delays, in 2005.[18]

Indirect evocations of Mussolini continued in the EUR complex, where the Palace of Civilisation building, that was designed by three architects working in the rationalist style, applied a similar concept of *romanità* that was intended to encompass past, present and future. The rows of arches that marked each of the six stories of the monumental building referred directly to the arches of the Colosseum. The six vertical and nine horizontal rows of arches were, however, of more contemporary significance as they corresponded to the number of letters respectively in the Duce's first name and surname.

The fate of these monuments did not follow any very predictable pattern. While the incomplete EUR was not subjected to any anti-fascist attacks, it would be wrong to assume, on the grounds that many of the monuments of the Foro Mussolini (renamed the Foro italico) are still extant today, that these too escaped any danger of demolition. It could be that, by not directly depicting Mussolini, Moretti inadvertently ensured that his creations did not face the sort of direct destructive attacks that many figural representations did. Their story, in this sense, was similar to that of some of the statues discussed in Chapter 9. However, in fact, the representations were explicit enough for Romans to want to demolish both the sports complex and the obelisk. Rather it was the Allies that prevented any dismantling, as they had set up a recreational centre for their troops on the site.[19] The question was again raised after the Allies left, though the decorative spaces remained largely unaltered and indeed were subsequently restored for sporting events. There were efforts to erase evocations of the dictator by eliminating the lettering on the obelisk in the 1950s, but a cost-effective solution proved elusive. The matter however remained open. Proposals to cover or remove the mosaics for the 1960 Olympic Games resulted in political protest, controversy and only minimal changes, so that Mussolini's sublimated presence was preserved behind the superficial renaming of the complex.

The complexity of this history shows, perhaps, a lack of determination in dealing with the legacies of Mussolini's personal impact on the built environment. But it also highlights the ways in which practical considerations bore on the question, along with issues of cost.[20] For many, it was simply not a priority to rid the capital, as it would not be for other cities, of the visual signs of a defunct regime. As life moved on, politics took a different course and the effort of reconstruction gave way to a period of unprecedented growth. Pulling down buildings and monuments, even those which had initially been targeted for destruction, was not a priority. Repurposing was always a more viable and accessible option than ideologically motivated destruction. It was simple, effective and less controversial. However, each case presented different considerations and gave rise to debates that were heavily influenced by local concerns. In a big city like Milan, massive urban development rendered much of the Fascist architectural legacy functionally invisible, while in the Marche region unregulated and unaesthetic development meant that it continued to determine the image of small and medium-sized towns.[21]

A common attitude, albeit with particular local permutations, seems to have been one of removal; that is, not removal in any physical sense, although this unsurprisingly was also widely urged, but rather removal or repression in a psychological sense. Buildings and monuments, especially where explicit references to the dictator were sublimated or absent, quickly lost the impact that they were supposed to have. They were no longer 'seen' by people who had decided, whether consciously or otherwise, that they did not wish any longer to see them, or see them for what they were. Sometimes psychological and physical removal went hand in hand; as, for example, when Fascist-themed murals were covered over, or statues and busts were simply stored away in deposits rather than destroyed. Removed from view, they could easily be forgotten and the awkward question of the artistic value of a given object, that needed to be determined negatively by the Superintendence of the Belle Arti for destruction to be approved, elided. The problem with mental removal was that this was dependent on a particular state of mind that, no matter how definitive it may have seemed, was timebound. This would become clear from the 1990s, when some covered representations were once more uncovered. In the 2000s, there were occasional news stories concerning the 'discovery' of overlooked monuments, such as a collection of large bronze heads of Mussolini that had been consigned to storage in the EUR. In other instances, like the case of the huge 7.5-metre neoclassical marble monument of an athletic naked young man in Brescia, that was known locally by the affectionate nickname Bigio, rediscovery of the removed statue in 2013 led to calls for it to be restored to its original site in Piazza della Vittoria. Created in 1932 by the sculptor Arturo Dazzi, the monument did not in any way depict the Duce, though it was praised by him as a fine representation of the 'Fascist Era', a denomination that became its official name. The desire after the war to rethink the city and allocate new meaning to places was only ever partially accomplished despite the efforts of small numbers of committed individuals.[22] This was due to many factors including a certain reluctance to take part in a public recognition of the defeat of Fascism by eliminating visual markers and renaming streets and squares.[23]

After Palazzo Venezia, the Roman location that was most identified with Mussolini's person was Villa Torlonia. In contrast to the former, with its explicit political connotations, the latter was the dictator's private residence in the capital. Located on the Via Nomentana, it was built in the early nineteenth century by the neoclassical architect Giuseppe Valadier for the aristocratic Torlonia family. Mussolini rented the spacious villa and gardens for the nominal sum of one Lira per year. It served as the family home for some eighteen years from 1925, and Mussolini's two youngest children were born and raised there. Villa Torlonia did not enjoy a high public profile, though some significant family moments and occasions, notably the wedding of Edda Mussolini to Count Galeazzo Ciano in 1930, gave rise to newsreels and photographs that depicted the exterior in all its columned neoclassical glory. It was never used as a location for entertaining as neither the dictator nor the family took any part in the social life of the capital, though Edda was known to frequent high society. Rachele Mussolini turned the villa and its grounds into a more homely dwelling reminiscent of her own house near Predappio. During the war she maintained an ample kitchen garden that was held up in the press as an example to others in the time of autarky.

After Mussolini was deposed and arrested, and Rachele and her younger children were taken into custody, the villa was left empty. When the Allies liberated Rome in June 1944, the property was requisitioned by the Allied High Command, which remained there until 1947. There then began a long period of abandonment and decay that testified to the ties that still existed in the imagination between the villa and the Mussolini family. This period of abandonment only ended when the villa was bought by the Municipality of Rome in 1977. The following year, the gardens and house were opened to the public though many of the buildings were still in a run-down state. Restoration was initiated in the 1990s to complement a museum containing some items that had once been part of the Torlonia family's substantial art collection. The association with Mussolini at this point was residual but not forgotten. A section of the museum contains the reconstructed bedchamber of Giovanni Torlonia, who had made the villa available to the dictator, featuring pieces of furniture that were used by Mussolini during the years he resided there.[24] Explanatory panels and videos currently in the villa provide disconcertingly anodyne descriptions of the life of the dictator's family. This curious limbo position between history and nostalgia was threatened from the 1990s when discussions began about a Holocaust memorial, discussions that were taken up again during the administration of mayor Walter Veltroni in 2005. This matter was sensitive because it implicitly raised the issue of Fascist complicity in the deportation and extermination of Italy's Jews. An important step forward occurred in 2014, when it was announced that a Holocaust Museum designed by the architect Luca Zevi was to be located in the park of the villa, also on the grounds that these were home to ancient Jewish catacombs. After several delays, in 2019 it was announced that work would begin in 2020 and last for three years.[25] Nothing in fact happened until the project was approved by the government in October 2023. However, the only Shoah memorial in Italy in existence until that museum is finally opened is located deep in Milan's central station by the platform from which Jews were deported directly to Auschwitz.

Mussolini was associated during the regime with many different locations in the peninsula. In contrast to Hitler, who addressed crowds in sports stadia and specially constructed arenas, he preferred to hold his rallies in the historic squares that for centuries had been the focus of civic life. Indeed, historian Mario Isnenghi notes in his history of the Italian piazza: 'the itinerant practice and the success of these periodic encounters between the Duce and the crowd in canonical places of civic sociability owe much to the culture of the piazza'.[26] 'The ubiquitous oratory of Mussolini', he adds, 'was rooted in the deep texture and in the specific character of many urban histories and town squares'.[27] For the most part, these encounters did not leave deep traces. The Italian culture of the piazza preceded Fascism and persisted after the war, when different political leaders would impress their oratory on the crowds of the republican era. In the city of Milan, where Mussolini began and ended his national career, the link he always cultivated and cherished with the city was broken. Only in some of the new towns founded under the regime was there a more lasting link though this too underwent modification. The small town inaugurated in Sardinia by King Vittorio Emanuele III in 1928 under the name Villaggio Mussolini in honour of the Duce (modified in 1930 to Mussolinia di Sardegna), was the result of a land reclamation programme dating back to the time of prime minister Giovanni Giolitti (1842–1928). Like many new towns, it was populated by migrants loyal to the regime and benefited from significant investment in its infrastructure, including Fascist-branded public buildings that evoked more the Bergmanesque origins of the engineer, Carlo Avanzini, who planned the centre, than the Sardinian tradition. In 1944, the town's name was officially changed to the inoffensive Arborea, though only after the end of the war did the complex process of detachment from Fascism begin in earnest with the Mussolini name being removed from public buildings.[28]

It was Mussolini's home region of Romagna that hosted more instances of the absent presence of the Duce than anywhere else. He remained a regular visitor throughout his rule and even thought of retiring to Predappio after he was ousted from power in 1943. Predappio-Forlì was, outside Rome, the place most closely associated with Mussolini. A medieval fortress, the Rocca delle Caminate, served as his local residence. It was given to Mussolini in 1927 as a gift by local authorities, who had launched a popular subscription for the purpose. The family's private home, Villa Carpena, which was Rachele's domain, was located on the outskirts of Forlì. During the regime, Predappio enjoyed special status as it was transformed into a site for the celebration of the personality cult. Founded as a town in 1925, it was formed from the merger of two medieval villages, Predappio Alta and Dovia. The new town was created for propaganda purposes and as a showcase for the myths surrounding the popular image of the Duce.[29] New buildings and facilities were constructed with monumental architecture, including an enormous Casa del Fascio (containing a restaurant, a library, reception and meeting rooms) that was situated in Piazza 28 October (the date of the March on Rome) at the end of the 'Viale Benito Mussolini', the main thoroughfare and one of very few roads to bear the name of the Duce himself. This huge building was perhaps the only significant one ever to be inaugurated by the Duce's wife Rachele. The population grew from a few hundred to around ten thousand while the town became a key centre for the promotion of the cult. In the 1920s and 1930s, it enjoyed special status and paying a visit—or rather making a pilgrimage there—was considered almost obligatory, a sign of loyalty to the regime. Even the king undertook an official visit in June 1938, when he was filmed ascending the steps to the simple house where Mussolini was born. This was a key site for visitors, as was the building which had housed the school run by his mother, Rosa Maltoni, and where the family lived, and his parents' reburial place in the San Cassiano cemetery. The visitors book to the house, which is now preserved in the Central State Archive in Rome, contains the signatures of many dignitaries as well as common people. The Duce retained a strong attachment to the town and encouraged investment, the most significant result of which was the Caproni aircraft factory. Efforts to put Predappio on the map included imposing a detour on the Giro d'Italia cycle race in 1928.

After the war, Predappio's fortunes declined quickly. Pilgrimages, which had reached hundreds per day and had a positive impact on the local economy, had been brought to a halt during the conflict. With the overthrow of Mussolini, all special regard ended. The Allies entered Predappio in October 1944. By that time, some items had been stolen from the Rocca but enough remained for troops to be photographed amid pictures of the Duce.[30] It was looted by the Poles and the British as well as the local population, some of whom acted to preserve items from theft. The area had a strong Resistance movement and after the war it was governed by left-wing administrations that were forced to deal with a legacy that was problematic as well as with sharp economic decline. 'Predappio today is the poorest and most abandoned of towns, the saddest and most miserable in Italy', wrote Fascist sympathiser Vittore Querel in 1954.[31] Predappio, from a place of cult, became an object of national shame, a place that was an embarrassment to be dismissed from the mind and forgotten. Local politicians sought to address the problem of the place of the town within Fascism by arguing that it had had a Fascist identity imposed on it, though in fact this really only referred to the previously socialist pre-existing village of Predappio Alta. Left-wing local leaders worked to recover the socialist traditions of the old town, while inhabitants sought to find a way to reassert an ordinariness that would allow them to distance themselves from ongoing disputes over a burdensome history.[32] In an effort to reassert an original identity, roads and institutions were renamed and some even sought to change the town's name. The monumental Casa del Fascio that dominated the town's entrance remained closed and disused, save for some small businesses that occupied part of the rear ground level.[33]

However, the ties to Mussolini remained. His local roots had been stressed under the regime and they were not cancelled by its fall. There was a strong possessive memory of Mussolini in the town that was based on a unique proximity to the dictator before his rise to power and which was based on kinship and family ties.[34] This memory was less inflected with myth than that cultivated by those for whom he was a remote, if admired, ruler. The family connection would be reprised strongly in 1957 with the return of Rachele Mussolini to the town and the final burial of Mussolini's mortal remains in the family crypt in the cemetery (see Chapter 6).

Corporeal relics both living (Mussolini family members) and dead (Mussolini's remains at the cemetery) were essential elements in Predappio's controversial revival as a site of dark tourism from 1957. The pilgrimages that had been a characteristic of the 1930s resumed on a smaller scale. Although many visitors were Fascist sympathisers, the benevolent, watered-down memory of Fascism that prospered in the 1950s favoured the flow of less ideological visitors. The town was soon attracting 80,000 to 100,000 visitors per year, with nostalgic Fascists being the most numerous on the key anniversaries of the March on Rome and Mussolini's birth and death. On these occasions, what was referred to as 'a carnival of Mussolini' flourished, which was experienced by locals as a tiresome burden.[35] The restoration of a political identity to the town was not welcomed by the local government, which, for decades, sought to correct and balance it, not least because, in the 1970s, there were frequent clashes between far-left groups and neo-fascists, which received national news coverage. These eventually ebbed and the centenary of Mussolini's birth in 1983 gave rise to largely uncontested, if officially ignored, celebrations. The event provided an impulse to the commercial exploitation of the Duce's memory via the sales of souvenirs, gadgets, flags, reproductions of Fascist clothing, weapons and other items, including specially labelled wine. Local administrators intervened at various intervals to prohibit the sale of such goods in the street or by the cemetery, but they proved unable to prevent the supply of items whose sheer banality both trivialised Fascism and turned it into de-ideologised consumable folklore.[36]

The political buildings and sites of Predappio were nothing like as awkward as Hitler's Berghof in the Bavarian Alps (which was demolished) or the Nazi rally grounds in Nuremberg, which came to be regarded as 'difficult heritage'.[37] But they bore some of its traits, as the enormous, abandoned Casa del fascio testified. Andreas Huyssen's notion that 'buildings are palimpsests, of what we sense as being there before, as well as alternatives to what is there now', informed the decisions by successive local mayors to seek in some way to re-appropriate, contextualise and use a physical heritage that was inconvenient but also impossible to eliminate.[38] Recognising that it was not easy in the context of Mussolini's birthplace to make Fascistic buildings and markings functionally invisible, they opted to condition visibility, in a way that confirmed Huyssen's observation that 'visibility and invisibility became the categories of architectural discourse about the built legacies of the fascist and communist states'.[39] The decision to create an urban museum of Fascist architecture in Predappio, in which key locations were signposted and furnished with explanatory panels, was the sign of a desire to acknowledge the town's history and open a historical debate about it. The house where Mussolini was born was restored and reopened as an exhibition space in 1999, while the Rocca delle Caminate castle, which had had a double function as private residence of the Mussolini family and an alternative seat of government during the summer, eventually became a conference centre. A small and not easily found plaque commemorating partisans who were killed there—but making no reference to its notorious former resident—displays a desire to acknowledge the past while also sidestepping it.[40] Unlike these reconversions, which occurred with little local debate and none at all at national level, the bold initiative of left-wing mayor Giorgio Frassineti to turn the enormous and decaying Casa del Fascio into a Museum of Fascism provoked an extended debate in the 2010s that testified to the extreme sensitivity around any institutionalisation of the memory of Fascism and its leader (see Figure 12).[41] Frassineti's idea was to accept Predappio's historical identification with Mussolini but in a critical, reflective way rather than a celebratory one. Considered by many to be a 'dead monument', the mooted revival of the building had a number of local justifications, though these were given no

Figure 12. Mayor Giorgio Frassineti inside the abandoned Casa del Fascio in Mussolini's home town of Predappio. The mayor sought support to turn the building into a museum of Fascism, but his proposal ran into objections and did not come to fruition. Screenshot from the documentary directed by Vanessa Roghi for the AHRC project 'The Cult of the Duce: Mussolini and the Italians' that was led by the author from 2006 to 2011. Author's own image.

importance by those at national level who would have preferred the building to remain forgotten and for Predappio once more to drop out of the headlines.[42]

While Fascism constituted a toxic legacy for many, it offered a political resource for others and a commercial opportunity for yet more. One location that served political and commercial ends was Villa Carpena, the house to which Rachele Mussolini returned in 1957 (see Chapter 6). With help from local friends and sympathisers, who had hidden items for safekeeping, and some purchases, she was able to fit it out with original furniture and mementoes.[43] The relics of Mussolini that filled the house and garden served as a reminder of the glories of the Fascist regime and helped instil in young members of the family a sense of pride in the achievements of the man who was said to have been devoted selflessly to the good of his country.[44] Rachele provided an affective focal point for numerous family events that took place in Predappio, including the 1962 wedding of her son Romano to film star Sophia Loren's sister Maria, and the wedding of their daughter, and future politician, Alessandra in 1989. After her death in 1979 Villa Carpena remained largely disused until, in 2001, the villa and grounds were bought by a Milanese businessman Domenico Morosini, who proceeded, with his wife, to restore it and turn it into a museum of Mussolini's memory. Entirely ignored by local left-wing politicians, who never visited it, the house was preserved much as it had been when Rachele was alive save for the explicitly political connotation it was now given, collapsing the distinction that had once obtained between family and territory on the one hand, and politics and memory on the other. Renamed Villa Mussolini—Casa dei ricordi (House of memories), it attracted visitors who were given guided tours in which they were shown a mixture of domestic artefacts, objects once owned by family members and political symbols and images. The villa became a Mecca for curious visitors and the nostalgic fascists who continued to frequent the birthplace of the dictator, render homage at his tomb and purchase trinkets that, by virtue of being bought in that particular location, carried special value. Setting foot in spaces once inhabited by Mussolini and his family was a commercial proposition that was further embellished by occasional claims that the dictator's spirit haunted the house.[45] Such claims were comforted by the knowledge that, for the Mussolini family, the villa had been 'home to many memories' and represented 'a spiritual landscape'.[46] Many of the busts that occupy the garden are the same as those placed there in Mussolini's day, while the objects displayed in the house feature a mixture of artefacts like his violin, his Bianchi motorcycle and items of clothing, together with other pieces acquired at auction.

Villa Carpena has none of the grandeur and monumentality of Villa Torlonia or Palazzo Venezia, both of which were furnished in a manner that reflected the Fascist gift for conferring a melodramatic quality on interiors as well as buildings.[47] Villa Carpena by contrast sentimentalises and sugar-coats dictatorship in a manner that is in keeping with a diffuse idea of kitsch.[48] The taste on display is not that of Mussolini but rather that of his widow. In contrast to the domesticity of the bachelor Hitler, which was constructed as a normalising tool of propaganda, Mussolini largely concealed his home life. While images of his domestic ménage occasionally appeared in the foreign press, no propaganda for domestic consumption ever showed him in any domestic environment.[49] By highlighting the normality of the domestic spaces of Villa Carpena, the present owners confirm the function that Rachele played, between the late 1950s and her death in 1979, of turning Mussolini from tyrant into a political leader who was also a regular husband and father. In this way, the kitchenware, furniture and bric-a-brac close the gap between the cultural experience of the mass of people and the everyday existence of the man who led their country for twenty years before bringing it to disaster.[50]

With the decline in the once dominant culture of anti-fascism in the 1990s and 2000s, a number of other buildings and locations associated with the fallen dictator in his native Romagna and elsewhere were returned to the realm of visibility. Not far from Predappio, in the local seaside resort of Riccione, a villa where the family had vacationed was turned into a restaurant in the 1960s. After this closed, the property risked demolition. Instead, it was turned into a conference and exhibition centre and once more baptised Villa Mussolini, the name that it had always preserved in local usage.[51] The final chapter of Mussolini's political career as head of the doomed RSI was never coated with the peculiar hew of nostalgia that surrounded the places which he had inhabited in the 1930s. But the strange phenomenon of dark tourism provided opportunities to some of the sites associated with the final months of Fascist rule in the north of Italy. Only Piazzale Loreto, the site of Mussolini's bodily desecration avoided macabre exploitation of this type. The centre-left administration of the town of Salò announced in 2008 that it would offer guided tours of buildings and locations associated with the RSI. The local museum has since then hosted exhibitions of a historical nature on the Nazi-dominated puppet regime which, while seeking to avoid overt tendentiousness, have granted space and dignity to the experiences and memories of those who threw in their lot with the losing side in Italy's civil war.[52] The touristic reconfiguration of even this extreme and final example of Fascist government, a phenomenon heavily geared to

German tourists, did not pass up the chance to offer visitors opportunities to inhabit the very spaces of the protagonists of the impending collapse. The luxury Art Nouveau–style hotel Villa Fiordaliso at Gardone Riviera, where Mussolini's mistress spent the final weeks of her life, offers guests the chance to occupy the 'Claretta suite', which one British newspaper reported, is 'wonderfully preserved with Damasco wallpaper, yellow Siena marble and wooden furnishings'.[53] This sort of tourism is difficult to classify, as elements of transversal and ideological nostalgia mix with voyeuristic curiosity. While the former may condition a whole outlook, the latter is transient. The persistence and revival of a Fascist–Mussolini heritage testifies not only to the impossibility of consigning the dictator to oblivion but also to the ideological and de-ideologised currency that he continues to have. Commerce and memory, history and voyeurism all rub shoulders in ways that are not always predictable. In this hybrid heritage, the dictator's posthumous cult finds a mixture of material and immaterial expressions.

II

Fascist art and kitsch

'Incredible decorations painted on the walls, horrible busts of coloured plaster in every corner, colourful emblems and banners in lieu of tapestries, gilded plaster Fascist symbols, chromolithographs of the Duce in impossible positions, huge sabres and wooden spears painted in charcoal. These are the Fascist headquarters and the offices of the syndicates and local councils...living monuments to bad taste'.[1] Fascist government minister Giuseppe Bottai's withering remarks in his diary on the proliferation of Fascist art and artefacts of questionable taste indicate how issues relating to the quality and quantity of images of Mussolini were closely bound up with the construction and management of the cult of the Duce.[2] The devotion which resulted in the production of this visual hodgepodge and which created the overload of images of the Duce was never managed solely from above. It was a complex and multifaceted process to which there were many spontaneous contributions. Commercial enterprises, professional and amateur artists, inventors, photographers and others all sought to get in on the act. Many artistic homages were sent directly to Mussolini himself, the act of homage sometimes occurring disinterestedly but also on many occasions in the hope of receiving some preferment or endorsement.

The kitsch aspects of Fascism have often not received much attention on account of the relatively high reputation of some if not all of the art and architecture that was produced in Italy under the regime. In contrast to Nazism, which resisted modernism and embraced a conservative aesthetic in the realm of the arts, there was no dramatic fall in the standing of the artistic production that was closest to the regime in the post-1945 period.[3] Fascism allowed a variety of tendencies to flourish and encouraged rationalism in architecture as well as modern and abstract currents in painting. Thus, a significant part of the production of the period continued to enjoy a standing in the postwar years, and still does so today. While the most blatant examples of Fascist propaganda in art and obsequiousness to Mussolini were often concealed, deleted from artists' curriculums or in some instances destroyed, many works produced under the regime, whether or not they were infused with Fascistic themes and visual motifs, continued to be displayed and valued. In a context in which there was little attempt to dictate style, artistic work produced for the regime was sometimes difficult to distinguish from artistic work created under the regime.

One area in which art and kitsch encountered each other was the representation of Mussolini. Encouraged by Margherita Sarfatti, the art expert who was his lover and advisor, the dictator took an interest in his own iconography. He regularly posed for sculptors, painters and photographers.[4] Many others, who either did not seek or did not receive an audience with the man himself, created his likeness from still and moving images or from their own imaginations. Among these works were some by important artists whose efforts won plaudits and recognition not so much for the literal accuracy of their portrayals as for the way their works confirmed or enhanced the iconic status of the Duce. But there were also vast numbers of works that had little or no artistic merit which represented the attempts of their creators to translate the hyperbole surrounding the Duce's genius and achievements into pictorial or material form. Some of these were commissioned for installation in the numerous public buildings that were built in the 1930s. Many such edifices, like the Case del Fascio centres and the Case Balilla youth clubs, but also the council buildings and the syndicates referred to by Bottai, were politically connotated spaces that included various visual signs of their allegiance to Fascism and its leader. Others were entirely spontaneous tributes to the man who was often said to embody the best qualities of the Italian people.

Perhaps the biggest single collector of these dubious products was Mussolini himself. This is not to say that he was necessarily keen on them, though there is little doubt that that some of the most striking pieces, such as Adolfo Wildt's 1924 marble portrait, Ernesto Thayat's 1932 'Dux' bust and Renato Bertelli's 1933 'Continuous Profile of Mussolini', had his approval and became symbols of Fascism. Indeed, he very publicly endorsed Thayat's work by writing the words 'Questo è Benito Mussolini così come piace a Benito Mussolini' (This is Benito Mussolini as approved by Benito Mussolini) on a printed image of the iconic bust. The bulk of the works that came into Mussolini's possession did so as unsolicited gifts and homages. Foreign and domestic artists, artisans and craftsmen, and many others sent or gave him images of every size and in every form, from weaponry and ornamental animals to domestic furnishings and ceramic plates. Many of these items were shipped periodically to the Rocca

Figure 13. The so-called 'chamber of horrors' at the Rocca delle Caminate castle where Mussolini was accustomed to store craft items and artistic works of dubious merit that were sent to him as personal homages. Courtesy of the Fondi Antichi della Biblioteca Aurelio Saffi di Forlì, Sezione Mussoliniana (G L 01 917).

delle Caminate where they were gathered in a vast storage space that was, in a reflection of the questionable taste of some items, dubbed by Mussolini himself—perhaps light-heartedly—'the chamber of horrors' (see Figure 13).[5] One person who took an active interest in the gifts, however, was the Duce's wife Rachele. She selected pieces that aroused her curiosity or which seemed to her to underline Mussolini's historical significance, and installed them in the interiors and garden of the family home, Villa Carpena. From her point of view, the objects had material value and were a sign of power. Though she maintained a network of allies and informers and received thousands of letters begging for favours or assistance, all the power that she had derived from the identity of her husband.[6] Having the Duce's ear was a source of influence in the age of the cult of personality. Cultish objects served to remind her and others of this influence, which otherwise would not have been readily perceptible and which, given Mussolini's remoteness from his family, may even have been doubted.

After Mussolini was deposed, some of these pieces went missing. Publication in August 1944 of the government decree relating to sanctions against Fascism led to the confiscation of properties belonging to leading members of the Fascist Party and their families. To avoid treasured possessions also being requisitioned once the decree was applied, Rachele arranged for several lorries full of furniture and objects from the Rocca to be transported to northern Italy, though she rejected as false rumours that these had included jewels and furs (which she claimed never to have owned).[7] Much remained, however, and was left at the mercy of looters. Items that were not taken away by local residents were often seized by the forces of liberation.[8] A few weeks after Rachele's departure, on 27 October 1944, wrote local author Antonio Mambelli, 'the "liberation" of Predappio was effected by Polish troops backed up by the partisans of the Garibaldi Brigade. The news of the time reported that these were the first to enter the Rocca delle Caminate'.[9] A little later, English soldiers belonging to the Eighth Army reached Predappio, where they found residues of the personality cult (see Chapter 3).

Allied soldiers eagerly appropriated souvenirs of the battle against Fascism, as they would subsequently collect up souvenirs of Nazism. The predilection of both regimes for branding objects with political symbols and for images of their leaders ensured that there were many items large and small that could be taken home to show off. Some of these ended up in official possession, like the boots of the Tripoli statue of Mussolini housed in the Royal Electrical and Mechanical Engineers (REME) museum in England (see Chapter 9) or the metallic bust of a helmeted Duce by the German sculptor Friedrich Fröbel that is currently displayed in the white tower of the Tower of London. Many other objects of little ostensible value were treated by soldiers as war booty and were retained by them, sometimes as potential gifts for family members.[10] Helmets, knives, uniforms, badges and other small items that had been produced in very large numbers were easy to pack up and transport. Some of these souvenirs would later form the basis of the first collections of memorabilia.[11]

The practice of impressing political symbols and motifs on objects was not a new one and nor, certainly, was the desire of victors to seek out such objects as mementoes of their triumph. Louis XIV is regarded as the first monarch to have made extensive use of the reproduction of his own image.[12] Under Napoleon, an even wider plethora of images, symbols and objects had been produced.[13] Busts, coins, drawings and portraits were among the most diffuse. Such was the demand for Napoleonic objects in Britain in the period after the defeat of the one-time emperor at the battle of Waterloo that French merchants made good business supplying large quantities of small receptacles like tobacco boxes to soldiers to take home with them.[14] In France, there were several different attitudes towards this material culture. One of these was destructive. As the Bourbons struggled to re-establish their authority, a ban was placed on books and pamphlets about Napoleon and there was also strict censorship of any pictorial representation that was deemed by the government to be threatening. In the early months of 1816, there was a widespread purge of objects and symbols of the Napoleonic era that entailed the burning of art works, portraits and so on.[15] Another attitude was conservationist. Some officials hid busts and artefacts rather than destroy them. For example, an official in Angers hid a bust of Napoleon by Canova that was discovered twenty years later. Sometimes there was a tussle between these attitudes, as when objects that had been hidden were discovered and subjected to 'purging' ceremonies. Such actions testified to a belief that objects were impregnated with a magical aura and that their destruction or preservation would have an impact on persistence or otherwise of the Napoleonic legend.

Those who arrived in Predappio and set about taking possession of items that might have been personally owned or used by the fallen—but not yet finally defeated—Duce were not interested in any possible 'live' political significance of the objects. Rather, they were interested in what are sometimes called representative relics.[16] This term refers to items that have had contact with the figure in question—in this instance an authoritarian dictator who had been likened to a god—or with the places they inhabited. Usually such objects, which combine the sacred and the ephemeral, would be of value only to devotees. In this instance, they were of interest as trophies or as curious bearers of a negative ideology whose defeat was imminent. Similar objects, in other hands, later helped to sustain a post-cult of Mussolini in which ideological, sentimental and even supernatural preoccupations figured.[17]

The objects that had signified the cult of the Duce to the Mussolini family would have a long and complicated afterlife. Some of them were re-assembled by Rachele Mussolini when she took possession once more of the family properties. Other objects remained in private hands and would sometimes come on to the market for sale in Italy and abroad. In this market context, items became to some degree alienated from their political past and, like Nazi artefacts, acquired new value as status objects for collectors who believed that through them they were touching history.[18] Some of the story of the political artefacts is known; other aspects have not yet been fully documented. In 2015, the researcher Elena Versari found eleven objects in a storeroom of the state archive in Forlì.[19] These were what was left of twenty-six items that had been confiscated by the Italian authorities in 1950 (five from Villa Carpena, nineteen from the Rocca). They included a metal head of Hitler, some metal plaques a hand-embroidered portrait of Mussolini, a framed painting and a broken ceramic plate, both featuring his image, and a gift from the city of Bari and a wooden sculpture of an eagle. Over the sixty years that they had lain in the storeroom, some pieces of note had gone missing. These included the monumental semi-abstract painting 'The March on Rome' by the Futurist artist Tato and the sword of Islam that was presented to Mussolini on his visit to Tripoli in 1936. As Versari has noted, the items remaining had no particular value; they represented Fascist visual culture at a low level. They were not so much propaganda items as gifts, homages and commercial products.

The interplay of art and propaganda, official and unofficial, high art and low culture was common under the regime. It was especially in the fields of manufacture and reproduction that these fluid relationships were defined. The Central State Archive in Rome conserves all the requests that were submitted by artists, designers, photographers, entrepreneurs and others to commercialise Mussolini's name or image.[20] These were generally brought to the Duce's personal attention and received from him either approval or denial of permission. The sheer variety of proposals conveys something of the extent to which Mussolini became a centre of commercial activity following one or two endorsements, such as the one he granted to Baci Perugina chocolates.[21] Among them were several from factories of ceramics asking to be allowed to reproduce and sell terracotta busts and medallions; there was a proposal for a leather wallet featuring his image, a car radiator-grille cover shaped like the famous profile, drinking glasses featuring Mussolini's image (and bearing the legend 'Toast your Duce with the fine wine of Italy').[22] In all cases, prefects submitted reports on the conduct and political standing of the applicant. By no means all requests were accepted, and where (as in the case of the glasses) the sole end appeared to be financial gain, rejection was usual.[23] There was a continuous tension between commercial enterprises seeking to exploit Mussolini's fame and popularity and close collaborators of the Duce, and Mussolini himself, who were concerned to avoid trivialisation and banalisation of Fascism's greatest asset.[24]

The example of Bertelli's 'Continuous Profile of Mussolini' is of interest in this regard. The head was one of a handful of abstract evocations that powerfully demonstrated the iconic potential of the Duce. A spherical object on a stand in which regular indentations around the surface gave the impression of the features of a face, a mere glance brought to mind the iconic head of the Duce. It was never conceived as a one-off item or even as a limited edition, and there was considerable demand for copies among cultured Fascists and senior regime members. It was produced in several types of material in significant numbers and Bertelli even proposed a table lamp version made of glass. The modernist object in this version would have become a domestic decorative piece.[25] In this case, it was Mussolini himself who vetoed the proposal to avoid the descent of a representation that stood apart from the mass of propaganda art into the realm of the mass-produced object of dubious taste.

Precisely because it had become an icon of modernist art, in the aftermath of the regime Bertelli's head retained value as a collectable piece and examples were not disposed of like many busts, heads and portraits. Private individuals who were the possessors of heads tended not only to retain them but to continue to display them. Indeed, their aesthetic originality trumped their devotional aspect with the result that they were prized even by non-fascists. The catalogue entry in a 2006 Paris exhibition on Italian art in the first half of the twentieth century boldly claimed of Bertelli's Profilo: 'It is one of the most interesting examples of the art of the fascist period, because it does not respond to the canons and the rhetoric of official sculpture to which the artists of the regime submitted themselves'.[26] This statement, which entirely separates Bertelli and his creation from the cultural production of the regime, elaborates a view of the sculptor that is also to be found in a recent study that—in spite of considerable evidence to the contrary—downplays his relationship with the regime and with Mussolini in particular.[27]

The first occasion on which art and artefacts depicting Mussolini were put on open public display in the postwar period was in 1997 when the municipal art gallery of the northern Tuscan town of Seravazza hosted an exhibition with the title 'The Man of Providence: iconography of the duce, 1923–1945'. Among numerous exhibits of every level of quality were paintings, drawings, sculptures, cartoons, photomontages and medallions which, by virtue of their sheer quantity, testified to the scale and variety of a phenomenon that had been glossed over and de-realised. The exhibition caused surprise and outrage because of its embarrassing subject matter and because it gathered many celebratory works that had disappeared after the fall of the regime and were assumed to have been destroyed or lost. It also indirectly highlighted the complicity of the artistic community with the cult of Mussolini after decades of critical work and testimony that had sought to affect a post-facto separation between art and the regime. The exhibition, which also included anti-fascist artworks (by Tono Zancanaro and others), had no overt fascistic or nostalgic intent; indeed, the aim, it was stated, was to 'document the mentality of an era which, admittedly, is hardly exhilarating from a historical, and in this case cultural viewpoint'.[28] It was also asserted that 'it should not be thought that the inglorious end of Mussolini fizzled out in the minds and hearts of those who had faith in him and hailed him in the form of "ducemania" '.[29] In other words, it was controversially asserting that the entanglement of the cult of the Duce and the national psychology had not ended in 1945. The acknowledgement that some examples of the cult were still being produced in the immediate aftermath of Mussolini's death carried the implication that the cult itself was not a top-down imposition and that it might still contain some residual mobilising potential.[30]

There seems no doubt that the Seravazza exhibition had the consequence—intended or unintended—of legitimising the return to the public sphere of many of those objects which had vanished from view after 1945. The organisers, who claimed not to be offering 'tools for a reading of history', but rather, more modestly, 'a contribution to the knowledge and learning of each of us', perhaps did not bargain for the revival of interest in Fascist art that followed the exhibition.[31] Unsurprisingly, the main motors of this revival were those who remained attached to the historical memory of Fascism. The writer and journalist Duilio Susmel (1919–84), who was best known for his devotional faith in compiling and editing, with his father Edoardo, an edition of Mussolini's *opera omnia* in thirty-six volumes in 1951 was one the main early collectors.[32] He was an example of a certain type of collector who, far from being interested in objects and art for their curiosity value or market worth, wanted to recover and preserve the story of the Italians' intense involvement with their dictator. He made it his personal mission to salvage and preserve discarded paraphernalia of historical interest that he found at flea markets and in junk shops.[33] His collection later formed part of several hundred objects related to Mussolini and artworks testifying to the revival of interest in the iconography of the Duce that were put on display in the MAGI '900 museum in Pieve di Cento, near Bologna.[34] The museum was opened three years after the Seravazza exhibition by the collector Guido Bargellini, who was thanked in the catalogue for his assistance with the exhibition. The section dedicated to Mussolini was inaugurated nine years later, uniting several private collections including Bargellini's own.

Although the MAGI '900 collection contained many objects and celebratory images including watches, statuettes and bottle openers that were unquestionably kitsch, that is to say they were examples of the trivialisation of art by politics, it was asserted that they were works of art of aesthetic value.[35] The art discourse was deployed to ennoble the display and deflect accusations that it was politically motivated. The collection, however, highlighted the ambiguities of collecting as well as the slippage between a hobby and a political project. Owning objects of historical interest was deemed to be worthy and their display a publicly spirited act, but some ideologically inclined collectors deployed aesthetically enticing artefacts to conceal or downplay the violence that had been a hallmark of Fascism throughout its history.[36]

There was of course no continuation of the production of Fascist art after 1945, although some one-time Fascist artists continued to work in similar idioms and aesthetics as before. For the most part the art scene of the1950s and 1960s and after was aligned with international artistic tendencies that eschewed the political and the representational. In the political context of the 1990s and 2000s, however, a new generation of artists began to take an interest in the artistic production of the regime. Most of those who engaged with the Fascist material and artistic legacy did so from a critical position. Contemporary artists on several occasions sought to employ examples of Fascist art, or use Fascist themes, to completely subvert their original meaning. This itself was not out of line with a growing interest in the most rhetorically charged examples of totalitarian art, which served as inspirations to artists precisely because they challenged most directly our capacity to resist persuasion. It is mostly Soviet propaganda, posters especially, that have been subjected to re-proposition, and Nazi works that have received least attention from artists. Fascist works have been the object of occasional interest. For example, Rossella Biscotti has engaged with the theme of the reactivation of fading or inconvenient memories. She has tackled these by opening up past time to new perspectives and creating contemporary reinterpretations in the light of the present. In the project 'Cities of Continuous Lines', in which she worked with Dutch artist Kevin van Braak, a variety of means including photography, restoration and even the reconstruction of selected fragments of Fascist architecture were used to explore the meanings of that architecture in the present. The two artists were concerned to inquire whether somewhere like the Foro italico (ex-Mussolini) in Rome or the many new towns created throughout the peninsula by the regime could contain Fascist impulses or house political ghosts, in other words function as storehouses of memory.[37] By using a variety of media, Bisciotti and van Braak aimed to raise issues and to provoke reactions rather than offer ready answers to troubling questions.

The discovery in the early 2000s in a storage space at the Palazzo degli Uffici in the Fascist-conceived EUR district in Rome of five bronze heads of Mussolini and Vittorio Emanuele III inspired Biscotti to conceive a show that was hosted by the Nomas Foundation in Rome in 2009.[38] As with other works created by the artist, the project developed in relation to the bronze heads envisaged the reuse of archive material and the analysis of the relationship obtaining between artistic creation and historical context. It began with the journey of the five bronzes from the deposit at the EUR up until the moment they were placed in the exhibition space of the Foundation, where they were situated on a modern-style wooden platform that, it was claimed, was 'the architectonic element that permits a real meeting between the public and the artist, who share in the process of the discovery of something that has been long buried and was unknown to most people'. The dialogue between the neoclassical monumentality of the heads and the modernist architecture of the platform was said to highlight not only the way the relationship between artist and commissioner had evolved but also the function of the work of art in different historical and cultural contexts.

This exhibition was different and perhaps clearer in its intent of engaging the spectator than an earlier work by Fabio Mauri. This did not reuse art objects; rather it restaged a crucial event in the history of Fascism. The work consisted of a life-size recreation of the meeting of the Fascist Grand Council of 25 July 1943 in the form of a waxwork installation. The waxwork was a form of popular representational art that began in the era of the French Revolution and which enjoyed a long heyday through to the second half of the twentieth century. It was an early example of a modern cult of celebrity that typically presented subjects solely on the basis of their fame.[39] For many years, a wax reconstruction of the meeting of the Grand Council could be viewed at the Rome Waxworks Museum, just a stone's throw from the Palazzo Venezia where the meeting took place (see Chapter 15). However, the medium has also attracted avant-garde artists. Born in 1926, Mauri grew up under Fascism and had precociously founded a cultural magazine in 1941 with his friend—and later famous writer, film-maker and polemicist—Pier Paolo Pasolini. He worked experimentally in several media, tackling issues of ideology and memory. His installation entitled 'Oscuramento—il Gran Consiglio' (Darkening: The Grand Council, 1975) featured twenty-nine figures in military dress, several

Figure 14. 'Oscuramento—il Gran Consiglio' (Darkening: The Grand Council, 1975). Detail of Fabio Mauri's art installation of the Great Council of Fascism of 1943 at which a motion critical of Mussolini was passed. Author's own photograph.

but not all of them made in the likeness of an actual historical figure (see Figure 14). The men are seated around the outer perimeter of a horseshoe-shaped table in a confined space that is decorated with striped wallpaper and several scenic paintings. 'Mussolini' is seated at the centre on a raised platform and is doubly flanked by waxworks of Emilio De Bono and Carlo Scorza and busts of nineteenth-century political figures. The restaging, it was stated, invited the public 'to consider the powers that governed the fate of so many, and to inspect and scrutinise this covert and sinister event, exposing the perpetrators of fascism'. The accompaniment of a loud soundtrack of Fascist speeches provided a forceful additional stimulus to reflection. The work raised the question of censorship and repression in relation to the theme of war that Mauri later treated from different points of view in various other multimedia creations. When 'Oscuramento' was shown at a private gallery in London in 2016 it was described by the *Financial Times* as 'a strange mise-en-scène, stunning, chilling and absurd in equal measure' that alluded to 'any closed world of power and corruption'.[40] The work was re-presented to the Italian public by the MAXXI gallery in Rome in 2022.[41]

The questions these artists sought to ask about the heritage of Fascism arose in contexts in which a heritage that had been forgotten and removed was coming back into the public realm in ways that seemed to grant it a spectral appeal. While Mauri was concerned with power and evil, Biscotti was seeking to tackle the complex meanings that attached to objects and buildings that had either literally been made invisible or from which the collective gaze had turned. In this sense they challenged a situation, which had obtained for many years, in which it was only among the closed circles of neo-fascism or of committed collectors that the material legacy of the regime aroused interest.

Debates around Fascist art are often shaped by two assumptions; first, that the art is still dangerous and, second, that the motives for examining or displaying it must be somehow politically questionable or sympathetic to Fascist ideology.[42] Even artists like Biscotti, who seek to escape from this limited view to provoke debate and reflection, run the risk of being criticised for publicising Fascist artefacts. However, this atmosphere of suspicion can be disrupted by an alternative perspective that treats propaganda art as an object of legitimate and necessary interest. The motivating rationale behind the Wolfsonian Museum of Miami Beach and Genoa is critical and philological, akin to the critical conservation viewpoint raised in relation to the question of the architectural preservation of Nazi works in Munich.[43] It is to highlight the ways in which in the nineteenth and twentieth centuries artistic works, which could be of great intrinsic beauty, were imbued with nationalist, fascist or communist ideology.[44] Dedicated to the design, decorative and propaganda arts of the period 1885–1945, the collection's research initiative is accompanied by an educational mission that avoids the ambiguities of other collections. The purpose of museum founder, businessman and collector Mitchell Wolfson Jr, whose father was the first Jewish mayor of Miami Beach in 1943, was to inform future generations about the past to alert them to art's potential for political manipulation. Thus, exhibition of objects related to Mussolini in the foundation's two sites occurs in a context that is not conducive to nostalgia. An exhibition about the 'Duce-mania' of the 1930s here has specific educational purposes that it would not necessarily have elsewhere. The perspective of propaganda art has the added advantage of downplaying the distinction between art and kitsch by interpreting serious works, design objects and bric-a-brac in terms of their relation to ideology. Bertelli's 'Continuous Profile' and an anonymous statuette or bottle-opener in the shape of Mussolini's head may have little in common in terms of their artistic standing, but they have a deep connection as products of the twentieth century's first major cult of personality. They were all contributors to a dangerous mass enthusiasm that profoundly shaped the course of Italian history and which critical contemporary artists and collectors have felt needed to be understood and analysed if it were not to be repeated in some form. This was all the more true in a context in which an object like Bertelli's Profilo grew in influence and became almost a classic. A new generation of artists and designers were influenced by it and turned the continuous concept to new ends. The American photographer Robert Mapplethorpe, who owned a copy, worked on a photodynamic self-portrait which was inspired directly by Bertelli's work ('Self-portrait', 1985).[45] The British sculptor Tony Cragg talked of his fascination with the copy of the Profilo on display at the Imperial War Museum (IWM), London, that was formerly owned by Galeazzo Ciano, and echoes can be found in 'Rational Beings', his series entitled 'Articulated Column' and his 2006 work 'Divide'.[46]

It is striking how few revisitations of the Mussolini cult in contemporary art deal with the macabre end of the dictator. The painting by Luciano Boccardini with which the preface to this book begins is a rare example of a treatment of the hanging corpse of Milan's Piazzale Loreto by an artist, albeit one with little affinity with realism.[47] In contrast to certain reservations within the country, outside of Italy this powerful and gruesome event has been taken as a warning to actual and potential dictators of the end that may await them. Thus, it is perhaps not surprising that the only extended artistic reflection on the final public appearance of Mussolini as a vilified corpse has come not from an Italian artist but from a British one. Thom Winterburn's *Redux: The Exhibition of Mussolini* is an exhibition in the form of a book that consists of many tens of photographs of the scenes at Piazzale Loreto.[48] These are preceded by images illustrating the heyday of the personality cult of the Duce and are interspersed with reflections, extracts from comic strips and depictions of death in the history of European art. Many of the images of the living dictator are printed upside down to establish a critical point of view and anticipate visually the spectacle of the hanging bodies in Milan (see Figure 15). Published in 2008, it is an unflinching attempt to stage a trial of Mussolini using images from his period of dominance and from his end. The book takes inspiration from the 1942 *Trial of Mussolini* by 'Cassius' (Michael Foot) discussed in Chapter 8 and the more recent trial of the Serbian dictator Slobodan Milošević.[49] It presents the political life and the death of Mussolini as a choreographed sequence of displays of all four of the dictator's bodies (see Introduction). It is an artistic installation that does not shy away from the grim, macabre nature of the key event recorded in the photographs. Like some American observers of Piazzale

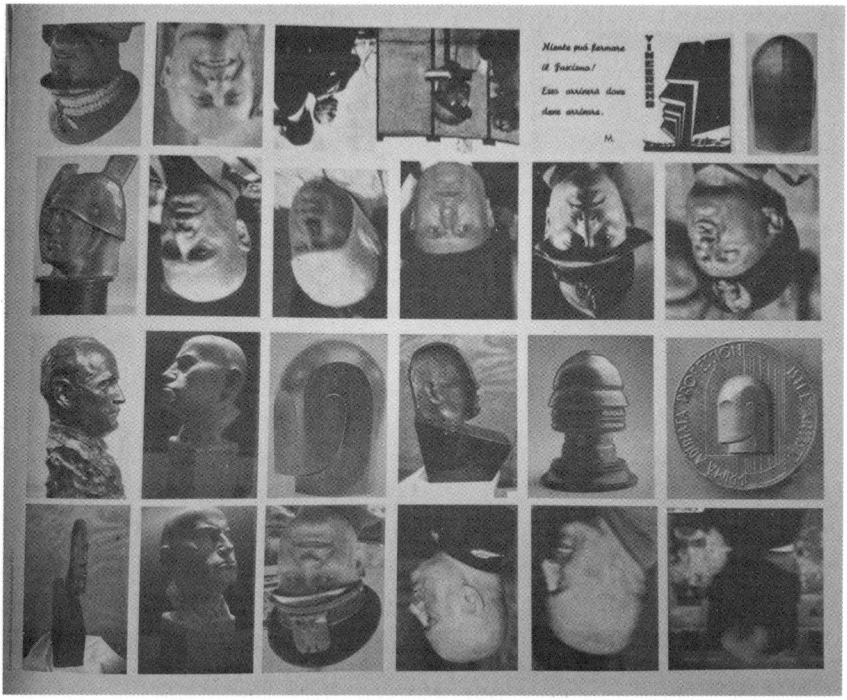

Figure 15. Extract from Thom Winterburn's exhibition-book *Redux: The Exhibition of Mussolini*, which revisits the display of Mussolini's cadaver in Milan in 1945. The composition inverts images of the live dictator, while keeping busts upright, to allude to the posthumous upside-down hanging that would be his final public appearance. Courtesy of Thom Winterburn.

Loreto, including Colonel Charles Poletti, the appointed Allied governor of Lombardy, who was not at all scandalised by the treatment accorded the dictator's corpse and indeed recalled that similar scenes had occurred at the end of the American Civil War,[50] Winterburn does not recoil; rather he seeks to grasp the meanings of a spectacle that was a gruesome act of repudiation conditioned by ritualistic aspects and a sense of crude justice. He does not condemn the people who vented their fury against a fallen and defeated dictator; however, he underlines the uncomfortable fact that, in his heyday, Mussolini found legions of admirers and that he still drew an audience in death. In contrast to Boccardini, who removes the horror in order to turn the hanging body of the dead Mussolini into a semi-abstract reminder that troubles more on account of its implications rather than its content, Winterburn dwells on the brutal scenes of bloodied, battered and displayed corpses to show how Fascism was a movement that was marked by violence and blood to the very end, finishing in an obscene pile of dehumanised human remains. Presented with little context or explanation, his repetitive use of images conforms to the practice of displaying photographs of death on the assumption that these are capable of speaking for themselves.[51] Fascism's epitaph was a horrible spectacle centred on a dictator whose extensively photographed posthumous desecration, the artist implies, was the final act of judgement that definitively deprived him of all power to enchant.

12

Political ghost signs

In January 2021, some council officers belonging to the local electoral commission in the town of Jesi in the Marche region of central Italy noticed high on the wall of the municipal register office some faded words, followed by the signature 'Mussolini'. The barely visible and possibly incomplete phrase read: 'della potenza e della gloria del lavoro' (of the power and glory of labour).[1] Evidently, the slogan had been whitewashed over in the postwar period, but the durability of the original black paint was such that, as the former began to wear away, the words reappeared, a faint and ghostly reminder of the period when even the most bland of Mussolini's pronouncements were treated as gospel (see Figure 16). The unexpected appearance of the slogan raised questions as to what action should be taken. The first to intervene was a town councillor who proclaimed that the words should be 'preserved as a by now more or less unique and exemplary testament of a period of the history of our country whose historical and cultural aspects should be protected'.[2] She called on the regional superintendence of public assets to back her view and consider the possible restoration of the writing, citing the opinion given by an association of former partisans in the Veneto region that the wall slogans of the Fascist period should be preserved as objects to be studied, discussed and criticised by future generations. By contrast, several cultural associations in Jesi, including the local branch of the former partisans' association, took the view that the writing should be covered or, alternatively, that an unspecified anti-fascist phrase attributed to Benedetto Croce should be added to it.

This debate was not the first to flare up in Jesi. Just two months previously, a wall motto on a highway leading to the town centre dating from the 1930s had been unceremoniously destroyed in the course of building work.[3] On this occasion, the faded catchphrase read 'È destino che Roma torni ad essere la città direttrice della civilità in tutto l'Occidente d'Europa. Mussolini' (Rome is destined once more to become the leading civilised city in the whole of Western

Figure 16. The wall slogan that was uncovered during restoration work in the municipal register office of the town of Jesi in the Marche region in 2021. Barely legible, the slogan gave rise to controversy over what should be done about it. Author's own photograph.

Europe). Although it was too late to remedy the situation, a controversy ensued in which the removal was condemned as an act of vandalism or, less polemically, regretted for the failure to take account of the potential educational uses of such writings. The question was raised as to why such mottos were still part of the urban environment. 'The post-fascist and anti-fascist Italy of 1945 was right to leave those slogans as a warning...so that the population reading them would have before its eyes its own stupidity, because you had to be rather foolish to have given credence to those banal mottos', read one reader's letter to a local newspaper.[4] The publicity given to this episode led to a campaign to restore a further Mussolini motto that was still extant on another building façade.

Like many towns in the peninsula, Jesi's civil society had been profoundly shaped by Fascism in the 1920s and 1930s.[5] The Fascists had taken over ex-combatants' associations and had absorbed memorial practices relating to World War I into their own system of commemorations and homages to the fallen. The piazzas that had once been sites of protest and spontaneous gatherings were now regimented and 'governed by a geometric order'. As the town's historians Amoreno Martellini and Barbara Montesi wrote of the change that dictatorship brought:

> Little boys in military uniform were organised into a square formation on one side of the piazza; beside them there was the formation of the little girls in a different uniform; behind them, in ascending order, came the other age groups, each one with its own space, each with its own uniform, from the fez caps of the Balilla [Fascist youth] up to the black shirts of the Militia. There were no more angry cries, unless they were expressly demanded of the crowd by the orator of the day, no more excited and noisy demonstrations demanding rights and better wages. Instead there were parades at a marching pace through the town's streets with right arms raised and rigid; applause and shouts of joy now marked with a regular rhythm the close relationship between the 'infantilised people' [popolo bambino] and their Duce.[6]

The children themselves were, as was the case throughout the peninsula, subjected to an education that was designed to turn them into 'fighter-believers'. The cult of Mussolini was one of the fundamental principles of this and the 'obsessive repetitivity of his presence' was a part of the life of schools. 'The discourse aimed at children', write Martellini and Montesi, 'usually took the form of a fable about the childhood of the Duce, who thus became a child among children to aid the process of identification'.[7] Changes to the urban environment in terms of new street names, public buildings, parks, sports facilities and monuments impressed on the town's citizens the progress that was being made under the new order.[8] Initiatives, such as the planting of a tree in 1932 to commemorate the death the previous year of Mussolini's brother Arnaldo (who had been president of the National Forestry Committee), that were required of municipal authorities, served to bring small towns into the Fascistised national community.[9]

In the aftermath of the war, all those who had held any position in the local Fascist hierarchy were barred from holding public office, at least until the amnesty proposed by the then justice minister and Communist leader Palmiro Togliatti in 1946 put an end to the purge. Resentments remained, however, and former Fascists and Nazi collaborators were subjected to attacks, which included a case of lynching. The victim was a former municipal official, a founding member of the Republican National Guard, who became known for terrorising those suspected of anti-fascism and subjecting random citizens to violent and degrading assaults.[10] His reappearance in Jesi in July 1946 provoked intense reactions that the forces of order were not able to contain. The anger culminated in an act of collective aggression that resulted in the man's death a few weeks later. In a moral reversal that was typical of the time, two years later some former partisans were arrested and tried for inciting the crowd. Their trial gave rise to demonstrations of solidarity at national as well as local level. As in many towns, the desire to revisit and correct the injustices of the Fascist period was strong, though the chances of achieving this by legal means were remote in a context in which Fascist officials had returned to their posts and in which there was pressure from the Church and the government to bury past divisions and look to the future. In 1967, a 'monument to the fallen' was inaugurated in Jesi's municipal gardens that ostensibly conformed to this imperative since it was dedicated to the memory of the fallen of all wars.[11] However, the monument had a complex history as it was originally conceived during the Fascist period as a memorial for the fallen of World War I. Today it stands as silent testimony to these contradictory origins and purposes. It is not the sole example in Jesi of historical amalgamation. In the municipal cemetery a memorial to 'The Martyrs for Liberty' (the fallen of the Resistance), including some tombs, stands within a special 'mausoleum of honour' inaugurated in 1928 where the dead of the World Wars I and II, including numerous civilian victims, are interred along with one Ernesto Galeazzi, who did not die in any war and was hailed by the town's Fascists as their founder.

In the aftermath of the liberation, the town's topography was radically altered as street and square names were modified to replace references to Fascist heroes and dates with anti-fascist and republican figures and moments.[12] These changes were hotly debated, with some championing a return to pre-fascist names while anti-fascists moved swiftly to make alterations and affix plaques to walls to mark Resistance martyrs. There is no record of the mottos that provoked such interest seventy-five years after the war having received any attention, though writings such as the one that reappeared in the register office were systematically destroyed. Perhaps because they were not painted on public buildings and were also difficult to reach, the two wall mottos were left in peace. It is also possible that, as in other locations, they were left to act as a reminder and warning to future generations.

The controversies over the reappearance of slogans on walls in a provincial town of 40,000 people constitute an example of the way in which one aspect of Mussolini's legacy plays into larger questions about the place of the Fascist experience in contemporary Italy. As this case shows, the matter is complex and is certainly not reducible to a difference of opinion between nostalgic preservationists on the one hand and anti-fascist abolitionists on the other, although the former faction certainly exists. Those demanding the eradication of mottos do so on the grounds that vigilance is required in a context in which the anti-fascist values of the postwar years no longer command the degree of support that they once did within the political system.[13] The written slogans are a reminder of a time when Mussolini's words were seen to have a unique power to mobilise the spirits of the masses and propel the nation towards the regime's proclaimed goals. They also provide testimony of the commitment to using every available means to communicate Fascism's messages to people who lived far away from the major urban centres. Unlike radio broadcasts, newsreels or print media, slogans on walls required only a minimum of attention and, in the best of cases, stuck in the minds of those who read them. The assumption was that most mottos would be seen many times by the same people as well as occasional travellers. They would therefore become imprinted on people's consciousness in true totalitarian fashion. Their authoritative verbal origin—and indeed the grandiloquent rhetorical character of some of them—distinguished them from commercial advertising, but they belonged to the same universe of mass communication and the art of persuasion.

During the regime, the walls of public buildings, houses and even churches were adorned with hand-painted slogans and symbolic images. Most of the phrases were brief sayings or affirmations of Mussolini himself.[14] To communicate a political sense of purpose as widely as possible, Mussolini's words, like his appearance, became standardised in the sense of being reduced to a limited range of concepts that facilitated a specific way of seeing and relating to him. 'The spoken and wall slogans, the mottos, the photographic and sculptural reproductions worked in the same way', the historian Mario Isnenghi argues: 'they exhibited continuously the image of the Duce; they hammered home and repeated the point that he was inseparable from the people and the destiny of the people; they re-stated incessantly the right and duty of everyone to place their trust in him'.[15]

The aim of the wall slogans was to carry the mottos and watchwords of the Duce to the remotest areas as part of the effort to shape the consciousness of the population. Unusually for a propagandistic innovation of the 1930s, it was a practice that owed nothing to Nazi Germany.[16] The Fascists were aware that, in mass politics, great leaders can only make an impression in general terms through the means of communication that shape the fantasies and sentiments of millions. It was necessary to propose gestures and words with the sort of reiteration that was typical of photography and cinema. Giuseppe Bottai was one senior Fascist who understood the parallels between modern advertising and politics and the need for political forces to learn from the communication techniques of the former.[17] Fascists took ideas and techniques from commercial advertising in order to manipulate and direct public opinion.[18]

The practice of using walls was initiated in 1930 and expanded dramatically in 1936, when party secretary Achille Starace gave the order that even walls had to don a blackshirt.[19] To this end, the party leadership identified the most important phrases from the Duce's speeches and ordered local officials to make them visible in interior spaces that were used for assemblies. From here they spread to the exterior environment.[20] It is striking that their appearance was quite uniform. The slogans and phrases were never amateurish or spontaneous in appearance; often they were hand-painted in a professional manner by companies specialised in signwriting that developed and rented a wide range of stencilled symbols, images and phrases. Slogans were assigned methodically to Case del Fascio, to the youth centres (GIL), to the recreation clubs of the OND (National Afterwork Organisation), to factories and Fascist union offices. Later they extended to barracks and military establishments, Mussolini himself noted, after his arrest on 26 July 1943, the wall inscription in the courtyard of the Carabinieri barracks to which he was taken in an ambulance, ostensibly for his own protection.[21] The slogans were numerous, not only because Mussolini gave many speeches and his peremptory catchphrases also multiplied, but also because mayors sought to incentivise citizens to host writings on their property through payments that went from 30 to 100 Lire according to the length of the phrase and the size of the letters.[22] Among the most diffuse were: 'Mussolini (or Il Duce) ha sempre ragione' (Mussolini is always right, a phrase famously coined by Leo Longanesi which the author later claimed to have been ironical), 'Chi si ferma è perduto' (He who stands still is lost), 'Molti nemici molto onore' (Many enemies, much honour), 'Roma doma' (Rome rules), 'Credere obbedire combattere' (Believe, obey, fight), while others were more cumbersome. In the war years: 'Vincere' (To be victorious) triumphed over other slogans. There were signs in big cities and more in smaller centres or the countryside. Many were placed on buildings situated at the start of villages or at the end. There was a particular flurry of them during the Duce's journeys to the regions, such as that to Piedmont in 1937, where they adorned the itineraries that he followed.[23]

The slogans were widely observed at the time. Henri Béraud noted that the walls of the capital and the larger cities were covered with posters and slogans lauding Mussolini, the institutions, and events of the regime.[24] These seemed to be ever fresh and constantly renewed. He noted a contrast between the walls that shouted their unanimous enthusiasm for the regime and the Duce, and the people who seemed sullen and silent. The regime imposed an 'obligatory optimism' that was supposed to infuse everyday life with enthusiasm, though this was not easy to maintain. The Englishman John Gibbons in 1933 travelled from north to the south and recounted that everywhere the walls were covered with posters with the slogan 'W il Duce' and by portraits of Mussolini, drawn with chalk or stencilled.[25] Mussolini's image was to be found in waiting rooms, in offices, everywhere. He concluded that the dominant motive was the representation of a 'total and inflexible power', of a propulsive force that had taken charge of the nation and, in a short time, had transformed it by imposing order and inculcating a new collective awareness. A few can be spotted in the background of films shot in real locations, though these were not numerous in an age when most feature films were made entirely in the studio. One example, however, is Alessandro Blasetti's proto-neorealist comedy *Quattro passi tra le nuvole* (Four steps in the clouds, 1942) in which the delayed departure of a bus entails an extended scene in a village square, one wall of which has been adorned with one of Mussolini's sayings.

As war events took a turn for the worse, printed posters and hanging banners provided an immediate complement to wall mottos. 'The walls of Milan are covered with posters on which you read how and why "it is necessary to hate the enemy"', wrote journalist Andrea Damiano in his diary. 'On the posters you can see the big wings of a bomber, amid a blood-coloured wake of smoke. The aim is to provoke hatred, taking as a starting point the bombardment by enemy planes'. He saw this as a major psychological error, since stoking hatred by means of posters affixed to street corners was equivalent to admitting that the hatred was not there.[26] Occasionally, anti-fascist writings would appear at night, a practice that would increase in the final stages of the war and afterwards.[27] Official wall mottos were in this sense an inadvertent incitement to opponents to use the same means. In November 1940, Piero Calamandrei noted in his diary that opposition writings were appearing on walls including 'Viva la fame' (Long live hunger) and 'Abbasso Ciano' (Down with Ciano). 'Abbasso M' (Down with M) had been seen stencilled in public toilets. These, he wrote, were signs of an 'ever more desperate general situation'.[28] By 1941, 'M a M', a code for 'Morte a Mussolini' (Death to Mussolini) had appeared.[29]

The regime's wall writings were still there of course, but they had an ever more hollow ring to them. The former Fascist Party secretary Giovanni Giuriati observed in his memoirs that:

> In the days preceding 25 July 1943, whoever had occasion to travel along one of our great carriageways and re-read Mussolini's sentences and precepts reproduced in box-style letters on almost all rural houses could not avoid making a

> comparison between the genial, almost impeccable reasoning of those mottos and the tremendous reality into which the country had fallen ....From this pointed comparison one logical, necessary and instinctive question emerged: how come a man so capable of such clear and convincing intuitions was able to drag his people into such a state of ruin?[30]

The return of the Fascists to power, backed by the Germans, witnessed a last hurrah of Fascist wall writings and banners. In every district of Milan, the slogan 'Tenere fede alla parola data' (Honour the commitment that has been pledged) was emblazoned on walls in capital letters. In Rome, the Nazi occupation led to a proliferation of graffiti. Giovanni Artieri noted in his diary that the lack of bread, which led to raids by women on bakeries, also produced wall protests: 'PANE, MORTE AI FASCISTI E AI TEDESCHI. VIVA STALIN' (Bread, death to the Fascists and the Germans. Viva Stalin) was one that struck him for its large red capital letters.[31] However, hideous damage caused during bombardments of August 1943—'pure terror bombings' intended to force Badoglio's hand—led to a certain change of mood.[32] Later, during the Allied occupation, Fascist-style writings appeared once more on the walls of Milan. American writer and critic Edmund Wilson noted 'Museo distrutto' (museum destroyed), 'Casa incendiata dai liberatori anglo-sassoni. Milanesi riflettete' (House burned down by the Anglo-Saxon liberators. People of Milan—reflect!), 'Anglosassoni assassini' (Anglo-Saxon assassins).

In the period between 1943 and 1946, many writings were defaced or painted over, though a number of them feature prominently in the documentary film *Giorni di Gloria* (Days of Glory, Mario Serandrei and others, 1945), that was made by the partisans' association soon after the war. The motto 'Se avanzo seguitemi, se indietreggio uccidetemi. M' (If I advance, follow me. If I retreat, kill me. M) stood as a sign of destiny fulfilled. In Allied propaganda films shot during the liberation, wall images and writings also feature, sometimes being pelted with rotten fruit and vegetables by angry townspeople. Such scenes are likely to have been staged, but they still provide testimony of the ubiquity of the mottos and the feelings they aroused in the aftermath of Fascism's defeat.

In the immediate aftermath of Fascism, the slogans were painted over or simply forgotten as people turned their attention to other things. Even a one-time minister in the Italian Social Republic and leading member of the neo-fascist MSI, Giorgio Almirante, admitted that the regime had furnished 'an infinity of slogans that were useless and sometimes false'.[33] They were not seen to carry any effective charge after the catastrophe of the war.[34] Where indifference did not render them all but invisible, they came to be seen as part of the built environment, an aspect of the fabric of life as it had once been in another age. Decades later, they would stand out as remnants of a period that seemed increasingly remote.[35] In some instances, mottos were seen not in an ideological key but rather as something that was part of people's mental world, a part of the furniture as it were. Preserving them was akin to keeping an old toy.[36] Few thought they were dangerous as, more than anything, they recalled a failure, even a tragedy. They acted as reminders of the rhetorical illusions that the regime produced in large doses and the peremptory tone of its injunctions.

Only in the 1990s, when National Alliance, the post-fascist successor party to the MSI, entered a right-wing government coalition did the legacy of Fascism begin to undergo a certain re-evaluation. Journalist Enrico Deaglio noted that 'suddenly those writings on the walls of the houses appeared to me in a different light'.[37] 'In effect they have been there since you were small, you got used to those writings, fading but never cancelled' that were to be found by the roadside as you entered villages, or on farmhouses and the walls of trattorias. He wondered why 'those stupid writings' had never been properly erased, and discovered that, although attempts had been made, 'the magic formula of "fascist paint"' had proved more resistant over time than the covering paint: 'in the end they left them where they were and forgot them'. But the question remained in his mind as to why precisely this was. 'Because there were other things to do, it has always been said, but perhaps also because people liked them', he concluded.

At the turn of the millennium, journalists and photographers, some of them also local historians, began to document the phenomenon of Fascist wall slogans. The fading writings possessed something of the fascination of ruins, and the knowledge that they were gradually heading towards complete disappearance only added to the interest they aroused. Two photographic books were published in 2000 and 2010 aiming to capture the incidence of wall mottos mainly in Piedmont (see Figure 17).[38] The books intended to provide a record not only of the invasiveness of Fascist propaganda but of what remained, more than fifty years later, of its efforts to impress the thoughts of its leader on the minds of the people. The slogans were, as the subtitle of Giovanni Bosca's volume clarified, 'a historical memory of the twentieth century'. Neither Bosca nor his fellow author, Ariberto Segala, had any sympathies for Fascism. Bosca's publisher saw his work, at a time of renewed controversies over war memories, as 'a way of remembering that the price of these words has been the lives of millions of innocent men and women'.[39] The book constituted 'a small contribution to keeping alive the sense of a freedom that it was a struggle to win back

Figure 17. A wall slogan in Piedmont in 2000, in a reasonable state of preservation. Author's own photograph.

and that we must remember never to take for granted'. Segala felt no sentimental attachment to mottos that would soon be no more:

> Goodbye, then, old, stupid writings. Your world is no more and you do nothing but perpetuate the death of those who conceived you. Therefore we salute you, abandoning you forever to your destiny. Thinking about it, you are even formulated in a prose that is nasty, crude and rhetorical. And your past of infallible pronouncements and categorial imperatives is nothing but a dead planet, wrapped in silence. Collapse by all means, crumble away, disappear, old words that have stayed around in a world that is no longer yours.[40]

His salute was heartfelt and measured, a just conclusion to the documentary project that formed his book. But his view was not universally shared and, as the Jesi controversies show, the passage of a further twenty years led to a heightened sense of the rarity value of all the remaining wall slogans (see Figure 18). They attracted interest and gave rise to a need to take decisions about possible preservation that had not been on the agenda in previous decades. Letting them decay and disappear no longer seemed an option to some when that

Figure 18. A wall slogan in Jesi in 2023, in such a poor state of repair that it is virtually illegible. The passing of time has turned such examples of Fascist propaganda into the political equivalent of ghost signs. Author's own photograph.

disappearance implied the vanishing from the built environment of some towns and villages of all explicit evidence that Italy had once been ruled by a regime headed by a war-mongering dictator. Preserving this memory was seen as important by people who held different, and by no means pro-fascist, viewpoints.

The mottos can, in this sense, be equated in some respects to the 'ghost signs' that have been studied by scholars of the history of advertising. They consist of the faded painted advertisements that adorn the sides of buildings in towns and cities that no longer bustle with economic activity and which are afflicted by post-industrial decay. According to one definition, ghost signs are advertisements hand-painted on the walls of buildings that are at least fifty years old and which publicise products that are no longer commercially available.[41] In the process of fading away, these signs take on a spectral nature, they become icons of times past that cannot return. They are remnants of an era that is on the brink of slipping away and disappearing forever. Though they are often associated with economic failure—they may exist in de-industrialised wastelands—they invite curiosity. Sometimes they are the subject of conservation efforts.[42] They can be seen as tradition, evoking the craft of signwriting or an oddly fascinating early approach to mass persuasion. As one commentator has said, 'ghost signs cast spells'.[43]

Only very few of the photographs in the Segala and Bosca volumes portray faded wall adornments that once must have been colourful and visually striking. The vast majority are of repetitive slogans and affirmations that, beyond their spectral curiosity value, are purely of political interest. In contrast to the architecture and advertising of the Fascist period, they are not heritage or tradition but legacy. It is for this reason that the polemics around them are always and exclusively the result of evaluations of the political opportunity of preserving them as warnings or as historical testimony. There can be no attempt of the type often encountered in relation to the rationalist buildings of the 1930s to subtract them from the ideology of the regime, for they have no intrinsic aesthetic merit. The writings do, however, have a capacity to act independently of human agency. In common with commercial signs, they exhibit a tendency to rebel against hasty cancellation, to reappear over time, suggesting a haunting, a refusal to die.[44]

In this respect, they have something in common with the few, but not insignificant, propagandistic impressions that the regime left on the natural landscape. As far as the Mussolini cult was concerned, these were not numerous. However, they were products of a time when the cult was at its apex and Mussolini came to be identified ever less with his human history than with what historian Luisa Passerini terms 'the "eternal" part of the nation, Italian nature and landscapes... representing himself as linked by sacred bonds to the heritage of the earth, water and the sky'.[45] As one Fascist author expressed it, the secret of Mussolini's genius lay in 'an immense, unprecedented will, a mysterious spring of great vigour hidden in the heart of a man instead of in the bowels of the earth: in short a force of nature, a prodigy of the force of nature'.[46] 'Ideas and ideologies count for little in this extraordinary life', he continued, 'but the fundamental impulses like attachment to the earth, to mother and to the family will count very much'. Interventions in the environment took a number of forms and existed in a realm that was somewhat different to the physical locations and buildings associated with the Duce (discussed in Chapter 10). They constituted an early example of what would come to be known in the United States in the 1960s as land art.

The Gola del Furlo pass near Fermignano in the Marche region—some 95 kilometres by road from Jesi—became known during the regime because Mussolini passed through it on his journeys from Rome to Predappio and the Adriatic coast. Its fame was enhanced by the fact that the side of the Pietralata mountain, which stood at the pass, featured a sculpted profile of Mussolini himself. At 180 metres long, it was visible even from several kilometres' distance. This was not entirely a natural, if curious, feature of the landscape. After the dictator developed the habit of pausing his journey at Furlo, a local sculptor named Oddo Alimenti conceived the project as a homage to the then highly popular leader. The work was commissioned and executed in 1936 by the Forest Militia by means of some dry walls. Mussolini himself was not over-enthusiastic about this tribute and expressed disapproval of the sculpted profile on the grounds that it depicted him horizontally, in a resting position, in contrast to his ever-active image.[47] He was somewhat assuaged by the ingenious riposte given to his objection that the figure was not resting but staring up at the sky, in a reference to the Duce's known passion for aviation. Nevertheless, it attracted many visitors, a fact which ensured it received attention during the war of liberation. In 1944, partisans firing heavy weaponry destroyed the nose, without effecting much damage to the overall profile. No significant damage was done by a subsequent attempt to dynamite it. The sculpted head should have been destroyed in 1946 on the orders of the then minister of public works, but the money set aside for this was instead used for road maintenance. The profile remained broadly visible for years, though the construction of the new Flaminia road in the 1960s, that bypassed the Gola through a tunnel in contrast to the ancient Roman road, dramatically reduced the passing traffic.[48] In the 1980s, there was talk of promoting the restoration of the profile, and this went further in 2006 when nostalgic Fascists backed by the prominent neo-fascist politician Pino Rauti urged it. In March 2007, the municipality of Fermignano approved a motion to restore the profile of Mussolini on Mount Pietralata, though nothing in fact was done. The rock face's survival led to an increase in its curiosity value, with it being described as an icon of land art.[49]

Another example is the devotional homage to be found at Monte Giano in the Appenines at the border between Lazio and the Abruzzo regions in the province of Rieti. The mountain is overshadowed by the much larger Terminillo (where the dictator was accustomed to go skiing to encourage Italians to take up mountain sports) and would be little known were it not for a large number of pine trees that were planted in 1939 by the students of the

Forest Militia School in Cittaducale with the help of volunteers from the area.[50] As part of an initiative of re-forestation, these trees were planted in patterns to form the letters of the word DUX. The inscription dominated the Velino valley and on a clear day was visible at a distance of several kilometres. It could even be seen, it was said, from as far away as Rome. After the war, proposals to intervene to disguise or obscure the Monte Giano DUX letters were consistently resisted on one pretext or other.[51] Even though only a few years had passed since their planting, they had come to be regarded by some as part of the landscape and the history of the place. In the 1950s, further forestation was undertaken which resulted in a rectangular configuration of pines beneath the word DUX. This de-emphasised the word which, however, remained. In the years that followed, emigration and depopulation led to the abandonment of the area, while natural forces made the letters ever less visible. Neglect, avalanches and rockfalls in the following years created potential dangers that compelled the Lazio regional government to intervene. In 1995, approval was given for restoration of the pine wood. The funds were approved in 1998 and the work carried out in 2004. By this time, it was barely possible to make out the letters. In 2017, a fire, possibly caused by arson, seriously damaged the wood. As a consequence, the attempt to imprint the Italian landscape with the sign of Mussolini's rule prompted interest and calls to action. In early 2018, tens of volunteers from the neo-fascist grouping Casa Pound, a civil defence group and an ecological association, undertook the planting of one thousand pine trees on the mountain to refurbish the inscription. This curious mixture of the political and the ecological, of memory and conservation, testifies to the range of concerns that can bear on decisions regarding those traces of a once potent personality cult that persist in the physical environment, as well as to a strangely widespread attachment to them.

PART IV

History and memory

13

Biography as monument

On 28 April 1976, on RAI-2, the second Italian state television channel, the historian Renzo De Felice was brought face-to-face with the British historian Denis Mack Smith, one of his most prominent and vociferous critics (see Figure 19). De Felice was an eminent figure, a full professor at the Sapienza University in Rome and the author of an ongoing multi-volume biographical study of Mussolini that encompassed almost all aspects of Fascist policy. The encounter between the two historians occurred following the recent publication of a book interview, entitled *Intervista sul fascismo* (Interview on fascism), which had brought De Felice's view of Fascism to a far wider audience than

Figure 19. Historian of Fascism Renzo De Felice debates with his British counterpart Denis Mack Smith (on television screen) in the course of their 1976 television debate. Screenshot by the author.

had read the lengthy volumes of his biography, the first of which had appeared in 1965.[1] In this short text, De Felice had responded to questions put to him by the American Michael Ledeen, setting out some ideas that aroused great controversy. Already, prior to publication of the interview, the first five books (volume one, volume two—parts one and two, volume three—parts one and two) of his projected eight volume biography had caused a stir. The titles alone of volume one (*Mussolini il rivoluzionario*—Mussolini the revolutionary) and volume three part one (*Mussolini il duce: Gli anni del consenso*—Mussolini the Duce: the years of consensus) challenged established views by asserting that Mussolini remained a revolutionary even after he abandoned Socialism for interventionism and Fascism, and by highlighting the alleged mass support that Mussolini's regime succeeded in securing from the population. At the time, it was still commonplace to see the Italians as having been victims of an oppressive regime.

Mack Smith was best known for his iconoclastic works on the Risorgimento, beginning with *Cavour and Garibaldi, 1860: A Study in Conflict* (1954) and his biographies of Garibaldi (1956) and Vittorio Emanuele II (1975). Just months before the television debate, his *Mussolini's Roman Empire* had appeared in Italian with the title *Le guerre del duce*. It would be followed in 1981 by his own single-volume biography of Mussolini.[2] In a review entitled 'A monument for the Duce', that was published in the *Times Literary Supplement*, Mack Smith praised De Felice's dispassionate and serene description of controversial events, but charged that 'an overriding and almost obsessive preoccupation with documents has interfered with and even inhibited the search for plausible criteria of interpretation'.[3] Moreover, De Felice had, like many biographers before him, ended up idealising his subject, leaving the impression that 'Mussolini has been given the benefit of too many doubts'. 'His picture of the Duce differs too little from the legendary image that the Fascist apparatus spent so much time inventing and propagating', Mack Smith judged. He pointed out that De Felice failed to mention the dictator's cruelty and misinterpreted the facts in arguing that he derived no financial benefit from his position. These were matters he would take up again in the television debate, which proved to be acrimonious and demonstrated little or nothing in the way of common ground.

De Felice was undoubtedly a scrupulous historian, an extraordinary pioneer in the identification and consultation of official and private documents relating to Fascism. On the back of his interview with Ledeen, he also became a public figure, a position he had begun to acquire with his previous short book, *Interpretazioni di fascismo* (Interpretations of fascism), published in 1969.[4]

However, he was not the sort of intellectual who readily accepted debate or contradiction. He proclaimed that his approach was objective, insofar as it was rooted in historical research. Interpretation, in his view, was something that would come after the preliminary phase of documentation in which he was engaged. It should not precede it. But critics found that his work was not as objective as he claimed. In his responses to Ledeen, De Felice drew attention to the distinction he had made between Fascism as a movement (which was marked by radical impulses deriving from the rise of a new middle class) and as a regime (based on compromise with established elites). He set out his objections to the notion of 'Nazi-Fascism' (a term that was widely used, particularly on the left), which implied that Nazism and Fascism shared a common set of principles and beliefs, especially in the period in which they were closely allied. Instead, he favoured a clear distinction between the two movements, with Fascism seen as revolutionary and Nazism as conservative or reactionary. In his view, Fascism was not a purely reactionary phenomenon that served to forestall the legitimate advance of the lower classes. It was first of all a vehicle for the affirmation of an emergent middle class. This was not the same as the view articulated by Croce in the closing years of the war, which had portrayed the Nazi regime as a product of German history and culture while Fascism was interpreted as a transient deviation from the best qualities of liberal Italy. But it worked on the view that was forcefully asserted during the final stages of the war and immediately afterwards by Croce and others that Nazism and Fascism were fundamentally different.

De Felice's attitude towards Mussolini was complex. Some of his critics went so far as to accuse him of seeking to re-evaluate him or to rehabilitate Fascism.[5] In some respects, he was forthright in his condemnation: 'I am convinced that if an individual comes out of all my work intimately and deeply criticised, and in many ways destroyed, that person is Mussolini'.[6] That the dictator possessed great tactical and political abilities was beyond doubt, he claimed, but the patient, concrete work of writing the history of Fascism was, in his view, the best way to critique it. The objective method was to be contrasted with the necessary, but also momentary, needs of political debate: 'Mine is the deepest critique of Mussolini from within, beyond the fine-sounding phrases, the true and sometimes false accusations that have been levelled at him to destroy him summarily, but which do not destroy anything. I believe that this is the concrete work that needs doing; facts are a good deal more eloquent and persuasive than the haranguing of a certain politically-motivated anti-fascism and of many schematisations that don't hold water at all'.[7] His much-vaunted impartiality, his self-proclaimed 'serenity in judging certain people and events as though they were things that happened two or three centuries before' were, he was well aware, stances that annoyed many for whom recent history was not remote but rather a factor that bore on the present.[8]

That a historian should seek to look beyond polemics of a conjunctural political nature was a view that many might have shared, if taken in isolation. But De Felice's assertion of impartiality was a provocative position, an eminently political detachment from the founding values of the postwar republic. In his account, the patient gathering of facts could not sit with any sort of value judgement and was therefore incompatible with an anti-fascist stance. In short, he sought to look at Fascism not only without regard for the dogmas of anti-fascism but in such a way as to imply that any sort of anti-fascism was an impediment to knowledge. However, the idea that the political forces which had established themselves after the end of Mussolini's regime, and which acquired a measure at least of their legitimacy via the Resistance, should leave the dictatorship and the events of the war period to the historians—long before they had faded from living memory—was an absurd presumption. This was so not least because these forces in some cases were alert to the recrudescence of a fascism that had never been fully uprooted from society and which was still present in the state and the political system. Far from having occurred two or three centuries before, they happened only thirty to fifty years previously. The problem, from De Felice's point of view, was that the political had invested the cultural; the left, in other words, had set down positions and frameworks that straightjacketed historical research. 'When the political climate will become calmer, the historiography of Fascism will gain much in terms of objectivity', he proclaimed.[9] But, in Italy, culture was politicised, and to a large degree this was a consequence of the regime's own extensive interventions in this sphere. If postwar political forces, including the Italian Communist Party, had gone out of their way to cultivate the educated and to develop a cultural policy, it was at least in part with the aim of assisting the conversion to democracy of groups formed or courted assiduously by the regime and its cultural bigwigs.[10]

How far Fascism was still a factor in Italy was a much debated point. For some, the presence within the state and the economic elite of officials and others who had loyally served the regime was a problem. Others were of the opinion that the more worrying phenomenon was the presence within the political system of a party—the Italian Social Movement (MSI)—that openly and explicitly derived from the Italian Social Republic and which consistently sought to legitimate that experience as a patriotic one.[11] De Felice did not have a consistent opinion on this. On the one hand, he was dismissive of nostalgic neo-fascism, which he regarded as minor and unimportant.[12] On the other hand, he acknowledged that residues remained. A certain political intolerance was one inheritance, though this was attributed to the left insofar as it levelled accusations against himself. There had been, he argued, a 'moral breakdown' under the regime that resulted from mass depoliticisation under the guise of mass politicisation; engagement and participation were replaced by formal adherence and conformism.[13] This had had a negative impact on the political culture of the postwar years as it inherited some of the models of mass participation of the dictatorship.

The left was indeed critical of the historian and there were various reasons for this.[14] His taste for challenging shibboleths and advancing unconventional hypotheses was undoubtedly one. But there were others. Among them was the use that was made of his work and his authority by an ambiguous current of centre-right opinion that had long cultivated an indulgent memory of the regime.[15] The veteran journalist Indro Montanelli, who conducted his own personal cultural battle in defence of the support that men of his generation had given to the regime and its imperial adventures, was among those who counterposed the historian's work, or at least a shorthand version of it, to an official anti-fascism that had always grated with him.[16] In a reply to a newspaper reader that was later reprinted with the heading 'A hero who fought against ideology', Montanelli praised the objectivity of the historian and his courage in refusing to demonise Mussolini 'at a time when for careerists it was obligatory'.[17] For those of similar opinions, De Felice bravely championed dispassionate history against ideology. However, while De Felice the historian may arguably have been objective, the public figure was not. Citing his commitment to scholarship, he refused offers of political positions or candidacies, but he did not shy away from intervening publicly on political matters and his antipathy to anti-fascism only increased over time. In this way, he politicised his own work and made it difficult for his research to be separated from his public position. People who criticised his politics were accused of attacking him as a historian.

Another issue was that De Felice's work placed Mussolini at the centre of the study of Fascism in a reading that saw the dictator as the key component of a complex interaction of many forces.[18] The destruction of the personality cult in the aftermath of the dictator's fall had required that Mussolini be seen as an ordinary and worthless individual, a charlatan more than a statesman. But De Felice did not demolish or demonise his subject. His insistent focus on

Mussolini, and his expansion of his biography into a multifaceted study of Fascism, preserved something of the dictator's charisma, his exceptionality and his capacity for leadership. He made the dictator seem like an original thinker, a man of great intellectual gifts as well as unusual energy. De Felice spent much time trying to penetrate Mussolini's mind, in keeping with his view that 'the personality of Mussolini, which is decisive for the understanding of fascism' was both intriguing and a suitable topic for research.[19] This followed from his view that 'without Mussolini 'the very fascist regime would not have been possible and it was always strictly linked to the physical life of Mussolini and his permanence at the head of the regime'.[20] Thus, as a historian, he became bound up obsessively with the man, with trying to see things from his point of view. 'The Italians suffered Mussolini for twenty years and I have for twenty more', he once said.[21] In his view, the dictator was, for all his errors, and imprisonment in his own myth, a talented politician with a 'great gift for understanding the masses'.[22] The task, as he saw it, was to face up to Mussolini historiographically, not polemically or in way that was conditioned by the fascist/anti-fascist dichotomy.[23] The problem was that in consequence Mussolini was portrayed in the best possible light and often from a point of view that was his own or that of the Fascists.[24] 'We do not deny that Mussolini had his notable personal magnetism', wrote the anti-fascist historian and politician Leo Valiani, adding that it was a matter of concern that it was 'exactly that magnetism that even decades later still dazzles De Felice'.[25]

De Felice's wide influence was great and extended into television coverage of Mussolini and his regime. The state network RAI began to broadcast television documentaries about the Fascist period from the late 1950s and these soon became a staple of its output.[26] Many of those made in the 1960s and 1970s were conceived by the journalist and broadcaster Sergio Zavoli, who called on historians of various political affiliations to develop a balanced approach to controversial questions that aimed to inform but not offend.[27] Zavoli was keenly aware of the sensitivity of the issue; before embarking on a series of documentaries of his own, he contributed to the texts of documentaries in others. He cautiously exploited the freedom that followed from the entry of the Socialist Party into government in 1963 and the creation of a second public television channel to introduce elements of debate and some perspectives that departed from the template of the 1950s.

The De Felice–Mack Smith television debate therefore did not come out of nowhere. It stood as testimony to the serious engagement of Italian television with the themes of contemporary history. The date selected for the broadcast, 28 April, was richly significant, for it was the thirty-first anniversary of the dictator's execution. The encounter between the historians took place against a striking mise en scène that did not disguise the televisual nature of the clash. The two men sat far apart, on either side of the moderator, each with a television set beside him on which the image of the other could be seen.[28] There was no handshake or greeting between them, either at the start or the end. De Felice sat slumped in his chair, with a cigar clenched between his teeth, looking considerably older than his forty-seven years. He spoke profusely, seeking to develop complex extended responses to the forceful, direct criticisms that his British antagonist levelled at Mussolini and at De Felice's failure to tackle some of the more unsavoury aspects of his rule. He adopted an unpleasant air of superiority, as though Mack Smith, eight years his senior, were a pupil who needed to be educated to see Mussolini correctly as a figure to be understood in the context of his time rather than an evil dictator to condemn. Such an attitude could only have been adopted for the benefit of the Italian public since, for the British of the war generation—Mack Smith was born in 1920—Mussolini could never be anything but a negative political leader and a thoroughly reprehensible individual.

The controversy surrounding De Felice did not subside in the 1980s and nor did it end with his death in 1996. Indeed, it became accentuated through a period that saw a significant ebbing of the influence of the left and a multiplication of the challenges that were levelled at the settled view on matters concerning Fascism, war, civil war and the Resistance. Nine years after the historian's death, the right-wing newspaper *Il Giornale* claimed that he had been the victim of 'a hostility that was at times ferocious' on account of his refusal to kowtow to 'anti-fascist orthodoxy'.[29] In other words, it was claimed that he had courageously pursued his goal of furthering the understanding of Fascism in the face of the sustained opposition of those who refused to acknowledge its profound impact on Italian society. The odd thing about the position of De Felice's right-wing defenders was that they were not motivated by a similar desire to understand Fascism, except insofar as they saw understanding as incompatible with condemnation. They took the view that a better knowledge of Fascism informed by De Felice's scholarship would aid their cause of delegitimating the anti-fascist consensus on which the left founded its moral authority. This would open the way to the full re-admission to the national political community of forces and currents that took a positive view of Fascism's impact on Italy at least up until World War II. Their intention was not condemnation, and it was for this reason that De Felice faced deep scepticism among those who opposed any dilution of anti-fascism.

To attribute Fascist sympathies to De Felice would be far-fetched, though Mack Smith was not alone in finding that he treated Mussolini with sympathy. One of his sharpest Italian critics, the historian Nicola Tranfaglia, also accused him of producing an apologetic 'monumentalisation' of Mussolini.[30] De Felice's own background was more on the left than the right. He joined the Italian Communist Party in the postwar years, though he was among the many intellectuals who quit the party in 1956. His father-in-law, Guido De Ruggiero, was a university professor of the history of philosophy who in 1925 signed Benedetto Croce's Manifesto of Anti-Fascist Intellectuals and was imprisoned in 1942 for his activities. Later he was a founder of the liberal Action Party and was the minister of public education in the Bonomi governments of 1944. Despite this left-liberal milieu, the operation in which De Felice was engaged, if that is not too programmatic a word, was one that attributed weight and significance—in the sense of granting dignity and serious value—to a particular political and cultural experience that was the fruit of the abolition of democracy and the establishment of dictatorship. The accusation that De Felice was seeking to 'rehabilitate' Fascism was articulated most directly by Tranfaglia, who denounced not only his omissions regarding violence and colonialism but also his arrogance and 'superiority complex'.[31] The author of *Processo a Mussolini* (Mussolini on trial), Paolo Pavolini, noted: 'this too has happened, that certain substantial studies begun with a genuinely anti-fascist spirit have ended up, inexplicably, as authentic apologias for Mussolini'.[32] While any biographer must see things from the point of view of their subject, De Felice seemed to have fallen under Mussolini's fateful spell, as Mack Smith claimed.

In 1995, *Rosso e nero*, a second book-length interview with De Felice, further accentuated controversy. By this time, irritated by attacks from the left on his work, he was firmly positioned on the right. In it, he went beyond the period thus far covered by the biography to question the widely held view that the Resistance had been a genuinely popular, a national movement by means of which the Italians had freed themselves of dictatorship. Instead, De Felice argued that it had been a minority phenomenon. The civil war of 1943–45 had seen most Italians stand on the sidelines, he asserted, occupying a 'grey zone' unaligned with either the Resistance or the Nazi-backed forces of the Italian Social Republic. In other words, he seemed to be saying that, while Fascism was an important and integral feature of national history, fully deserving of the attention of historians, the Resistance had limited significance as it did not concern the majority. The valorisation by De Felice of the 'grey zone' contributed to a powerful current of opinion that was seeking to undermine the Resistance as a relevant national force. De Felice asserted that, 'contrary to what the pro-resistance vulgate has always argued, it is not possible to consider the Resistance a mass popular movement. The partisan movement grew rapidly in numbers a few days before the German surrender, when a simple red handkerchief tied around the neck was sufficient for someone to feel like a fighter and join the victory parade'.[33] 'In the accounts of the protagonists', he continued, 'the drama experienced by the Italians between 8 September [1943] and 25 April [1945] has been distorted by a historiography that has reduced the Resistance to a cult object'.[34] The historian Giovanni De Luna commented, referring to *Il rosso e il nero*, that De Felice had, with this book interview, assumed a new role that, while substantially independent of his historical work, used the authority which derived from it to speak in the name of 'the people'.[35] The historian no longer identified himself, then, with a school of thought or a historiographical movement but rather asserted that he was an opinion leader.

Although he was anything but an authority on the Resistance, which was itself the object of a rich self-reflective historiography, De Felice had very firm views about the way a minority phenomenon had been used to grant a democratic patent to forces that did not merit it.[36] Whereas in France the Resistance had been led by General de Gaulle, a national figure who was not aligned with any political force, the first head of the Committee for National Liberation in northern Italy, Alfredo Pizzoni—an equally apolitical figure, who was by profession a banker—had been displaced by the Socialist Rodolfo Morandi, signalling the politicisation of the entire phenomenon of the Resistance.[37] These views downplayed the role of armed resistance (in which the Communists played a very prominent role), not only in hastening the end of the war Italy but also in redeeming the Italians in the eyes of the Allies. This role was important in ensuring that the country did not receive the same sort of punitive treatment that was meted out to the Germans during their occupation. The much smaller place occupied by discussions around collective guilt in postwar Italy stemmed precisely from the fact that there had been a Resistance movement and that the people had not remained attached to their dictator until the bitter end. In this respect, the dogma of a people united in resistance to Fascism, while historically inaccurate, was vital in securing for Italy a greater measure of autonomy over the country's affairs during the Allied occupation than their German counterparts, as well as a far swifter rehabilitation in the eyes of the world.

Like Croce—to whom some admirers likened him by virtue of his supposed solitary intellectual stance in the face of conformism—De Felice did not address the idea of collective guilt.[38] He also insisted, as Croce had done, on the differences between Fascism, which he interpreted with great subtlety, and Nazism, which he tended to see in far more simplistic terms.[39] In other respects, though, his position was completely different to the philosopher-historian's in that he situated Fascism very precisely within the context of Italian history instead of seeing it as an foreign contamination or a short and regrettable parenthesis. Moreover, he did not dismiss Mussolini as a buffoon. Even the last phase of his leadership was seen by the historian as having some merit. By accepting Hitler's persuasive invitation to head the puppet regime of the RSI, he sacrificed his desire to stand aside from politics and ultimately gave his life. He succumbed to pressure in order to mitigate the impact of the Nazi occupation on the Italians, to preserve the population from brutal repression. Without his republic, northern Italy might have been turned into a new Poland instead of something akin to Vichy France. In De Felice's opinion, the issue of loyalty was also not to be discarded. Italy was allied to Germany and had gone to war at its side. By abandoning the alliance and switching sides in September 1943, Badoglio and the king had thrown away the concept of national honour, which it became the task of others to redeem. The historian clearly felt that Mussolini's position was honourable. He did not dwell on the pathetic pretence that the Republic was engaged in reviving Fascism on the basis of a socialistic anti-bourgeois programme that recalled its origins. Nor, more tellingly, did he pay attention to the brutal reprisals that were inflicted on the population in response to Resistance activity, not only by Germans but by Italians belonging the Republican National Guard and the so-called Black Brigades.[40] Mussolini may have used honour as a mobilising tool, but he had hoped that the secret weapons Germany was developing, and which Hitler had told him about, would be ready in time to lead to a sudden reversal of the war situation and herald a resurgence of the Axis. Instead, however, he would go down to ignominious defeat and a suffer a degrading death.

In an article published in 2000, twenty-four years after the television encounter, Denis Mack Smith returned to the question of De Felice's biography and accused him of taking Mussolini at his word and of praising him—mistakenly—for his supposed realism.[41] The historian was guilty of absolving him of the Matteotti killing and of ignoring the atrocities that were committed by his troops in Ethiopia, which included not only violent reprisals but also the use of illegal poison gas. Though there was much evidence to the contrary,

De Felice denied that Mussolini was cruel and vindictive, as when he encouraged the Germans to destroy Italian cities in response to the July 1943 jubilation. 'The Mussolini of this biography was immensely industrious in the service of his country', Mack Smith argued.[42] De Felice understated the dictator's inefficiency and that of a regime in which corruption and dishonesty flourished.[43] He ignored the military catastrophe in Africa and the incompetent management of the war. For Mack Smith, De Felice seemed to share Mussolini's own view that one day history would prove him right. His Mussolini was too close to the myth, he concluded, suggesting implicitly that it was more a product of the personality cult than a demystification of it.

If this is true, then it must be asked whether De Felice's opus can be considered a contribution to the elaboration of mourning for Mussolini that signally failed to occur in the postwar years, that mourning which the Mitscherlichs had considered to be impossible for the Germans and which the Italians had not seen to be necessary. By operating within a framework that was governed by the point of view of the dictator and the Fascists, De Felice attracted criticism on methodological as well as political grounds, but it must also be recognised that his work opened up the way to new types of study that would prove to be richly productive. These included Emilio Gentile's many works on ideology and Fascism as a political religion that were stimulated by De Felice's insistence on looking at the regime and the movement from the inside.[44] This point of view brought Fascism within the national experience and in practice acknowledged that the Italian people had lived and breathed Fascism and participated in the events of the regime with enthusiasm. De Felice's focus on the psychology of the dictator left somewhat out of the frame the matter of the collective psychology. However, this was occasionally alluded to. Despite a reluctance to embrace psycho-sexual interpretations of the dictator and the relationship he enjoyed with the crowds, he dimly acknowledged that the transformation of Mussolini into a collective ego-ideal was a factor in the regime's stabilisation and success.[45] This all points in the direction of a significant contribution on the part of De Felice to the working through process that is required of a people if they are to detach from the mystique of dictatorship. The historian's prominent position, his centrality in press debates on Fascism and in television coverage, accorded him a unique platform that was reinforced by his refusal to demonise the dictator and his regime.

It may be argued that, ultimately, De Felice's work did not constitute a conventional working through. Rather, it went in the direction of de-realisation in the sense that it downplayed the very worst aspects of the regime and made as if these had not existed. Although he did not portray Fascism as a departure from the noble history of the nation or seek to ridicule or diminish it, he cannot be said to have favoured any sort of meaningful reckoning with the Fascist experience. By omitting many negative aspects of the regime and its chief, and indeed in finding good in them, he gave Italians a view of them that they could live with, a view that was negative within limits but not one that made them feel that they should be ashamed, if not for themselves then for their parents or grandparents. De Felice developed a perspective on Fascism that kept the Italians in an ambiguous relationship of complicity with the dictatorial past. 'It is embarrassing, in the absence of any Italian debate on revisionism comparable in scale to the *Historkerstreit*', the historian Luisa Passerini remarked, referring to the German historical debate of the 1980s over how to incorporate the Nazi regime and the Holocaust into national historiography, 'that the leading expert on Mussolini, holder of a key position in the system of academic power, should contemporaneously declare that he believes the distinction between Fascism and anti-fascism to be outdated along with the anti-fascist affirmations included in the Italian republican constitution'.[46] An object of a cult of personality himself of sorts, De Felice proclaimed objectivity but was methodologically and morally a man of his time, one who arguably can and perhaps should be historicised in relation to the problems encountered in the postwar decades in coming to terms with the legacy of Fascism.[47]

14

Performing the Duce

When the film director Carlo Lizzani was preparing his film *Mussolini ultimo atto* (The Last Days of Mussolini, 1974), he went to considerable lengths to ensure that the portrayal of the dictator's final days was properly researched and that his impending end would not be represented in a way that might arouse sympathy. As a leftist, Lizzani was concerned to take a role in demystifying the Duce at a time when a right-wing backlash against the social protests of the 1968–73 period was in full swing. Born from the director's conviction that 'the figure of Mussolini...needed further reflection, especially regarding the time when the Duce was nearing the end',[1] the film was intended to be a dramatised account of the circumstances which led to the dictator's being sentenced to death by the leadership of the northern Resistance. Lizzani bore a special responsibility as his film offered the first full re-enactment of Mussolini in cinema.[2] With *Mussolini ultimo atto*, he concentrated the treatment on the final phase of the dictator's life up to his death on 28 April 1945. Having already made a film of the trial and execution in Verona in August 1944 of the Duce's son-in-law Galeazzo Ciano and other senior figures who had voted for Dino Grandi's motion in the Fascist Grand Council of July 1943,[3] the director was well placed to take the step of centring a film on the figure of Mussolini. When he began to work on his new project, he formed the idea that a 'great actor' was called for to convey the tragedy of the man who led his country to ruin.[4] The actor he cast was certainly of high standing. Rod Steiger had been nominated for an Academy award in 1954 for *On the Waterfront* (Elia Kazan) and had won one in 1967 for his role in *In the Heat of the Night* (Norman Jewison). His profile was particularly interesting because he specialised in closed, difficult characters. He had played an emotionally withdrawn Holocaust survivor in *The Pawnbroker* (Sidney Lumet, 1964) and a late Napoleon in *Waterloo* (Sergei Bondarchuk, 1970), as well as a corrupt property developer in Francesco Rosi's *Le mani sulla città* (Hands over the City, 1963).[5] These roles

Figure 20. Rod Steiger as Mussolini and Lisa Gastoni as Claretta Petacci in Carlo Lizzani's film *Mussolini ultimo atto* (The Last Days of Mussolini, 1974).

had shaped his screen persona and ghosted his interpretation of Mussolini in the final, tragic phase of his life (see Figure 20).[6]

In portraying the dictator facing final defeat, Lizzani took steps to ensure that the broken man would not arouse compassion. 'The screenplay of the film was filled with unequivocal clues—through some flashbacks and dialogue—as to the responsibility of Mussolini in the disastrous conduct of the war, and in the guilty subservience to the Germans', he later wrote.[7] Alert to the need to avoid leading the audience too blatantly, Lizzani added that 'the public was stimulated, it *had* to be stimulated to judge without the assistance of excessively obvious signposts'.[8] Steiger prepared for the role under the director's supervision by watching newsreel footage of Mussolini. A method actor, he immersed himself in the part and produced a performance that was widely praised. Indeed, his Mussolini was convincing enough for the Syrian-American director Moustapha Akkad to cast him once more as the dictator in *Lion of the Desert* (1980), a powerful anti-colonial film that for many years would be banned in Italy on account of its highly critical treatment of the Fascist colonial experience. The historian Denis Mack Smith was the consultant on this film. Although it was set during the dictator's heyday, Akkad conferred an aura of charisma not on Mussolini but on the rebel leader Omar Mukhtar, who offers in the film a compelling model of honesty, inner strength and simplicity. His courage in refusing to surrender to colonial troops led to his capture and hanging in 1931, events which are featured in the film and which highlight the cruelty of Mussolini and the Italian army commander General Graziani.

Lizzani took care to eliminate from the mise en scène all elements that might have evoked or inadvertently revived the personality cult. Mussolini is presented as isolated and defeated. The fallen dictator's only devoted supporters are his lover Claretta and a handful of desperate Fascists including Alessandro Pavolini, who has been lying to him about the number and quality of soldiers prepared to make a final stand. As his car travels among the villages in the hills above Como, in the real locations of those days, several wall slogans of the type discussed in Chapter 12 (painted or refreshed for the purposes of the film) underline the delusions that the regime had peddled. The only evidence that Mussolini was once adored is provided by newsreel footage of crowds roaring their support as he delivered one of his speeches. But this footage is not deployed to show that the dictator and his regime had once been able to count on widespread support. Rather, it serves to reveal his own fantasies of past glory as he journeys along the deserted streets of Milan before he abandons the city on 25 April.

Mussolini was not a conventional subject for a biographical film. The genre was conceived by its pioneers as having a strong educational and moral impulse. In both France, which produced some early films of the lives of Napoleon and Joan of Arc, and the United States, the desire to convey a positive national story was strong. For the producers of early biographical pictures of Abraham Lincoln, such as *Young Mr Lincoln* (John Ford, 1939), spectators had to be given a 'rooting interest' in the life of the famous person.[9] For this reason only worthy subjects were given film treatments. However, for countries in which dictatorship was a part of national history, negative leaders could not be permanently ignored. In postwar Germany, there was a reluctance to represent the deceased dictator in screen drama that only crumbled in the 1970s.[10] There were a number of reasons for this reserve. First, there was the problem that Hitler has been removed and forgotten; no one wanted to be reminded that he had once been the ego-ideal of the Germans. There was also the problem that he had passed into history as a symbol. 'Hitler' was not a man but a monster; he was the very embodiment of evil.[11] As a result, any attempt to present him in a human dimension was regarded with deep suspicion. This reduced the possibility of portraying him to a few stock gestures or situations including ranting, acts of great cruelty and the exercise of megalomania, or to the final phase of his rule when he was broken and defeated. Only gradually was this taboo overcome, first abroad and then in Germany.

A further complication derived from the fact that the German dictator had been heavily represented; in his time he was a media star.[12] Mussolini arguably had a less sure grasp of cinema, although he was also a creature of the media age and his prewar American image as a political celebrity had not been entirely erased.[13] As with Hitler, the huge stock of images that the regime created of its leader presented a problem. Not only did the way of representing the dictator on film seem to have been established once and for all by the regime itself, but almost all actual footage of him was created with the aim of perpetuating his personality cult. Moreover, still and moving images of Mussolini were so widely seen under the regime, and had been so frequently reproduced since its fall, for example in television documentaries, that every spectator felt they 'knew' Mussolini. Unlike actors playing Napoleon, who only had to compete with painted portraits, or Garibaldi, whose image was widely reproduced in popular prints, actors who played Mussolini had to do so in the knowledge that they would constantly be compared to moving images of the dictator himself. The matter is further complicated by the fact that the first person to play the part of Benito Mussolini in a way that met the public's expectations was undoubtedly Mussolini himself.[14] This made it challenging for actors playing the late Mussolini. They had not only to capture the man, but the man playing the man, and do so without offering a caricature that, instead of seeming like a sophisticated elaboration of a real situation, would appear like an amateurish cameo.

In his lifetime many found Mussolini readily imitable. For some, like Galeazzo Ciano who saw himself as a potential successor, he was a human and political model.[15] Others just picked up on a limited repertoire of characteristics that included facial mimicry, poses (hands on hips, jutting jaw) and speaking via brief, declamatory phrases.[16] Even children postured and posed in the manner of the Duce, as the writer Italo Calvino later recalled (see Chapter 1). The phenomenon of the 'lookalike', that is the systematic adoption of the style and attitudes of Mussolini in order to in some way pass for him, was noted by observers.[17] These did not disappear entirely with the fall of the dictator and the end of the war, and the illustrated magazines occasionally ran features on better known imitators. Postwar popular cinema also testified to the fact that images and ideas of Mussolini continued to be present in the collective mind and in ways that were by no means always negative. The popular Neapolitan comedian Totò (Antonio De Curtis) alluded to him in several of the many films he made in the 1950s and after. In *Totò e Carolina* (Mario Monicelli, 1955), his character, a police officer, is shown painstakingly employing breadcrumbs to construct a Mussolini-style bust of his superior in order to ingratiate himself with him.[18] In *Totò diabolicus* (Steno, 1962), one of the six characters the actor plays is General Scipione, a nostalgic Fascist still in thrall to Mussolini who has not reconciled himself to the fall of the regime.[19] The Roman comic actor Alberto Sordi—whose persona has been seen as a complacent embodiment of national vices, a celebration rather than a critique of widely acknowledged shortcomings in the national character—was even said to have considered making a film adaptation of Mussolini's attendant Quinto Navarra's highly anecdotal volume of memoirs.[20] These approaches testify to the fact that while the dictator might have disappeared he had not fallen out of mind to the extent that he could be freely represented.

The allusions, comedic references and tangential approaches present in the films of Totò and Sordi occurred in a context in which Mussolini himself, although he was remembered indulgently in the press and some quarters of public opinion, was a taboo subject in audio-visual media. This was not a case of 'out of sight, out of mind' but rather the opposite: out of sight and very much still in mind, rather as theorist Theodor Adorno found with the postwar German will to forget.[21] The problem at one level was one of political sensitivity and therefore of censorship on the part of Italy's new rulers, but there were also broader unresolved issues of complicity and consent. For two decades, Mussolini's biography had been the biography of the nation. As the collective ego-ideal, he had attracted a high level of identification that, to be sure, had been terminated but which remained as memory even if problematic or watered down. Representing Mussolini on screen therefore risked reviving not just the life of an individual but the fact that the whole nation had been bound up with that individual. In other words, it entailed a potentially inconvenient collective reflection. In a highly politicised country, the subject of a political biopic unavoidably became the vehicle for the treatment of tensions, emotions and conflicts present in the community.[22]

Deconstructing the relationship between the Italians and their dictator and his regime was one of the themes that ran though the auteur cinema of the 1970s. Directors and screenwriters adopted a critical stance which they elaborated in different ways. Lizzani showed the gulf that had opened by the end, leaving Mussolini isolated and defeated. In *Il conformista* (Bernardo Bertolucci, 1970), the screen adaptation of Moravia's novel, *Una giornata particolare* (A Special Day, 1975), Ettore Scola closely examined the forms and sources of consent, while Federico Fellini portrayed provincial life under the regime in *Amarcord* (1973). His film was thought by some to offer too affectionate a picture, although one perceptive critic, the novelist Natalia Ginzburg, pointed out that it acutely underlined the way that Fascism became interwoven with the life of a community that lacked the resources to defend itself against its seductions and deceptions.[23] Critical films were at one level provocations in a context in which there was still a residual nostalgia for the Fascism of the 1930s. They looked back to analyse society's entanglement with a dictator. In this sense, they ran counter to television documentaries that were often narrowly political and rather ecumenical in their treatment of the past.

Lizzani took the bold step of making Mussolini the central protagonist of a feature film. He would not have anticipated that the dictator would become a staple fixture of television drama in the following decade and beyond. After the phase of documentaries there came a new entertainment-oriented trend towards the dramatisation of history on television. In the 1980s, RAI-TV invested heavily in drama as it sought to compete with private networks and to contrast with Silvio Berlusconi's rising Fininvest company.[24] It produced lavish biopics of Marco Polo, Giuseppe Verdi, Garibaldi and others. Regarding Fascism, the focus remained firmly on Mussolini, whose drawing power as a subject remained undiminished. He was in a way the odd one out in the gallery of great Italians, the one subject whose career was not the stuff of dreams but of everyday compromises and base conduct.[25] However, the events that marked Mussolini's rise to power and which accompanied his fall in July 1943 and its tragic epilogue possessed undeniable dramatic potential.

The first drama, Pasquale Squitieri's *Claretta* (1984), approached Mussolini via the figure of his lover. It was a lavish RAI-2 international co-production which also had a theatrical release. Starring Claudia Cardinale in the title role, it was presented at the Venice film festival where it won the prize for best actress. In contrast to the past, the treatment accorded greater importance to the domestic sphere and to women in keeping with television's conventional stress on family and entertainment. It was followed the next year by Alberto Negrin's *Io e il duce* (broadcast in the United States as *Mussolini: The Decline and Fall of Il Duce*), in which Bob Hoskins as Mussolini was flanked by Anthony Hopkins (Ciano) and Susan Sarandon (Edda). These multi-part dramatic historical reconstructions were later joined by *Il giovane Mussolini* (1993, broadcast in the USA as *Benito Mussolini: His Rise and Fall*) and by *Edda* (2005, broadcast in the USA as *Mussolini's Daughter*). The films saw RAI forge new foreign partnerships. For example, *Io e Mussolini* was an Italian (RAI)-American (HBO)-French (Antenne 2)-Spanish (TVE)-Swiss (RTSI) co-production with an input from Beta film (a leading international distributor of TV licensing rights).

These films were made at a time when a backlash against anti-fascism in public opinion was accompanied by a significant revival of interest in the Fascist period. A variety of popular histories of Fascism, part-work publications, exhibitions and biographies contributed to a trend that was denounced as an attempt to create a cheerful and nostalgic perception of the period.[26] The films themselves, however, all used a variety of devices to try to establish their authenticity and through this their seriousness. Lizzani was the pioneer in this sense. He spoke at length about the research he undertook before writing his script with Fabio Pittorra, while Squitieri enlisted the help of historian Arrigo Petacco. *Io e Mussolini* was described as 'original story by Nicola Badalucco', a former collaborator of Visconti and the author of several television screenplays, while the narrative revolved around the diaries of Ciano (ostensibly the main 'Io' of the title) and their fate. *Mussolini: The Untold Story* claimed to be based on Vittorio Mussolini's memoirs while publicity suggested that the author had directly availed himself of Vittorio's advice. *Edda* dramatised the story of Mussolini's daughter, drawing on her published memoirs and a documentary interview. *Il giovane Mussolini*, like many of the RAI documentaries, benefited from the consultancy of historian Renzo De Felice. All the films made use of plausible locations, and a few were able to use authentic ones. Lizzani conducted location research in and around Como and filmed Mussolini's execution in the very place it happened in Giulino di Mezzegra. The same location was used in *Edda*. *Io e Mussolini* secured permission to partially restore and use Villa Torlonia, where the Mussolini family resided in Rome from 1929 to 1943, while *Io e Mussolini* and *Edda* were both able to use the Sala del Mappamondo in Palazzo Venezia for the Duce's office.

A further device to assert authenticity was the insertion of documentary footage in the narrative flow of a biopic, which was on a par with the use of montages of news headlines.[27] Footage is sometimes employed diegetically to explore Mussolini's relationship with his own image. Such episodes serve both to indicate his power over the media but also to highlight the extent to which his charisma was a media effect or he was himself a construction of the media, 'a one-man cinema' as his one-time associate Giovanni Giuriati succinctly put it.[28] Newsreel material is often subject to manipulations of various types. Original footage is sometimes intercut with faked material in which a film's actors take the place of the historical originals. In *Io e Mussolini*, Bob Hoskins is inserted into footage of the devastation of San Lorenzo in the aftermath of the Allied bombing of Rome in 1943. *Mussolini: The Untold Story* includes the most creative manipulations. Gabriel Byrne and Robert Downey Jr as Vittorio and Bruno Mussolini are spliced into original footage of the invasion of

Ethiopia, while colourised footage of Nazi troops on parade and Nazi rallies is fused with staged material. Aside from *Mussolini ultimo atto*, this is the only film to take the risk of including, briefly, footage of Mussolini himself, shown in profile at the Munich peace conference together with other national leaders. All these devices are geared to bringing spectators into a situation in which they can immerse themselves in the events, a sensation that in these instances also brings the unsettling effect of forcing a proximity—if not an identification—with Mussolini's milieu.[29] Lizzani's work was influential in this regard, as he had been the first to centre a narrative on female characters and bring the Mussolini family to the screen in his 1962 film *Il processo di Verona*, a film which in keeping with the attitudes of the time had avoided a focus on the dictator.[30]

One of the concerns of critics was that the accent the films placed on the domestic was in tune with a well-known approach to the famous of the past which typically mobilised an anecdotal repertoire that was not necessarily truthful.[31] The focus on the domestic was primarily motivated by the fact that the family as an institution 'reigns supreme' in a consumer-based medium such as television.[32] In the field of biopics, narratives organised around a great man or woman were often replaced by ones focused on more commonplace individuals in which a so-called 'tabloid point of view' (extra-marital lovers, unflattering images, tragedies)—which in fact was a medium-specific bias typical of television—triumphed. Where historical figures were the subjects, they tended to be seen from this viewpoint too. In France, television explorations of the private Napoleon contributed to an image of very questionable authenticity of 'the housewife's emperor', a respectable husband and father who emanated solid bourgeois values.[33] The transformation of the avowedly anti-domestic Mussolini into a 'housewife's dictator' who was shown eating and relaxing with members of his family, as well as being situated in a variety of ordinary domestic contexts (kitchens, bedrooms, dining rooms), worried historians. The need to entertain viewers was seen to contain certain biases and lead on occasion to pure invention, for it entailed an engagement with those areas of life like the domestic or the intimate for which there was no historical record or (until the publication years later of Claretta Petacci's diaries) much significant testimony.[34]

This approach to televisual historical dramas was explicitly identified by historian Guido Crainz as a 'new sort of revisionism', which was something that 'television in part recorded and in part helped to manufacture and spread'.[35] Revision, however, if such it was, did not take the form of an acritical rehabilitation of prewar Fascism. Most films, in fact, were concerned exclusively or predominantly with the period 1943–45, that is to say the period of Fascism's decline and defeat. In this sense, the image of Fascism they offered broadly dovetailed with the anti-fascist idea of the people united in the Resistance that was the founding myth of the republic.[36] Rather, the sense that revisions were occurring in the representation of Fascism was related to the discovery of the human and familial side of the dictator. In this way, the negative premise deriving from a focus on the later war years was mitigated, turning Mussolini into object of compassion.[37]

In fact, the focus on family did not necessarily mean normalisation.[38] Humanisation may entail a highlighting of flaws and moral defects that erode charisma. As Duce, Mussolini is known to have disliked film treatments of great men which demeaned and 'de-sacralised' them by making them seem ordinary, typically by showing them in their domestic environments.[39] As Sergio Luzzatto, the author of an influential study of Mussolini's body has commented, 'it is really by digging into the private life of the Duce that the intrinsically perverse public life of the fascist period emerges'.[40] In drama, Mussolini was rarely shown as a good father and husband, as regime propaganda had portrayed him. The presence of Claretta already undermined this image, although it may be argued that it reinforced another, that of the virile, sexually potent dictator. But the importance of family to a regime which in a number of ways shaped and directed private life meant that the theme offered various opportunities for criticism or deconstruction. This was exploited most effectively some years later in Marco Bellocchio's film *Vincere* (2009), which revealed a dark underside to Mussolini's family relations in the form of a lover (and possible wife, Ida Dalser) who was interned and an illegitimate son who was repudiated.[41] Hauntingly, the son is shown in the presence of busts of his alienated father and responding to requests from other youngsters to 'make like the Duce'.

The task of capturing Mussolini's flaws and contradictions as well as his appeals fell to actors who, like Rod Steiger, were all foreign and well known. Their foreignness meant that they might have approached the part to some degree like any other, with a certain detachment. In reality the actors cast as Mussolini were apprehensive about playing an Italian of such notoriety and were aware of the challenges, as well as the responsibility they bore to convey a sense of promise betrayed and moral defectiveness.[42] None except Steiger, who played the sixty-year-old Mussolini at the age of forty-seven, was young. Bob Hoskins, at age forty-three in 1985, was the youngest, while George C. Scott was aged fifty-eight and Claude Brasseur, who played Mussolini in *Edda*, was seventy. Scott was an actor of undoubted talent and screen presence, who had famously played General Patton in *Patton* in 1970. Truculent and difficult, he seemed well suited to the part. Only the playing of the forty-year-old Mussolini of 1922 seemed daunting; for the French veteran Brasseur, the challenge was even greater. Hoskins had established a reputation for playing rough characters with a streak of charm and a capacity for violence or forcefulness. Short of stature and round-headed, the qualities that would commend him to the producers of *Io e Mussolini* in their efforts to capture a resemblance to the Duce would also lead him to be cast as Churchill, Khrushchev and, for Italian television, Pope John XXIII as well as Pinocchio's creator Geppetto. *Il giovane Mussolini*, which only covered the period up to Italy's entry into World War I, was unusual in requiring a young actor of energy and vitality to play the future dictator. Physical resemblance was not so important since visual familiarity with the young Mussolini was much vaguer. The choice of Antonio Banderas thus presented more advantages than difficulties, although this film was in some ways the most ambiguous since it featured a vigorous and handsome young actor as its hero and only alluded very indirectly to future disasters.

Actors playing historical figures are expected to confirm the icon memory of a character by offering references to well-known visual traits and mannerisms, but also to elaborate an interpretation that is not limited to impersonation.[43] To produce a convincing portrayal, they need to explore the personal or psychological aspects of the person behind the image. Typically, actors stress the need to penetrate and understand a character in order to play them well and bring insight into their conduct.[44] To be convincing they have to master exterior aspects and transcend them. Thus considerable preparation is needed. Like Steiger, Scott and Hoskins watched hours of documentary film on their subject and read about him.[45] Scott developed a perception of Mussolini as an actor and used this as a key to character. The films were not exercises in the revisitation of the grandeur of a leader but rather meditations on the theme of destiny thwarted or derailed, of botched greatness or debased genius rather than true greatness.[46] They used dramatic licence to turn the focus back on the man and address the question of how he experienced the collapse of his charisma. This question would have been a narrow one of relatively limited interest were it not for the fact that this introspection entailed the interrogation of a realm of national experience that raised issues of how defeat and catastrophe were interpreted in cultural memory.

In 2024 the question of representing Mussolini was approached in a different way in the Sky Studios' television adaptation of Antonio Scurati's non-fiction novel *M—Son of the Century*.[47] The combination of Italian director and foreign actor that marked most previous screen representations of Mussolini was in this case reversed, with actor Luca Marinelli being guided by the British film director Joe Wright. Some aspects of Marinelli's preparation were the same as those of his predecessors: he read widely, watched video material and sought to find the human aspect behind the public image.[48] His Mussolini is constantly centre-stage, as had been the case before but, strikingly and unprecedentedly, he breaks the fourth wall at frequent intervals, addressing the audience directly. A century after the events that are portrayed, the Mussolini of this production still wants to charm and seduce. However, Wright brought into play the buffoonish aspects that had always been a part of the dictator's image abroad and which Scurati had rigorously avoided. He thus diverted Mussolini's charisma towards the grotesque. Marinelli, under Wright's close supervision, captured the deep theatricality of a man who always seemed to be performing for someone. The series focuses exclusively on Mussolini's rise to power and his eventual abolition of democracy; it shows his opportunism and unscrupulousness, his complicity in violence and indifference to murder. The intent is unambiguously demystifying; the director provides a lesson from history on the perils of populism that was fully endorsed by the actor, who proclaimed his anti-fascist convictions and his discomfort at radically altering his appearance to play a character for whom he felt no sympathy.[49]

In heroic biographical pictures death scenes serve various purposes. Often, the death of the hero is not so much the conclusion of the story as the beginning of the passage to immortality. Clearly this could not be the case with Mussolini since his story ended in disaster and defeat and his posthumous exhibition was obscene. The films that dealt with the final phase of his career treated the problem in different ways. While Lizzani ended *Mussolini ultimo atto* with a declaration of the justification for the dictator's execution, other films carried the family narrative over into the treatment of the dictator's death. *Claretta* includes ample references throughout to the end that awaits its protagonists. This is conveyed in a contemporary framing narrative. The film ends days before the well-known *dénouement* with a scene in which Claretta explains to her distressed sister Myriam how she finds the strength to face difficulty. Her short speech is delivered in close-up, with intercutting to long shots of the darkened dormitory where they find themselves detained and to a small picture frame on a table containing twin photographs of a younger Mussolini playing the violin and Claretta herself. As she finishes, the screen is filled with another long shot of the room while the rain beats down in gloomy anticipation of the events that will shortly come to pass. The effect of this solution is to depict Claretta as admirable and to contrast her humanity with the brutality of her death. *Io e Mussolini* ends with Edda in mid-range standing in a Swiss clinic as the foreground is occupied by residents and a nun who are seated listening to the radio. She stands emotionless as Radio Free Milan broadcasts the news that that her father and his lover have been shot. The statement by the Northern Resistance that appears in written form at the end of *Mussolini ultimo atto* is read out as part of the bulletin. In *Edda* the same device is used, except on this occasion Edda is sitting alone at home playing solitaire and smoking. As the announcement is broadcast, she ceases playing cards, clasps her hands to her head and, as the soundtrack rises to a crescendo, utters a long, silent scream. The scene is intercut with images of her children playing outside in the garden. The final moments consist of Edda standing at the window looking down on them as the youngest shouts up to her that spring has arrived. Her face is stern and drained but resolute. This is followed by a voiceover reading text, which also appears on the screen, which informs the spectator of the basic facts of the transition to peace. Information is also provided about the fate of Edda and her mother. The dramatisation of the reception of the news of Mussolini's death by his daughter is effective in terms of the narrative, but it has two consequences: first, it privatises an event that was a complex national watershed and, second, it projects the Mussolini family members into the postwar era in the role of bereaved sufferers, which is of course precisely how they sought to position themselves.

Piazzale Loreto presented a challenge for authors of biopics who wished to carry the story through to its conclusion. The display of Fascist bodies in Milan on 29 April 1945 had not formed a basis of national rebirth and it remained an embarrassment that was not part of the collective patrimony.[50] It remained a troubling memory, and in some respects an unrepresentable experience that provided a stark reminder that Italian political history was, to use historian Giacomo Tagliani's graphic expression, spattered with 'flesh, blood and shit'. In fact, only the American drama starring George C. Scott dared to include a re-enactment of the macabre scenes. Decisions by Lizzani and other filmmakers to omit them may be taken less as a sign of restraint than the expression of a concern to avoid a tendency noted by anti-fascists in the postwar years whereby people were moved to pity Mussolini in Piazzale Loreto rather than by the victims of Fascist violence.[51] However, while the decision may have been motivated by anti-fascist sentiments, the effect of this omission was to downplay a shocking but vivid watershed. The gruesome display of the hanging bodies was execrated by right-wing commentators in the postwar years, but it crucially symbolised the nation's detachment from Mussolini and the opening of a new political season.[52]

The omission and the sensitivity around this event signalled the absence of any widespread recognition that the dictator had formed the central linchpin of a collective super-ego. Even in the 1980s and after, a form of psychological subordination persisted in cultural memory. Few in those years indulged in any form of mourning for Mussolini beyond those who felt a political affinity to Fascism. In such circles mourning was in any case rejected in favour of a more positive sentiment of nostalgia that kept Mussolini in the imagination of the living. For the national community, it was by then too late for a process of mourning to occur in the way that it had been conceived by Freud and his followers. But the fact that it had not done so meant that the consequences of the repression and denial of a historical psychological entanglement with the dictator still reverberated. The repeated visual reproduction and re-enactment of Mussolini was the sign of an inconvenient dependency. It was a product of a past in which a dictatorship had moulded lives and minds and still occupied a large place in collective and cultural memory.

Over ten years after the last major television drama of 2000 and six years before Joe Wright's adaptation of *M*, a provocative film was released that was centred not on Mussolini's story but rather on his persistent presence in the imagination. *Io sono tornato* (I have come back, Luca Miniero, 2018) adapted the theme of an earlier film imagining the return of the historical Hitler to present-day Germany to the Italian context. Discarding the historical scrupulousness of the biopics, it had the Mussolini of Piazzale Loreto, played by actor Massimo Popolizio, miraculously return to life.[53] Disorientated, the revenant asks for directions to Piazza Venezia and lets himself into the uninhabited Villa Torlonia, where he spends the night and is awakened the next morning by a visiting party of schoolchildren. Greeted as he wanders the streets by a mixture of scripted and ostensibly spontaneous reactions from a public seemingly obsessed with the negative impact of immigration on Italian identity, Mussolini finds to his satisfaction that some of his habitual themes still have currency. He becomes the star of a television show and a famous personality all over again. A disturbing historical rewind, the film does not so much exorcise Mussolini's posthumous hold over the imagination as exploit it to present the Italians with a figure who is less an unwelcome reminder of the past than a distorted and paradoxical mirror image of some of the ways in which the Mussolini cult still resonated.

15

Pop culture and cultural memory

The live Mussolini figured in the Italian imagination in several ways: as figure of power, as fantasy, as projection and as a being at once remote and seemingly close at hand. He was a conscious presence, a protagonist of news and events, as well as an unconscious one, a spectral resident of dreams and desires. Death brought an end to his earthly existence but not to his fantasy one. Mussolini's posthumous reverberations in a variety of media and social and political spheres testify to a vitality which took different forms in different periods. Mussolini's image was commodified throughout his time as dictator and that commodification did not cease with his death. 'Mussolini' continued to be a resource for artists, writers and film-makers as well as tourist agencies, souvenir manufacturers and purveyors, bric-a-brac dealers and collectors, and exhibition curators. In the 2000s, the internet would add a whole new dimension to this ghosting by offering a place where an established iconic repertoire could be reproposed and the trade in memorabilia and reproduced artefacts flourish.[1]

How does historical knowledge relate to these developments? Does it provide them with any framework and context? This is a complex matter that is itself conditioned by a range of factors including the receptiveness or otherwise of historians to new sources of information and means of communication, the influence of a range of imperatives including the political and the commercial, and the permeability of cultural context by old and new ideas.[2] Also significant are the triggers and interests that ensure Mussolini retains an iconic currency. Icons are not neutral or exclusively visual. They belong to—and themselves create—shared heritages, they develop identities and create or perpetuate myths. They are dense images in that they are formed over time and emerge from decisive and sometimes traumatic experiences. They occupy a place in memory and are reproducible in a variety of contexts that are real and imaginative. In some, perhaps all, instances they downplay or remove the responsibilities of the past by turning it into a receptacle in which memory often competes successfully with historiography.[3]

In the mid-1990s, Renzo De Felice asserted that, 'The problem of Mussolini, in Italy today, should be a matter only for specialist historians. However, the opposite is the case: historians continue to circle around the Mussolini case without ever wanting to deal with it once and for all. As a result, the field is open and vulnerable to the raids of journalists, eager amateurs, collectors, profiteers, antiquarians'.[4] De Felice perhaps attributed too much influence to historians, for neither his own monumental works nor those of other historians after him stemmed the flow. For historians of a later generation who reflected on this matter, the issue in part was the responsibility of the many scholars who remained aloof from innovation and were not very receptive to new forms of communication and new sites of historical knowledge.[5] Engaging with a plurality of sources, sites and voices, for an older generation especially, was challenging. Pop culture especially lay largely beyond their reach, not only for its content but also for the way it mixes and blends the pseudo-historical and the para-historical. Through it, the past inhabits the present in a way that does not dovetail with any idea of linear historical progression. Rather, it seems to conform to Michel Serres and Bruno Latour's idea that time 'filters', that is to say its passage is better thought of in vertical rather than horizontal terms.[6] As a spatially foldable phenomenon, time loses its conventional specificity: what is near and what is far is subject to change, and the past can never be scythed off from present and future. Modern media keep the past alive in myriad ways that are always selective, often creative and sometimes misleading, ensuring that it is always present and never truly 'over'.

This is not a new phenomenon, as one of the most suggestive ways that the past remains present is through the long-established medium of wax sculpture. Mussolini was represented in international waxwork museums like the London Madame Tussauds in the 1920s and 1930s and featured in Italian museums after their establishment in the postwar era. In keeping with the strongly political sense of the national community, the scenes and personalities featured in the Rome museum, founded in 1958, were related to key moments in national history.[7] The second most important museum was for many years located within Milan's monumental central station. Rather small, it accorded a prime position to the presidents of the Italian republic. However, it closed at the end of the 1990s as it could no longer compete with major European museums in terms of scale or quality of the models. The statues were bought by a private foundation and are today to be found a long way from their original home in a museum in Gazoldo degli Ippoliti in the province of Mantua.[8]

Today wax figures of the Duce are present in Rome, Madrid and San Francisco, among other locations, although the contexts in which the statues are to be found varies. The Rome museum, which is centrally located close to Piazza Venezia, for many years featured a reduced version of the famous meeting of the Fascist Grand Council on 25 July 1943 in the Sala del Pappagallo in Palazzo Venezia. This was dismantled some years ago and today a Mussolini waxwork (not the one that was previously seated at the Grand Council) is to be found standing in the company of a small number of international leaders. He has Donald Trump to his right, Hitler to his left and Mao Tse Tung and Barack Obama to his far left. He is bare-headed and attired in a simple grey uniform (see Figure 21). Although the resemblance is not perfect, as it seldom is with waxworks, he is recognisably the Duce of the 1943–45 RSI period, grim and unsmiling. The decontextualised setting removes the implication of impending

Figure 21. Wax figure of Mussolini in the Rome waxworks museum. Author's own photograph.

defeat and arrest that was present formerly. Instead, he is configured in a curiously ahistorical fashion as belonging to a generic category of 'world leaders' that makes no distinction between past and present, democrats and tyrants. All five figures are male twentieth- or twenty-first-century figures, but otherwise they have little in common beyond their strong place in either memory or the present-day international imagination, as befits an attraction that is geared mainly to tourists. The positioning of Hitler in a similar grouping in the Berlin Madame Tussauds, which was inaugurated in 2008, provoked questions as to why he was not set apart as a monster or placed together with great criminals of the past in a chamber of horrors.[9] Beyond the fact that macabre rooms of this type are not as popular as they once were, the answer is simply that for waxworks museums the only thing that matters is fame, regardless of whether that is moral or immoral, deserved or undeserved.[10] In fact, to keep up with changing tastes and interests, the larger international museums regularly remove from display statues depicting men and women whose celebrity has declined.

As a waxwork figure, Mussolini is both easy and difficult. An icon in his lifetime, who was reducible to a handful of ready traits (the round head, jutting jaw, hands on hips), he should not pose a great challenge to wax figure artists. Yet wax figures are mainly about the face and head rather than the body or the pose, except in so far as a figure is associated with obvious props. The faceless killer Jack the Ripper, for example, has to be defined by his Victorian clothing and a weapon.[11] Hitler has his hair and moustache, as well as the swastika, Trump an orange face and blonde back-combed hair. Mussolini has none of these, and so much depends on the rendering of a face that was less a site of symbolic value than a body that, by contrast, was considered an asset or even the essence of the leader's authority.[12] The tableau of the Fascist Grand Council captured the end of the myth while the RSI Mussolini presents the politically posthumous leader. Other waxworks of the Duce, however, attempt to capture Mussolini in his heyday but can never convey the charismatic one man show who dominated the Fascist regime. Instead, they present a reduction, that is to say a figure that has neither iconic value nor photogenic charisma.[13] Unlike Roland Barthes's Abbé Pierre—the subject of one of the short essays in his *Mythologies*—whose iconography was imbued with 'all the signs of apostleship' and saintliness, but in a predictable and ready-made way,[14] waxwork Mussolinis fail to elevate the man to the status of symbol and—perhaps fittingly—leave him looking like a thug in uniform.

Waxwork statues have an eerie quality to them. Quasi-human and yet devoid of life, they have an affinity with marble and metal sculptures that have been erected to many great figures. Yet they are both more lifelike, in the sense that they possess realistic human features and are made of softer material, and less impressive in that they are not idealised or placed on pedestals. The statues do not command respect and are often mocked and ridiculed for their failure to capture an accurate likeness and their stiff artificiality. They are the product of a hyper-real art that often, paradoxically, fails to correspond fully to our perception of the real. If hyper-realism is, as French thinker Jean Baudrillard states, 'the meticulous reduplication of the real, preferably through another reproductive medium',[15] with each transmedial step simultaneously volatising and reinforcing the real, then wax art represents an interruption, for the end result is not 'reality for its own sake' but something that is still evidently an approximation, an imperfect simulacrum or an embalmed version of reality.

Wax figures bring a deceased personality into the present but in a way that is neither flattering nor truly enduring. They are alive in appearance but dead in all other respects. In this they have something in common with shop mannequins, dolls, ventriloquists' dummies and puppets, though they lack the visual or verbal expressiveness of the last two of these. They attract the curious and offer a take on celebrity that coincides with contemporary hierarchies of value while also being a leftover of an era when the effigy had the power to offer a semblance of life and thus to startle. They are a legacy of an earlier era of personalisation, before the age of the ready reproduction of images, when the living struggled to find satisfactory prompts to venerate a deceased figure of respect like a monarch. The nineteenth-century French author and art critic Champfleury found that waxwork figures were excessively descriptive, obsessed with surface detail at the expense of character.[16] They evoked in him a primitive fear that derived from their being simultaneously less and more complete than painting and sculpture. The source of this fear lies in the fact that, while they may be three dimensional, unlike painting, and more lifelike than sculpture, wax figures more closely resemble dead human beings than either of these media. He likened them to the assembled corpses in a morgue and compared the injections used to make cadavers seem alive to the make-up of wax faces. 'For Champfleury', critic Sarah Pappas argues, 'wax figures reproduce the most horrifying human reality: our own inevitable demise, both inciting his curiosity and repelling him at the same time'.[17]

Waxwork figures communicate no message about the role in history or politics of those they depict beyond confirming their fame or notoriety. In a way though they offer the potential to act as a source of understanding on account of the questions they raise about celebrity and power, good and evil, mass tastes and popular culture, animate and inanimate, life and death. In his extraordinary seven-hour-long film *Hitler—Ein Film aus Deutschland* (Hitler—A Film from Germany, 1978), Hans-Jürgen Syberberg conducted a thorough interrogation of the significance of the Führer in the German imagination. Conceived as a response to the supposed objectivity of journalist Joachim Fest's well-received television documentary *Hitler, eine Karriere* (Hitler, a career, 1977) which (like the documentaries of RAI TV discussed in Chapter 13) relied heavily on images created by the Nazi propaganda machine, he produced a hybrid that shattered conventional aesthetic and genre categories and challenged established interpretations of the political problem of Hitler by invoking high and mass culture.[18] His film is a deconstructed, fragmented total work of art that offers up different Hitlers: a waxwork, a puppet, an automaton, a ventriloquist's dummy, a toy dog and a zombie-like figure rising from the grave, and as well as a crazed dictator. Syberberg, in other words, constructs a personal chamber of horrors featuring declinations of one exhibit that, in the contemporary imagination, is the most horrifying of all.

Controversially, *Hitler—Ein Film aus Deutschland* grants space to Hitler, as well as Goebbels, Speer and Himmler to offer self-justifications and explanations, thereby giving rise to the suspicion that the director was too sympathetic to a figure he clearly saw not as a usurper or brutish interloper but as a figure who 'belonged' to the Germans, who was the product of their shared culture and whose allure lingered ghoulishly in the imagination. Syberberg, it has been argued, refused to treat Hitler as a historical subject like any other or to indulge the market for Hitler material. Instead, he was interested in the Hitler who had wormed his way into the collective psyche, the blank cypher. For some observers the mass psychological aspects of the film evoked the writings of Adorno and the Mitscherlichs, but the focus is more on the genesis of a myth rather than on its impact and duration. The film positions German historical figures like King Ludwig of Bavaria and Wagner as a backdrop, but a master of ceremonies calls on a range of real and imaginary characters including Napoleon, Charlie Chaplin, Caligula and Frankenstein to present themselves and to play Hitler. Hitler is an amalgam of elements drawn from the circus, the toyshop, the fairground and cinema. While Leni Riefenstahl's propaganda films, starting with the film of the 1934 Nuremberg rally, *Triumph of the Will*, contained elements drawn from the world of entertainment that were refashioned to achieve a specific purpose, Syberberg's aim was to examine how this sort of assemblage had been achieved.[19] His film explores the relationship between Hitler and cinema, taking in the way the medium impacts on identity and structures of feeling, channelling spectatorship and stimulating emotional engagement.[20]

Syberberg embraces Max Picard's view of the modern age as being fundamentally fragmentary, in which different disjointed elements are seeking recomposition. 'Only in a world of total discontinuity could a nullity such as Hitler become Fuehrer', Picard declared.[21] He was the one stable point in world in constant flux. Propaganda uses visual politics to create the impression of such a reunification in a way that is political and not yet fully dependent on the commodity and consumerism. Syberberg is interested in cinema as phantasmagoria and for this reason he makes connections between Hitler and Hollywood, in contrast to Siegfried Kracauer who, in his famous 1947 book *From Caligari to Hitler*, saw the unsettling German expressionist films of the 1920s as premonitions of Hitler's rise.[22]

No film of the power and originality of *Triumph of the Will* was produced in Italy and nor was any film like Syberberg's.[23] But the director's reflections have an application, for he did not limit the relevance of his investigations to Germany. He believed that anyone who wants the support of all of the people, the mass, or to have a big impact on them, is an incipient Hitler. There are Hitlers everywhere, in his view.[24] 'I think the systems we know from history—either Hitler, or the Soviet Union, or the western society of consumer ideas—do not want individuals', he stated: 'They want each being to sacrifice part of its own substance. They want us to follow the lines of only one idea, of buying things, or the ideology of Hitler, Franco, Mussolini, Lenin, Stalin, or what follows'.[25] In contrast to those who sought to separate Fascism and Nazism, he argued for the unity of all regimes. He saw his film as an antidote against uniformity, against the single idea, seeing it as a film *from* Germany that offered a warning, rather than a film *about* Germany. The Nazi regime bequeathed to posterity a morbid fascination with everything to do with Nazism, he claimed, whether that was tourism, publishing, the production of souvenirs or entertainments.[26] '"Our" Hitler belonged not just to Germany but to cinema audiences and even to the West as a whole'. His legacy as universal object of interest testifies to this.

This was a challenging argument, for Mussolini is rarely seen in this way, as a product of mass psychology in the age of mass culture. As a leader, he was always more tangible, more real, more human, than Hitler. Nonetheless, the world of cinema and the media was important to his cult of personality and the more complex and articulated media world of the twenty-first century have been the prime arena for the repurposing of Mussolini as a celebrity in a later era. To focus on Mussolini as a star or celebrity is not to shift the focus of analysis of the personality cult to a terrain that ignores the political and underplays the Fascist system of organised acclamation of the Duce. It is rather to add layers to the analysis which assist in understanding the nature of the hold he achieved in popular culture as well as the persistence of a posthumous cult that extended, in some of its forms, well beyond the sphere of neo-fascism. Mussolini rose to power before Hitler in an age that witnessed modern innovations in communications, transport and the sensory environment. It was one that brought extraordinary fame and acclaim to a limited number of people including film stars like Charlie Chaplin and Mary Pickford, aviators like Charles Lindbergh and sports champions including baseball hero Babe Ruth and boxer Jack Dempsey.[27] In Italy, it was people like the cinema strongman Maciste, the diva Francesca Bertini or the poet turned aviator and politician Gabriele D'Annunzio who achieved mass attention. Mussolini, the magnetic embodiment of national redemption, emanated from this cultural environment as much as from the sphere of popular politics.

Fascism opposed aspects of commercial culture while embracing and manipulating others. This phenomenon was not wholly separate from the regime's own propaganda efforts, but nor was it entirely reducible to these. Magazines and postcard manufacturers were among those who exploited Mussolini's popularity for commercial ends by using his image on the covers or in endless series of postcards. The majority of the eight million postcards of Mussolini that entered circulation during the life of the regime were not produced by the Fascist Party or official organisations; they were made and sold by private companies.[28] As early as 1922, vendors of toiletries were selling a soap bar in the shape of Mussolini's head, while shopkeepers placed his image in their window displays. More than Hitler, whose opposition to the avant-garde ensured the conventional nature of Nazi art, Mussolini developed an image that was expanded and reworked by modern artists. The avant-garde contributions to the cult remain striking, as are the photomontages that not only transmitted a political message but also turned Mussolini into a modernist icon. These hold a place in art history and had an influence on commercial culture. In their time, images that presented fusions of leader and mass had the purpose of 'casting the image of the masses in the image of the leader and/or the state and vice versa'.[29] Mussolini's profile drawn over a mass crowd, or his face composed of, or his body immersed in, a crowd, now belong to the history of photomontage and the documentarist aesthetic. Already in the 1930s, this type of representation was not confined to propaganda but spread to advertising.[30] Today it has a marked period feel because the mass aesthetic does not function in the same way. Nevertheless, similar motifs are occasionally employed. Mussolini himself has sometimes reappeared in such unlikely locations as advertisements for Venice's Excelsior Hotel, in detective novels or in films like Guillermo del Toro's stop-motion animated fantasy *Pinocchio* (2022), which moves the tale's setting from the nineteenth century to the Fascist period and deploys a pompous Duce-like figure as a signifier of censorship and repression.

Such was his gift for self-promotion that some have compared Mussolini to the promoter Barnum or to the director of big-budget cinematic spectaculars, Cecil B. de Mille. Historians have noted the simultaneous sacralisation and commercialisation of politics under Fascism, a point evident in photographs of a god-like Mussolini addressing crowds in squares adorned with large advertisements for Martini and Cinzano.[31] 'The star-as-god and the star-as-merchandise, which are two facets of the same reality, refer, in the first case, to a fundamental anthropology and, in the second, to the sociology of the twentieth century', the sociologist Edgar Morin noted.[32] Despite efforts to conceptualise Fascism as an all-consuming religion, the people who gathered to hear and see the Duce were people who also went to the cinema, read magazines, took an interest in fashion and looked at advertisements and shop windows.[33] Mussolini was a feature of an emergent mass culture no less than he was a politician.

A multiplicity of media including photography, cinema, the illustrated press, radio, gramophone records and posters, as well as architecture, wall inscriptions, sculpture and painting, were harnessed to the task of bolstering the personality cult. Mussolini was seen and heard by millions of people, both in person and through mass communications. To some extent, therefore, it can be said that he became a permanent feature of the mediatic repertoire of the nation. He was a 'massifier' rather than a 'democratiser', a tyrant who drew people into a form of community while dramatically restricting free expression. What happened after his death? If a historian as prominent as Renzo De Felice presented in his works a Mussolini that not completely detached from the image of the dictator transmitted by the regime itself, then it cannot be surprising that aspects of this image remained in wider circulation or still have some currency today. For De Felice, Mussolini's disappearance was an interruption more than a repudiation or a detachment. 'Without the catastrophe, the Italian ruling class, the fascist bourgeoisie and even the popular classes would have had neither the interest nor the force to cast off fascism. Or even

Mussolini', he argued.[34] The only mass repudiation that occurred was of his dead body in Piazzale Loreto, but, while this was important symbolically, it was a complex event that did not involve directly or indirectly the whole population. In parts of the community, instances of silence and resignation testified to continuing ties and dependency. After repudiation came not oblivion but reabsorption into a memory sphere in which simplified or tendentious narratives often prevailed over historiography.

The star aspects of Mussolini as a public personality of his time provide a key to the way in which he occupied a place in the star system of the postwar years. This sort of posthumous remediation should not be surprising as even *Triumph of the Will*, which was perhaps the single most significant contribution to the creation of the cult of the Führer, can be seen both in terms of its contribution to Fascist aesthetics and its later impact on cinematic imagery, advertising and pop videos.[35] Nazi propaganda did not stand in isolation from popular culture and therefore could not easily be made wholly taboo after the war. Mussolini was a product of Italian political culture, but also a formative figure in the nation's mass consciousness.

In this respect he can be likened to one of the 'strange angels' that critic Andy Bull discusses in his exploration of the posthumous resonance of some celebrities.[36] Seeking to explain the permanent place occupied in the western imagination by Marilyn Monroe, Elvis Presley and James Dean, Bull identifies four contributory factors: they achieved fame at a time that in hindsight seemed simpler, optimistic, affluent and idealistic; they were at the pinnacle of a popular culture the world loved and envied; the seamy side of their lives was concealed while they lived and its later exposure came too late to alter their image; they emerged at a time when relatively few stars were known to all.[37] The biggest idols of the present come from the past for a reason, he argues: 'We want them to embody all the rosy-tinted appeal of a lost time of perceived hope and happiness'.[38]

Mussolini is hardly surrounded by a rosy aura of past happiness. His place in the imagination was eroded in this last years of his rule by a number of factors: the alliance with and subordination to Hitler, military setbacks, war weariness, hardships and dissatisfaction with the inefficiency and corruption of the regime. Subsequently, the brutality of the German occupation of northern and central Italy, his cowardly attempt to flee, his death and desecration in April 1945 were all devastating blows. Despite all this, he is wrapped in a strange and irrational aura, a haunting reminder of a past that was and is far from being seen by everyone as the worst time in national history.

The role of echoes and evocations in Bull's notion of the strange angel points to the complex connection between the historical existence of the cult of Mussolini and the mass cultural universe that took shape in the postwar period. Fascist aesthetics aimed to transcend commercial culture to invest the everyday with mythic resonance. Its practitioners rejected the ironic, the temporary and the ugly and treated the relationship between the individual and the mass in a hierarchical way that precluded dreams of personal fulfilment. However, hybridity was always a feature of it: there was space for consumerist dreams, the star system was not entirely dominated by the regime and nor was popular entertainment. As in Germany, elements of Fascist popular culture, that was itself eclectic and sponge-like, persisted into the postwar years.[39] There was no sharp break or radical new departure although there were substitutions and a new horizons that came with the transition to the democratic era. New cultural forms linked to the Resistance, including cinematic neorealism, were more influential than they were in Germany.

Analyses of representations and treatments of Hitler in contemporary culture suggest that the themes and fragments that passed into the postwar period, after remaining semi-dormant, contributed in the 1980s to a normalisation of the Nazi past and even of Hitler. This accelerated in the new millennium so that a figure once seen as the epitome of evil became something more ambiguous and multifaceted, a resource for comedy and entertainment, a hook for counterfactual history, a meme.[40] In this way Hitler was humanised and the view of the Nazi regime as exceptional was replaced by an understanding of it as a part of the national past that was perhaps neither better nor worse than other parts. Long-standing efforts in right-wing German culture to normalise the Nazi period and not judge it morally—which always ran up against efforts to accept responsibility and atone—were boosted by a series of factors.[41] These included a generational turnover, that brought to prominence those with no personal memory of the 1930s and 1940s, the increasing remoteness of the period in question (and therefore its passage into cultural memory), a shift in representation from documentary to dramatic reconstruction, and the trend towards aestheticisation, as well as relativisation and universalisation.[42] The last-mentioned word refers to the commercial exploitation of Nazi symbols and the Hitler image emptied of content, and to the focus in films on the early political years (when he was still an outsider) and the late period (when he was broken and defeated). The focus on these two periods humanises the Nazi leader by avoiding any representation of him in his prime.[43] In this, German films followed the same pattern as the Italian ones examined in Chapter 14. The criminality and the guilt of the subject are elided in treatments which use the dictator to express grievances or consider possible alternate histories. Narratives of the young activist, struggling and making his way, or the aged and isolated dictator, provided the raw material for subsequent portrayals that mocked him or turned him into something different from what he was. No one ever dreamed of portraying the instigator of the Holocaust as a Jew, but the chameleon-like Mussolini was sometimes blended in the melting pot of popular media with the forms and traits of the victims of Fascist aggression: in the comic art series *Quando c'era lui* (When he was around) the Duce returns to life thanks to the genetic engineering of a Nazi scientist who is engaged by a hapless gang of Fascist sympathisers. However, in a telling paradoxical reference to colonial atrocities and present-day racism, he returns with black skin (see Figure 22).[44]

Figure 22. Mussolini returns to life, thanks to the marvels of science, '...but he is black!' From the comic book fantasy *Quando c'era lui* by Stefano Antonucci, Daniele Fabbri and Mario Perrotta (Brescia: Shockdom, 2017). Illustration courtesy of Stefano Antonucci.

The mainstreaming of Mussolini in present-day culture produced a shift away from him in sectors of the far right. With Mussolini no longer cast as dangerous Other, some sought something less acceptable and more radical. This led to a proliferation in certain of Nazi symbols and swastikas in certain circles in place of the more conventional busts and trinkets featuring the Duce.[45] But even these groups were not immune to cultural eclecticism. One journalist who visited the meeting places of a neo-fascist group called Blocco studentesco (Student Bloc), whose members greeted each other with raised-arm Fascist salutes, was surprised to find what he called 'extraneous bodies' among the range of their iconographic references: 'alongside the Futurism of Marinetti, in many sections of the Blocco images of Mussolini and Nietzsche sit together with those of Marx, Che Guevara and Arbore, yes Renzo Arbore' (a popular Neapolitan entertainer and musician not known for his right-wing sympathies).[46] The wax museum-style jumbling of icons and personalities testified to the range of possible reference points within the contemporary mass cultural universe that can be mobilised by the far right. However, Mussolini's old charisma still has a power in certain spheres. Politicians, mostly of the right, have channelled Mussolini since the 1980s, and the aggressive masculinity he symbolises has also been associated with football and crime. Groups of die-hard fans ('Ultras') of some football clubs have been known to chant Fascist slogans and give raised-arm salutes during matches while also engaging in hooliganism during and outside of them. This applied notably to Lazio, at one time Mussolini's own favoured team, several of whose players at various times declared their support for the MSI.[47]

Historian Richard Bosworth has referred to a process of 'de-ideologisation' of the Fascist dictatorship's history and 'the cancelling of a moral stance towards the relatively recent events of the past'.[48] In relation to Mussolini specifically, this process has occurred in such a way that the historical judgement on the role he played has struggled to assert itself in some areas against indulgent memory and the resonances of material culture. Paradoxically, the indulgent attitude towards him is characteristic of what has been referred to as the 'feminine phenomenon' of nostalgia.[49] This embraces all and promises a mythic reunification of fragmented elements of a conflictual past on the basis of a sense of restored plenitude. Nostalgia, psychoanalysts have argued, occupies an intermediate position between mourning and melancholy.[50] It is a compensatory mechanism that mingles acceptance of loss with denial of any investment in what has been lost. It is marked by forward and backward movements between different spatial and temporal contexts.[51] It has a dual nature, being bound up with feelings of well-being in another time or place and a sense of loss regarding the present.[52] In its reunifying impulse it bears a resemblance to the response to disjointedness that Fascism itself offered. When it hinges on a view of the past that has not been digested through mourning, it is likely to be self-serving. Nostalgia works against 'real history' in ways that can also be dangerous. The danger lies in the residual appeal of authoritarian leadership in periods of flux and uncertainty, especially in countries with experience of it. For this reason, it has been argued that unreflective nostalgia breeds monsters.[53] On the other hand, contaminations with popular culture and commercialisation make it difficult for the ghost of Mussolini to exercise a mobilising role for anything other than ever less specific editions of itself. The cult of Mussolini in this sense continues to have a complex popular cultural aftermath that is multifaceted and can be pulled in different directions. Casting off the dictator's ghost may be urged by anti-fascist historians and others, but his being embedded in popular culture and an ongoing ability to gather devotees makes this a difficult task.

16

The shadow of M

When the writer Antonio Pennacchi won the prestigious Strega prize for his novel *Canale Mussolini* in 2010,[1] he received acclaim for his rich portrayal of a peasant family that relocates from the Veneto to the Lazio region seeking to improve its economic fortunes by farming land awarded to it for political merits by the regime. The title refers to the main canal of the reclaimed area of the Agro Pontino that was named after Mussolini under the regime, but which today is called Canale delle Acque Alte. It is situated not far from the new town of Latina which was inaugurated with the fascistic name of Littoria in the 1932. The draining of swamp land was one of the much-boasted achievements of the regime, a sign of its investment in the modernisation of long-abandoned areas that were infested with malaria-bearing mosquitoes. The real extent of the achievement has been questioned, but in popular memory the reclamation is seen as one of the positive legacies of the regime. The Peruzzi family of the novel is an example of a new class of peasant proprietors that was created precisely through the reclamation of land and the foundation of new towns in Lazio, Sardinia and other regions. This process would represent Fascism's solution to the problems of over-population and under-employment in parts of the peninsula and was the prelude to external imperialism that would find new impulse with the invasion of Ethiopia in 1935. The conquest of new territories at home and abroad was seen as important for national prestige as well as for economic and political reasons.

Initially Socialist, the Peruzzi family turns Fascist after the local Socialists set fire to its haystacks as a reaction to its refusal to take on more labourers. In response, the Peruzzi men burn down the local labour exchange and become bound up with the movement of *squadristi* that constituted the violent grass roots of Fascism. After an economic setback, the family seeks help from the Mussolini government of which they are keen supporters, and it is with the response to these pleas that the novel's odyssey begins. Like many other early beneficiaries of the foundational and imperialist urge, they are rewarded for their loyalty to the regime. Pennacchi was himself born in Latina in 1950 and the novel is a fictionalised version of the story of his own family. Although his politics swung over the years from the far left to the centre left, his initial political involvement, motivated by family tradition, was with the neo-fascist Italian Social Movement (MSI). Pennacchi was interested in memory, and his novel seeks to bear testimony to a rarely recounted experience of political population movement that in the postwar years was, if not precisely an embarrassment, then no longer something to be celebrated in itself. While the Italian empire, lost during World War II, was for years widely ignored or misleadingly remembered, the new towns lost their heroic aura and became routine provincial centres different from others only for their recent creation. One of Pennacchi's repeated complaints is that, with few exceptions, historians have ignored or misrepresented an experience that he felt intensely to be his own, even if he was born after the pioneer phase that saw thousands of families migrate from the Veneto and other regions to resettle in areas that were treated under the regime with special interest and attention.

For many years, it was said that Fascism as a period of history had not inspired any great literature. Mussolini's odyssey did not give rise to novels of the stature of Victor Hugo's *Les Misérables* or Tolstoy's *War and Peace*, both of which featured battles from the Napoleonic era and were influenced by the legend of Napoleon. However, these novels were published respectively in 1862 and, following earlier serialisation, 1869, some fifty years after Waterloo. Neither was centred on Napoleon. The most significant literary treatments of dictators of the twentieth century have been in Latin America, where the 'dictator novel' genre has had some important exponents including Tomas Eloy Martinez (*Saint Evita* and *The Peron Novel*) and Mario Vargas Llosa (*Year of the Goat*).[2] In postwar Italy, there were many novels dealing with various experiences of war and Resistance, some of the latter becoming modern classics. Fewer turned back to the Fascist period and addressed it a self-reflexive way, although Ennio Flaiano's pioneering novel of 1947 *Tempo di uccidere* (Time to Kill) reflected on less than edifying aspects of the colonial experience (see Chapter 5). Some of Alberto Moravia's works including *Il conformista* (The Conformist) were widely read and have been hailed for their frank posing of the question of guilt and of Fascism.[3]

In popular literature, however, Mussolini had a significant presence, mostly in thrillers and minor historical novels. A significant genre in Germany and in time also in Italy was the counter-factual novel and specifically narratives that imagined alternative histories of the war and its outcome. A few examples were published in the 1940s but the bulk of this production dates from the 1980s or after. Mostly remote thematically from the historical experience of the dictatorships, these novels blend elements of fact and fantasy, wishful thinking and dystopian scenarios. In his examination of the normalisation of Nazism in contemporary culture, historian Gavriel Rosenveld devotes some attention to counter-factual narratives, the most popular of which entail the Nazis winning World War II.[4] These narratives, he acknowledges, have different purposes ranging from the critique of present-day trends to relativisation and aestheticisation of the Nazi past. Fictions formulated in the first postwar decades often had a moral resonance that became dulled by the passage of time, leaving the way open to unorthodox and even humorous representations. For obvious reasons, Germany conventionally produced fewer alternate histories on the topic of a Nazi victory in the war, while many were produced in the English-speaking world. Hitler sometimes figured in these narratives, but his presence was not necessary for such books to have a market appeal. In Italy, as in Germany, counter-factual narratives for many years were rare. The first writer to imagine the return of Mussolini to power in Rome was Marco Ramperti, a film journalist of some renown who adhered to the Italian Social Republic, where his anti-semitic views found free reign. From Venice, he poured sarcastic vitriol on those who had benefited from Fascism and then turned their backs on it. Placed in custody at the end of the conflict, Ramperti published a diary of the months he passed, as he put it, 'al fresco' (out in the cold).[5] A supporter of the newly formed MSI, he published a novel in 1950 of clear propagandistic intent, *Benito I imperatore* (Benito I Emperor).[6] In this text, he imagined the return of Mussolini to Rome following a last-minute German victory brought about by secret weapons, where those who had converted to anti-fascism were obliged to perform a further volte-face and once more indulge in adulation of the Duce.

Ramperti's novel has been seen as a key inspiration for a current of imaginative 'fantafascist' fiction that prospered mainly from the 1990s.[7] As in Germany, narratives constructed around visions of alternative outcomes to the war became a minor popular genre. Some fictions of this type envisage a Fascist Italy as it saw itself: powerful, highly militarised, imperialist and internally united.[8] Such imaginary reconstructions have a variety of purposes. While some have critical intents, others bolster the view that the only thing Mussolini got wrong was his decision to go to war. Some novels accord value to minoritarian or marginalised pro-fascist experiences and seek to rescue them from oblivion. In this sense, they practise a form of revisionism infused with exculpation.[9] Yet others have displayed a satirical or parodic intent in keeping with the trend in Germany noted by Rosenveld and seen by him as examples of trivialisation.[10] The works of one of few significant authors to contribute to this current, Enrico Brizzi—*L'inattesa piega degli eventi* (An Unexpected Turn of Events) and *La nostra guerra* (Our War)—imagine a Fascist regime that remains neutral in 1940 and in 1942 joins the Allies in the war against the Third Reich. It secures a place among the victors and Mussolini remains in power for many years afterwards.[11]

Pennacchi's fictionalised reconstructions have nothing to do with this genre. But there is a slim common thread because his writing is clearly shaped by the wish that events had turned out differently to the way they did. The Peruzzi family was happy under the protection of a regime that its members felt had their interests at heart. Though Mussolini figures only occasionally in *Canale Mussolini*, the novel is permeated by his presence as the head of Fascism, as a benevolent force and as a figure who is perceived by the migrants to the reclaimed lands to be close. In a way that bore a distant resemblance to the inclusion of Napoleon in great novels of the nineteenth century, his novel brought Mussolini into the picture as a supporting literary character. He is first mentioned when the narrator recounts his opposition to the creation of new urban centres in the areas of reclamation. His objection is based on the fear that new towns will undermine the ruralist thrust of the policy, a stance that is modified when he is persuaded that the new populations will require some basic public services and administration. The change of heart is sealed in December 1932, when he comes to the Agro Pontino to inaugurate the city of Littoria, the first of the new foundations, and promises assistance and justice in return for obedience.[12] This is a moment of great communion between the leader and a people grateful for the spartan homes and facilities which have been bestowed on them.[13] The crowd delights in his presence and chants 'Du-ce! Du-ce! Du-ce!' in a noisy chorus of approval. There is a belief that he is an exceptional man, one of those rare figures 'who had the features of a man but who inside had the spirit of a whole people and a whole era', a man with a capital M, 'a Man-God, a Demiurgo, a cosmic power incarnated in a single man, completely different from a normal man'.[14] The narrator—perhaps speaking for the author—adds that 'the real problem—unfortunately—was that at a certain point he himself really believed it', though he does not believe the initial faith in him was misplaced.

The Duce is not a distant figure for the Peruzzi family. Littoria was located only 55 kilometres from Rome, and residents are transported to the capital to fill out the 'oceanic crowds' that are assembled in Piazza Venezia on select occasions to acclaim him. Mussolini also pays off-duty visits to the town, arriving unescorted by car or motor bike. On these occasions—probably more the fruit of fantasy than testimony—he mingles easily with the loyal locals, even drinking wine with them.[15] Like many Italians of the 1930s, the head of the family, Pericle, writes to Mussolini when things are not going as they should, in the knowledge that the matter is likely to be investigated and, he expects, corrected.[16] People who are anyway grateful for the land received also see great improvements to their quality of life with the construction of sports and recreational facilities, buildings for official institutions of various types and the provision of practical services. There is great pride when the Duce decides to come to Littoria to take part in a publicity-driven exercise of harvesting.[17] Images of the shirtless leader threshing the grain would constitute one of the most striking and memorable pieces of propaganda of the entire regime.[18] They testified at once to the regime's ruralist vocation and to the physical prowess of the leader.

In Pennacchi's prose, Mussolini is a benevolent, paternalistic figure. When he comes to Littoria, it seems, the sun always shines. In the book, 'Duce' is spelt with a capital D, not the lower case 'd' that was the Italian convention in the postwar years. The author captures the sense of a family whose life is transformed and turned into an epic by their participation in one of Fascism's heroic achievements. The feeling of being indebted to the regime is exemplified by the fact that, after Mussolini's fall, there are no joyous acts of destruction: 'In fact no-one touched anything on 25 July, not even the marble Fascist symbols on the walls, not even a bust of the Duce—we were the only ones in the whole of Italy, probably because of the story of the debt and the land. Elsewhere already at 6.00 in the morning people were there with chisels in hand'.[19] When Mussolini was reinstated to power with Hitler's support, it was as though normality was restored. Hundreds volunteered enthusiastically to fight for the RSI without having to wait to be called up.[20] Referring to the head of the republic's army, Pennacchi's narrator reports with pride that 'Graziani would have had to shoot us to stop us going to join up', adding—in a rare criticism of the policies of the regime—that if the land had been distributed to the peasants more widely then maybe the Resistance would never have expanded in the way that it did.[21] Littoria is subjected to repeated aerial bombing that results in the destruction of many of the town's symbolic buildings on which men and boys had worked with pride. The Peruzzi men defend their land alongside the Germans against the Americans, the Mussolini canal forming the front line of a four-month-long trench war that leaves 30,000 dead and the whole area devastated.[22]

The end of Mussolini is recounted in detail in neutral prose, with a negative judgement being given on the behaviour of the Milanese people who had acclaimed him for a final time on 16 December 1944 only to deride his cadaver on 29 April 1945.[23] Pennacchi seems to speak for himself when it is stated that 'That scorn—that horrendous evil of Piazzale Loreto, that out-and-out ancestral purification—enabled the Italian people, enabled the Nation, to rid itself of twenty years of support for Fascism'.[24] In Littoria, the matter was not digested easily: for the older people, Mussolini 'was one of the family at certain moments';[25] the very idea of the fatherland was closely bound up with the Fascist political religion. The change of name from Littoria to Latinia occurred in November 1944, before the name was then modified to Latina in April 1945. No longer blessed with special attentions, the residents of the new towns needed a new protector. After some time has elapsed there is some acknowledgement of the liberty that the Americans brought along with health improvements and other tangible benefits.[26] Politically, the choice was not difficult as the orientation had always been pro-government: 'Those of us who hailed from the Veneto region all became Christian Democrats'.[27]

Pennacchi's narrator, a member of the Peruzzi family who tells his story in colloquial Italian with occasional recourse to a bastardised Veneto dialect, is not exactly the author's own, although his emotions are inflected by those of the author. Mussolini is seen to still inhabit the mental universe of the people of Littoria after the war and, in the words of the author of the preface to *Canale Mussolini*, Lucio Carraciolo, his ghost—a phantasm who still visits 'Littoria' and who continues on his night-time excursions to speak with people there—is grateful to Pennacchi. Following the journalist Indro Montanelli and the author of the first substantial Italian imaginary trial of Mussolini, Mario Caudana, Carraciolo resurrects the voice of Mussolini, in this case to pay tribute to the author: 'At last someone who understands me! If he had been born earlier, I would have appointed him to the Minculpop [Ministry of Popular Culture], with the brief for Public Works!', he has the ghost exclaim.[28] In fact, Pennacchi was a chronicler and posthumous witness rather than a politician or propagandist; his perspective was not properly a Fascist or a neo-fascist one. His writings, which include a volume of narrative accounts of a selection of the many new towns founded under Fascism, are works of fiction that are infused with memories and presented as historical legacy.[29] He was a writer who turned himself into a historian in order that his family experience and that of the community of which it was a part should become recognised and acknowledged. His was not a working through that had as its end goal a detachment from a historical experience but rather the opposite: a working through that was designed to remedy a repression, a de-realisation, that had been operated by a historiography shaped by the postwar anti-fascist consensus.[30] His reconstructions were simultaneously detached, in the sense that he had no personal experience of the events described, and deeply attached in the way they evoked without judging and gave voice to those he believed to have been overlooked. Before his death in 2021, he contested historians at numerous turns, always drawing on memory and sometimes on archives too to deliver a sympathetic account of places and people who had been filtered out of postwar history.

Despite Pennacchi's passionate portrayal of the land reclamation, it is a matter of some dispute whether Mussolini should be credited with the status of a project that became central to Fascist propaganda.[31] Initiatives to tackle the swamplands and the disease that prospered there began before Fascism came to power and would continue long afterwards, reaching an acceptable level of achievement in the postwar period with the aid of funds from the Marshall Plan and the Italian government's Southern Development Fund. It is beyond doubt that Fascism invested vast resources in the project and provided financial incentives of all kinds to those engaged in working the reclaimed land. The historian De Felice, however, dismissed the results as inferior to both the original plan and to the expectations that had been raised by the publicity that accompanied reclamation and the establishment of new towns.[32] In brief, the regime's true achievements in this area were modest. However, in Pennacchi's prose, the Fascist phase is a heroic, formative one, even if it is not without illusions and self-deception. The sense of pride and even gratitude lingers in his account of the towns. Despite the Christian Democrats becoming the new reference point from the late 1940s, the neo-fascist MSI acquires a strong base of support because of this. Fascism was not something that could be wiped away: 'In the entire body of the country—in every small stratum of the Italian people—except for miniscule exceptions—people shared to the last all the faults, the glories, the good things and the bad things of Fascism—Pennacchi argues—even those like me who were not born and those who have not been born yet… [because] in the same identical conditions we would have done exactly the same identical things'.[33] In his interpretation, Mussolini's was not a dictatorship founded on repression; he did not divide and rule but rather united and socialised in order to rule: 'The Mussolinian dictatorship is nothing other, in substance, than a tribunate of the plebeians', he judges. 'It is founded on the masses. On the consent of the masses. And the fact that this unanimous consent lasted without interruption... [until] the Americans arrived in Sicily and our legions melted in the sun, is the glaring demonstration of this fact'.[34]

The new towns promoted a vigorous, spartan lifestyle to the position of model as part of the regime's effort to change the character of the Italians. Their creation was informed by, and served as preparation for, the imperialist drive that that would see Italy invade Ethiopia in 1935 and proclaim a new Italian empire. Motivated by a desire to avenge the humiliations of the past and assert Italy's rightful status as a great power, the occupation of the horn of Africa was portrayed as a form of popular imperialism in which the people were fully drawn into a noble and timely collective endeavour. Emotional engagement in this historic enterprise was promoted by myriad forms of propaganda. The task of Luce Institute newsreels was not so much to inform as to actively form opinion.[35] Other media gave striking visual impulse to an enterprise that commanded widespread consent. The cult of the Duce was given cartographic form through images of areas and territories in which a collective hero formed of masses of people was guided by an all-seeing leader.[36] Just as those who settled in the new towns were loyalists who owed allegiance to Mussolini, so the colonists, whether soldiers or civilians, were strongly infused with the idea that they were going to Africa 'with Mussolini'. The brutal violence that characterised first conquest and then Italian rule was concealed from the domestic population while the huge effort of infrastructural development carried out by the Italian 'civilisers' was widely proclaimed. Convinced that Ethiopia was 'theirs for good', the emigrants built roads and railways, schools, factories, hospitals, hotels and so on, giving rise to self-justifying perceptions of a noble Italian endeavour that would long linger in popular memory and that would be promoted after the war by a network of associations which defended the Italian role in Africa.[37] The colonial novel enjoyed a heyday during the regime and, albeit with some modifications, it continued to prosper in minor form long afterwards.[38]

Pennacchi in some ways had more in common with the authors of these works than with the writers who tackled the legacy of empire in the late twentieth and early twenty-first centuries and did so in a critical key. Overturning the imperial idea of Africa as an empty space, these later writers concentrated on the peoples and territories that were colonised, elaborating highly critical perspectives on the violence and repression that accompanied Italian rule from the outset and the forms of apartheid that marked it from 1938. These experiences were of course absent in the Italian new towns. Fictional works, some of them authored by writers with family connections to colonists, scrutinised familial and national legacies. Many of them were authored by women and some in English rather than Italian. Such texts provided a means of working through experiences that had been documented by revisionist researchers following in the footsteps of pioneering anti-colonial historian Angelo Del Boca.[39] Memories of atrocities, poison gas attacks and massacres such as those which followed the assassination attempt on the first viceroy of Ethiopia Rodolfo Graziani in 1937 loom large, as does the Italian sense of racial superiority and impunity. In novels such as *Sangue giusto* by Francesca Melandri, *The Shadow King* by Maaza Mengiste and *The Fourth Shore* by Virginia Baily, the portrayal of the empire as a civilising mission is dismantled to give voice or representation to those who were the victims rather than the beneficiaries of Italy's brief presence in Eastern Africa.[40] These novels also seek to project the history of Italian imperialism into public consciousness and provoke a long-overdue reflection. Melandri's novel in particular, it has been argued, with its explicit aim of challenging the mystifications of journalist Indro Montanelli—who was accustomed to flights of nostalgia about his colonial adventures, which included a form of marriage to an adolescent Ethiopian girl—permits the reader to understand how the history of involvement in Africa was inscribed within Italy's transcultural past, its present and its possible future.[41]

In most of these narratives, the paternal presence of Mussolini that is evoked by Pennacchi is remote if not absent. Only in *The Shadow King* does a figure dubbed Mussoloni [*sic*] find mention. 'Mussoloni' is the mental image that Ethiopians have formed of the Italian leader, the modified name conveying a sense of great size and of the oppressiveness of the foreign dictator who was determined to fascistise their country. There is a touch of the grotesque in the less than deferential distortion of the nomenclature. This imagined figure exists alongside and is informed by the historical Mussolini, who is recalled as 'narrow-eyed and stern-jawed' appearing on film on a white horse before a statue of Julius Caesar.[42] Photographs as well as newsreels link past and present in a novel that is alert to the power of representation. The camera's gaze is seen in terms of a 'beam of light' casting itself across 'Africa's dark borders, ushering men toward greatness', while western foreign correspondents are seen as complicit in the depiction of the Duce as a reformer and redeemer.[43] A mysterious, imaginary 'shadow king' spurs on the Ethiopian resistance after the exile of Haile Selassie, who is seen as a more suggestive and complex figure than the posturing demi-god who is constantly acclaimed by the Italians during and outside of the many political rituals they have imported.

The demystificatory approach was alien to Pennacchi, who failed to see connections between what he depicts as a heroic endeavour and the brutal practices of Mussolini's imperial drive. He achieves his elevation of a localised experience by radically excluding less savoury aspects of Fascist rule and everything beyond Italy's borders. It would fall to another, younger writer, Antonio Scurati, to integrate colonial aggression into a broader treatment of Fascism and its founder. Scurati embraced the notion of the 'documentary novel' to describe his method of bringing documents and proofs into his text to support his narration and demonstrate that it was based on truth. Quotations from speeches, newspaper articles and documents of various sorts provide the aspect of documentation. More systematically and ambitiously than Pennacchi, he would apply the documentary method in a series of novels devoted to the figure of Mussolini. Published between 2018 and 2022, *M—Il figlio del secolo* (M—Son of the Century), *M—l'uomo di provvidenza* (M—The Man of Providence) and *M—Gli ultimi giorni d'Europa* (M—The Last Days of Europe) offer fictionalised accounts of three key phases in Mussolini's career: his rise to power and the establishment of a dictatorship, his becoming the infallible leader at the centre of a personality cult, and the events which led to him taking Italy to war alongside Germany in 1940.[44] A further two volumes, *M—l'ora del destino* (M—The Hour of Destiny) and *M—La fine e il principio* (M—The End and the Beginning) dealing with the aftermath of his removal from power and final drawn-out demise were published respectively in 2024 and 2025.[45] Each volume is between four hundred and around seven hundred pages long, making the work the first sustained effort on the part of a writer of fiction to turn Mussolini's rise and decline into a compelling and troubling national story. The books are presented to some degree as the fruit of imagination—the word *romanzo* (novel) appears on the cover of each volume—but they are largely factual accounts of events and persons that are real. They respect history and proclaim their accuracy, even though they are the work of a novelist engaging with historical material that is remote in time.

What was Scurati trying to do? His aims were not those of Pennacchi. In some respects, his work could be compared for its scale and ambition with Renzo De Felice's enormous biography of Mussolini that appeared in eight volumes over a thirty-year period. However, as a writer of novels, his approach and indeed his aims were different. His purpose was to shed light on historical events by merging historical investigation and imaginative recreation. Moreover, his perspective is avowedly anti-fascist and this does not waver; no one could accuse him of undue sympathy for his subject in the way that the historian was accused of taking too forgiving a view. Scurati's narrative is, as the reviewer for the French magazine *Esprit* observed, 'democratic'.[46] In 2019, the novel was awarded the prestigious Strega prize that had been awarded to Pennacchi in 2010. The author dedicated the prize 'to those who fought against Fascism'. Mussolini is never excused or justified; he is nailed to his responsibilities. Scurati was aiming at a far wider readership than most historians. De Felice achieved great influence beyond his professional peers—in part through his book interviews—but his readership was circumscribed. His prose was often difficult and his argumentation contorted; his extended meticulous reconstructions required a level of interest and concentration that was beyond most. Denis Mack Smith and many other biographers succeeded better in attracting the general reader, but their reach paled by comparison with what could be achieved by a best-selling author. In fact, it was reported that *M—Il figlio del secolo* was being translated in forty countries and later that it had sold 600,000 copies, a success that would lead to the commissioning of the international television adaptation directed by Joe Wright (see Chapter 14).[47]

Born in Naples in 1969, Scurati grew up at a time when Fascism, though still very much a part of the collective memory of the old, was for members of his own generation a historical experience that carried still a present threat. He was imbued with the anti-fascist culture that was thoroughly institutionalised in the 1970s.[48] With the weakening from the 1980s of the anti-fascist sensibility that was so important in the decades after World War II, more positive discourses around Mussolini acquired currency in public debate. There was also a concerted effort to grant legitimacy and citizenship to the memories of those who fought in Fascism's wars, believing that they were honourably serving the fatherland.[49] The vast amount of historical work on some of the criminal aspects of the regime—aspects that had been minimised or glossed in the work of De Felice and others—had a limited incidence on public opinion, which was still conditioned by the rose-tinted representation of Fascism that held sway in popular culture.[50] Scurati aimed to correct an understanding of Fascism that downscales the violence that marked its rise and consolidation as a regime. This had not been fully accepted by public opinion because much of the violence occurred out of view, in the countryside and at night, or in the colonies, which Pennacchi ignored.[51] Taking account of a new focus in historiography on imperialism, he devotes striking attention to the Italian actions in Libya, which became a colony in 1912 and which in the 1920s gave rise to constant rebel attacks on Italian authority. The violent response to these actions is not glossed. The campaigns led by Graziani in the late 1920s, marked by systematic violence in an effort to establish military supremacy, are described in grim detail including the use of chemical weapons. Official documents are quoted to confirm this use, which was denied by the authorities even decades after the loss of the empire and the end of World War II. Describing a ceremony in which King Vittorio Emanuele honours Graziani for his effective campaign of re-conquest, the author notes that the suppression of acts of rebellion entailed mass aerial bombing, hundreds of summary executions and the requisition of cereal harvests with the resulting famine of the civilian population.[52]

Death and violence are seen as core features of Fascism. At the culmination of the second volume, Mussolini is inspecting the exhibition in Rome's Palazzo delle esposizioni that was staged to mark the tenth anniversary of the Fascist Revolution. He comes to Sala U, a circular space with an enormous metal cross at its centre that contains the names of those of sacrificed their lives during the violent conflicts that marked Fascism's ascendancy. Each one is marked by a single sculpted word 'Presente!' that points to the significance of martyrs to the movement. 'The chorus of the dead, with that obsessive repetition, that sing-song lie of presentness', Scurati writes, 'for whoever is capable of turning their ear to its resonance—and Benito Mussolini, however incapable he may be of other things, can do this—reaches Sala U not from the past but from an imminent future'.[53] *M—Gli ultimi giorni d'Europa* traces the events that lead to this future of death and destruction through the formation of the alliance with Germany and then the declaration of war in 1940. In the fourth volume, the horrors of a war conducted with supreme incompetence and disdain for human life—whether Italian or foreign—are illustrated in pitiless detail. It ends with the deposed Mussolini, the man who for decades had sought to position himself at the centre of the course of History regardless of the human cost, stripped of all manufactured heroism, lying sleeplessly and in pain on a camp bed in a prison cell following his loss of power.

Scurati does not disdain reference to the Mussolini of anecdotes. The presence in the novels of a secondary cast of family members, lovers and servants aligns his prose with the point of view of anecdotal history. The driver Ercole Boratto, the domestic servant from Villa Torlonia Cesira Carocci, and above all Quinto Navarra, his attendant at Palazzo Venezia—the man who knows all his ruses and weaknesses—are brought in as characters to convey the everyday ordinariness of the great leader, whose health is not as robust as his image. While Margherita Sarfatti and Claretta Petacci play more substantial parts, these supporting figures are introduced not to humanise the Duce in a false way but in order to show aspects of his personality that reveal his fallibility. There is a dialectic in the novel between the elevation to the status of idol and the flawed qualities of the man; the author presents the construction of the cult of personality without allowing the myth to take over. Banality and tragedy are present in numerous ways. The atrocities committed in Libya on the orders of the commander of the Italian military Graziani in pursuit of imperial ambitions are juxtaposed to the grandiose efforts to turn Rome into a city worthy of the ambitions that Fascism is pursuing in the name of Italy's glorious history. The failure to fully instal 'in everybody a will as sharp as the blade of a dagger',[54] an aim attributed to Fascist Party secretary Augusto Turati, is conveyed by the observation that, at the inauguration of the new Via dell'Impero linking the Colosseum and Piazza Venezia in 1932 on the anniversary of the March on Rome, many of the young people gathered for the solemn occasion are secretly killing time playing with yo-yos—'the fad of the moment, an innocent pastime based on the hypnotic repetition of the same completely pointless gesture that had been condemned by fascists for its triviality'.[55]

The final episode in the third volume is one of the most powerful and ominous. To set the scene for Mussolini's declaration of war against Britain and France from the balcony of Palazzo Venezia at 18:00 on 10 June 1940, he first explores the way he decides to dress, depicting the ageing dictator as a man who is fast losing his once legendary vigour.[56] His lover Claretta and the faithful Navarra attend to him as he nervously awaits the appointed hour. The announcement that war has been declared, as expected, is greeted with noisy acclamation, but then Scurati introduces a warning as well as the doubts and fears among the crowd that have been recorded in some testimonies. 'The speech proceeds without hitches, the script is performed with precision, yet there is something that seems to be broken; the diction is crisp but mechanical, as if the Duce of fascism had swallowed a tape recorder on which his own voice had been recorded'.[57] 'The shadow of doubt lengthens over the hour of destiny', he continues, the instinct for interpreting the mind of the masses had perhaps abandoned him. 'Maybe, after all, he who murmurs that you cannot forever live off the fat of your own myth is right; you cannot navigate for all your life on the basis of petty dealing and perhaps fascism, like a ripe fruit, has detached itself from the country'.[58]

In the final two volumes of the biography Scurati maps the dictator's return at the head of the Hitler-backed Italian Social Republic. The brutal civil war that marked this period brings Fascist violence once more to the centre of the narrative; the final period of Mussolini's career as a weak and dependent head of government is fatally tainted by extreme manifestations of the very hatred, blood and terror against fellow Italians that had been the sickening hallmark of his rise to power. While the dictator's actual death is omitted, those of his associates—some of whom were shot while others expired years later in their beds—are described in a set of concluding vignettes. Piazzale Loreto is interpreted not as a final detachment but as the first of many posthumous returns, including of what I have referred to in the Introduction to the present volume as the fourth body of the dictator and of the Mussolinian idea of power, of the strong leader and of the simplification of problems in the identification of an enemy to loathe and to destroy.[59] The very last note of the final volume, however, is dedicated to Liliana Segre, the Holocaust survivor, born in 1930, who was made a life senator by the President of the Republic in 2018.[60] Scurati praises her courage and underlines the vile abuse to which she was continually subjected for her determination to present witness to the horrors in which Fascism was complicit and of which those who do not condemn it prefer not to be reminded.

In Pennacchi's prose, the Fascist movement and the dictator have been embraced and internalised by the population to the extent that they are in symbiosis. The Italians, or at least those whose story he is telling, are inscribed within Fascism. By contrast, Scurati, on the basis of a viewpoint that is markedly more critical, recoils from stressing the close alignment between people and dictator or exploring the dependency of the former on the latter. He is nuanced in his attribution of responsibilities, though most of them are laid unequivocably at the door of Mussolini and those who were close to him. This is markedly the case in the fourth and fifth volumes, when the dictator's isolation is a recurrent theme. However, Scurati's address is not to memory; rather it is to the Italian readers of the present and to these he offers no alibis for the Italians of an earlier generation who backed Mussolini. The Italians of today, in other words, have in his view to carry the responsibility that their forebears chose to remove or veil and acknowledge that, without working through an unadmitted relationship, the national conscience will continue to be haunted, as in a ghost story, by 'a great repressed presence'.[61] 'I hope that the incredulity and dismay that will understandably be provoked by reading [the book]', he mused, 'will not be due to the fact that, in the events that are recounted, the fierce, demented dogs of war were us'.[62] He argued in 2023 that, if the Italians were to 'reckon with the past', it would be necessary for it to be accepted that 'we, the Italians, were fascists, that fascism was invented by us, that fascism was and would remain not a deviation from the regular course but the central moment of contemporary history'.[63] In short, they had to accept the uncomfortable fact that Mussolini was one of them.

Conclusion

Why does Mussolini linger in the Italian imagination? Why are there so many arguments and discussions concerning the legacies of Fascist rule and the place of these in the perception of Italians and others of the role of the country in the history of the twentieth century? The question of the contemporary currency of ideas about Fascism, many of them strangely positive, is important for a variety of reasons, the most pressing being the way these are employed in the political realm. When parties of government and prime ministers express positive views about aspects of Mussolini's dictatorship or diminish its violence, it suggests that a very particular, and improbably mild, vision of it has taken hold in public opinion. When the background of some of the country's leading politicians includes membership of the party that emerged from the final experience of Fascism during the civil war of 1943–45 and some of its various successor formations, it indicates that those experiences have been normalised within commonly held ideas of national history and that the Fascist regime itself is no longer seen as wholly or predominantly negative.

It has become common to explain these things by drawing attention to the way inaccurate and misleading ideas about Fascist Italy, some of them originating in its own propaganda, continue to circulate and enjoy credibility. Notions that the regime was a mild form of dictatorship compared to Nazi Germany, that its colonial wars were motivated by civilising ideals, that it achieved much in the realm of social reform and welfare, that it unified and modernised the country with its investments in education, infrastructure, land reclamation and communications all play into the view that Fascism achieved much and was not after all so bad.

This book has taken a different approach to explaining why Fascism is seen in this rose-tinted light. Specifically, it has focused on the figure of Mussolini and examined how his spectre continues to haunt Italy more than three quarters of a century after his death. It has applied ideas drawn from psychology that were first developed to analyse German attitudes towards the Nazi past. The intention has not been to imply or suggest that Fascist Italy and Nazi Germany were the same or that analysis of them should downplay significant differences. But nor has the view been adopted that they were so completely different that comparisons are misleading or that tools of analysis cannot, with due adjustment, be transferred from one context to the other. The idea that the two regimes were fundamentally different gained currency towards the end of the war, as efforts were made to downplay the role of Fascism in Italian national history. The true Italy had never been Fascist, it was argued, but liberal and democratic. This notion was stressed during the phase in which the Allies were determining the conditions of Italy's readmission to a reconfigured international order. Subsequently, it was taken up and elaborated by historians, most notably Renzo De Felice, who stressed the specificity of Italian Fascism as a modernising force compared to a more backward-looking Nazism. The idea that Fascism had little in common with Nazism has played a comforting, reassuring role in Italian self-perceptions. It was bolstered by a discourse on national character that counterposed the fundamental goodness of the Italians to the supposed intrinsic evil of the Germans. This idea contributed to a veiling of the less savoury aspects of the Fascism and its wars, including atrocities in Africa and the Balkans, the anti-semitic racial laws (viewed as a German imposition), contributions to the Holocaust, and violence and repression in everyday life.

After the war there was great interest in the question of how the Germans had succumbed to Hitler. What had led a whole people to embrace a terroristic vision of the national mission and pledge themselves so completely to a charismatic leader who promised them everything? And, once it was over, how had they reacted to that leader's exposure as an evil monster? The way in which the Germans experienced the end of the Nazi dictatorship was a matter that the world cared about and paid attention to. The transition to democracy was a process that was carefully supervised and monitored. It was felt that there was a lot to explain and that sophisticated tools were needed to explore culture, the national character and collective psychology. In Italy, this impulse was lacking. The interpretation of Fascism as mild and lacking roots, in contrast to the ruthlessness of Nazism and its profound rooting in German culture and society, meant that internally and externally the issue was less pressing. Unlike the Germans, the Italians had taken an active role in casting off their dictator and contributed to the war of liberation. What was there to explain that could not be accounted for by political history? If the people had mainly been oppressed and only for a short period been seduced by a showman-dictator before reverting to their true liberal-democratic vocation, there was no need to interrogate anything beyond the facts of the circumstances that brought a tyrant to power and those which marked his fall.

For many years and still today, it has not been widely accepted that there was a close psychological bond in Italy between the people and the dictator. This despite the fact that the Italians, like the Germans, had in very large numbers given their support to dictatorship and had developed an extraordinarily intense mental relationship with its figurehead. Conventional narratives around Mussolini's overthrow in 1943, the civil war and the spectacle of Piazzale Loreto have minimised this relationship. The consequence has been that few of the ways in which a psychological dependency was negotiated and digested after the war have been investigated. Some of these had much in common with the way the Germans emerged from the shadow of a tyranny in which they had been active participants. Dealing with a situation in which a regime that had seemed to embody the national mission and seen a despot hailed as a figure of providence, which had been condemned in the eyes of the world, was challenging. It gave rise to responses that often avoided conscious acceptance of historical reality.

The Germans of the postwar years had seemed to have succeeded in putting the Nazi past behind them and becoming once more a European country like any other. This certainly was the self-perception of West Germany, although doubts persisted and questions were raised at home and abroad. In their pioneering and controversial work, Alexander and Margarete Mitscherlich argued that the Germans had not properly detached from Hitler. Faced with the crimes of the Nazi regime, they had not engaged in a process of mourning for a figure they had loved intensely and who they had internalised as part of their super-ego. Instead, they behaved as though this attachment had never existed and the Nazi order itself had never been. There were perfectly good explanations for this act of suppression, the Mitscherlichs argued. While mourning would have allowed the Germans to work through their love for Hitler and eventually detach from it, placing themselves in a position to be able to move forward and develop new political attachments, it would also have entailed acknowledgement that they had idolised a criminal. To avoid the melancholia and sense of worthlessness that this would have caused, they preferred to go into denial, turning the Nazi past into a 'dim and ghost-like' memory. The consequence was that a great deal of psychic energy went into repression, leading to a passive engagement with democratic institutions and a convenient embrace with American-style economic growth as a source of national pride and identity. All the while, though, the Mitscherlichs contested, the bond with Hitler remained unaddressed and unresolved as a concealed undercurrent in national life.

It has been argued here that the Italians too failed to mourn their dictator and therefore that they did not constructively detach from him psychologically. They too made him vanish and acted as if Fascism as a brutal tyranny had never existed. There were other parallels too. Italy embraced passively the new political leadership of the Christian Democrats in the postwar years and placed extraordinary emphasis on economic recovery and growth as a source of national identity. However, the mechanisms and processes were different and the detailed examinations of many different spheres of postwar culture and society in this book have illustrated the complex ways in which elements of mourning and working through occurred in a context in which Fascism as a totalitarian regime was reinterpreted as mild and Mussolini was turned from a tyrant into something more manageable and familiar. In Italy, silence did not fall over the dictator as it did in Germany; instead, he was painted in a false way and domesticated. In the end though, it may be argued that the lack of any genuine collective process of mourning meant that the bond was not broken and Mussolini continued to cast a spectral spell.

It might be asked what a mourning process might have looked like. Would it have entailed an acceptance of guilt and a need for atonement? In Germany, this was a central issue that also carried economic implications in relation to the new state of Israel. That country's leaders and intellectuals wrestled with the question in a context of moral pressure and the expectations of the international community, although the mass of the population was less receptive to it. In Italy, guilt was an issue that was occasionally raised but never given the importance it was in Germany. Colonial atrocities and war crimes in the Balkans never came to the forefront of the national conscience. No Nuremburg trial forced matters into consideration and the Holocaust did not trigger a moral reckoning. Precisely the question of national responsibility, therefore, might have been handled in a more honest and self-reflexive way. Albeit for entirely explicable reasons, an opportunity was missed. The matter of Italy's relationship with Fascism and Fascism's impact on the world stands unconfronted at a time when the governments of some other countries have apologised for slavery and colonialism. For the Mitscherlichs, mourning entails overcoming the defence mechanisms that prevent full acceptance of a loss. Overcoming is not simple; it is something that has to be struggled for, learned and accomplished. Complication arises where the lost object has been a narcissistic one that has become part of the self via what in psychoanalytic terms can be called a collectivised super-ego. In this case, the loss involves feelings of impoverishment and a potential collapse of self-esteem, although this type of emotional attachment is more likely to occur in a context where the attachment itself is a means of confirming one's own self-esteem.

In Germany, the immobilism of the 'inability to mourn' was overcome in the period after the Mitscherlichs were writing. In the 1970s, a great deal of effort went into re-examining the Nazi past, which entailed a confrontation between generations and a wide variety of cultural re-elaborations of Nazism. Whether this was as extensive and complete as it might have been is an open question. Even in the 2000s, there were questions about the way the German leadership following reunification handled the Nazi past. In Italy, that process was not embarked on except in a highly fragmented way. There was no national assessment that, even if unofficial, was recognised as such. For this reason, an unmourned Mussolini constitutes an awkward posthumous presence. The haunting, to be sure, has something to do with the way the past in the contemporary mediatic and cultural context no longer appears as something final and finished. It troubles the present, occupying it and shaping it, moulding it and reinventing it. The chapters of this book explore how the ghosts of the past return in different ways and forms, as unresolved trauma, template, material leftover, memory or icon. In such a context, the afterlife of Mussolini has consisted not simply of narrations of his history but also of the persistence, survival, revival and re-elaboration of stories, memories and images.

Would a mourning process have laid Mussolini to rest and deprived his ghost of this capacity to haunt? At one level, perhaps not. In his controversial speech to the Bundestag in 1988, German politician Philipp Jenninger suggested that Hitler and Nazism would be associated in the global mind with Germany until the end of time. No matter how much self-examination, atonement and repentance occurred, nothing could be done to abolish this burden inherited from the past. The same may be true of Italy and Mussolini. What Jenninger suggested, though, was that this fact entailed a responsibility to the past and to the future. What was required was constant self-scrutiny and honesty. Exculpations and desires to pretend horrors had not occurred needed to be set aside in favour of an acknowledgement of the persistence within the interstices of a democracy of the cultural constructions of an authoritarian dictatorship and the potential of these inheritances to act on the present. Such a recognition is not reassuring, but it is as well to be alert to this long-range threat; better, certainly, than to be oblivious to it.

Endnotes

NOTES TO PREFACE

1. See Mimmo Franzinelli, *Il fascismo è finito il 25 aprile 1945* (Rome: Laterza, 2022), pp.101–6.
2. Filippo Focardi, *Nel cantiere della memoria: Fascismo, Resistenza, Shoah, Foibe* (Rome: Viella 2020), p.93.
3. John Borneman, 'Preface' to Borneman (ed.), *Death of the Father: An Anthropology of the End of Political Authority* (New York and Oxford: Berghahn, 2004), p.vi.
4. See, for example, Michele Battini, *The Missing Italian Nuremberg*: *Cultural Amnesia and Postwar Politics* (New York: Palgrave Macmillan, 2007) and Focardi, *Nel cantiere della memoria*, pp.95–114.
5. For a critique of this view, see Nicola Tranfaglia, *Labirinto italiano: il fascismo,l'antifascismo, gli storici* (Florence: La Nuova Italia, 1989), p.506.
6. Filippo Focardi, *Il cattivo tedesco e il bravo italiano: la rimozione delle colpe della seconda guerra mondiale* (Rome: Laterza, 2016).
7. Il Gazettino, 'Docente di Ca' Foscari posta la Meloni a testa in giù. Fdi chiede all'ateneo di allontanarlo, il rettore si dissocia, e lui: «Attacco strumentale»', 28 May 2021 https://www.ilgazzettino.it/nordest/venezia/ricercatore_ca_foscari_simon_levis_sullam_post_libro_meloni_testa_in_giu_fdi_insorge-5988678.html (consulted 12/9/23).
8. Sandro Gerbi and Raffaele Liucci, *Indro Montanelli*: *una biografia (1909–2001)* (Milan: Hoepli, 2014), p.219.

NOTES TO INTRODUCTION

1. See Jeffrey K. Olick, *The Politics of Regret: On Collective Memory and Historical Responsibility* (New York: Routledge, 2007).
2. See Jeffrey Herf, *Divided Memory: The Nazi Past in the Two Germanys* (Cambridge, Mass.: Harvard University Press, 1997); Jeffrey K. Olick, *In the House of the Hangman: The Agonies of German Defeat, 1943–1949* (Chicago: University of Chicago Press, 2005); Jeffrey K. Olick, *The Sins of the Fathers: Germany, History, Method* (Chicago: University of Chicago Press, 2016).
3. See Renato Moro, *Il mito dell'Italia cattolica: nazione, religione e cattolicesimo negli anni del fascismo* (Rome: Studium, 2021).
4. See Tony Judt, *Postwar: A History of Europe Since 1945* (London: Vintage, 2010), Chapter 1.
5. Filippo Focardi, *La guerra della memoria: la Resistenza nel dibattito politico italiano dal 1945 a oggi* (Rome: Laterza, 2005); Luca La Rovere, *L'eredità del fascismo: gli intellettuali, i giovani e la transizione al postfascismo, 1943–1948* (Turin: Bollati Boringhieri 2008); Guri Schwartz, *Tu mi devi seppellir: riti funebri e culto nazionale alle origini della Repubblica* (Turin: UTET, 2010); Mariuccia Salvati, *Passaggi: italiani dal fascismo alla Repubblica* (Rome: Carocci, 2016). Guri Schwartz, *Tu mi devi seppellir: riti funebri e culto nazionale alle origini della Repubblica* (Turin: UTET, 2010).
6. Filippo Focardi, *Nel cantiere della memoria: Fascismo, Resistenza, Shoah, Foibe* (Rome: Viella, 2020).
7. Michele Battini, *The Missing Italian Nuremberg: Cultural Amnesia and Postwar Politics* (New York: Palgrave Macmillan, 2007); Roy Palmer Domenico, *Italian Fascists on Trial 1943–1948* (Chapel Hill, N.C.: University of North Carolina Press, 1992).

8. For example, see Davide Conti, *Gli uomini di Mussolini: prefetti, questori e criminali di guerra dal fascismo alla repubblica italiana* (Turin: Einaudi, 2017). For a general overview of older and more recent trends in the historiography of Fascism, see Claudia Baldoli, *Italian Fascism 1914–1945: Themes and Interpretations* (Cham: Palgrave Macmillan, 2023).
9. Alexander and Margarete Mitscherlich, *The Inability to Mourn: Principles of Collective Behaviour* (New York: Grove Press 1975; first published in 1967).
10. Ibid., p.22.
11. Ibid., pp.24–5.
12. See Sigmund Freud, *On Murder, Mourning and Melancholia* (London: Penguin 2005).
13. Ibid., p.26.
14. Ibid., p.31.
15. Ibid., p.52.
16. Ibid., p.66.
17. Susan Neiman, *Learning from the Germans: Confronting Race and the Memory of Evil* (London: Penguin, 2019).
18. See Olick, *In the House of the Hangman*, *The Politics of Regret* and *The Sins of the Fathers*. See also Eric Santner, *Stranded Objects: Mourning, Memory and Film Iin Postwar Germany* (Ithaca, N.Y.: Cornell University Press, 1990), p.xi.
19. Christopher Duggan, 'Coming to terms with Italy's war', *History Today*, December 2013; Ruth Ben-Ghiat, 'Why are so many Fascist monuments still standing in Italy?', *The New Yorker*, 5 October 2017.
20. This will not be the first attempt to apply the Mitscherlichs' approach to a different context: sociologist Paul Gilroy has used it in his work on colonial legacies. See *After Empire: Melancholia or Convivial Culture?* (London: Routledge, 2004). It has also been applied to a study of *The Great Gatsby*. See Greg Forter, 'Against melancholia: contemporary mourning theory, Fitzgerald's *The Great Gatsby*, and the politics of unfinished grief', *differences*, 14:2, 2003, 134–70.
21. Although Freud himself argued that 'the contrast between individual psychology and social or group psychology, which at first glance may seem to be full of significance, loses a great deal of its sharpness when it is examined more closely' for an individual is always related to others, with the result that the psychology of one person 'is at the same time social psychology as well'. Sigmund Freud, *Group Psychology and the Analysis of the Ego* (New York: Norton 1989), p.3.
22. The Mitscherlichs' book was translated into Italian in 1970 by the publisher Sansoni (*Germania senza lutto: psicoanalisi del postnazismo*), but it received almost no attention. It did not fare much better in the English-speaking world. *The Inability to Mourn* was never published in the UK, though an English translation appeared in the USA in 1975, since when it has been out of print. The book was published in French in 1972 in an edition that was republished in 2004. On the matter of cultural history and psychoanalysis, see Peter Burke, 'Freud and Cultural History', *Psychoanalysis and History*, 9:1, 2007, 5–15 and Joan W. Scott, 'The incommensurability of psychoanalysis and history', *History and Theory*, 51, 2012, 63–83.
23. For one view of this from within the field of psychology, see David Stewart, 'Are Freud and psychoanalysis still relevant?' https://www.alliant.edu/blog/are-freud-and-psychoanalysis-still-relevant (consulted 20/8/24).
24. Ennio Di Nolfo, *Le paure e le speranze degli italiani (1943–1953)* (Milan: Mondadori, 1986); Rosario Forlenza, *On the Edge of Democracy: Italy, 1943–1948* (Oxford: Oxford University Press, 2019); Simonetta Falasca-Zamponi, *Fascism, the War, and Structures of Feeling in Italy, 1943–1945: Tales in Chiaroscuro* (Oxford: Oxford University Press, 2023).

25. Filippo Focardi, *Il cattivo tedesco e il bravo italiano: la rimozione delle colpe della seconda guerra mondiale* (Rome: Laterza, 2016). English edition: *The Bad German and the Good Italian: Removing the Guilt of the Second World War* (Manchester: Manchester University Press, 2023).
26. Anon., 'Editoriale', *Educazione sentimentale*, 27, 2017, p.5.
27. Freud, *On Murder, Mourning and Melancholia*, p.203.
28. Emilio Gentile uses the term 'totalitarian Caesarism' as the title of the second part of his book, *La via italiana al totalitarismo: il partito e lo Stato nel regime fascista* (Rome: Carocci, 2018).
29. See my 'Remembering Berlinguer: mourning, nostalgia and the left' in John Foot and Stephen Gundle (eds), *Paul Ginsborg and the Historiography of Modern Italy* (London: Palgrave Macmillan, 2024).
30. Martha Hodes, *Mourning Lincoln* (New Haven and London: Yale University Press, 2015).
31. See Jean Lipman-Blumen, *The Allure of Toxic Leaders* (New York: Oxford University Press, 2006).
32. Ibid., p.205.
33. See Gundle, 'Remembering Berlinguer'.
34. Hodes, *Mourning Lincoln*, p.62.
35. It is less common to see the Duce as a 'star' than Hitler, who Leni Riefenstahl's artistic expertise turned into 'Adolf Hitler superstar'. See Steven Bach, *Leni: The Life and Work of Leni Riefenstahl* (London: Abacus, 2008), p.44. But some of the most renowned historians of Fascism, including Renzo De Felice and Luisa Passerini, have recognised this aspect of Mussolini's public profile. See Renzo De Felice, *Mussolini il duce*. Tomo I: *Gli anni del consenso 1929–1936* (Turin: Einaudi, 1974), pp.576–8; Luisa Passerini, *Mussolini immaginario: storia di una biografia, 1915–1939* (Rome: Laterza 1991), pp.126–7. See also my 'Mass culture and the cult of personality' in Stephen Gundle, Christopher Duggan and Giuliana Pieri (eds), *The Cult of the Duce: Mussolini and the Italians* (Manchester: Manchester University Press, 2013).
36. Anthony Elliott, *The Mourning of John Lennon* (Berkeley: University of California Press, 1999), p.141.
37. Ibid., p.58.
38. Ibid., p.143.
39. Andy Bull, *Strange Angels* (London: Black Swan, 1995).
40. Alessandra Antola Swan, *Photographing Mussolini: The Making of a Political Icon* (Basingstoke: Palgrave Macmillan, 2020). On Mussolini as an American celebrity, see John P. Diggins, *Mussolini and Fascism: The View from America* (Princeton: Princeton University Press, 1972).
41. Another work of considerable interest is Cristina Baldassini, *L'ombra di Mussolini: l'Italia moderata e la memoria del fascismo (1945–1960)* (Soveria Mannelli: Rubbettino, 2008). More recently, there have been some books by journalists that have investigated the dictator's posthumous resonances. See Sergio Rizzo and Alessandro Campi, *L'ombra lunga del fascismo: perché l'italia ancora ferma a Mussolini* (Milan: Solferino, 2022) and Sara Lucaroni, *Sempre lui: perché Mussolini non muore mai* (Milan: Pienogiorno, 2022).
42. Sergio Luzzatto, *Il corpo del duce* (Turin: Einaudi, 1997).
43. Ernst Kantorowicz, *The King's Two Bodies: A Study in Mediaeval Political Theology* (Princeton: Princeton University Press, 1957).
44. Burkhard Schnepel, *The King's Three Bodies: Essays on Kingship and Ritual* (London: Routledge, 2022), pp.15–137.

45. Frank Dikotter, How To Be a Dictator*: The Cult of Personality in the Twentieth Century* (London: Bloomsbury, 2019), p.ix.
46. Ronald Wintrobe, 'The tin pot and the totalitarian: an economic theory of dictatorship', *American Political Science Review*, 84:3, 2014, 849–72.
47. Dikotter, *How To Be a Dictator*, p.x.
48. Luisa Passerini, 'Mussolini' in Mario Isnenghi (ed.), *I luoghi della memoria: personaggi e date dell'Italia unita* (Rome: Laterza, 2010), p.182.
49. Joseph Roach, *It* (Ann Arbor; University of Michigan Press, 2007) refers to the 'cinematic body' of the film actor, suggesting that 'celebrities, then, like kings, have two bodies' (p.36). For dictators, I have preferred to conceptualise this as a third body.
50. Michel Serres with Bruno Latour, *Conversations on Science, Culture and Time* (Ann Arbor: University of Michigan Press, 1995), p.59.
51. Serres with Latour, *Conversations*, p.59.
52. Roach, *It*, pp.12–13.
53. See David Broder, *Mussolini's Grandchildren: Fascism in Contemporary Italy* (London: Pluto Press, 2023).
54. See Franzinelli, *Il fascismo è finito il 25 aprile 1945*, p.130.
55. For an assessment of these myths, see Francesco Filippi, *Mussolini ha fatto anche cose buone* (Turin: Bollati Boringhieri, 2019).
56. Berlusconi made this declaration to Nicholas Farrell. See 'Diary', *The Spectator*, 13 September 2003. https://www.spectator.co.uk/article/diary-13-september-2003/ (consulted 10/11/24).
57. Christopher Duggan, *Fascist Voices* (London: Bodley Head, 2012), pp.198–215.
58. The debate flourished following publication of Silvana Patriarca's *Italian Vices* (Cambridge: Cambridge University Press, 2010).

NOTES TO CHAPTER I

1. Italo Calvino, 'I ritratti del Duce', in *Saggi (1945–1985)*, edited by Mario Barenghi (Milan: Mondadori, 2022), p.2879. The article was originally published under the title 'Cominciò con un cilindro' in *La Repubblica*, 10–11 July 1983.
2. See, for example, Renzo De Felice, *Mussolini il duce.* Tomo I: *Gli anni del consenso 1929–1936* (Turin: Einaudi, 1974), pp.49, 798, 801. See also Renzo De Felice, Mussolini il fascista. Tomo 1: La conquista del potere 1921–1925 (Turin: Einaudi, 1966), pp.461–2.
3. De Felice, *Mussolini il fascista*. Tomo 1: *La conquista del potere*, p.461.
4. De Felice, *Mussolini il duce*. Tomo I: *Gli anni del consenso*, pp.761–7. On the psychological subordination of Galeazzo Ciano, see pp.807–8.
5. See, for example, Christopher Duggan, 'The internalisation of the cult of the Duce; the evidence of diaries and letters' in Stephen Gundle, Christopher Duggan and Giuliana Pieri (eds), *The Cult of the Duce: Mussolini and the Italians* (Manchester: Manchester University Press, 2013). See also, Duggan, *Fascist Voices: An Intimate History of Mussolini's Italy* (London: The Bodley Head, 2012), pp.229–31. Two special issues of the journal *Educazione sentimentale*, published in 2017, were dedicated to the analysis of Fascism from a psychoanalytical point of view. The psychological is taken into consideration to some degree in Rosario Forlenza, *On the Edge of Democracy: Italy, 1943–1948* (Oxford: Oxford University Press, 2020).
6. Gustave Le Bon, *The Crowd* (New Brunswick: Transaction, 1995; first published 1895), p.58.
7. Ibid., p.140.
8. Serge Moscovici, *The Age of the Crowd* (Cambridge: Cambridge University Press, 1983), p.295.

9. Ibid., pp.292–3.
10. See Urs Stäheli, 'Seducing the Crowd: The Leader in Crowd Psychology', *New German Critique*, 114, 2011, 63–77. For Freud's critique of Le Bon, see his *Group Psychology and the Analysis of the Ego* (New York: Norton, 1989), pp.6–18; on leaders, pp.17–18.
11. Mario Isnenghi, *Storia d'Italia: i fatti e le percezioni dal Risorgimento alla società dello spettacolo* (Rome: Laterza, 2011), p.639.
12. See Stephen Gundle, 'The death (and rebirth) of the hero: charisma and personality cults', *Modern Italy*, 3:2, 1998, 173–89.
13. See Mario Isnenghi, 'Aspetti del rituale di massa fascista: stampa e dintorni' in Riccardo Redi (ed.), *Cinema italiano sotto il fascismo* (Venice: Marsilio, 1979), pp.52–3.
14. Giordano Bruno Guerri (ed.), *Rapporto al Duce: l'agonia di una nazione nei colloqui tra Mussolini e i federali nel 1942* (Milan: Bompiani, 2020), p.46.
15. Mario Isnenghi, *L'Italia in piazza: i luoghi della vita pubblica dal 1848 ai nostri giorni* (Milan: Mondadori, 1994), p.313.
16. Antonio Beltramelli, *L'uomo nuovo* (Milan: Mondadori, 1923), p.12.
17. Ibid., p.47.
18. Simona Storchi, 'Margherita Sarfatti and the invention of the Duce' in Gundle, Duggan and Pieri, *The Cult of the Duce*, p.42.
19. Philip Cannistraro and Brian Sullivan, *Il Duce's Other Woman* (New York: Morrow, 1993), p.303. Emilio Gentile, *Fascismo: storia e interpretazione* (Rome: Laterza, 2002), pp.218–19.
20. Quoted in Pier Giorgio Zunino, Interpretazione e memoria del fascismo*: gli anni del regime* (Rome: Laterza, 2000), pp.131–2.
21. Ibid., pp.134–5.
22. Ibid., p.135.
23. Carlo Emilio Gadda, *Eros e Priapo* (Milan: Adelphi, 2016; first published 1967), p.37.
24. Ibid., p.136. This judgement appeared in the journal *La Critica* in 1923, in a review of Gaetano Mosca's *Elementi di scienza politica*.
25. Fathali M. Moghaddam, *The Psychology of Dictatorship* (Washington, D.C.: American Psychological Association, 2013), p.133.
26. Benedetto Croce, 'La sottomissione all'universale', *La Critica*, 1938, p.157. Cited in Zunino, *Interpretazione e memoria del fascismo*, p.138.
27. Curzio Malaparte, *Muss: il grande imbecille* (Milan: Luni, 1999), p.43.
28. Ermanno Rea, *La fabbrica dell'obbedienza: il lato oscuro e complice degli italiani* (Milan: Feltrinelli, 2011), p.27.
29. Pier Giorgio Zunino, *La Repubblica e il suo passato* (Bologna: Il Mulino, 2003), pp.62–3.
30. Luisa Passerini, *Mussolini immaginario: storia di una biografia 1915–1939* (Rome: Laterza, 1991), p.125.
31. Ibid., pp.60–1.
32. A liberal anti-fascist, Marcello Soleri reported this observation of a 'religious observer' in *Memorie* (Ravenna: Edizioni Moderne, 2013; first published 1949), p.269.
33. Emilio Gentile, *Il culto del littorio: la sacralizzazione della politica nell'Italia fascista* (Rome: Laterza, 1993), p.293.
34. Pino Nicoloso, *Mussolini architetto: propaganda e paesaggio urbano nell'Italia fascista* (Turin: Einaudi, 2008), p.7.
35. Cesare Musatti, 'Super-io individuale e super-io collettivo' (1961) in Musatti, *Libertà e servitù dello spirito: diario culturale di uno psicanalista (1945–1971)* (Turin: Boringhieri, 1971), pp.208–25.
36. Ibid., p.219.

37. The idea of the regression of the super-ego or ego-ideal under dictatorships was discussed by Joachim Fleischer in 'Political life and super-ego regression', Psychological Review, 36:4, 1949, 416–28.
38. Musatti, *Libertà e servitù dello spirito*, pp.216–17.
39. 'In this orgy of civic festivals, in this self-serving logic made of dates to remember and heroes to sanctify in public events—that, beyond filling the squares, helped to widen and the same time manage consent—' Amoreno Martellini and Barbara Montesi argue in their critical history of the town of Jesi, 'streets, squares and public parks became spaces in which the rituals of the regime were dramatized and in which its liturgies were spectacularised'. Amoreno Martellini and Barbara Montesi, *Il Novecento in provincia: storia di Jesi tra memorie e oblii 1900–1970* (Milan: Franco Angeli, 2020), pp.114–15.
40. Freud, *Group Psychology and the Analysis of the Ego*, pp.32–3.
41. Laura Malvano, *Fascismo e politica dell'immagine* (Turin: Bollati Boringhieri, 1988), p.63.
42. See Jacqueline Reich, *The Maciste Films of Italian Silent Cinema* (Bloomington: Indiana University Press, 2015).
43. Dino Biondi, *La fabbrica del duce* (Bologna: Cappelli, 1973), pp.88–9.
44. Camillo Berneri, *Mussolini: psicologia di un dittatore* (Milan: Edizioni Azione comune, 1966).
45. Isnenghi, 'Aspetti del rituale di massa fascista: stampa e dintorni', p.53.
46. Martellini and Montesi, *Il Novecento in provincia*, p.115.
47. Giovanni Giuriati, *La parabola di Mussolini nei ricordi di un gerarca* (Rome-Bari: Laterza, 1981), p.48. In Italian the term used is 'un cinematografo'.
48. Passerini, *Mussolini immaginario*, p.125.
49. What Christopher Duggan calls the 'internalisation' of the cult was facilitated by the fact that 'no matter how extraordinary Mussolini was claimed to be', he was 'nonetheless a figure whom men, women and children, of all ages and backgrounds, felt they could relate to—and often in an extremely intimate way'. 'The internalisation of the cult of the Duce', p.130. Duggan made ample use of diaries held at the Italian national diary archive in Pieve Santo Stefano.
50. Three teenage girls, members of the Giovani italiane, wrote in early 1941 to inform him: 'we can no longer contain the ardent beating of our hearts and the passionate yearning of our spirits in these days of struggle and sacrifice for all and especially for You who are our hope, our luminous and courageous guide, our glory…Every day we make a prayer to God for You, for the Fatherland, for victory'. Letter dated 13 February 1941. Reproduced in Vacca, *Duce! Tu sei un Dio!*, pp.226–7.
51. Letter dated 25 February 1941. Ibid., pp.230–1.
52. Letter dated 9 October 1941. Ibid., p.243.
53. Passerini, *Mussolini immaginario*, pp.37, 94, 98. For another example of a dictator with a feminine dimension, see Lauren Derby's study of Rafael Trujillo, *The Dictator's Seduction: Politics and the Popular Imagination in the Era of Trujillo* (Durham, N.C.: Duke University Press, 2009), Chapter 3.
54. Letter dated 21 February 1942. Reproduced in Vacca, *Duce! Tu sei un Dio!*, p.260.
55. Ibid., p.218. Jung argued the same thing about the anti-fascist Germans residing in Switzerland that he saw. See Stephen Spender, *European Witness* (London: Hamish Hamilton, 1946), p.161.
56. Ibid., p.219.
57. Franco Ciarlantini, *Mussolini immaginario* (Milan: Sonzogno, 1933), p.6.
58. Musatti, 'Super-io individuale e super-io collettivo', p.200.

59. Angelo Michele Imbriani, *Gli italiani e il duce: il mito e l'imagine di Mussolini negli ultimi anni del fascismo (1938–1943)* (Naples: Liguori 1992), pp.90–4.
60. Carlo Delcroix, *Un uomo e un popolo* (Florence: Vallecchi, 1928), p.327.
61. De Felice, *Mussolini il duce*, p.761.
62. Paul Corner, *Mussolini Myth and Memory* (Oxford: Oxford University Press, 2022), pp.43–62.
63. Paul Ginsborg, *Family Politics: Domestic Life, Devastation and Survival, 1900–1950* (New Haven and London: Yale University Press, 2014), p.355.
64. Luca Baldissara, *Italia 1943: la guerra continua* (Bologna: Il Mulino, 2023), pp.109–30.
65. For the idea that 'if only Mussolini knew, things would be different', see Paolo Monelli, *Roma 1943* (Turin: Einaudi, 2012; first published 1963), p.29 and Duggan, *Fascist Voices*, pp.352–4.

NOTES TO CHAPTER 2

1. Luce D'Eramo, *Il 25 luglio* (Rome: Elliot, 2013). First published in 1999, this text by the future writer Luce Mangione (D'Eramo was her surname by marriage) was composed in August 1943 shortly after the events it recounts.
2. Ibid., p.7.
3. Ibid., p.27.
4. See Luca Baldissara, *Italia 1943: la guerra continua* (Bologna: Il Mulino, 2023), pp. 100–9.
5. D'Eramo, *Il 25 luglio*, p.51.
6. Ibid., pp.55–6. The events in Rome were written up much later as the original pages were lost.
7. See Melton S. Davis, *Who Defends Rome? The Forty-Five Days, July 25–September 8, 1943* (London: George Allen & Unwin, 1972), pp.151–62.
8. George Axelsson, 'Wild rejoicing in Rome's streets hailed end of Mussolini regime', *New York Times*, 30 July 1943, p.3.
9. Davis, *Who Defends Rome?* p.156.
10. Rachele Mussolini, *Ma vie avec Benito* (Paris: Editions du Cheval Ailé, 1948), pp.179–80.
11. Axelsson, 'Wild rejoicing in Rome's streets', p.3.
12. On events in Milan, see Barbara Bracco, 'I segni littori di Milano: costruzione, distruzione e rinascita del volto di una città' in Giulia Albanese and Lucia Ceci (eds), *I luoghi del fascismo: memoria, politica, rimozione* (Rome: Viella, 2022), pp.153–4.
13. Nazario Sauro Onofri, 'Il mio 25 luglio 1943 (con il seguito del 8 settembre)', Quaderni della Resistenza oggi, *Vol.1* 1943: Cade il fascismo, 2003, 69–81, p.73.
14. See Simona Storchi, 'Mussolini as monument: the equestrian statue of the Duce at the Littoriale Stadium in Bologna' in Stephen Gundle, Christopher Duggan and Giuliana Pieri (eds), *The Cult of the Duce: Mussolini and the Italians* (Manchester: Manchester University Press, 2013), p.202.
15. Piero Calamandrei, *Diario 1939–1945*, Vol.1 (Florence: La Nuova Italia, 1997), p.159.
16. Ibid., p.156.
17. Rosario Forlenza, *On the Edge of Democracy: Italy, 1943–1948* (Oxford: Oxford University Press, 2019), p.24.
18. Onofri, 'Il mio 25 luglio 1943', p.157.
19. Ibid., p.159.
20. '"Testone è caduto": testimonianza di Antonio Bortolotti', *I Quaderni della Resistenza oggi*, Vol.1 *1943: Cade il fascismo*, 2003, p.83.
21. Calamandrei, *Diario 1939–1945*, p.157.

22. Renzo De Felice, *Mussolini il duce*. Tomo 1: *Gli anni del consenso 1929–36* (Turin: Einaudi, 1974), p.51.
23. See Baldissara, *Italia 1943: la guerra continua*, pp.21–2.
24. Lucio Villari, 'Prefazione' to Monelli, *Roma 1943* (1954), p.ix.
25. Dino Grandi, *25 luglio: quarant'anni dopo*, ed. by Renzo De Felice (Bologna: Il Mulino, 2013), pp.336–7. The volume was written in 1944, forty years before it was published.
26. Paolo Cacace, *Come muore un regime; il fascismo verso il 25 luglio* (Bologna: Il Mulino, 2021), p.8.
27. Renzo De Felice, *Mussolini l'alleato 1940–1945*. Tome 1: *L'Italia in guerra 1940–1943*, Tomo 2: *Crisi e agonia del regime* (Turin: Einaudi, 1996), pp.1398–401.
28. De Felice, *Mussolini il duce*, p.304.
29. Ibid., p.765.
30. Ibid., p.798.
31. Ibid., pp.798–9.
32. Ibid., p.181.
33. Monelli, *Roma 1943*, p.16.
34. Ibid., pp.505–6.
35. Ibid., p.419.
36. Baldissara, *Italia 1943*, pp.91–7.
37. The diaries and memoirs of senior Fascists attest to this. See especially Giuseppe Bottai, *Diario 1935–1944* (Milan; Rizzoli, 1989), pp.278, 328.
38. Monelli, *Roma 1943*, p.223.
39. Bottai, *Diario 1935–1944*, p.337.
40. Giordano Bruno Guerri (ed.), *Rapporto al Duce: l'agonia di una nazione nei colloqui tra Mussolini e i federali nel 1942* (Milan: Bompiani, 2020), p.57.
41. Ibid., p.45.
42. Aldo Cesaraccio, testimony in Cesaraccio, Antonello Mattone and Giuseppe Melis Bassu (eds), *Mussolini in Sardegna* (Cagliari: Gia editrice, 1983), page unnumbered.
43. Giuseppe Melis Bassu, testimony in ibid.
44. Bottai, *Diario 1935–1944*, p.305.
45. Forlenza, *On the Edge of Democracy*, pp.30–1. Duggan, *Fascist Voices*, p.xvii.
46. Simona Colarizi, *L'opinione degli italiani sotto il regime, 1929–1943* (Rome: Laterza, 1991), p.400.
47. Benito Mussolini, *Storia di un anno: il tempo del bastone e della carota* (Rome: Libero, 2004; first published 1944), p.54.
48. Reynolds and Eleanor Packard, *Balcony Empire: Fascist Italy at War* (New York: Oxford University Press, 1942), p.366.
49. Bottai, *Diario 1935–1944*, p.379.
50. Giovanni Giuriati, *La parabola di Mussolini nei ricordi di un gerarca*, edited by Emilio Gentile (Rome and Bari: Laterza, 1981), p.220.
51. As Giurati wrote in his memoirs, 'You went from one regime to another as if it were a matter of turning the page of a detective novel'. Ibid., p.3.
52. Monelli, *Roma 1943*, p.112.
53. Benito Mussolini, *Pensieri pontini e sardi* (Bologna: Libreria Piani 2022; first published 1943), thought number 7, page unnumbered.
54. Anti-fascists were caught by surprise. They had not expected that Mussolini would be removed in a palace coup, though in 1942 two American correspondents in Italy published a book in which they stated that 'the only kind of coup d'etat that would have a good chance of

success in Italy would be a "palace revolution"—that is, an agreement among the most prominent fascists to remove Mussolini and put another Fascist in his place'. Packard, *Balcony Empire*, p.368. Anti-fascists only inserted themselves into the public manifestations of joy during the day following the night of 25–26 July, mainly to direct action towards the call to release political prisoners.

55. The sheer speed with which people divested themselves of Fascism was viewed with a certain repulsion by some observers. See Calamandrei, *Diario 1939–1945*, p.389.
56. Davis, *Who Defends Rome?* p.160.
57. Ibid., p.155.
58. What was being repudiated was the representation of the Duce, in keeping with the medieval ritual of dethroning. In the medieval period it was a widespread practice to reject the body or person of a king—as the mystical embodiment of a community—when he became a threat to the cohesion of the community. In the absence of the king, rituals of dethroning were enacted by attacking statues and imagery that were regarded as containing something of his spirit. In the case of Mussolini, the ritual rejection of the symbols of the regime accompanied the repudiation of its leader, whose ejection from power had brought about the end of a whole system of rule. See Sergio Bertelli, *The King's Body: Sacred Rituals of Power in Medieval and Early Modern Europe* (Philadelphia: Pennsylvania University Press, 2001), p.247. This question is discussed, with special relevance to the Bologna equestrian statue of Mussolini, in Storchi, 'Mussolini as monument', pp.202–3, which has been used here.
59. Maria Pia Di Bella, 'From future to past: a Duce's trajectory' in John Borneman (ed.), *Death of the Father: An Anthropology of the End of Political Authority* (Oxford: Berghahn, 2003), p.34.
60. Mussolini, *Storia di un anno*, p.75.
61. Monelli, *Roma 1943*, p.30.
62. Christopher Duggan, in *Fascist Voices: An Intimate History of Mussolini's Italy* (Oxford: Oxford University Press, 2013), outlines the practice of exempting Mussolini himself from blame whenever something went wrong.
63. Colarizi, *La seconda guerra mondiale e la Repubblica*, p.192.
64. Simonetta Falasca-Zamponi, 'Ordinary anti-Fascism: Italy and the fall of Fascism, 1943–1945', *Journal of Modern Italian Studies*, 24:1, 2019, 171–89.
65. Ibid., p.176.
66. Cited in Pier Giorgio Zunino, *La Repubblica e il suo passato* (Bologna: Il Mulino, 2003), p.206.
67. Monelli, *Roma 1943*, pp.166–7.
68. Sigmund Freud, *Group Psychology and the Analysis of the Ego* (New York: W.W. Norton & Company, 1959), p.38.
69. Joshua Arthurs, 'Vivere il fascismo: politica e vita quotidiana durante il regime' in Giulia Albanese (ed.), *Il fascismo italiano: storia e interpretazioni* (Rome: Carocci, 2021), pp.237–53. See also Joshua Arthurs, 'Settling accounts: retribution, emotion and memory during the fall of Mussolini', *Journal of Modern Italian Studies*, 20:5, 2016, 617–39, pp.623–5.
70. Giannetto Magnanini, *Il regime badogliano a Reggio Emilia: 25 luglio–8 Settembre 1943* (Rome: Teti, 1999), p.75.
71. D'Eramo, *Il 25 luglio*, p.27.
72. Ibid., p.28.
73. Ibid., pp.19–22.

74. Ibid., p.23.
75. Duggan, *Fascist Voices*, p.30.
76. Ibid., p.391.
77. Magnanini, *Il regime badogliano a Reggio Emilia*, pp.32–5.
78. Christian Goeschel, *Mussolini and Hitler: The Forging of the Fascist Alliance* (New Haven and London: Yale University Press, 2020), p.258.
79. Private citizens were encouraged to denounce instances of unjustified wealth among officials and their families and report suspicions of money or goods being concealed or transferred to third parties. *La Stampa*, 28 August 1943, p.1.
80. Mussolini was taken into custody and was later transferred to Ponza and then Sardinia before being imprisoned in the Abruzzo.

NOTES TO CHAPTER 3

1. Gian Franco Venè, *Coprifuoco: vita quotidiana degli italiani nella guerra civile 1943–1945* (Milan; Mondadori, 1989), pp.63–4.
2. Renzo De Felice, *Mussolini l'alleato 1940–1945*. Tome 1: *L'Italia in guerra 1940–1943*. Tome 2: *Crisi e agonia del regime* (Turin: Einaudi, 1990), pp.1407–8.
3. Ibid., p.1410.
4. Renzo De Felice, *Mussolini l'alleato 1940–1945. La guerra civile 1943–1945* (Turin: Einaudi, 1996), p.19.
5. Ibid., pp.65–6.
6. Pier Giorgio Zunino, *La Repubblica e il suo passato* (Bologna: Il Mulino 2003), p.213.
7. For a fictionalised account of these feelings, see Carlo Mazzantini, *In Search of a Glorious Death* (London: Carcanet, 1992; first published Milan 1988).
8. Ibid., p.31.
9. Ornella Stellavato, 'I giovani romani e la Repubblica sociale' in IRSIFAR, *Roma tra fascismo e liberazione* (Milan: Franco Angeli, 2006), 49–66, p.64.
10. Ibid., p.65.
11. Ibid., p.65.
12. Giuseppe Bastianini, *Uomini cose fatti: memorie di un ambasciatore* (Milan: Vitalgiano, 1959), p.138.
13. Ibid., p.70.
14. Maria Fraddosio, 'The fallen hero: the myth of Mussolini and the fascist women in the Italian Social Republic (1943–5)', *Journal of Contemporary History*, 31:1, 1996, 99–124, p.101.
15. Ibid., p.103.
16. Ibid., p.104.
17. Ibid., p.106.
18. Ibid., pp.109–11.
19. Mimmo Franzinelli, *Il prigioniero di Salò: Mussolini e la tragedia italiana del 1943–45* (Milan: Mondadori, 2012), p.113.
20. The Germans never acknowledged it as a possible tool; where invitations to collaboration and cooperation were resisted, repression was employed.
21. Franzinelli, *Il prigioniero di Salò*, p.116.
22. Barbara Bracco, 'I segni littori di Milano: costruzione, distruzione e rinascita del volto di una città' in Giulia Albanese and Lucia Ceci (eds), *I luoghi del fascismo: memoria, politica, rimozione* (Rome: Viella, 2022), pp.149–51.
23. Ibid., p.117.

24. Archivio Centrale dello Stato (henceforth ACS), Segreteria Particolare del Duce (henceforth SPD), Carteggio Riservato (1922–1943), b.105, letter of P. Cambié to G. Vigorelli. 18 December 1944.
25. ACS, SPD, Cart. Ris. (1922–1943), b.105, Bruno (illegible) to Anita Quadrelli, 18 December 1944.
26. Rachele Mussolini, *Ma vie avec Benito* (Paris: Editions du Cheval Ailé, 1948), p.232.
27. Mazzantini, *In Search of a Glorious Death*, p.144.
28. Ibid., p.145.
29. Ibid., p.146.
30. Ibid., p.70.
31. Andrea Mammone, 'Gli orfani del duce: i fascisti dal 1943 al 1946', *Italia contemporanea*, 239:24(2), 2005, 249–74.
32. Venè, *Coprifuoco*, p.157.
33. De Felice, *Mussolini l'alleato 1940–1945*. Vol. 2: *La guerra civile 1943–1945*, pp.19, 53.
34. See Giovanni Contini, 'Novelists, historians and the memory of the Italian Resistance' in John Foot and Stephen Gundle (eds), *Paul Ginsborg and the Historiography of Modern Italy* (London: Palgrave Macmillan, 2024).
35. On the 'three Italies' of the 1943–45 period, see Federico Chabod, *Italia contemporanea (1918–1948)* (Turin: Einaudi, 1961), p.119.
36. David. W. Ellwood, *Italy 1943–1945* (Leicester: Leicester University Press, 1985), p.35.
37. Ester Lo Biundo, *London Calling Italy: BBC Broadcasts During the Second World War* (Manchester: Manchester University Press, 2022).
38. Emilio Gentile, *In Italia ai tempi di Mussolini: viaggio in compagnia di osservatori stranieri* (Milan: Mondadori, 2014), p.17.
39. Ibid., p.154. See also Mauro Canali, *La scoperta dell'Italia: il fascismo raccontato dai corrispondenti americani* (Venice: Marsilio, 2017), pp.319–21.
40. P.G. Edwards, 'The Foreign Office and Fascism 1924–1929', *Journal of Contemporary History*, 5:2, 1970, 53–61, pp.153–4.
41. Maurice Bedel, *Fascsime an VII* (Paris: Gallimard, 1929), pp.9–11.
42. Henri Béraud, *Ce que j'ai vu a Rome* (Paris: Editions de France, 1929), p.38.
43. Emil Ludwig, *Colloqui con Mussolini* (Milan: Mondadori, 2000; first published 1932), p.80.
44. John P. Diggins, *Mussolini and Fascism: The View from America* (Princeton: Princeton University Press, 1972), p.47. For Norman Manea, 'totalitarian tragedy' and 'totalitarian comedy' are inextricably linked. See Clown: il dittatore e l'artista (Milan: Il Saggiatore, 1995), p.10.
45. See Nicola Zapponi, *Il fascismo nella caricatura* (Rome and Bari: Laterza, 1981).
46. S. Gundle, 'Satire and the destruction of the cult of the Duce' in Gundle and others, *Against Mussolini: Art and the Fall of a Dictator* (London: Estorick Collection, 2010), p.18.
47. See Anna Fiaccarini et al. (eds), *The Great Dictator: Il grande dittatore di Charlie Chaplin* (Bologna: Cineteca di Bologna, 2002).
48. On Maccari's Dux exhibition on 6–7 September 1943, see Calamandrei, *Diario 1939–45*, p.224. See also Gundle, 'Satire and the destruction of the cult of the Duce', pp.15–35.
49. Sexual derision also came into it. In one image, a Mussolinian figure is shown groping the bare breasts of a young woman while, in the background, a figure resembling the national female symbol Italia adjusts her stockings. See Gundle, 'Satire and the destruction of the cult of the Duce', pp.20–1, 53.
50. Tono Zancanaro, Introduction to *Tono Zancanaro* (Ferrara: Galleria Civica d'Arte Moderna, 1973), page unnumbered.

51. Carlo Emilio Gadda, *Eros e Priapo* (Milan: Adelphi , 2016; first published 1967).
52. The two quoted expressions appear respectively on p.137 and p.356 of ibid.
53. Editorial, 'Twilight of the Gods', *Daily Mail*, 26 July 1943, p.1.
54. *A Bell for Adano* was a fictionalised version of a real episode from the Allied occupation of Sicily. Joppolo is the fictional alter ego of the American military governor of Licata named Frank E. Toscani, who in civilian life was a clerk in the New York City Sanitation Department. Licata, like Adano, was a fishing port, and the 700-year-old bell of the Church of Sant'Angelo had been taken away to be melted to make weapons and ammunition.
55. The film in fact was not shot on location in Sicily, but rather in California at Brent's Crags (thirty miles from Hollywood, near Malibu).
56. The inscription read as follows: 'To Benito Mussolini, pacifier of peoples and redeemer of the land of Libya, the populations, proud and in memory of where the sword of Islam flashed, consecrate in the sign of the Littorio a faith that challenges destiny'.
57. Mike Sibbons, *From the Archives: An Eclectic Mix of Stories from the History of REME* (Oxford: Osprey, 2016), pp.115–16.
58. Romano Mussolini, *My Father Il Duce* (Carlsbad, Calif.: Kales Press, 2006), p.144.
59. Ibid., p.43.
60. On the looting, see Vittore Querel, *Il paese di Benito* (Rome: Corso editore, 1954), pp.29–31.
61. Ellwood, *Italy 1943–1945*, p.71.
62. Paul Ginsborg, *A History of Contemporary Italy: Society and Politics, 1943–1988* (London: Penguin, 1990), p.37.
63. Ibid., p.37.
64. Curzio Malaparte, *La pelle* (Milan: Adelphi, 2010; first published 1949), p.48.
65. On Matthews, see Canali, *La scoperta dell'Italia*, p.385; Ellwood, *Italy 1943–1945*, p.72.
66. Herbert Matthews, The *Education of a Correspondent* (Westport, Conn.: Greenwood Press, 1946), p.482.
67. Ibid., p.482.
68. One of Mussolini's collaborators in the North, Asvero Gravelli, informed him of this slogan. 'He opened his eyes wide and began to laugh in his characteristic way', Gravelli later wrote, 'that is to say accompanying his laugh with a highly personal movement of his shoulders'. Asvero Gravelli, *Mussolini aneddotico* (Rome: Latinità 1951), p.289.
69. Giovanni Arteri, *Prima durante e dopo Mussolini: memorie del Novecento* (Milan: Mondadori, 1990), p.522.
70. Falasca-Zamponi, 'Ordinary anti-Fascism', p.179.
71. Ginsborg, *A History of Contemporary Italy*, p.38.
72. Ibid., p.38.

NOTES TO CHAPTER 4

1. Mirco Dondi, 'Piazzale Loreto' in Mario Isnenghi (ed.), *I luoghi della memoria: simboli e miti dell'Italia unita* (Rome: Laterza, 1996), p.494.
2. Sergio Luzzatto argues that he did this when he accepted responsibility for the killing of opposition deputy Giacomo Matteotti in 1924. See *Il corpo del duce* (Turin: Einaudi, 1998), p.6.
3. Challinor James, 'Dead Duce kicked by Milan crowds', *Daily Mail*, 30 April 1945, p.1.
4. Milton Bracker, 'Slain by partisans; Italy's former dictator shot after trial, other fascists executed', *New York Times*, 30 April 1945, p.1.
5. Colonel Valerio's real name, Walter Audisio, was revealed later. He became a public figure and the object of a hate campaign by the far right. See Giovanni Scirocco, 'Piazzale Loreto

29 aprile 1945: la memoria' in Elisabetta Colombo, Anna Modena and Giovanni Scirocco, *Il nostro silenzio avrà una voce: Piazzale Loreto—fatti e memoria* (Bologna: Il Mulino, 2021), pp.237 and 237n.

6. The French historian Pierre Milza offers the most serious and complete review of the many different accounts that have over the years been furnished by witnesses and others. See Les derniers jours de Mussolini (Paris: Fayard, 2010).
7. Benito Mussolini, *Storia di un anno: il tempo del bastone e della carota* (Rome: Libero, 2004; first published 1944), p.33.
8. Luigi Salvatorelli, *Leggenda e realtà di Napoleone* (Turin: UTET, 2007; first published 1944).
9. Ibid., p.6.
10. Ibid., p.4.
11. Ibid., p.124.
12. Quoted in Guri Schwartz, *Tu mi devi seppellir: riti funebri e culto nazionale alle orgini della Repubblica* (Turin: UTET, 2010), p.28. For a more personal angle on Nenni's pronouncements on Mussolini's death, see Duilio Susmel, *Nenni e Mussolini: mezzo secolo di fronte* (Milan: Rizzoli, 1969), pp.351–2.
13. Ibid., p.28n.
14. Renzo De Felice, *Mussolini l'alleato 1940–1945*. Vol. 2: *La guerra civile 1943–1945* (Turin: Einaudi, 1996), pp.32–3.
15. Ibid., p.118.
16. Raffaele Cadorna, *La riscossa* (Turin: Bietti, 1975), pp.203–4.
17. 'When tyrants are put to death, it should be by their own subjects', George Orwell remarked in a reflection on how dictatorial regimes end and the fate of their leaders. See S. Orwell and I. Angus (eds), *Collected Essays, journalism and Letters of George Orwell*, Vol. 2, *My Country Right or Left 1940–1943* (London; Secker and Warburg, 1968), p.324. See also John Foot, *Blood and Power: The Rise and Fall of Italian Fascism* (London: Bloomsbury, 2022), p.295.
18. Colombo, 'Resistenza e rappresaglia: i fatti di viale Abruzzi e piazzale Loreto' in Colombo, Modena and Scirocco, *Il nostro silenzio avrà una voce*, p.151.
19. Massimo Castoldi, Piazzale Loreto: *Milano, l'eccidio e il 'compromesso'* (Rome: Donzelli, 2020), p.157.
20. Colombo, 'Resistenza e rappresaglia', pp.153–4.
21. Scirocco, 'Piazzale Loreto 29 aprile 1945', p.237. On Parri's use of this term, see Dino Messina, 'Piazzale Loreto, la "macellaria messicana" che indignò i partigiani', *Corriere della sera*, 24 April 2015. See also Valiani, *Tutte le strade*, p.276. See also *L'Avantì*, 30 April 1945, p.1.
22. *L'Avantì*, 30 April 1945, p.1.
23. Ibid., p.1.
24. Milza, *Les derniers jours de Mussolini*, p.216.
25. Bertoldi, *Piazzale Loreto*, p.259.
26. Luigi Meneghello, *Bau-sète!* (Milan: Bompiani, Milano 1996), p.38.
27. Caterina Bianchi, 'Il nudo eroico del fascismo' in Sergio Bertelli and Cristiano Grottanelli (eds), *Gli occhi di Alessandro: potere sovrano e sacralità del corpo da Alessandro Magno a Ceausescu* (Florence: Ponte alle Grazie, 1990), pp.166–7.
28. Aldo Palazzeschi, *Tre imperi... mancati: cronaca 1922–1945* (Milan: Mondadori, 2016; first published 1945), p.220.
29. Silvio Bertoldi, *Piazzale Loreto* (Milan: Rizzoli, 2001), p.228.
30. Scirocco, 'Piazzale Loreto 29 aprile 1945', p.248.

31. Christopher Duggan, *Fascist Voices: An Intimate History of Mussolini's Italy* (London: The Bodley Head, 2012), p.417.
32. Milza, *Les derniers jours de Mussolini*, p.217.
33. Mimmo Franzinelli, *Il prigioniero di Salò: Mussolini é la tragedia italiana del 1943–1945* (Milan: Mondadori, 2012), p.16.
34. Emilio Radius, *Personaggi del secolo* (Milan: Palazzi, 1970), p.161.
35. Foot, *Blood and Power*, p.288.
36. Radius, *Personaggi del secolo*, p.162.
37. Bertoldi, *Piazzale Loreto*, p.250. For a discussion of Montanelli, see Scirocco, 'Piazzale Loreto 29 aprile 1945', pp.252–3.
38. Foot, *Blood and Power*, p.287.
39. Carlo Mazzantini, *In Search of a Glorious Death* (London: Carcanet, 1992; first published 1986), p.132–3.
40. Silvio Lanaro, *Storia dell'Italia repubblicana* (Venice: Marsilio, 1992), pp.28–9.
41. Mirco Dondi, cited in Scirocco, 'Piazzale Loreto 29 aprile 1945', p.243.
42. The demolition of the petrol station was reported in *Illustrazione italiana*, 19 September 1948. The article 'Il tempo passa su Piazzale Loreto' was authored by R.C., in reality former fascist journalist Giovanni Ansaldo, according to Scirocco. See 'Piazzale Loreto 29 aprile 1945', p.254. On the idea of the square as a non-place, see Anna Modena, 'I morti illimitati: le scritture di piazzale Loreto' in Colombo, Modena and Scirocco, *Il nostro silenzio avrà una voce*, pp.163–4.
43. Mazzantini, *In Search of a Glorious Death*, p.155.
44. Duggan, *Fascist Voices*, pp.418–19.
45. Ibid., pp.419–20.
46. The only instance of a Fascist committing suicide for Mussolini was the journalist Manlio Morgagni, who took his own life after the dictator was toppled in July 1943.
47. Volker Ullrich, *Hitler: Downfall 1939–1945* (London: The Bodley Head, 2020), p.603.
48. Alexander and Margarete Mitscherlich, *The Inability to Mourn: Principles of Collective Behaviour* (New York: Grove Press, 1975), p.26.
49. Ibid., p.26.
50. Milza, *Les derniers jours de Mussolini*, p.217.
51. Ibid., p.219.
52. https://fondazionefeltrinelli.it/piazzale-loreto-tra-memoria-e-oblio/ (consulted 28/1/21).
53. For Montanelli's writings on Mussolini over a long period, see his *Io e il duce*, edited by Mimmo Franzinelli (Milan: Rizzoli, 2018).

NOTES TO CHAPTER 5

1. Herbert Matthews, 'Hitler-Mussolini ideas still endanger Europe', *The New York Times*, 6 May 1945, p.E4.
2. Ibid.
3. Herbert Matthews, *The Education of a Correspondent* (New York: Harcourt, Brace & Co., 1946), p.493.
4. Ibid., p.498.
5. George Murray, 'Duce has made his niche in history', *Daily Mail*, 26 July 1943, p.2.
6. Ibid.
7. Rosario Forlenza, *On the Edge of Democracy: Italy, 1943–1948* (Oxford: Oxford University Press, 2020), p.29.
8. Luisa Passerini, 'Mussolini' in Mario Isnenghi (ed.), *I luoghi della memoria: personaggi e date dell'Italia unita* (Rome: Laterza, 1997), p.176.
9. Ibid., p.7.

10. Alexander and Margerete Mitscherlich, *The Inability to Mourn: Principles of Collective Behaviour* (New York: Grove Press, 1975).
11. Luca La Rovere, *L'eredità del fascismo: gli intellettuali, i giovani e la transizione al postfascismo (1943–1948)* (Turin: Bollati Boringhieri, 2008), p.358.
12. Franco Baldasso offer an interesting analysis of a variety of intellectuals, including Curzio Malaparte, Giuseppe Berto and others, who reflected on the responsibilities of the Italians and sometimes (though less frequently) on their own culpability. See *Against Redemption: Democracy, Memory, and Literature I Post-Fascist Italy* (New York: Fordham University Press, 2022). See also Michael Caesar, 'Writing and the real world: Italian narrative in the period of reconstruction' in Nicholas Hewitt (ed.), *The Culture of Reconstruction: European Literature, Thought and Film, 1945–50* (Basingstoke: Macmillan, 1989).
13. Benedetto Croce, 'L'Anticristo che è in noi' in Ilario Bertoletti (ed.), *La fine della civiltà, l'Anticristo che è in noi* (Brescia: Morcelliana, 2022; essay first published 1946), p.34.
14. Ibid., p.36 and p.34.
15. Ibid., p.40. By this time, Croce was thinking also of communism, as the reflection on fascism 'now passed gradually to the second level', Giuseppe Galasso, *Croce e lo spirito del suo tempo* (Rome: Laterza, 2002), p.420.
16. Benedetto Croce, 'The Fascist germ still lives', *The New York Times*, 28 November 1943, p.9.
17. Massimo Bontempelli, *Dignità dell'uomo (1943–1946)* (Milan: Bompiani, 1946), p.80.
18. Filippo Focardi, *Il bravo italiano e il cattivo tedesco: la rimozione eelle colpe della seconda guerra mondiale* (Rome: Laterza, 2013).
19. Guido Lami, *La psiche tedesca: osservazioni sulle psicogenesi del totalitarismo* (Brescia: Morcelliana, 1948), p.7.
20. Ibid., p.8.
21. The super-ego—or the ego-ideal (for Freud the two terms are inter-changeable)—is the psychic instance that is identified with moral conscience which should temper the impulses of the instincts. Sigmund Freud, *The Ego and the Id* (London: Hogarth Press, 1950), pp.44–9.
22. Lami drew on the work of Joachim Fleischer, who would move to the United States in 1950, and later elaborated his views on this topic in 'Political life and super-ego regression', *The Psychoanalytic Review*, 36:4, 1963, 416–28.
23. Lami, *La psiche tedesca*, pp.44–5.
24. Croce, cited and discussed in Pier Giorgio Zunino, *La Repubblica e il suo passato* (Bologna: Il Mulino, 2003), pp.293–4.
25. Lami, *La psiche tedesca*, p.45.
26. Ibid., p.45. This is precisely the view of Fascism developed in R.J.B. Bosworth, *Mussolini's Italy: Life Under the Fascist Dictatorship, 1915–1945* (London: Allen Lane, 2005).
27. Christian Goeschel, *Mussolini and Hitler: The Forging of the Fascist Alliance* (New Haven and London: Yale University Press, 2018), p.4.
28. David W. Ellwood, *Italy 1943–1945* (Leicester: Leicester University Press, 1985), p.117.
29. The potential confusion between different sorts of guilt—moral, political, metaphysical, individual and collective—led one of the country's leading philosophers—Karl Jaspers—to intervene to bring some clarity to the terms of the debate. See Jaspers, *The Question of German Guilt* (New York: Fordham University Press, 2000; first published 1946). On Jaspers, see Jeffrey K. Olick, 'In the ashes of disgrace: guilt versus shame revisited' in Efrat Ben Ze'ev, Ruth Ginio and Jay Winter (eds), *Shadows of War: A Social History of Silence in the Twentieth Century* (Cambridge: Cambridge University Press, 2020).
30. Luca La Rovere, 'The "examination of conscience" of the nation: the lost debate about the "collective guilt" in Italy, 1943–5', *Totalitarian Movements and Political Religions*, 9:2–3, 2008, 187–202. More of this debate has been brought to light and examined by Franco

Baldasso in *Against Redemption: Democracy, Memory and Literature in Post-Fascist Italy* (New York: Fordham University Press, 2022).

31. Ibid., p.16.
32. La Rovere, 'The "examination of conscience"', p.189. One of the few who had been implicated in the rise of Mussolini who took responsibility was Margherita Sarfatti, although her volume *My Fault*, in which she demolished the man she had built up in *Dux*, was not published in 1947, as she had hoped. It only appeared, and in English, in 2014. See Margherita Sarfatti, *My Fault: Mussolini as I Knew Him*, ed. by Brian Sullivan (New York: Enigma Books, 2014). See Sullivan's introduction for her efforts to publish the book in Italy after the war. More generally, Baldasso discusses intellectuals who refused to embrace the credo of national redemption and sought instead to reflect on a defeat that involved them personally. See *Against Redemption*.
33. Focardi, *Il cattivo tedesco e il bravo italiano*, p.xvii.
34. Ibid., p.74.
35. Focardi, *Il cattivo tedesco e il bravo italiano*, p.xviii.
36. Aldo Palazzeschi, *Tre imperi... mancati: cronaca 1922–1945* (Milan: Mondadori, 2016), p.210. Gadda's sarcastically satirical denunciation of the collective enslavement to Mussolini had a similar premise. See Carlo Emilio Gadda, *Eros e Priapo* (Milan: Adelphi, 20916; first published 1967).
37. Tony Judt, *Post-war: A History of Europe Since 1945* (London: Heinemann, 2005), p.808.
38. Focardi, *Il cattivo tedesco e il bravo Italiano*, p.53.
39. Norberto Bobbio, 'Le colpe rimosse di noi italiani', *La Stampa*, 6 December 1988, p.1. Also contained in Pirani, *Il fascino del nazismo*, pp.112–15.
40. Christopher Duggan, *Fascist Voices: An Intimate History of Mussolini's Italy* (London: Vintage, 2013).
41. Ibid., p.543.
42. See ibid., p.420.
43. Gian Maria Capuani, *Ricordi di tempi fascisti* (Milan: Jaca Book, 1995), p.52.
44. Mitscherlich and Mitscherlich, *The Inability to Mourn*, pp.26–7.
45. R.D. Laing, *The Divided Self: An Existential Study in Sanity and Madness* (London: Penguin, 1960).
46. Salvatore Satta, *De Profundis* (Milan: Adelphi, 1980; first published 1945), p.43. See also Vitaliano Brancati, *Diario romano* (Milan: Bompiani, 1984; first published 1961), p.125 in which the Sicilian writer argued that Italians who applauded the dictator in mass rallies were behaving like theatrical extras.
47. Andrea Damiano, *Rosso e grigio* (Milan: Muggiani, 1947), pp.33–4.
48. On the attempts to redress this cancellation, see Francesco Germinaro, *L'altra memoria: l'estrema destra, Sal e la Resistenza* (Turin: Bollati Boringhieri, 1999).
49. On the novels of the Axis war, see Guido Bartolini, *The Italian Literature of the Axis War: Memories of Self-Absolution and the Quest for Responsibility* (Basingstoke: Palgrave Macmillan, 2021).
50. Simona Colarizi, 'Fascism-qualunquism-neofascism: the rise of neo-fascism in Italy in the first postwar period, until the foundation of the neo-fascist political party' in Stein Larsen (ed.), *Modern Europe after Fascism, 1943–1980s* (New York: Columbia University Press, 1998), p.500.
51. Ibid., p.511.
52. Ibid., p.508.
53. Bontempelli, *Dignità dell'uomo*, p.14.

54. Ibid., p.15.
55. See Simona Storchi, *Massimo Bontempelli e la cultura italiana fra le due guerre: l'intellettuale, il fascismo, la modernità* (Milan: Mimesis, 2024), pp.287–90. See also Paolo Aquilanti, *Il caso Bontempelli* (Palermo: Sellerio, 2020).
56. Pier Giorgio Zunino (ed.), *Scritti politici di Alcide De Gasperi* (Milan: Feltrinelli, 1979), p.300. Speech of 14 December 1946.
57. Renato Moro, Il mito dell'Italia cattolica: *nazione, religione e cattolicesimo negli anni del fascismo* (Rome: Studium, 2021), pp.549–50.
58. Ibid., p.551.
59. Ibid., p.551.
60. Forlenza, *On the Edge of Democracy*, p.72. On the way American ideas and popular culture were received in postwar Italy and clashed with Soviet-derived ideas, see Pier Paolo D'Attore (ed.), *Nemici per la pelle: sogno americano e mito sovietico nell'Italia contemporanea* (Milan: Franco Angeli, 1991).
61. Ibid., p.105.
62. Theodor W. Adorno, *Guilt and Defense: On the Legacies of National Socialism in Postwar Germany* (Cambridge, Mass.: Harvard University Press, 2010), p.213.
63. Ibid., p.220.
64. Cited in Jeffrey Herf, *Divided Memory: The Nazi Past in the Two Germanys* (Cambridge, Mass.: Harvard University Press, 1997), p.300.
65. Ibid., p.370. Speech of 8 August 1951.
66. Mitscherlich and Mitscherlich, *The Inability to Mourn*, p.271.
67. Carlo Mazzantini, *In Search of a Glorious Death* (Manchester: Carcanet, 1992; first published 1986), pp.161–2.
68. Caesar, 'Writing and the Real World', p.40.
69. Forlenza, *On the Edge of Democracy*, pp.145–6. On the private worlds of the supposedly former Fascist fathers of two journalists, see Pierluigi Battista, *Mio padre era fascista* (Milan: Mondadori, 2016) and Andrea Cangini (ed.), *La camicia nera di mio padre: riflessioni sulla morte della patria* (Bologna: Minerva, 2018).
70. See Baldasso, *Against Redemption*, pp.118–25. The phenomenon of the 'home museum' of colonial souvenirs and artefacts is discussed by Angelo Del Boca in 'Impero' in Mario Isnenghi (ed.), *I luoghi della memoria: simboli e miti dell'Italia unita* (Rome: Laterza, 1996), p.436.
71. See Baldasso, *Against Redemption*, pp.51–64.
72. Simon Levis Sullam, *I fantasmi del fascismo: le metamorfosi degli intellettuali italiani nel dopoguerra* (Milan: Feltrinelli, 2021), p.133.

NOTES TO CHAPTER 6

1. Archivio Centrale dello Stato (ACS), Presidenza del Consiglio dei Ministri (PCM), 1934–36, 14.5.
2. Sebastian Hauffner, *The Meaning of Hitler* (London: Phoenix, 2011; first published 1978), p.4.
3. Max Picard, *Hitler in Ourselves* (Hinsdale, Ill.: Regnery, 1947), p.28.
4. Cristina Baldassini, *L'ombra di Musssolini: l'Italia moderata e la memoria del fascsimo (1945–1960)* (Soveria Mannelli: Rubbettino, 2008), p.20.
5. See Emilio Gentile, *Chi è fascista* (Rome: Laterza, 2019), pp.10–12.
6. Paul Ginsborg, Family Politics*: Domestic Life, Devastation and Survival, 1900–1950* (New Haven and London: Yale University Press, 2014), p.169.

7. Quinto Navarra, *Memorie del cameriere di Mussolini* (Milan: Longanesi, 1946), pp.70–1.
8. Luisa Passerini, 'Mussolini' in Mario Isnenghi (ed.), *I luoghi della memoria: personaggi e date dell'Italia unita* (Rome: Laterza, 1997), p.185.
9. Ibid.
10. Alberto Mario Banti, *Sublime madre nostra: la nazione italiana dal Risorgimnto al fascismo* (Rome: Laterza, 2011), pp.39–40. Vitaliano Brancati discussed him as 'the head of the family' of the entire nation. See *Diario romano* (Milan: Bompiani, 1984; first published 1961), p.73.
11. Luisa Passerini, *Mussolini immaginario: storia di una biografia, 1915–1939* (Rome: Laterza, 1991), p.94–8.
12. See Christopher Duggan, *Fascist Voices: An Intimate History of Mussolini's Italy* (London: The Bodley Head, 2012), pp.216–37.
13. Picard, *Hitler in Ourselves*, p.28.
14. John Borneman, 'Introduction', in Borneman (ed.), *Death of the Father: An Anthropology of the End in Political Authority* (Oxford: Berghahn, 2004), p.4.
15. Maria Pia Di Bella, 'From future to past: a Duce's trajectory' in Borneman (ed.), *Death of the Father*, p.40.
16. *Il Meridiano d'Italia illustrato*, 25 July 1951, p.2.
17. Passerini, *Mussolini immaginario*, p.125.
18. Joachim Fleischer in 'Political Life and Super-Ego Regression', *Psychological Review*, 36:4, 1949, 416–28.
19. Passerini, *Mussolini immaginario*, p.125.
20. Rachele Mussolini, 'Mussolini vent'anni dopo', third part, *Gente*, n.16, 1964, p.27.
21. Ibid.
22. Renato Moro, *Il mito dell' Italia cattolica: nazione, religione e cattolicesimo negli anni del Fascismo* (Rome: Studium, 2020).
23. Ginsborg, *Family Politics*, p.193.
24. Edda Ciano, *La mia vita: intervista con Domenico Olivieri* (Milan: Mondadori, 2001), pp.94–5.
25. See Antonio Spinosa, *Edda: una tragedia italiana* (Milan: Mondadori, 1995), pp.337–48.
26. 'After the death of Bruno, our whole family gave its tragic and bloody contribution to death', Rachele Mussolini wrote in *Ma vie avec Benito*, p.239.
27. Romano Mussolini, *My Father Il Duce* (Carlsbad, Calif.: Kales Press, 2006; first published in Italian in 2004), pp.49–56; see Bruno D'Agostini, *Colloqui con Rachele Mussolini* (Rome: O.E.T Edizioni del Secolo, 1946), pp.12, 27–8.
28. On the cultural standing of war widows and the translation of this into political value in support of a defeated order—in a very different context—see Angela Esco Elder, *Love and Duty: Confederate Widows and the Emotional Politics of Loss* (Chapel Hill, N.C.: University of North Carolina Press, 2022), pp.2–5.
29. Rachele Mussolini, *La mia vita con Benito* (Milan: Mondadori, 1948). Family photographs were published in Rachele Mussolini, 'Il mio album', *Tempo*, 25 August 1962.
30. Mino Caudana, 'Edda mi ha detto', *Oggi*, 24 June to 27 July 1947.
31. Cristina Baldassini, L'ombra di Mussolini*: l'Italia moderata e la memoria del fascismo (1945–1960)* (Soveria Mannelli: Rubbettino, 2008), pp.285–6.
32. Guri Schwarz, *Tu mi devi seppellir: riti funebri e culto nazionale alle origini della Repubblica* (Turin: UTET, 2010).
33. Sergio Luzzatto, *Il corpo del duce: un cadavere tra immaginazione, storia e memoria* (Turin: Einaudi, 1998), pp.120–1.

34. In her memoirs, *Ma vie avec Benito* (Paris: Edition du Cheval Ailé, 1948), Rachele Mussolini asserted that during the regime, 'I took care to avoid professions of faith. I repeated that politics was not my business and that I was only the wife of Mussolini; his wife and nothing more.... This attitude, adopted right from the start, helped create the legend that I was not interested in my husband's official and political life. But the reality was completely different and even the opposite: Benito continued to confide in me and I, because I was proud to have his trust, knowing that it was the depository of his aspirations and plans, decided to jealously keep to myself everything that he told me', p.65.
35. Rachele Mussolini, 'Il mio album', p.18.
36. See Anne Wingenter, '"Mothers of the Fallen" between symbolic and experienced political participation' in Karen Lauwers, Sami Suodenjoki and Marnix Beyen (eds), *Subaltern Political Subjectivities and Practices in the Nineteenth and Twentieth Centuries* (London: Routledge, 2023).
37. Rachele Mussolini, quoted in *Tempo*, 9 September 1962, p.16.
38. Renzo De Felice, *Mussolini l'alleato 1940–1945*. Tomo 2: *Crisi e agonia del regime* (Turin: Einaudi, 1990), p.1345.
39. Renzo De Felice, *Mussolini il duce*. Tomo I: *Gli anni del consenso 1929–1936* (Turin: Einaudi, 1974), p.798.
40. Se Luigi Romersa, 'È in vendita la Rocca della Caminate', *Tempo*, 2 July 1955, 16–17.
41. Mussolini, *My Father Il Duce*, pp.59–69.
42. Mussolini, *Ma vie avec Benito*. The volume contains various photographs of Rachele in domestic settings. On Sarfatti's *Dux*, see Simona Storchi, 'Margherita Sarfatti and the invention of the Duce' in Stephen Gundle, Christopher Duggan and Giuliana Pieri (eds), *The Cult of the Duce: Mussolini and the Italians* (Manchester: Manchester University Press, 2013).
43. According to the Duce's attendant Quinto Navarra, she only ever referred to him while he was in power as 'Mussolini'. *Le memorie del cameriere di Mussolini*, p.85.
44. Baldassini, *L'ombra di Mussolini*, p.289.
45. See Romano Mussolini, *Il Duce, mio padre* (Milan: Rizzoli, 2004).
46. Sudhir Hazareesingh, *The Legend of Napoleon* (London: Granta, 2004), p.232.
47. Alexander and Margarete Mitscherlich, *The Inability to Mourn: Principles of Collective Behaviour* (New York: Grove Press, 1975), pp.62–3.
48. Rivista romana (ed.), *Mussolini* (Rome: Centro editoriale nazionale, 1958), p.15.
49. Teodorani married Arnaldo Mussolini's daughter Rosa. Having played a part in the press of the RSI, and narrowly escaped execution at Dongo, after the war he was a contributor to, and then editor of, the Fascist satirical weekly *Asso di bastoni*.
50. Vanni Teodorani, 'il segreto di Mussolini' in Rivista romana, *Mussolini*, p.585.
51. Ibid., p.590.
52. Ibid., p.591.
53. Luzzato, *Il corpo del duce*, pp.218–19.
54. See Laura Impert and Margaret Rubin, 'The mother at the glen: the relationship between mourning and nostalgia', *Psychoanalytic Dialogues*, 21, 2011, 691–706.
55. Orianne Aymard, *When a Goddess Dies: Worshipping Ma Anandamayi after Her Death* (Oxford: Oxford University Press, 2014), p.129.
56. Ibid., p.153.
57. Ibid., p.155.
58. See Stephen Gundle, 'The "civic religion" of the Resistance in postwar Italy', *Modern Italy*, 5:2, 2000, 113–32, p.127.

59. Baldassini, *L'ombra di Mussolini*, pp.8–9.
60. Rachele Mussolini, 'Per due volte le nostre pene', *Gente*, 16 April 1964, p.26. On Celentano, see Stephen Gundle, 'Adriano Celentano and the origins of rock and roll in Italy', *Journal of Modern Italian Studies*, 11:3, 2006, 367–86.

NOTES TO CHAPTER 7

1. For Victoria De Grazia, 'No European leader of the period was more involved than Mussolini in a competition of virility, none as aware of the importance of image'. See *Storia delle donne nel regime fascista*, new edition (Venice: Marsilio, 2023), p.438.
2. Barbara Spackman, *Fascist Virilities: Rhetoric, Ideology and Social Fantasy in Italy* (Minneapolis: University of Minnesota Press, 1996), p.2; Sandro Bellassai, 'The masculine mystique: antimodernism and virility in fascist Italy', *Journal of Modern Italian Studies*, 10:3, 2005, 314–35.
3. Spackman, *Fascist Virilities*, p.xii.
4. Bellassai, 'The masculine mystique', p.315. For a wider view of Fascism, masculinity and the family, see Paul Ginsborg, *Famiglia novecento: vita famigliare, rivoluzione e dittature, 1900–1950* (Turin: Einaudi, 2013), pp.245–321.
5. This is recurrent theme in modern masculinity, as Christopher Forth shows in Masculinity in the Modern West: Gender, Civilisation and the Body (Basingstoke: Palgrave Macmillan, 2008).
6. See Giordano Bruno Guerri (ed.), *Rapporto al Duce: le interrogazioni delle organizzazioni provinciali del 1942* (Milan: Bompiani) 2020), pp.527–9. Emilio Gentile has referred to this as an attempt at an 'anthropological revolution'. See Gentile, *Fascismo: storia e interpretazioni* (Rome: Laterza, 2002), Chapter 10.
7. Giulietta Stefani, *Colonia per maschi: italiani in Africa Orientale—un storia di genere* (Verona: Ombre corte, 2007), pp.42–3.
8. On the failure of the idea of creating a new fascistic man, see Nicola Labanca, 'Constructing Mussolini's new man in Africa? Italian memories of the fascist war in Ethiopia', *Italian Studies*, 61:2, 2006, 225–32.
9. Sandro Bellassai, 'L'autunno del patriarca: insicurezze maschili nel secondo dopoguerra' in Penny Morris, Francesco Ricatti and Mark Seymour (eds), *Politica ed emozioni nella storia d'Italia: dal 1848 ad oggi* (Rome: Viella, 2012), p.193.
10. Patrizia Gabrielli, *Il 1946, le donne, la repubblica* (Rome: Donzelli, 2009), p.5.
11. Ibid., p.5.
12. Ibid.
13. Guri Schwarz argues that in postwar rituals 'it is striking that there is no centre, no figure capable of dominating the symbolic scene and act as the fulcrum around which action rotates. There was no authority that played a role comparable to that of the monarch in liberal Italy or the Duce in Fascist Italy'. See *Tu mi devi seppellir: riti funebri e culto nazionale alle origini della Repubblica* (Turin: UTET, 2010), p.110.
14. Michael Foley, *Political Leadership: Themes, Contexts and Critiques* (Oxford: Oxford University Press, 2013), p.1.
15. Oliver Logan, 'Pius XII: romanità, prophecy and charisma', *Modern Italy*, 3:2, 1998, 237–47.
16. Angelo Ventrone, 'Forme e strumenti della propaganda di masa nella nascita e nel consolidamento della Repubblica (1946–1958)' in Maurizio Ridolfi (ed.), *Propaganda e comunicazione politica: storia e trasformazione nell'età contemporanea* (Milan: Brunop Mondadori, 2004), p.221.
17. Renato Moro, *Il mito dell' Italia cattolica: nazione, religione e cattolicesimo negli anni del Fascismo* (Rome: Studium, 2020).

18. Luciano Cavalli, 'Considerations on charisma and the cult of charismatic leadership', *Modern Italy* 3:2, 1998, 159–71, p.167.
19. Marzia Marsili, 'De Gasperi and Togliatti: political leadership and personality cults in post-war Italy', *Modern Italy*, 3:2, 1998, 249–61.
20. Ibid. On Mussolini and mountains, see Marco Armiero, 'Making Italians out of rocks: Mussolini's shadows on Italian mountains', *Modern Italy*, 19:3, 2014, 261–74, p.263.
21. On the postwar Communist subculture, see Stephen Gundle, *Between Hollywood and Moscow: the Italians Communists and the Challenge of Mass Culture, 1943–91* (Duram, N.C.: Duke University Press, 2000).
22. Ruth Ben-Ghiat, 'Unmaking the Fascist man: masculinity, film and the transition from dictatorship', *Journal of Modern Italian Studies*, 10:3, 2005, pp.335–65.
23. Ibid., pp.31–2.
24. An extraordinary account of the much-interrupted speech given to a rally by the anarchist-turned-monarchist Maria Rygier in Ancona in 1946 is offered by Barbara Montesi in *Un 'anarchica monarchica': vita di Maria Rygier (1885–1953)* (Naples: Edizioni Scientifiche Italiane, 2013), pp.268–9.
25. Donatella Campus, 'Women in politics' in Erik Jones and Gianfranco Pasquino (eds), *The Oxford Handbook of Italian Politics* (Oxford: Oxford University Press, 2015), p.628.
26. Ibid., p.627.
27. Gabrielli, *Il 1946, le donne, la repubblica*, p.104.
28. Patrizia Gabrielli, *Il tempio della virilità: l'antifascismo, il genere, la storia* (Milan: Franco Angeli, 2008).
29. See Ulrike Sieglohr (ed.), *Heroines Without Heroes: Reconstructing Female and National Identities in European Cinema, 1945–51* (London: Bloomsbury, 2016).
30. Angelo Del Boca, 'Impero' in Mario Isnenghi (ed.), *I luoghi della memoria: simboli e miti dell'Italia unita* (Rome: Laterza, 1996), pp.420–1. See also R.J.B. Bosworth, *Mussolini and the Eclipse of Italian Fascism: From Dictatorship to Populism* (New Haven and London: Yale University Press, 2021), p.197. See also Daniela Baratieri, *Memories and Silences Haunted by Fascism: Italian Colonialism MCMXXX–MCMLX* (Bern: Peter Lang, 2010). On the memory of colonialism, see Giacomo Mancosu, 'Rituals of colonial memory: crafting imperial nostalgia in republican Italy', *Journal of Contemporary History*, 59:4, 2024, 660–85.
31. See Richard Dyer, *White* (London: Routledge, second edition 2017), pp.152–3, 163.
32. Gundle, *Between Hollywood and Moscow*, pp.83–4.
33. A. Ventrone, 'Forme e strumenti della propaganda di massa nella nascita e nel consolidamento della Repubblica (1946–1958)' in M. Ridolfi (ed.), *Propaganda e comunicazione politica: storia e trasformazioni nell'eta' contemporanea* (Milano: Bruno Mondadori, 2004), p.221.
34. Stephen Gundle, 'From Mussolini to Berlusconi: masculinity and political leadership in post-war Italy' in Christopher Fletcher and others (eds), *The Palgrave Handbook of Masculinity and Political Culture in Europe* (Basingstoke: Palgrave Macmillan, 2018), pp.436–42.
35. Angelo Del Boca, *The Ethiopian War, 1935–1941* (Chicago: Chicago University Press, 1966), p.276.
36. See Stephen Gundle, 'The aftermath of the Mussolini cult: history, nostalgia and popular culture' in Stephen Gundle, Christopher Duggan and Giuliana Pieri (eds), *The Cult of the Duce: Mussolini and the Italians* (Manchester: Manchester University Press, 2013), pp.245–6.
37. Curzio Malaparte, 'Deux chapeaux de paille d'Italie' appendix to *Ces sacrés Toscans* (Paris: Les belles lettres, 2014; first published 1948).

38. Ibid., p.215.
39. Writer Vitaliano Brancati referred to the continuing circulation of ideas of virile, sexualised images of leadership deriving from Mussolini. See *Diario romano* (Milan: Bompiani, 1984; first published 1961), p.79.
40. Giovanni Ansaldo, *Anni freddi: diari 1946–1950* (Bologna: Il Mulino, 2003), p.88.
41. R.J.B. Bosworth, 'Dictators strong or weak? The Model of Benito Mussolini' in Bosworth (ed.), *The Oxford Handbook of Fascism* (Oxford: Oxford University Press, 2010).
42. Jean Lipman-Blumen, *The Allure of Toxic Leaders* (Oxford: Oxford University Press, 2005).
43. Ibid., p.18.
44. Hannah Arendt, *The Origins of Totalitarianism* (New York: Schocken, 1948), pp.459, 490–1.
45. Ulrich Raulff, *Farewell to the Horse: The Final Century of Our Relationship* (London: Penguin, 2017), p.368.
46. Leo Longanesi, *Il destino à cambiato cavallo* (Milan: Ronda, 1951).
47. On the eclipse of the horse, and the nostalgia it gave rise to, see Alberto Theodoli, *A cavallo di due secoli* (Rome: la Navicella, 1950), p.197. For a more general cultural treatment, see Raulff, *Farewell to the Horse*.
48. See Stephen Gundle, 'The Death (and Re-Birth) of the Hero: Charisma and Manufactured Charisma in Modern Italy', *Modern Italy*, 3:2, 1998, 173–89.
49. Carlo Emilio Gadda, *Eros e Priapo* (Milan: Adelphi, 2016; first published 1967), p.60.
50. Camillo Berneri, *Mussolini: psicologia di un dittatore* (Milan: Edizioni Azione comune, 1966), p.73.
51. Vitaliano Brancati, *I fascisti invecchiano* (Milan: Longanesi, 1950), p.101.
52. Calipso, *Vita segreta di Mussolini* (Rome: unidentified publisher, 1944), p.27.
53. Stephen Gundle, 'Mussolini between hero-worship and demystification: exemplary anecdotes, *Petite Histoire* and the problem of humanization', *Comparative Studies in Society and History*, 64:1, 2022, 122–49.
54. Caroline Humphrey, 'Exemplars and Rules: aspects of the discourse of moralities in Mongolia', *The Ethnography of Morality*, 1997, 25–49, 39.
55. Andrea Martini, *Fascismo immaginario: riscrivere il passato a destra* (Rome: Laterza, 2024), pp.135–72.
56. Romano Mussolini, My Father Il Duce (Carlsbad, Calif.: Kales Press, 2008), p.64.
57. Quinto Navarra, *Memorie del cameriere di Mussolini* (Milan: Longanesi, 1946), p.200.
58. Ibid., pp.200–1.
59. Ibid., p.204.
60. Ibid., p.205.
61. The origins of the text were revealed many years later in a biography of Longanesi by Montanelli and another journalist, Marcello Staglieno, published in 1984, which stated that the memoirs were 'in reality dictated to Leo and one of the authors of the present book'. Indro Montanelli and Marcello Staglieno, *Leo Longanesi* (Milan: Longanesi, 1984), p.47.
62. 'The book was written in reality by Longanesi and Montanelli, following the verbal account and on the basis of notes by Navarra himself', Montanelli and Staglieno added. In fact, the fluid, ironical style of the memoirs needed the input of the two experienced journalists who understood the power of anecdotes and the impact they could have on public opinion. Ibid., p.310n2. The close colleague was Giovanni Ansaldo. See *Anni freddi: diari 1946–1950*, p.78. Ansaldo also recounts the story of the Navarra volume on pp.77–8.
63. Constant, *Memorie del cameriere di Napoleone* (Milan: Rizzoli, 1941).

64. First published in 1830 in six volumes, the text was in fact initially written by Jean-Baptiste de Roquefort-Flaméricourt and completed by the journalists Auguste Luchet and Désiré Nisard.
65. Constant, *Memorie del cameriere di Napoleone*, p.283.
66. Giordano Bruno Guerri, 'Mussolini, duce con i mutandoni', *Il Giorno*, 3 April 1983.
67. Paolo Monelli, *Mussolini: An Intimate Life* (London: Thames and Hudson, 1953), p.147.
68. Renzo De Felice, *Mussolini il duce*, II *Lo Stato totalitario* (Turin: Einaudi, 1981), pp.275–6 and 276n.
69. Pierre Milza, *Mussolini* (Rome: Carocci, 2000; first published Paris, 1999), p.511.
70. R.J.B. Bosworth, *Mussolini* (London: Bloomsbury, 2002), p.212.
71. Ruth Ben-Ghiat, *Strongmen: Mussolini to the Present* (New York: Norton, 2020), p.250: 'The strongman brand of charisma... attracts followers by celebrating male authority'.
72. See Bellassai, *L'invenzione della virilità*, pp.98–116. The author refers to the replacement of 'virilism' as a hegemonic force in Italian society in the 1960s by an 'informal virilism' that safeguards the same values.
73. See Stephen Gundle, 'From Mussolini to Berlusconi: masculinity and political leadership in postwar Italy' in Christopher Fletcher and others (eds), *The Palgrave Handbook of Masculinity and Political Culture in Europe* (London: Palgrave, 2018), pp.435–55.
74. Mario Isnenghi, *Storia d'Italia: i fatti e le percezioni dal Risorgimento alla società dello spettacolo* (Rome: Laterza, 2011), p.639.
75. A poll in 2019 showed 60 per cent of people supported the idea of a strong leader. See Ilvo Diamanti, *La Repubblica*, 28 January 2019, p.11. Discussed in 'Le lettere di Corrado Augias', *La Repubblica*, 30 January 2019, p.28.
76. Forth, *Masculinity in the Modern West*, pp.201–15.
77. Eugenio Scalfari, 'Una dittatura è una sciagura, un vero leader è una fortuna', *La Repubblica*, 22 December 2013, p.23.
78. David Ward, *Antifascisms: Cultural Politics in Italy 1943–46* (Madison, N.J.: Farleigh Dickinson University Press, 1996), p.33.
79. Scalfari, 'Una dittatura è una sciagura', p.24.
80. Gad Lerner, 'Da Bossi a Salvini la lingua leghista non è mai cambiata', *La Repubblica*, 28 May 2019, p.15.
81. Hilary Clarke, 'Italy's Salvini channels Mussolini in tweet on late dictator's birthday', CNN World, 30 July 2018. https://edition.cnn.com/2018/07/30/europe/salvini-mussolini-italy-intl/index.html (consulted 19/5/20).
82. Scalfari, 'Una dittatura è una sciagura', p.23.
83. On the post-fascist populist tendency to 'leap over' or ignore Mussolini and focus instead on less burdensome right-wing themes, see David Broder, *Mussolini's Grandchildren: Fascism in Contemporary Italy* (London: Pluto Press, 2023), pp.24, 43.

NOTES TO CHAPTER 8

1. Benito Mussolini, *Storia di un anno: il tempo del bastone e della carota* (Rome: Libero 2004; first published 1944), p.109. See also Romano Mussolini, *My Father Il Duce* (Carlsbad, Calif.: Kales Press, 2006) in which Mussolini's son claims that his father was tormented by the idea that the Americans would stage a show trial at Madison Square Gardens 'with the people in the stands looking at me as if I were a caged beast'. Apparently, he added: 'No, it is better to die with weapons raised. Only this can be an end worthy of my existence' (p.8).
2. Michele Battini, *The Missing Italian Nuremberg: Cultural Amnesia and Postwar Politics* (New York: Palgrave Macmillan, 2007).

3. For an account of how former fascists managed to find space for their views in the daily press, the illustrated magazines and the publishing world, see the Andrea Martini, *Fascismo immaginario: riscrivere il passato a destra* (Rome: Laterza, 2024), pp.135–72.
4. The risk of allowing the accused too much space, even in an imaginary trial, was a problem that George Steiner encountered—and later admitted—in his fictional trial of Hitler, *The Portage to San Cristobel of A.H.* (London: Faber and Faber, 1981).
5. Cassius, *The Trial of Mussolini* (London: Gollancz, 1943).
6. Ibid., p.1.
7. Ibid., p.2.
8. Ibid., p.3.
9. Ibid., p.4
10. Ibid., pp.4–5.
11. Ibid., pp.56–61.
12. Ibid., p.75.
13. Ibid., p.75.
14. Ibid., p.80.
15. See Battini, *The Missing Italian Nuremberg*.
16. Indro Montanelli, *Il buonuomo Mussolini* (Milan: Edizioni Riunite, 1947). On the right-wing journalism and publishing of the postwar years, see Martini, *Fascismo immaginario*.
17. Notorius, *Processo a Benito Mussolini* (Milan: Paneuropa, 1959).
18. Ibid., p.5.
19. Mino Caudana, *Il figlio del fabbro* (Rome: C.E.N., undated but elsewhere indicated as 1964).
20. Caudana, *Il figlio del fabbro*, p.425.
21. Ibid., pp.365–6.
22. Ibid., p.560.
23. Baldassini, *L'ombra di Mussolini*, p.72.
24. Ibid., p.170.
25. Caudana (whose real name was Anselmo Jona) would go on to author a number of other texts relating to the regime, including *1922* (Milan: Edizioni del Borghese, 1972) and *I fucilati di Verona* (Rome: CEN, 1973).
26. Caudana, *Il figlio del fabbro*, p.3.
27. Ibid., p.705.
28. Giovanni Ansaldo, *Anni freddi: Diari 1946–1950* (Bologna: Il Mulino, 2003), p.204.
29. Mino Caudana, *Processo a Mussolini* (Rome: C.E.N., 1964).
30. Ibid., p.5.
31. For a reflection on a similar exercise in Germany, see Gavriel D. Rosenfeld. *Hi Hitler! How the Nazi Past Is Being Normalized in Contemporary Culture* (Cambridge: Cambridge University Press, 2014), pp.193–205.
32. Caudana, *Processo a Mussolini*, p.29.
33. Ibid., p.76.
34. Ibid., pp.73–4.
35. Ibid., p.76.
36. Ibid., p.84.
37. The real Folke Bernadotte was engaged in negotiations to secure the release in the final stages of the war of prisoners from concentration camps. He would be appointed by the UN as mediator in the Arab–Israeli conflict of 1947–48 and was assassinated by a Zionist group in Jerusalem in 1948.

38. Caudana, *Processo a Mussolini*, p.1623.
39. Ibid., p.1620.
40. Ibid., p.62.
41. Paolo Pavolini, *Il processo Mussolini* (Milan: Beleguese edizioni, 2008; first published 1975).
42. Paul Ginsborg, *A History of Contemporary Italy, 1943–1988* (London: Penguin, 1990), pp.333–5.
43. Pavolini, *Il processo Mussolini*, p.15.
44. Ibid., p.33.
45. Ibid., p.42.
46. Ibid., p.60.
47. Guglielmo Sangiorgi was the name of a real partisan (battlename 'a Biondo'), who belonged to the 36th Bianconcini Garibaldi brigade and occupied the role of deputy political commissar of the battalion in the Bologna region. It is not known if Pavolini was aware of his existence. See https://www.storiaememoriadibologna.it/sangiorgi-guglielmo-506941-persona (consulted 6/2/23).
48. Pavolini, *Il processo Mussolini*, pp.84–5.
49. Ibid., p.316.
50. Ibid., p.317.
51. The series began on 21 March 1965 under the general title 'Il processo che non è mai stato'.
52. The magazine explained that the initiative began with a letter from a Milanese student who found that books had not helped him to understand how a figure often described as a buffoon had dominated the Italians for so long. The letter was published in *Epoca*, 21 March 1965, p.27.
53. Luigi Barzini Jnr, 'C'era in lui qualcosa di inesplicabile', *Epoca*, 21 March 1965, p.27.
54. Ibid., pp.31–2.
55. Ibid., p.32.
56. Ibid., p.32.
57. Mario Missiroli, 'Giocò tutti: dalla Monarchia alla Chiesa', *Epoca*, 28 March 1965, p.54.
58. *Epoca* n.760, 1965, p.128.
59. Ibid., p.130.
60. Ibid., p.129.

NOTES TO CHAPTER 9

1. Anon., 'Il monumento al "lavoro italiano" distrutto da una carica di dinamite', *La Stampa*, 31 January 1961, p.1. A more balanced description of the event was published by the Communist daily *L'Unità* under the title 'L'attentato dinamitardo alla statua di P. Gardena', 31 January 1961, p.2.
2. https://www.ilprimatonazionale.it/approfondimenti/ha-volto-del-duce-1961-attentato-distrusse-statua-del-genio-lavoro-italiano-102920/ (consulted 28/4/20).
3. For an account of the impact on one region, see Francesco Bartolini, Roberto Giulianelli and Amoreno Martellini (eds). *Fascismo e spazi urbani nelle Marche* (Ancona: affinità elettive, 2024).
4. Simona Storchi, 'Mussolini as Monument: the equestrian statue of the Duce at the Littoriale Stadium in Bologna', in Stephen Gundle, Christopher Duggan and Giuliana Pieri, *The Cult of the Duce: Mussolini and the Italians* (Manchester: Manchester University Press, 2013), pp.193–208.
5. Ibid., pp. 197–8.
6. Ibid., p.201.

7. Ulrich Raulff, *Farewell to the Horse: The Final Century of Our Relationship* (London: Penguin, 2017), p.9.
8. Ibid., p.244.
9. Ibid., pp.251–2.
10. On all aspects of Mussolini as photographic subject, see Alessandra Antola Swan, *Photographing Mussolini: The Making of a Political Icon* (Basingstoke: Palgrave Macmillan, 2020).
11. Dino Biondi, *La fabbrica del Duce* (Florence: Vallecchi, 1973), p.108.
12. Emilio Gentile, *Il culto del littorio* (Rome: Laterza, 1993), pp.90–2.
13. Benito Mussolini, 'prefazione' to Margherita Sarfatti, *Dux* (Milan: Mondadori, 1926), page unnumbered.
14. Michel Serres, *Statues* (London: Bloomsbury, 2015; first published 19887), p.48.
15. Ibid., pp.121 and 183.
16. Giuseppe Bottai, *Diario 1935–1944*, ed. by Giordano Bruno Guerri (Milan: Rizzoli, 1982), entry of 27 August 1936, pp.109–10.
17. Ibid., pp.131–2.
18. Storchi, 'Mussolini as Monument', p.43.
19. Serres, *Statues*, p.102.
20. Luisa Passerini, *Mussolini immaginario: storia di una biografia, 1915–1939* (Rome: Laterza, 1991), p.71.
21. Ibid., p.181.
22. See Patricia Gaborik, 'Brancati's Gigantic Mussolinis', *Laboratoire italien* 30, 2023. Online ref. See also Giovanni Morelli, *Vitaliano Brancati tra fascismo e gallismo* (Bari: Lacaita, 1989).
23. Morelli, *Vitaliano Brancati tra fascismo e gallismo*, pp.181–2.
24. Archivio Centrale dello Stato, Predienza del Consiglio dei Ministri, 1937–39, 20/1.
25. Like Napoleon before him, Mussolini sought to appear as a Muslim to Muslims as he had earlier wanted to appear Catholic before Catholics.
26. The exact fate of the stone head is not recorded. Information about has been taken from https://italiacoloniale.com/2020/05/27/adua-1935-chi-scolpi-nella-roccia-lenorme-effige/#:~:text=L'enorme%20testa%20di%20Mussolini,che%20ne%20cur%C3%B2%20la%20progettazione (consulted 27/12/23).
27. A photograph of the head appeared on the cover of *L'Illustrazione italiana*, 16 February 1936.
28. Mike Sibbons, *From the Archives: An Eclectic Mix of Stories from the History of REME* (Oxford: Osprey, 2016), pp.115–16.
29. Ibid., p.116. The sergeant, Arthur Turner, was subsequently photographed at the age of ninety-six with the boots in the museum.
30. Raulff, *Farewell to the Horse*, p.234.
31. Storchi, 'Mussolini as monument', pp.203–4.
32. Ibid.
33. For example, in the concluding pages of Gentile, *Fascismo di pietra* and Pino Nicoloso, *Mussolini architetto* (Turin: Einaudi, 2008). Developments in the study of iconoclasm across periods and contexts—including Eastern Europe after 1989—have occurred without reference to post-Fascist Italy. See Jeffrey Johnson and Anne McClanan (eds), *Negating the Image: Case Studies in Iconoclasm* (London: Routledge, 2005); Stacy Boldrick and Richard Clay, *Iconoclasm: Contested Objects, Contested Terms* (London: Routledge, 2007).
34. McClanan and Johnson, *Negating the Image*, p.3.
35. According to the testimony of Arturo Conti, a veteran of the Italian Social Republic (RSI) and in the early 2000s president of the Istituto Storico della Repubblica Sociale Italiana (an

association founded in 1986 with the aim of preserving and transmitting the memory of the RSI), a Fascist named Mario Mattioli (later a lieutenant in the Brigate nere) acquired the head with the cooperation of the Germans (Conti described his intervention as 'an intelligent act, a rescue operation'). Mattioli buried it in his garden at Via S. Vitale 72. See Storchi, 'Mussolini as Monument', pp.203–6.

36. The situation in Bologna was probably similar to that described by Edoardo Albinati in his autobiographical novel *La scuola cattolica*, which explores the cultural backdrop to the kidnap and rape in Rome in 1975 of two teenage girls and the murder of one of them—a shocking incident known as the Circeo crime. The author describes a visit to a branch of the far-right Italian Social Movement (MSI). The thirteen-year-old narrator is escorted into a dark and gloomy environment in a manner that he likens to an initiation rite: 'everywhere there were trophies, symbols, drooping pennants with a dusty appearance; everything was stuck in the past and old. The only bright objects were the white or ivory heads of the Duce that were like phosphorescent globes in the semi-darkness, one and a half times or twice life-size .... The largest and most spectral of them was on top of a wardrobe and from on high it sized up anyone who entered the room that was the last, and the most remote and dark, of the branch building'. Albinati, *La scuola Cattolica* (Milan: Rizzoli, 2016), pp.272–3.
37. In the room where Simona Storchi and I met Arturo Conti in 2006, the head of Graziosi's statue was positioned on a table in the corner; beneath it was draped an RSI flag. Behind it there was, on the left, a small, framed photograph of the casket containing Mussolini's remains and, on the right, a Fascist pledge, also framed. On the walls were a large, framed list of the 'martyrs' of the RSI and a large photograph of Mussolini visiting Bologna in 1926. For Conti and those of like mind, Mussolini's spirit clearly still inhabited the place. Graziosi's head dominated the room and was a disquieting reminder—as well as an uncanny, almost physical, embodiment—of the persistence of a cult that, in clandestine or minoritarian forms, still persisted. By 2013, the institute no longer occupied the rooms in Via Marconi and the head had once more disappeared. Storchi, 'Mussolini as Monument', pp. 205–6.
38. https://telenord.it/gaslini-una-storia-di-eccellenza (consulted 10/2/23).
39. Ibid.
40. See Stephen Gundle, 'Mussolini's appearances in the regions' in Gundle, Duggan and Pieri, *The Cult of the Duce*, pp.110–28.
41. See Patrick Duerden in Dan Dubowitz, Patrick Duerdon and Penny Lewis, *Fascismo abbandonato: The Children's Colonie of Mussolini's Italy* (Stockport: Dewi Lewis, 2009), p.5.
42. Storchi, 'Mussolini as Monument'. See https://www.fonderiabattaglia.com/ (consulted 10/2/23).
43. http://www.arthurchandler.com/paris-1937-exposition (consulted 1/5/20).
44. *La Domenica del Corriere*, 24 April 1938.
45. See Sergio Rizzo and Alessandro Campi, *L'ombra lunga del fascismo: perchè l'Italia è ancora ferma a Mussolini* (Milan: Solferino, 2022), pp.140–1.
46. Renato Nicoloso, Mussolini architetto:*propaganda e paesaggio urbano nell'Italia fascista* (Turin: Einaudi, 2011) .
47. The interview was given in 1961, following the destruction of the statue, to the Bolzano newspaper *Alto Adige*. Quoted in https://www.ilprimatonazionale.it/approfondimenti/ha-volto-del-duce-1961-attentato-distrusse-statua-del-genio-lavoro-italiano-102920/ (consulted 1/5/20).
48. Rizzo and Campi, *L'ombra lunga del fascismo*, pp.158–60.
49. Reports of these events appeared almost side by side in the press. See for example, *L'Unità*, 10 February 1961, p.2.

NOTES TO CHAPTER 10

1. Reynolds and Eleanor Packard, *Balcony Empire: Fascist Italy at War* (New York: Oxford University Press, 1942).
2. Laura Fermi, *Mussolini* (Chicago: Chicago University Press, 1961), p.292.
3. Renzo De Felice, *Mussolini il duce*. Tomo 1: *Gli anni del consenso 1929–1936* (Turin: Einaudi, 1979), pp.52–3.
4. Vittorio Vidotto, 'I luoghi del fascismo a Roma' *Dimensioni e problemi della ricerca storica*. n.2, 2005, 39–51, p.41. Franco Martinelli described Palazzo Venezia under the regime as 'the pulsating heart of Italy'. See *Mussolini ai raggi X* (Milan: De Vecchi, 1964), pp.241–2.
5. Patrizia Girolami, 'Il carro di Tespi: Teatro e fascismo' in Mario Biondi and Alessandra Borsotti (eds), *Cultura e fascismo: letteratura, arti e spettacolo di un Ventennio* (Florence: Ponte alle Grazie, 1996), p.265.
6. Massimo Cardillo, *Il duce in moviola* (Bari: Dedalo, 1983), p.97.
7. Angelo Del Boca, 'Impero' in Mario Isnenghi (ed.), *I luoghi della memoria: simboli e moiti dell'Italia unita* (Rome: Laterza, 1996), p.422.
8. Flavia Marcello, *After the Fall: The Legacy of Fascism in Rome's Architectural and Urban History* (London: Bloomsbury, 2024), pp.34–5.
9. Piero Saporiti, *Empty Balcony* (London: Gollancz, 1947), p.7.
10. Emilio Gentile, *Fascismo di pietra* (Rome: Laterza, 2007), p.256.
11. Dario Pasquini, *Ansia di purezza: il fascismo e il nazismo nella stampa satiri ca italiana e tedesca (1943–1963)* (Rome: Viella, 2014), pp.124–5.
12. Vidotto, 'I luoghi del fascismo a Roma', p.39.
13. Robert Hughes, *Rome* (London: Weidenfeld and Nicolson, 2011), pp.446–50.
14. Eugene Pooley, 'Mussolini and the city of Rome' in Stephen Gundle, Christopher Duggan and Giuliana Pieri (eds), *The Cult of the Duce: Mussolini and the Italians* (Manchester: Manchester University Press, 2013), p.213.
15. Renato Nicoloso, *Mussolini architetto* (Turin: Einaudi, 2011).
16. Pooley, 'Mussolini and the city of Rome', p.215.
17. See Michael Tymkiw, 'Floor mosaics, *Romanità*, and spectatorship: the Foro Mussolini's Piazzale dell'Impero', *The Art Bulletin*, 101:2, 2019, 109–32.
18. The story of the obelisk is told in Francesco Filippi, *Noi però gli abbiamo fatto le strade: le colonie italiane tra bugie, razzisimi e amnesia* (Turin: Bollati Boringhieri, 2021), pp.170–3.
19. Gentile, *Fascismo di pietra*, p.257.
20. The question of practicality, especially in the postwar years, is underlined and examined closely by Simona Storchi in relation to a key fascist building in Predappio. See 'The ex-Casa del Fascio in Predappio and the question of the "difficult heritage" of Fascism in contemporary Italy', *Modern Italy*, 24:2, 2019, 139–57.
21. On Milan, see Barbara Bracco 'I segni littori di Milano: costruzione, distruzione e rinascita del volto di una città' in Giulia Albanese and Lucia Ceci (eds), *I luoghi del fascismo: memoria, politica, rimozione* (Rome: Viella, 2022), pp.145–62. On the Marche region, see Ercole Sori, 'Prefazione: modernizzare? "Adwelante, con juicio"' in Bartolini, Francesco, Roberto Giulianelli and Amoreno Martellini (eds), *Fascismo e spazi urbani nelle Marche* (Ancona: affinità elettive, 2024), p.24.
22. Guri Schwarz, *Tu mi devi seppellir: riti funebri e culto nazionale alle origini della Repubblica* (Turin: UTET, 2010), p.215.
23. See Maurizio Ridolfi, *Storia politica dell'Italia repubblicana* (Milan: Bruno Mondadori, 2010) on topographical modifications.

24. See Flaminia Bartolini, 'Fascism on display: the afterlife of material legacies of the dictatorship', *EX NOVO Journal of Archaeology*, 5, December 2020, 19–37, pp.20–3.
25. https://www.lastampa.it/roma/2019/12/04/news/roma-dopo-vent-anni-prende-forma-il-museo-della-shoah-a-villa-torlonia-1.38059434 (consulted 23/4/20).
26. Mario Isnenghi, *L'Italia in piazza: i luoghi della vita pubblica dal 1848 ai nostri giorni* (Milan: Mondadori, 1994), p.313.
27. Mario Isnenghi, 'La piazza' in Isnenghi (ed.), *I luoghi della memoria: strutture ed eventi dell'Italia unita* (Rome: Laterza, 1997), p.50.
28. On Arborea, see Antonio Pennacchi, *Fascio e martello: viaggio per le città del duce* (Rome: Laterza, 2010).
29. Sofia Serenelli, '"It was like something you have at home and which becomes so familiar that you don't even pay attention to it": memories of Mussolini and Fascism in Predappio, 1922–2010', *Modern Italy*, 18:2, 2013, 157–75, p.58.
30. Vittore Querel, *Il paese di Benito* (Rome: Corso editore, 1954), p.29.
31. Ibid., p.22.
32. Serenelli, '"It was like something that you have at home"', pp.159–62. On the question of ordinariness in relation to Predappio, see Paolo Heywood, 'Ordinary exemplars: cultivating "the everyday" in the birthplace of Fascism', *Comparative Studies in Society and History*, 64, 2022, 91–121. The point here is made on p.96.
33. Querel, *Il paese di Benito*, p.23. See Storchi, 'The ex-Casa del Fascio in Predappio', p.143–4.
34. Serenelli, '"It was like something that you have at home"', p.164. There were also multiple local ties to members of the dictator's family. His brother Arnaldo, who died in 1931, was accustomed to pass his summers in a house near Cesena that belonged to his wife's family. The study he had created there for use during his sojourns remained intact and was opened to the public in 2023 on the occasion of a Fondo Ambiente Italiano (FAI) open day. I am grateful to Alessia Zampini for telling me about this and for facilitating on a private view of the study in June 2024.
35. Heywood, 'Ordinary exemplars"', p.103. On the 'carnival of Mussolini, see Paolo Heywood, 'Out of the ordinary: Everyday life and the "carnival of Mussolini"', *American Anthropologist*, 2022, pp.500–1.
36. Serenelli, '"It was like something that you have at home"', pp.167–8; Heywood, '"Ordinary exemplars"', pp.104–5.
37. Sharon MacDonald, *Difficult Heritage: Negotiating the Nazi Past in Nuremberg and Beyond* (London: Routledge, 2008).
38. Andreas Huyssen, *Present Pasts: Urban Palimpsests and the Politics of Memory* (Stanford: Stanford University Press, 2003), p.81.
39. Huysssen, *Present Pasts*, p.79.
40. Heywood, '"Ordinary exemplars"', p.112.
41. See Storchi, 'The ex-Casa del Fascio in Predappio', pp.145–51. Frassineti was mayor between 2009 and 2019. Frassineti was the subject of a number of documentaries, including *Predappio: Past and Present in Mussolini's Birthplace*, part two of *Mussolini: The Story of a Personality Cult* (Vanessa Roghi, 2011) and *The Mayor* (Piergiorgio Curzi, 2022).
42. Storchi, 'The ex-Casa del Fascio in Predappio', pp.145–51.
43. Edda Negrini Mussolini and Mario Russomanno, I Mussolini dopo Mussolini (Argelato: Minerva, 2022), p.175.
44. See Romano Mussolini, *My Father, the Duce* (Carlsbad, Calif.: Kales Press, 2006), p. 60.

45. See https://edition.cnn.com/travel/article/villa-carpena-italy-mussolini-ghosts/index.html (consulted 4/1/24). https://bologna.repubblica.it/cronaca/2022/11/01/news/la_cnn_rilancia_la_storia_inventata_del_fantasma_di_mussolini_a_villa_carpena-372504473/ (consulted 28/8/23).
46. Mussolini, *My Father Il Duce*, p.60.
47. Peter York, *Dictators' Homes* (London: Atlantic Books, 2005), p.21.
48. Ruth Holliday and Tracey Potts, *Kitsch! Cultural Politics and Taste* (Manchester: Manchester University Press, 2012).
49. See Despinga Stratigakos, *Hitler at Home* (New Haven and London: Yale University Press, 2015).
50. See Holliday and Potts, *Kitsch!*, p.63.
51. Negrini Mussolini and Russomanno, *I Mussolini dopo Mussolini*, pp.184–5
52. See for example the exhibition 'The Last Fascism 1943–1945: The Italian Social Republic' held in the Museum of Salo in 2022–23: https://museodisalo.it/lultimo-fascismo-1943-1945-la-repubblica-sociale-italiana/ (consulted 27/12/23).
53. https://www.telegraph.co.uk/travel/destinations/europe/italy/italian-lakes/lake-garda/hotels/villa-fiordaliso-hotel/ (consulted 28/8/23).

NOTES TO CHAPTER II

1. Giuseppe Bottai, 'Il regime per l'arte' in *Politica Fascista delle arti* (Rome: Signorelli, 1940). Cited in Giuliana Pieri, 'The destiny of the art and artefacts' in Stephen Gundle, Christopher Duggan and Giuliana Pieri (eds), *The Cult of the Duce: Mussolini and the Italians* (Manchester: Manchester University Press, 2013), p.227.
2. Pieri, 'The destiny of the art and artefacts', p.227.
3. Kitsch and Nazism have often been associated and were the subject of Susan Sontag's famous attack on 'fascinating fascism' in her *Under the Sign of Saturn* (London: Writers and Readers, 1980), pp.73–108.
4. On Mussolini and his photographers, see Alessandra Antola Swan, *Photographing Mussolini: The Making of a Political Icon* (London: Palgrave Macmillan, 2020).
5. See Maria Elena Versari, 'Tra iconoclastia e oblio: guerra e requisizioni alla Rocca delle Caminate', in Maria Giuseppina Di Monte, Giuliana Pieri and Simona Storchi (eds), *Visualizzare la guerra: l'iconografia del conflitto e l'Italia* (Milan: Mimesis, 2016).
6. Rachele Mussolini, *Ma vie avec Benito* (Paris: Editions du Cheval Ailé, 1948), pp.88, 116.
7. Mussolini, *Ma vie avec Benito*, p.181. The story of the trucks was later questioned by family members as the items they supposedly contained were never seen or used by them. See Edda Negrini Mussolini and Mario Russomanno, *I Mussolini dopo Mussolini* (Argelato: Minerva, 2022), p.177.
8. Vittore Querel, *Il paese di Benito* (Rome: Corso editore, 1954), pp.29–31.
9. Antonio Mambelli, *Diario degli avvenimenti in Forlì e Romagna dal 1939 al 1945*. See https://nerodichina.home.blog/2019/04/07/spariti-tanti-documenti-dalla-rocca-delle-caminate/ (consulted 28/4/20).
10. Michael Hughes, *The Anarchy of Nazi Memorabilia: From Things of Tyranny to Troubled Treasure* (London: Routledge, 2022), p.8.
11. Ibid., p.151.
12. See Peter Burke, *The Fabrication of Louis XIV* (New Haven and London: Yale University Press, 1992).
13. Sudhir Hazareesingh, *The Legend of Napoleon* (London: Granta, 2004), pp.74–80.
14. Ibid., pp.63–4.

15. Ibid., p.75.
16. Orianne Aymard, *When a Goddess Dies: Worshipping Ma Anandamayi after Her Death* (New York: Oxford University Press, 2014), pp.70–1.
17. Hughes, *The Anarchy of Nazi Memorabilia*, p.43. A curious example of the different values attributed to a Fascist relic occurs in an episode of the British television detective series *Lovejoy* ('Angel Trousers', 1992). A group of Italian fascist loyalists come to England to retrieve the nose of a statue of Mussolini that had been taken as a souvenir by Allied soldiers during the war of liberation. I am grateful to Charlotte Brunsdon for drawing my attention to this.
18. Hughes, *The Anarchy of Nazi Memorabilia*, pp. 153–7.
19. Maria Elena Versari, 'Fascist Spoils: Gifts to Mussolini', *Burlington Magazine*, no. 157, June 2015, pp.407–13.
20. See Stephen Gundle, 'Un Martini per il Duce: l'immaginario del consumismo in Italia negli anni Venti e Trenta' in Anna Villari (ed.), *L'arte della pubblicità: il manifesto italiano e le vanguardie 1920–1940* (Milan: Silvana editoriale, 2008), pp.46–69. See also Bianca Gaudenzi, *Fascismi in vetrina: pubblicità e modelli di consumo nel Ventennio e nel Terzo Reich* (Rome: Viella, 2023), pp.151–2.
21. The Baci Perugina, invented in 1922 (the year Fascism came to power) and originally termed *cazzotti* (punches), they were dubbed 'exquisite' by Mussolini, who allowed the company to use his endorsement in advertising. An advertising card designed by the illustrator Seneca for the company featured the phrase prominently.
22. Archivio Centrale dello Stato (ACS), Presidenza del Consiglio dei Ministri (PCM), 1937–39, b.20, f.1 (various subfolders).
23. ACS, PCM, 1937–39, b.20, f.1 subfolder 8404, 19 August 1939 contains a letter to Rachele Mussolini begging for support following the rejection of his application for permission to manufacture drinking glasses. See Stephen Gundle, 'Mass culture and the cult of personality' in Gundle, Duggan and Pieri, *The Cult of the Duce*, pp.84–5.
24. See Alessandra Antola Swan, *Photographing Mussolini: The Making of a Political Icon* (Basingstoke: Palgrave Macmillan, 2020), pp.329–35 and Gaudenzi, Fascismi in vetrina.
25. ACS, SPD, Carteggio ordinario 1922–43. B.1871, f. 5288777.
26. Cited in Marco Moretti, 'Profilo continuo' in Moretti, *Renato Bertelli (1900–1974)* (Florence: Masso delle Fate, 2007), p.70. See Pieri, 'The destiny of the art and artefacts', p.233.
27. See Moretti, 'Profilo continuo', p.73.
28. Giorgio Di Genova, 'Introduction' to Di Genova (ed.), *'L'uomo di provvidenza': iconografia del duce, 1923–1945* (Bologna: Edizioni Bora, 1997), p.10.
29. Giorgio Di Genova, 'Iconografia del duce (1923–1945)', in ibid., p.51.
30. The idea that the artistic cult of the Duce was a top-down phenomenon with meanings that were confined to political propaganda was the driving concept behind Renzo De Felice and Luigi Goglia (eds), *Mussolini: il mito* (Rome-Bari: Laterza 1983). For a critique of this view of the cult, see Stephen Gundle, Christopher Duggan and Giuliana Pieri, 'Special issue: the cult of Mussolini in twentieth-century Italy—Introduction', *Modern Italy*, 18:2, 2013, pp.111–15.
31. Lorenzo Alessandrini (mayor of Seravazza) in Di Genova, *'L'uomo di provvidenza'*, p.5.
32. B. Mussolini, *Opera Omnia*, 36 vols. (Florence: La Fenice, 1951). Between 1978 and 1980, eight volumes of appendices were added. Susmel's activity is explored at length in Andrea Martini, *Fascsimo immaginario: riscrivere il passato a destra* (Rome: Laterza, 2024), pp.173–206.
33. Collections of artistic objects produced in the fascist period have occupied an ill-defined place in postwar culture. Collecting itself is a 'fuzzy concept' (O. Phys, *Contemporary*

Collecting: Theory and Practice, 2011: 14) which is often split between 'socially admissible collecting' and outsider practices which aim to 'challenge the norm and cock a snoop at the accepted patterns of knowledge' John Elsner and Roger Cardinal (eds), *The Cultures of Collecting* (London: Reaktion, 1994) p.3.

34. Arrigo Petacco, *Mussolini ritrovato: storia di una collezione proibita* (Bologna: Minerva edizioni, 2009).
35. Giulio Bargellini, 'Introduzione' in Petacco, *Mussolini ritrovato*, p.11.
36. The ambiguities of collecting Nazi memorabilia and the whitewashing it can involve are discussed in Hughes, *The Anarchy of Nazi Memorabilia*, pp.113–14, 116–18, 124–7. On the role of kitsch and kitsch-ification in masking violence and death, see Ruth Holliday and Tracey Potts, *Kitsch! Cultural Politics and Taste* (Manchester: Manchester University Press, 2012), pp.13–14.
37. Stefanie Pilat, 'Occupying history: film, fascism, and architecture in the work of Kevin Van Braak and Rossella Biscotti', Where Do You Stand: *Where Do You Stand: 99th ACSA Annual Meeting Proceedings*, Washington, DC, ACSA, 2011, p.344.
38. https://nomasfoundation.com/mostre/rosasella-biscotti-le-teste-in-oggetto/ (consulted 28/4/20).
39. On the history of waxworks, see Michelle E. Bloom, *Waxworks: A Cultural Obsession* (Minneapolis: University of Minnesota Press, 2003).
40. Jackie Wullschlager, 'Oscuramento: the wars of Fabio Mauri, Hauser & Wirth, London—stunning, chilling and absurd', *Financial Times*, 5 January 2016.
41. On this occasion Mauri's works were presented in a way that highlighted his friendship with Pasolini and their common interest in fascism and power.
42. Not always are such suspicions entirely without foundation. The Museum of Salò (MuSa) hosted in 2023 an exhibition on the legacy of the final phase of fascism that included filmed testimonies of participants as well as objects including many testifying to the personality cult. The exhibition 'Arte e fascismo' held at the MART gallery in Rovereto in 2024 was unusual in not playing down the influence of the regime on the artistic production of the interwar period. On MuSa and its collections, see Flaminia Bartolini, 'Fascism on display: the afterlife of material legacies of the dictatorship', *Ex Novo Journal of Archaeology*, 5, December 2020, 19–32, pp.27–9.
43. Gavriel D. Rosenfeld, *Munich and Memory: Architecture, Monuments and the Legacy of the Third Reich* (Berkeley: University of California Press, 2000). The author explores in depth the treatment of remnants of the Nazi past, examining the different strategies to erase the memory of the Third Reich. These included adopting the modernism that it rejected and returning to tradition by reviving pre-Nazi styles (the latter option prevailed). Alongside these, a group of 'critical preservationists' argued for the preservation of remnants as a cautionary reminder.
44. See Matteo Fochessati, 'La Collezione Wolfson' in Silvia Barisone, Matteo Foxchessati and Gianni Franzone (eds), *La Collezione Wolfson di Genova* (Milan: Skira, 2005), pp.13–14.
45. Pieri, 'The destiny of the art and artefacts', p.233.
46. Ibid., pp.233 and 239 n.44.
47. A proposal in 2007 to install three enormous heads of Mussolini made from sugar in Piazzale Loreto, each in a colour of the Italian flag, accompanied by the legend Xud (Dux written in reverse) sounded like a joke, although it was not treated as such in Italian public discourse. See Giovanni Scirocco, 'Piazzale Loreto 29 aprile 1945: la memoria', p.257.
48. Thom Winterburn, *Redux: The Exhibition of Mussolini* (London: Jeffrey Charles Henry Peacock Gallery, 2008). An early work by artist Brian Clarke also focused on the upside-down bodies of Mussolini and his mistress at Piazzale Loreto. See Martin Harrison, *Brian Clarke* (London: Quartet, 1981), p.29.

49. Conversation with Thom Winterburn, 5 February 2024. Winterburn spent months making court drawings of the David Irving trial and the Milošević trial, which also informed his decision to conduct a retrospective 'trial' of Mussolini.
50. Poletti's views are cited in Leo Valiani, *Tutte le strade conducono a Roma* (Bologna: Il Mulino 1995), p.276.
51. Elena Stylianou and Theopisti Stylianou-Lambert, 'Approaches to displaying death in museums: an introduction' in Stylianou and Stylianou-Lambert (eds), *Museums and Photography: Displaying Death* (London: Routledge, 2017), p.2.

NOTES TO CHAPTER 12

1. https://www.qdmnotizie.it/jesi-scritta-mussoliniana-allanagrafe-chiara-cercaci-va-salvaguardata/ (consulted 1/4/22).
2. Ibid.
3. https://www.ilrestodelcarlino.it/ancona/cronaca/jesi-scritta-mussoliniana-cancellata-la-citt%C3%A0-si-divide-sull-opportunit%C3%A0-1.5742276 (consulted 14/3/23).
4. Ibid.
5. See Amoreno Martellini and Barbara Montesi, *Il Novecento in provincia: storia di Jesi tra memorie e oblii 1900–1970* (Milan: Franco Angeli, 2020).
6. Ibid., p.114.
7. Ibid., p.127.
8. Ibid., pp.115–16.
9. Ibid., pp.202–3.
10. Ibid., pp.183–5. The general picture of postwar retributions is drawn in Gianni Oliva, *La resa dei conti* (Milan: Mondadori, 1998).
11. The inscription on the monument reads as follows: 'Figli di questa terra col pensiero alle mura natie caddero nelle guerre di un secolo/diverse nel fine e nella sorte/uguali nel sacrificio/la città materna li onora traendo dall'altissimo esempio la speranza in un mondo piu umano la fede di un mondo giusto' (Sons of this land, thinking of a place they knew from birth, fell in the wars of a century/different in their causes and outcomes/yet equal in their sacrifices/their maternal city honours them, drawing from their noble example hopes for a more human world and faith in a better world'). I am grateful to Barbara Montesi for supplying me with this text as well as for introducing me to Jesi's memorials and helping me to interpret them. I also thank Jesi town councillor Samuele Animali for permitting me to view the slogan mentioned at the outset of the chapter and for discussing local reactions to it with me.
12. On topographical changes in general in this period, see Maurizio Ridolfi, *Storia politica dell'Italia repubblicana* (Milan: Bruno Mondadori, 2010), pp.25–49.
13. Enrico Deaglio, *Besame mucho* (Milan: Feltrinelli, 1995), pp.15–16.
14. Luca La Rovere, *Storia dei Guf: organizzazione, politica e miti della gioventù universitaria fascista 1919–1943* (Turin: Bollati Boringhieri, 2003), p.326.
15. Mario Isnenghi, 'Aspetti del rituale di massa fascista: stampa e dintorni' in Riccardo Redi (ed.), *Cinema italiano sotto il fascismo* (Venice: Marsilio, 1979), p.53.
16. In Nazi Germany, there were no wall slogans but instead 'words of the week', a propaganda newsletter that was posted up widely each week, often featuring anti-semitic material and political slogans as well as the sayings of Hitler.
17. Giuseppe Bottai, *Diario 1935–1944*, ed. by Giordano Bruno Guerri (Milan: Rizzoli, 1982), p.112.
18. The journalist Enrico Deaglio refers to the slogans as 'fascist advertising spots' in *Besame mucho*, p.16.

19. Ariberto Segala, *I muri del duce* (Lavis: Arca edizioni 2000), p.14.
20. On wall propaganda, see Anna Borrini, 'Firmato M: la propaganda murale' in Adolfo Mignemi (ed.), *Immagine coordinate per un impero: Etiopia 1935–36* (Turin: Gruppo Editoriale Forma, 1984).
21. Benito Mussolini, *Storia di un anno* (Milan: Mondadori, 2004; first published 1944), p.79.
22. Segala, *I muri del Duce*, p.16.
23. Ibid., p.20.
24. Henri Béraud, *Ce que j'ai vu à Rome* (Paris: Editions de France, 1927), pp.22–3.
25. Cited in Emilio Gentile, *In Italia ai tempi di Mussolini* (Milan: Mondadori, 2014), pp.243–4.
26. Andrea Damiano, *Rosso e grigio* (Milan: Muggiani, 1947), p.27.
27. See Guri Schwarz, *Tu mi devi seppellir: riti funebri e culto nazionale alle origini della Repubblica* (Turin: UTET, 2010), pp.209–10 and 209n.
28. Piero Calamandrei, *Diario 1939–1945*, Vol.1, ed. by Giorgio Agosti (Florence: la Nuova Italia, 1982), p.266.
29. Ibid., p.290.
30. Giovanni Giuriati, *La parabola di Mussolini nei ricordi di un gerarca* (Rome-Bari: Laterza, 1981), p.42.
31. Giovanni Artieri, *Prima durante e dopo Mussolini: memorie del Novecento* (Milan: Mondadori, 1990), p.522.
32. Edmund Wilson, *Europe Without Baedeker* (London: Rupert Hart-Davis, 1967), pp.219–20.
33. Giorgio Almirante, *Autobiografia di un 'fucilatore'* (Milan: Edizioni del Borghese, 1974), p.48.
34. Vitaliano Brancati, *I fascisti invecchiano* (Milan: Longanesi, 1950), p.96.
35. See Segala, *I muri del Duce* and Giovanni Bosca, *La propaganda murale del regime fascista: una memoria storica del XX secolo* (Mondovi: ArabAFenice, 2010).
36. Segala, *I muri del Duce*, p.27.
37. Enrico Deaglio, *Besame mucho* (Milan: Feltrinelli, 1995), pp.15–16.
38. Segala, *I muri del duce* and Bosca, La propaganda murale del regime *fascista*.
39. L'editore, 'Prefazione' in Bosca, *La propaganda murale del regime fascista*, p.6.
40. Segala, *I muri del duce*, p.31.
41. Sam Roberts and Geraldine Marshall, 'What Is a Ghost Sign?' in Stefan Schutt, Sam Roberts and Leanne White (eds), *Advertising and Public Memory: Social, Cultural and Historical Perspectives on Ghost Signs* (New York and London: Routledge, 2017), p.16.
42. David Bernstein, 'Bedrock' in Schutt, Roberts and White, *Advertising and Public Memory*, p.199.
43. Ibid., p.200.
44. Gary Warnaby and Dominic Medway, 'Ghost Fascias: Retail Corporate Identity Revenants in Urban Space' in Schutt, Roberts and White, *Advertising and Public Memory*, p.179.
45. Ibid., p.181.
46. Ugo D'Andrea, *Mussolini motore del secolo* (Milan: Hoepli, 1939), p.7. On Mussolini and the natural environment, see Marco Armerio, 'Making Italians out of rocks: Mussolini's shadows on Italian mountains', *Modern Italy*, 19:3, 2014, 261–74.
47. See R. Ranghieri, 'Il Furlo per non morire chiede aiuto al Duce', *Il Giornale Nuovo*, 5 February 1987, p.8.
48. The 'Mussolini camera doppia storica' (Mussolini historical room), with its period furnishings, wall graffiti and bust of the Duce, is advertised on the website of the Hotel Antico Furlo as offering an 'originale percezione di emozioni d'altri tempi' (an original perception

of the emotions of other times). See https://anticofurlo.it/prodotto/mussolini-suite-storica-albergo-anticofurlo/ (consulted 15/4/20).

49. https://www.paolofabbri.it/saggi/profilo_duce/ (consulted 31/8/23). The case of the profile is discussed in Sergio Rizzo and Alessandro Campi, *L'ombra lunga del fascismo: perchè l'Italia è ancora ferma a Mussolini* (Milan: Solferino, 2022), pp.148–51.
50. https://it.wikipedia.org/wiki/Monte_Giano (consulted 16/4/20).
51. Rizzo and Campi, *L'ombra lunga del fascismo*, pp.151–2.

NOTES TO CHAPTER 13

1. Renzo De Felice, *Intervista sul fascismo*, ed. by Michael Ledeen (Bari: Laterza, 1975). His Mussolini biography was published in eight volumes by Einaudi between 1965 and 1997.
2. Denis Mack Smith, *Mussolini's Roman Empire* (London: Weidenfeld and Nicolson, 1976); Denis Mack Smith, *Mussolini* (London: Weidenfeld and Nicolson, 1981).
3. Denis Mack Smith, 'A Monument for the Duce', *TLS*, 31 October 1975, p.1278.
4. Renzo De Felice, *Le interpretazioni di fascismo* (Bari: Laterza, 1969).
5. On the reactions to De Felice, see Donatello Aramini, 'Renzo De Felice e la recente storiografia italiana', *Studi Storici*, 55:1, 2014, 335–48. It has been pointed out that the far right did not regard De Felice as an ally, at least not until he began to criticise the Resistance. See Francesco Germinaro, *L'altra memoria: l'estrema destra, Salò e la Resistenza* (Turin: Bollati Boringieri, 1999).
6. De Felice, *Intervista sul fascismo*, p.82.
7. Ibid., p.83.
8. Ibid., p.83.
9. Ibid., p.84.
10. On the cultural policies of the Italian Communist Party, see Albertina Vittoria, *Togliatti e gli intellettuali: la politica culturale dei comunisti italiani (1944–1964)* (Rome: Carocci, 2014) and Stephen Gundle, *Between Hollywood and Moscow: The Italian Communists and the Challenge of Mass Culture, 1943–1992* (Durham, N.C.: Duke University Press, 2000).
11. See Davide Conti, *L'anima nera della Repubblica: storia del MSI* (Rome: Laterza, 2013).
12. On the far right's view of this attitude, see Germinaro, *L'altra memoria*.
13. Emilio Gentile, *Renzo De Felice: lo storico e il personaggio* (Rome: Laterza, 2003), pp.118–19. See also his 'Renzo De Felice: a tribute', *Journal of Contemporary History*, 32:2, 1997, 139–51.
14. For an overview of these critiques, see Aramini, 'Renzo De Felice e la recente storiografia italiana'.
15. The term 'indulgent memory' was widely employed by Cristina Baldassini in *L'ombra di Mussolini: l'Italia moderata e la memoria del fascismo (1945–60)* (Soveria Mannelli: Rubettino, 2008).
16. For a selection of Montanelli's articles on Mussolini, many of them published in the *Corriere della sera* newspaper, see *Io e il duce*, ed. by Mimmo Franzinelli (Milan: Rizzoli, 2018).
17. Indro Montanelli, 'Un eroe che combattè ideologia' https://www.ilgiornale.it/news/politica/eroe-che-combatt-lideologia-1194388.html (consulted 31/8/23).
18. Emilio Gentile, 'Fascism in Italian historiography: in search of an individual historical identity, *Journal of Contemporary History*, 21:2, 1986, p.183.
19. De Felice, *Intervista sul fascismo*, p.28.
20. Renzo De Felice, Mussolini il fascista. L'organizzazione dello Stato fascista (Turin: Einaudi, 1969), p.73. cit. Gentile, *Renzo De Felice*, p.96.
21. Ibid., p.9.
22. Ibid., p.40.

23. Ibid., p.20.
24. Borden Painter, 'Renzo De Felice and the historiography of Italian Fascism', *The American Historical Review*, 95:2, 1990, 391–405, p.394.
25. Leo Valiani, review of *Mussolini il duce: gli anni del consenso*, *Corriere della sera*, 7 February 1975, cited in ibid., p.394.
26. Guido Crainz, 'The representation of fascism and the resistance in the documentaries of Italian state television' in Richard Bosworth and Patrizia Dogliani (eds), *Italian Fascism: History, Memory and Representation* (Basingstoke: Palgrave Macmillan, 1999), p.126; Vanessa Roghi, 'Mussolini and postwar Italian television' in Stephen Gundle, Christopher Duggan and Giuliana Pieri (eds), *The Cult of Duce: Mussolini and the Italians* (Manchester: Manchester University Press, 2013).
27. Zavoli collaborated on the texts of the commentary on a 1962 documentary entitled simply *Benito Mussolini*, before branching out on his own in series that included the landmark *Nascita di una dittatura* (Birth of a dictatorship) in 1972, followed by *Quel tragico e glorioso '43* (That tragic and glorious '43) in 1973, *La repubblica di Mussolini* (The republic of Mussolini) in 1978 and *Piazzale Loreto* in 1980.
28. This self-reflexive approach was not unique. Television critic Aldo Grasso wrote of television documentaries: 'The attempt to be objective did not prevent Zavoli from unveiling the programme's narrative construction and the workings of television machinery in relation to its subject: the opening sequence highlighted the presence of cameras, monitors, and screens, leaving the studio setup itself open to question and implicitly suggesting to the viewer that, in spite of every effort to be neutral, each story told on the small screen was the result of an exact and unavoidable work of mediation.' Cited in Roghi, 'Mussolini and postwar Italian television', p.262.
29. Claudio Siniscalchi, 'Così iniziò il linciaggio di De Felice', *Il Giornale*, 4 November 2015.
30. Nicola Tranfaglia set out his position most clearly in *Un passato scomodo: fascismo e postfascismo* (Rome: Laterza, 1999). See Federico Finchelstein, 'The Fascist canon: Renzo De Felice and the writing of history', *Forum italicum*, 40:1, 2006, 85–102, pp.92–3.
31. Nicola Tranfaglia, *Labirinto italiano: il fascismo, l'antifascismo, gli storici* (Florence: la Nuova Italia, 1989), p.506. Andrea Martini has explored the interesting and little-known relationship between De Felice and Duilio Susmel, the postwar editor of Mussolini's collected works, who passed him many documents and introduced him to former leading Fascists, who provided him with many insights into the workings of the regime. De Felice only ever expressed his gratitude to Susmel—whose views he did not share—privately. See *Fascismo immaginario: riscrivere il passato a destra* (Rome: Laterza, 2024), pp.195–216.
32. Paolo Pavolini, *Il processo Mussolini* (Milan; Betelguese, 2008; first published 1975), p.11.
33. Renzo De Felice, Rosso e nero, ed. by Pasquale Chessa (Milan: Baldini & Castoldi, 1995), p.55.
34. Ibid., pp.60–1.
35. Giovanni De Luna, 'Revisionismo e resistenza' in Angelo Del Bocca (ed.), *La storia negata: il revisionismo e il suo uso politico* (Vicenza: neri Pozza, 2009). Cited in Roghi, 'Mussolini and postwar Italian television', p.264.
36. Especially influential was Claudio Pavone, *Una guerra civile: saggio storico sulla moralità nella Resistenza* (Turin: Bollati Boringhieri, 1991). See also Philip Cooke, *The Legacy of the Italian Resistance* (New York: Palgrave Macmillan, 2011).
37. De Felice *Rosso e nero*, pp.89–98.
38. Aramini, 'Renzo De Felice e la recente storiografia italiana', p.345.
39. Finchelstein, 'The Fascist canon', p.87.

40. See Philip Cooke, 'Recent work on Nazi massacres in Italy during the Second World War', *Modern Italy*, 5:2, 2000, 211–18.
41. Denis Mack Smith, 'Mussolini: reservations about Renzo De Felice's biography', *Modern Italy*, 5:2, 2000, 193–210, pp.194–5.
42. Ibid., p.197.
43. Ibid., pp.194–5. Mack Smith died at the age of ninety-seven in 2017. This was his last published article.
44. Aramini, 'Renzo De Felice e la recente storiografia italiana', p.345. Of Gentile's many works, the most important can be considered *Il culto del littorio: la sacralizzazione della politca nell'Italia fascista* (Rome: Laterza, 1993).
45. See Stephen Gundle, 'Mussolini between hero-worship and demystification: exemplary anecdotes, *Petite Histoire* and the problem of humanization', *Comparative Studies in Society and History*, 64:1, 2022, 122–49. What he dubbed the 'priapic' depiction of Mussolini received less truck from him than it did from some other historians.
46. Luisa Passerini, 'Mussolini' in Mario Isnenghi, *Luoghi di memoria: personaggi e date dell'Italia unita* (Rome: Laterza, 1997), p.180.
47. On the need to historicise De Felice, see Aramini, 'Renzo De Felice e la recente storiografia italiana', pp.344, 348.

NOTES TO CHAPTER 14

1. Valentina Innocenti (ed.), *Carlo Lizzani: l'ultimo spettatore* (Rome: Datanews, 2012), p.96.
2. The first important dramatic re-enactment of figures belonging to the Fascist elite took place in cinema when Carlo Lizzani made *Il processo di Verona* (The Verona Trial) in 1963. The project was highly contentious and it required the influence of the producer Dino De Laurentiis to override official and other reservations. The still-living Edda Mussolini raised objections and even went to court to try and block distribution (see Franca Faldini and Goffredo Fofi (eds), *L'avventurosa storia del cinema italiano: raccontato dai suoi protagonisti (1960–1969)* [Milan: Feltrinelli, 1981], p.107). These reactions stoked interest in a film which was judged to have 'found a just balance between document and melodrama, making a film of notable quality that had a lot of success' (Tullio Kezich and Alessandra Levantesi, *Dino: De Laurentiis, la vita e i film* [Milan: Feltrinelli, 2001], p.162). On that occasion, Mussolini was only briefly seen from behind while particular emphasis was given to Edda and Claretta Petacci. At this time and for some time afterwards, re-enactments of the Duce continued to be limited to cameos. Damiano Damiani's *Girolimoni il mostro di Roma* (The Assassin of Rome, 1972), for example, contains profile shots of the celebrated jutting jaw in a simple impersonation of well-known aspects of Mussolini's basic public persona.
3. *Il processo di Verona* (The Verona Trial, 1962).
4. Lizzani interview, extra on DVD *Last Days of Mussolini* (Eureka Entertainment Ltd, 2008).
5. In *Le mani sulla città* (Hands Over the City, 1963), Steiger's character, Edoardo Nottola, remarks at one point that flash photography makes him look like Mussolini. Whether this comment shaped his later casting as the Duce is unknown.
6. On 'ghosting', see Marvin Carlson, *The Haunted Stage: The Theatre as Memory Machine* (Ann Arbor: University of Michigan Press, 2001).
7. Carlo Lizzani, *Il mio lungo viaggio nel secolo breve* (Turin: Einaudi, 2007) p.235.
8. Any doubts about Lizzani's position was erased by his decision to cast the handsome, blue-eyed Franco Nero as Mussolini's material executioner Colonel Valerio, a hate-figure on the far right who the left press in the postwar years had been concerned to present not as an avenging hero but as 'an ordinary individual' (Sergio Luzzatto, *Il corpo del duce* [Turin:

Einaudi, 1998], p.164). Nero had also played the antifascist martyr Giacomo Matteotti in *Il delitto Matteotti* (The Assassination of Matteotti, Florestano Vancini, 1973), and thus had a pre-established anti-fascist screen aura. By shifting the site of charisma from Mussolini to Colonel Valerio, the director effected a transfer that was historically nonsensical but which, within the context of the screen narrative, served his broader purposes.

9. Dennis Bingham, *Whose Lives Are They Anyway? The Biopic as Contemporary Film Genre* (New Brunswick: Rutgers University Press, 2010) p.37.
10. Karolin Machtans and Martin A, Reuhl, 'Introduction' in Machtans and Ruehl (eds), *Hitler—Films from Germany: History, Cinema and Politics Since 1945* (Basingstoke: Palgrave Macmillan, 2012), p.4.
11. Ewa Mazierska, *European Cinema and Intertextuality: History, Memory and Politics* (Basingstoke: Palgrave Macmillan, 2011) p.63.
12. Ibid., p.63. 'Making films about Hitler is…so challenging because Hitler was probably the first statesman in history who perfectly understood the power of cinema, and contemporaneous cinema served him exceptionally well', she writes.
13. John P. Diggins, *Mussolini and Fascism: The View from America* (Princeton: Princeton University Press,1972), pp.55–6.
14. Luigi Somma, *Mussolini morto e vivo* (Rome: Vito Bianco, 1960), p.13.
15. This is taken up in Antonio Scurati, *M—L'uomo della provvidenza* (Milan: Bompiani, 2020).
16. Some of these clichés of the Mussolini pose are discussed in Alessandra Antola Swan, *Photographing Mussolini: The Making of a Political Icon* (Basingstoke: Palgrave Macmillan, 2020).
17. Luisa Passerini, *Mussolini immaginario; storia di una biografia, 1915–1939* (Rome: Laterza, 1991), p.58. In her view, this phenomenon was a matter of political modelling within Fascism and of the mass understanding of the dictator as highly suggestive public figure beyond it. Ibid., pp.126–7. Sociologist Edgar Morin, in *The Stars* (New York: Grove Press, 1960), p.95, noted that in the contemporary era the famous and the public fed off each other.
18. See Stephen Gundle, *Fame amid the Ruins: Italian Film Stardom in the Age of Neorealism* (New York and Oxford: Berghahn, 2019), pp.205–6. See also Emilio Gentile, *Caporali tanti, uomini pochissimi: la storia secondo Totò* (Rome: Laterza, 2022), pp.20–32.
19. General Scipione lives in Villa Littoriale and has a mini-army of militiamen. He drills them as a firing squad to 'execute' cardboard cutouts of Churchill, Roosevelt, Eisenhower, De Gaulle, Parri and Fanfani. On his desk he has portraits of Mussolini on horseback attired in the uniform of the Fascist Militia and a bust. He performs the ritual of the 'saluto al Duce' and, under his general's uniform and medals, he wears a black shirt on which is written 'Me ne frego' ('I don't give a damn', a fascist curse expressing bravado).
20. Quinto Navarra, *Le memorie del cameriere di Mussolini* (Milan: Longanesi, 1946). Silvana Patriarca, *Italian Vices: Nation and Character from the Risorgimento to the Republic* (Cambridge: Cambridge University Press, 2010), pp.2–3. For Rodolfo Sonego, co-writer of all his films from 1954 to 1960, the Sordi type 'is a confused personality because the sudden passage from dictatorship to democracy, which occurred during his formative years, prevented him turning into a mature, coherent man'. Rodolfo Sonego, cited in Goffredo Fofi, *Alberto Sordi, l'Italia in bianco e nero* (Milan: Mondadori, 2004), p.108.
21. Theodor W. Adorno, *Guilt and Defense: On the Legacies of National Socialism in Postwar Germany* (Cambridge, Mass.: Harvard University Press, 2010), p.213.
22. Giacomo Tagliani, *Biografie della nazione: vita, storia, politica nel biopic Italiano* (Soveria Mannelli: Rubbettino, 2019), p.32.

23. See the essay on *Amarcord* in Natalia Ginzburg, *Vita immaginaria* (Milan: Mondadori, 1974) and Stephen Gundle, 'The question of Italian national character and the limits of commedia all'italiana: Alberto Sordi, Federico Fellini, and Carlo Lizzani' in Frank Burke (ed.), *Italian Cinema: A Companion* (Oxford: Wiley Blackwell, 2017).
24. In this context, television drama 'took on the role of narrator of history…and took up the baton of documentaries' writes Milly Buonanno in *Italian TV Drama and Beyond: Stories from the Soil/Stories from the Sea* (Bristol: Intellect, 2012), p.210. While documentaries about Fascism were reliant on old black-and-white film footage, were typically shown late in the evening, and viewers were limited to those with an explicit interest in history, dramatic productions shot in colour brought historical issues to a 'generalist' television audience, albeit in a way that was 'more or less shaped by imagination'.
25. Tagliani, *Biografie della nazione*, p.64.
26. Nicola Gallerano, 'Critica e crisi del paradigma antifascista', *Problemi del socialismo*, 7, 1986, 106–33, pp.119–20.
27. Tobias Ebbrecht, '(Re)constructing biographies: German television docudrama and the historical biography', in Erin Bell and Ann Gray (eds), *Televising History: Mediating the Past in Postwar Europe* (Basingstoke: Palgrave Macmillan 2010), p.210.
28. Stephen Gundle, 'The death (and re-birth) of the hero: charisma and manufactured charisma in modern Italy', *Modern Italy*, 3:2, 1998, 173–90. See Giovanni Giuriati, *La parabola di Mussolini nei ricordi di un gerarca* (Rome-Bari: Laterza, 1981), p.48.
29. *Claretta* took this a step further by featuring in the cast the subject's younger sister Myriam, who had been groomed for film stardom in 1942–43. See the chapter 'The Duce's Whim: Miria di San Servolo' on Myriam Petacci in Stephen Gundle, *Mussolini's Dream Factory: Film Stardom in Fascist Italy* (New York and Oxford: Berghahn Books, 2013), pp.244–58.
30. On this question, see the declaration of producer Dino De Laurentiis reported in Nerio Minuzzo, 'Mussolini non avrà una parte nel film', *L'Europeo*, 13 April 1968, 12–13.
31. On the function and nature of anecdotes, see Stephen Gundle, 'Mussolini between hero-worship and demystification: exemplary anecdotes, *Petite Histoire* and the problem of humanization', *Comparative Studies in Society and History*, 64:1, 2022, 122–49.
32. George Custen, *Bio/Pics: How Hollywood Constructed Public History* (New Brunswick: Rutgers University Press, 1992), p.155.
33. Isabelle Veyrat-Masson, 'Staging historical leaders on French television: the example of Napoleon Bonaparte' in Bell and Gray, *Televising History*, p.103.
34. Luisa Cigognetti and Pierre Sorlin, 'History on Television: The Problem of Sources' in Bell and Gray, Televising History, p.31.
35. Guido Crainz, 'The representation of fascism and the resistance in the documentaries of Italian state television' in R.J.B. Bosworth and Patrizia Dogliani (eds), *Italian Fascism: History, Memory and Representation* (Basingstoke: Palgrave, 1999), pp.133–4.
36. Claudio Fogu, '*Italiani brava gente*: the legacy of fascist historical culture on Italian politics of memory' in Richard Lebow and others (eds), *The Politics of Memory in Postwar Europe* (Durham, N.C.: Duke University Press, 2006), p.149; Milly Buonanno, *Italian TV Drama and Beyond: Stories from the Soil/Stories from the Sea* (Bristol: Intellect, 2012). 2012), p.215; Philip Cooke, *The Legacy of the Italian Resistance* (New York: Palgrave Macmillan, 2011).
37. Luisa Passerini, 'Mussolini' in Mario Isnenghi (ed.), *I luoghi di memoria: personaggi e date dell'Italia unita* (Rome-Bari: Laterza, 1997), p.185.
38. See Paul Ginsborg, *Family Politics: Domestic Life, Devastation and Survival, 1900–1950* (New Haven and London: Yale University Press, 2014) for the development of a critique of fascism that starts from Mussolini's own dysfunctional family.

39. Claretta Petacci, *Mussolini segreto: diari 1932–1938* (Milan: Rizzoli. 2009), p.420.
40. Sergio Luzzatto, 'Così il duce distrusse la famiglia segreta', *Corriere della sera*, 14 January 2005. Cited in Tagliani, *Biografie della nazione*, p.110.
41. Tagliani, *Biografie della nazione*, pp.110–11. On Dalser's story, see Daniela Baratieri, 'Sanity from a lunatic asylum: Ida Dalser's Threat to Mussolini's image' in Gundle, Duggan and Pieri, *The Cult of the Duce*, pp.57–71.
42. David Sheward, *Rage and Glory: The Volatile Life and Career of George C. Scott* (New York: Applause, 2008), p.315; Karen Moline, *Bob Hoskins: An Unlikely Hero* (London: Sphere, 1988), p.195.
43. Tom Cantrell and Mary Luckhurst (eds), *Playing for Real: Actors on Playing Real People* (Basingstoke: Palgrave Macmillan, 2010), p.29.
44. Cantrell and Luckhurst, *Playing for Real*, p.70.
45. Moline, *Bob Hoskins*, p.196.
46. Eva Mazierska, *European Cinema and Intertextuality: History, Memory and Politics* (Basingstoke: Palgrave Macmillan, 2011), p.61.
47. Antonio Scurati, *M—Il figlio del secolo* (Milan: Bompiani, 2018). The novel and its successors are discussed in Chapter 16.
48. Gianmaria Tammaro and Georg Szalai, 'Luca Marinelli on revealing the "Man Behind the Mask," in "M. Son of the Century"', *The Hollywood Reporter*, 31 January 2025.
49. Ibid.
50. On Damiano Damiani's 1980 documentary *Piazzale Loreto*, see Crainz, 'The Representation of Fascism and the Resistance', pp.133–4.
51. Luzzatto, *Il corpo del duce*, p.183.
52. Mirco Dondi, 'Piazzale Loreto' in Mario Isnenghi (ed.), *I luoghi della memoria: simboli e miti dell'Italia unita* (Rome: Laterza, 1996), pp.487–99. For foreigners, the display of the bodies of the dictator, his lover and his associates was a crucial episode, a vital element of the Mussolini narrative, one that provided a warning to others seeking to impress themselves on their fellow countrymen by ruthlessness and over-weening ambition. For the Americans, Piazzale Loreto was not a taboo of any sort but an appropriate fate for a war-mongering dictator. Thus, the American film *Mussolini: The Untold Story* includes a re-enactment of the bodies of Mussolini and Claretta hanging from the petrol station featuring the actors who play them. After they have been hauled up and subjected to abuse, they are shown in upside-down close-up.
53. The German film, *Er is wieder da* (Look who's back, David Wnendt, 2015) was adapted from a satirical novel by Timur Vermes.

NOTES TO CHAPTER 15

1. On the ambiguous and disturbing presence of Mussolini and Fascism on the internet in the early 2000s and its impact on the young, see Barbara Montesi, 'Potrebbe essere storia, ma è vero? Sui problemi di studiare il fascismo in rete', *Storia e problemi contemporanei*, 20: 44, 2007, 101–26.
2. Ibid., especially pp.124–6.
3. See Marco Panico, 'Repetition, recognition, remediation, or Benito Mussolini *after* Benito Mussolini', *Ocula*, 21:22, 2020, 62–78.
4. Renzo De Felice, Rosso e nero, ed. by Pasquale Chessa (Milan: Baldini & Castoldi, 1995), p.135.
5. Montesi, 'Potrebbe essere storia, ma è vero?', p.126.
6. Michel Serres with Bruno Latour, *Conversations on Science, Culture and Time* (Ann Arbor: University of Michigan Press, 1995), p.59.

7. Giacomo Tagliani, *Biografie della nazione: vita, storia, politica nel biopic Italiano* (Soveria Mannelli: Rubbettino, 2019), p.31.
8. See https://www.museionline.info/musei/museo-delle-cere-della-postumia (consulted 8/9/23).
9. See https://www.theguardian.com/artanddesign/artblog/2008/jul/04/hitlerisbackinwax-atmadam (consulted 8/9/23).
10. The chamber of horrors of the London Madame Tussauds, for example, was closed between 2016 and 2022.
11. Lucyna Krawcyzyk-Zywko, 'On waxworks considered as one of the hyperreal arts: exhibiting Jack the Ripper and his victims', *Humanities*, 7:2, 2018.
12. Alessandra Antola Swan, *Photographing Mussolini: The Making of a Political Icon* (Basingstoke: Palgrave Macmillan, 2020), pp.255–7.
13. Ibid., p.260.
14. Roland Barthes, *Mythologies* (London: Paladin, 1972), pp.47–9.
15. Jean Baudrillard, 'Symbolic exchange and death' in Baudrillard, *Selected Writings*, ed. by Mark Poster (Stanford: Stanford University Press, 1988), p.144.
16. Champfleury. *L'homme aux figures de cire* (Paris: Gallimard 2004; first published 1885).
17. Sara Pappas, 'The lessons of Champfleury', *Nineteenth-Century French Studies*, 42:1–2, 2013, 51–73. The deadness of wax statues goes in two directions: the living presented as though they were dead while the dead are pulled back eerily into the realm of the living.
18. Roswitha Mueller, 'Hans-Jürgen Syberberg's Hitler an interview—montage', *Discourse*, Vol.2, 1980, 60–82, pp.60–1.
19. Georg Seesslen, 'Blood and glamour' in Mary Rhiel and Ingeborg Majer O'Sickey (eds), *Riefenstahl Screened: An Anthology of New Criticism* (New York: Continuum, 2008), p.20.
20. Thomas Elsaessar, 'Our Hitler: a film by Hans-Jürgen Syberberg' in Karolin Machtans and Martin Ruehl (eds), *Hitler—Films from Germany: History, Cinema and Politics since 1945* (Basingstoke: Palgrave Macmillan 2012), p.76.
21. Max Picard, *Hitler in Our Selves* (Chicago: Henry Regnery, 1947), p.31.
22. Siegfried Kracauer, *From Caligari to Hitler: A Psychological History of the German Film* (Princeton: Princeton University Press, 1947). Syberberg was in no doubt that cinema has a purchase on the collective mind that is unrivalled. He also took the elitist view that mass culture turned whatever was noble and idealist about Germany into kitsch, commercialism and trash. It distracted and destroyed at the same time. To avoid such a fate for his own film, and avoid any risk of mass acclaim, he deliberately made it difficult and experimental.
23. It is worth noting that Thom Winterburn (see Chapter 11) intended also to make a film about Mussolini to accompany his book exhibition on Mussolini and Piazzale Loreto. The film was not in the end made, but the conception had some elements in common with Syberberg. Conversation with Thom Winterburn, 5 February 2024.
24. Hans-Jürgen Syberberg, Beatriz Schiller and Rod Ott, 'Our Hitler as visual politics', *Performing Arts Journal*, 4:3, 1980, pp.50–8, p.55.
25. Ibid., p.57.
26. Ibid.
27. See Stephen Gundle, 'Mussolini and mass culture', in Stephen Gundle, Christopher Duggan and Giuliana Pieri (eds), *The Cult of the Duce: Mussolini and the Italians* (Manchester; Manchester University Press, 201.), pp.73–5.
28. Enrico Sturani, 'Analysing Mussolini postcards', *Modern Italy*, 18:2, 2013, 141–56.
29. Jeffrey T. Schnapp, 'Mob porn' in Schnapp and M. Tiews (eds), *Crowds* (Stanford: Stanford University Press, 2006), p.20. See also Luca Acquarelli, *Il fascismo e l'immagine dell'impero: retoriche e culture visuali* (Rome: Donzelli, 2022).

30. Schnapp, 'Mob porn', p.39.
31. R.J.B. Bosworth, *Mussolini* (London: Arnold, 2002), p.211; Massimo Cardillo, *Il duce in moviola: politica e divismo nei cinegiornali e documentari 'Luce'* (Bari: Dedalo, 1983), p.91. See Stephen Gundle, 'Un Martini per il Duce: l'immaginario del consumismo I Italian negli anni Venti e Trenta' in Anna Villari (ed.), *L'arte della pubblicità: il manifesto italiano e le avaguardie 1920–1940* (Milan: Silvana editoriale, 2008) for some reflections on this sort of juxtaposition.
32. Edgar Morin, *Les stars* (Paris: Seuil, 1957), p.9.
33. These issues are tackled at length in David Forgacs and Stephen Gundle, *Mass Culture and Italian Society from Fascism to the Cold War* (Bloomington: Indiana University Press, 2007).
34. De Felice, *Rosso e nero*, , p.18.
35. Seesslen, 'Blood and glamour', p.20.
36. Andy Bull, *Strange Angels* (London: Black Swan, 1995), p.20.
37. Ibid., p.23.
38. Ibid., p.175.
39. See Forgacs and Gundle, *Mass Culture and Italian Society*.
40. Gavriel D. Rosenfeld, *Hi Hitler! How the Nazi Past Is Being Normalized in Contemporary Culture* (Cambridge: Cambridge University Press, 2015), p.3.
41. Ibid., p.15.
42. Ibid., p.24.
43. Ibid., p.288.
44. Stefano Antonucci, Daniele Fabbri and Mario Perrotta, *Quando c'era lui* (Soveria Mannelli: Rubbettino, 2017).
45. Paolo Berizzi, *Bande nere: come vivono, chi sono, chi protegge i nuovi nazifascisti* (Milan: Bompiani, 2009), p.14.
46. Ibid., p.129.
47. John Foot, *Calcio! A History of Italian Football* (London: Fourth Estate, 2006), p.370.
48. Bosworth, *Mussolini*, p.422.
49. Rita Felski, *The Gender of Modernity* (Cambridge, Mass.: Harvard University Press, 1995), p.38.
50. Ludovica Grassi and Clelia De Vita, 2016. 'Nostalgia between mourning and melancholia', *L'Autre*, 17:3, 2016, 321–9, p.323.
51. Ibid., p.323.
52. Ibid., p.324.
53. Svetlana Boym, *The Future of Nostalgia* (New York: Basic Books, 2001), p.xvi.

NOTES TO CHAPTER 16

1. Antonio Pennacchi, *Canale Mussolini* (Milan: Mondadori, 2010). The novel has a sequel, *Canale Mussolini—Parte seconda* (Milan: Mondadori, 2015).
2. See Magali Armillas-Tiseyra, *The Dictator Novel: Writers and Politics in the Global South* (Evanston, Ill.: Northwestern University Press, 2019).
3. Simon Levis Sullam, *I fantasmi del fascismo: Le metamorfosi degli intellettuali italiani nel dopoguerra* (Milan: Feltrinelli, 2021), p.145.
4. Gavriel D. Rosenveld, *Hi Hitler! How the Nazi Past Is Being Normalized in Contemporary Culture* (Cambridge: Cambridge University Press, 2015), p.159.
5. Marco Ramperti, *15 mesi al fresco* (Milan: Ceschina, 1960).
6. Marco Ramperti, *Benito I imperatore* (Rome: Editrice Scirè, 1950).
7. The reference point for this genre is Gianfranco De Turris (ed.), *Fantafascismo! Storie dell'Italia ucronica* (Rome: Settimo Sigillo, 2005).

8. Interesting in terms of Fascism's vocation for war is Mario Farneti's trilogy, which includes *Occidente* (Milan: Editrice Nord, 2001), *Attacco all'Occidente* (Milan: Editrice Nord, 2002) and *Nuovo impero dell'Occidente* (Milan: Editrice Nord, 2006). In the first volume, Italy stays neutral in 1940, only to be drawn into a third world war, which it wins. The second novel is sent in 1992 after the death of Mussolini but with Fascism still in power. In the final volume, set forty years after the fictional death of Mussolini, a new Duce is at the head of a Fascist world superpower.
9. Marco Malvestio, 'Cronache del *fantafascismo*. L'ucronia in Italia e il revisionismo storico', *The Italianist*, 38:1, 2018, 89–107, p.101.
10. See Bruno Mongai, *'Il fascio sulle stelle' di Benito Mussolini* (Turin: Robin, 2005), in which an imagined Mussolini has become a writer of run-of-the-mill science fiction. The film parody *Fascisti su Marte* (Fascists on Mars, Corrado Guzzanti and Igor Skofic, 2006), shot in the style of the Istituto Luce newsreels of the 1930s, was based on Guzzanti's sketches for the 2002 television programme Il caso Scafroglia (The Scafroglia Case).
11. Enrico Brizzi, *L'inattesa piega degli eventi* (Milan: Baldini Castoldi Dalai, 2008) and *La nostra guerra* (Milan: Baldini Castoldi Dalai, 2009). See also Giampietro Stocco, *Nero italiano* (Genoa: Frilli, 2003).
12. Pennacchi, *Canale Mussolini*, p.254.
13. On the living conditions of the migrant families in the new towns, see Victoria De Grazia, *Storia delle donne nel regime fascista*, new edition (Venice: Marsilio, 2023), pp.444–5.
14. Ibid., pp.255–6.
15. Ibid., p.307. On wine-drinking, see Antonio Pennacchi, *Fascio e martello: viaggio per le città del duce* (Rome: Editori Laterza, 2009), p.141.
16. Pennacchi, *Canale Mussolini*, p.249.
17. Ibid., p.310.
18. On these images, see Alessandra Antola Swan, *Photographing Mussolini: The Making of a Political Icon* (Basingstoke: Palgrave Macmillan, 2020), pp.298–315.
19. Pennacchi, *Canale Mussolini*, p.287.
20. Ibid., pp.425–6.
21. Ibid., p.425. 'Graziani' is Rodolfo Graziani, mentioned later in the chapter, who became Minister of Defence of the RSI.
22. Ibid., p.444.
23. Ibid., p.270.
24. Ibid., p.271.
25. Ibid., p.256.
26. Pennacchi, *Canale Mussolini—Parte seconda*, pp.108–9.
27. Ibid., p.73.
28. Lucio Caracciolo, 'Presentazione aggratis' in Pennacchi, *Fascio e martello*, p.xi.
29. Pennacchi, *Fascio e martello*.
30. Pennacchi had a precise mission that was very different from what many writers who tackled the Fascist experience in the postwar decades tried to do. For those who had lived through Fascism as writers and intellectuals, often sharing in its enthusiasms and passions, minimising their own position was as much a priority as presenting an edulcorated view of the role of Italians in the axis war was for others. See Guido Bartolini, *The Italian Literature of the Axis War: Memories of Self-Absolution and the Quest for Responsibility* (Basingstoke: Palgrave Macmillan, 2021).
31. See Francesco Filippi, *Mussolini ha fatto anche cose buone: le idiozie che continiano a circolare sul fascismo* (Turin: Bollati Boringhieri, 2019), pp.18–30. See also Paul Corner, *Mussolini in Myth and Memory* (Oxford: Oxford University Press, 2022), pp.134–7.

32. Renzo De Felice, *Mussolini il duce.* Tome I: *Gli anni del consenso 1929–1936* (Turin: Einaudi, 1974.), p.146.
33. Pennacchi, *Fascio e Martello*, pp.152–3.
34. Ibid., p.149.
35. Gianmarco Mancosu, *Vedere l'impero: l'istituto Luce e il colonialismo fascista* (Milan: Mimesis, 2022), p.20.
36. Luca Acquarelli, *Il fascismo e l'immagine dell'impero: retoriche e culture visuali* (Rome: Donzelli, 2022), pp.250–1.
37. Angelo Del Boca, *The Ethiopian War, 1935–1941* (Chicago: University of Chicago, 1966), p.232. On the activities of the associations, see Gianmarco Mancosu, 'Rituals of colonial memory: crafting imperial nostalgia in republican Italy', *Journal of Contemporary History*, online first, 2024.
38. See Luca Somigli, 'From a place in the sun to the heart of darkness: contemporary crime fiction and Italy's colonial past', Italian Studies, 73:4, 2018, 413–31.
39. For an overview of some important contributions to this body of work, see David Forgacs, 'Italian massacres in occupied Ethiopia', Modern Italy, 21:3, 2016, 305–12.
40. Francesca Melandri, *Sangue giusto* (Milan: Rizzoli, 2017); Maaza Mengiste, *The Shadow King* (Edinburgh: Canongate, 2019); Virginia Baily, *The Fourth Shore* (London: Little Brown, 2019).
41. Charles Burdett, 'Secrets and lies: Francesca Melandri's *Sangue giusto* (2017) and the uncovered memory of Italian East Africa', *Forum for Modern Language Studies*, 56:1, 2019, 49–65, p.52. See also Serena I. Volpi, '"I wanted to become an Abyssinian": rewriting Indro Montanelli's memories of colonial Africa in Francesca Melandri's *Sangue giusto* (2017)', *Journal of Postcolonial Writing*, 58:5, 2022, 654–68.
42. Mengiste, *The Shadow King*, p.37.
43. Ibid., pp.64 and 144.
44. Antonio Scurati, *M—Il figlio del secolo* (Milan: Bompiani, 2018), M—l'uomo *della* provvidenza (Milan: Bompiani, 2020) and M—Gli ultimi giorni d'Europa (Milan: Bompiani, 2022).
45. Antionio Scurati, *M—L'ora del destino* (Milan: Bompiani, 2024) and M—La fine e il principio (Milan: Bompiani, 2025).
46. Nicholas Léger, 'Un roman démocratique: M. L'enfant du siècle d'Antonio Scurati', *Esprit*, 7, 2021, 57–62.
47. The Sky series based on Scurati's first volume and directed by Joe Wright was made in 2024. The performance of Luca Marinelli in the role of Mussolini is discussed in Chapter 14.
48. De Felice was born in 1929 and therefore, if only as a child, experienced the downward phase of the dictatorship first hand. Scurati later revealed that he had 'never been affected by a fascination for the figure of the *duce* of fascism'. Antonio Scurati, *Fascismo e populismo: Mussolini oggi* (Milan: Bompiani, 2023), p.19.
49. Francesco Germinario, *L'altra memoria* (Turin: Bollati Boringhieri, 1999).
50. Filippo Focardi, *Nel cantiere della memoria: Fascismo, Resistenza, Shoah, Foibe* (Rome: Viella, 2020), p.93. See also Emilio Gentile, *Chi è fascista* (Rome: Laterza, 2019) on the 'defascistisation of fascism'.
51. 'Without violence, before and during the regime, fascism would never have come close to power. It was fundamental, visceral, epochal and life-changing: both for those who experienced it, and those who practised it. Fascist violence brought something fundamentally new to the political scene: a militia party, whose use of murder, beatings, intimidation and destruction swept aside all opposition. Revolvers, nail-studded cudgels, fire and castor oil

were all part of the weaponry of the blackshirts. In their wake they left thousands of terrified opponents, and hundreds of ransacked and charred buildings'. John Foot, *Blood and Power: The Rise and Fall of Italian Fascism* (London: Bloomsbury, 2022), p.3.

52. Scurati, *M—l'uomo della provvidenza*, p.368.
53. Ibid., p.625.
54. Ibid., p.269.
55. Ibid., p.621.
56. Scurati, *M—Gli ultimi giorni d'Europa*, pp.397–9.
57. Ibid., p.402.
58. Ibid., p.403.
59. Scurati, *M—La fine e il principio*, pp.284–5.
60. Ibid., pp.403–5. Under the Italian Constitution up to five life senators, who act as full members of the upper house of Parliament, may be appointed by the President of the Republic. Nominations are made 'for outstanding patriotic merits in the social, scientific, artistic or literary fields'.
61. Antonio Scurati, *Fascismo e populismo: Mussolini oggi* (Milan: Bompiani, 2023), p.26.
62. Scurati, *M—Gli ultimi giorni d'Europa*, page unnumbered (page after title page).
63. Scurati, *Fascismo e populismo*, p.26.

Bibliography

PRIMARY SOURCES

Archives

Archivio Centrale dello Stato (henceforth ACS), Segreteria Particolare del Duce (SPD), Carteggio Riservato (1922–43), b.105

ACS, SPD, Carteggio ordinario (1922–43), b.1871, f.528777

ACS, Presidenza del Consiglio dei Ministri (PCM)

1934–36, b.14, f.5 and b.20, f.1 (various subfolders)

1937–39, b.20, f.1 (various subfolders)

Press

Avanti, L'

Corriere della sera

Daily Mail

Epoca

Gente

Giornale, Il

Giornale Nuovo, Il

Giorno, Il

Illustrazione italiana, L'

Meridiano d'Italia illustrato, Il

New York Times, The

Oggi

Repubblica, La

Stampa, La

Tempo

Unità, L'

Memoirs and testimonies

Almirante, Giorgio. *Autobiografia di un 'fucilatore'* (Milan: Edizioni del Borghese, 1974)

Ansaldo, Giovanni. *Anni freddi: diari 1946–1950* (Bologna: Il Mulino, 2003)

Arteri, Giovanni. *Prima durante e dopo Mussolini: memorie del Novecento* (Milan: Mondadori 1990)

Bastianini, Giuseppe. *Uomini cose fatti: memorie di un ambasciatore* (Rome: Vitagliano, 1959)

Battista, Pierluigi. *Mio padre era fascista* (Milan: Mondadori, 2016)

Bottai, Giuseppe. *Diario 1935–1944*, ed. by Giordano Bruno Guerri (Milan: Rizzoli, 1982)

Brancati, Vitaliano. *Diario romano* (Milan: Bompiani, 1984; first published 1961)

Cadorna, Raffaele. *La riscossa* (Turin: Bietti, 1975)

Calamandrei, Piero. *Diario 1939–1945*, Vol.1 (Florence: La Nuova Italia, 1982)

Calamandrei, Piero. *Diario 1939–1945*, Vol. 2 (Florence: La Nuova Italia, 1982)

Cangini, Andrea (ed.). *La camicia nera di mio padre: riflessioni sulla morte della patria* (Bologna: Minerva, 2018)

Capuani, Gian Maria. *Ricordi di tempi fascisti* (Milan: Jaca Book, 1995)
Ciano, Edda. *La mia vita: intervista con Domenico Olivieri* (Milan: Mondadori, 2001)
D'Agostini, Bruno. *Colloqui con Rachele Mussolini* (Rome: O.E.T Edizioni del Secolo, 1946)
D'Eramo, Luce. *Il 25 luglio* (Rome: Elliot, 2013)
De Felice, Renzo (ed.). *Benito Mussolini: quattro testimonianze* (Florence: La Nuova Italia, 1976)
de Musset, Alfred. *La Confession d'un enfant du siècle* (Paris: Bonnaire, 1836)
Giuriati, Giovanni. *La parabola di Mussolini nei ricordi di un gerarca* (Rome-Bari: Laterza, 1981)
Grandi, Dino. *25 luglio: quarant'anni dopo*, ed. by Renzo De Felice (Bologna: Il Mulino, 2013)
Lizzani, Carlo. *Il mio lungo viaggio nel secolo breve* (Turin: Einaudi, 2007)
Malaparte, Curzio. *Muss: il grande imbecille* (Milan: Luni, 1999)
Matthews, Herbert. The *Education of a Correspondent* (Westport, Conn.: Greenwood Press, 1946)
Monelli, Paolo. *Roma 1943* (Turin: Einaudi, 2012; first published 1945)
Montanelli, Indro. *Io e il duce*, edited by Mimmo Franzinelli (Milan: Rizzoli, 2018)
Mussolini, Rachele. *Ma vie avec Benito* (Paris: Editions du Cheval Ailé, 1948)
Mussolini, Romano. *Il Duce, mio padre* (Milan: Rizzoli, 2004)
Mussolini, Romano. *My Father Il Duce* (Carlsbad, Calif.: Kales Press, 2006)
Navarra, Quinto. *Memorie del cameriere di Mussolini* (Milan: Longanesi, 1946)
Negrini Mussolini, Edda and Mario Russomanno. *I Mussolini dopo Mussolini* (Argelato: Minerva, 2022)
Petacci, Claretta *Mussolini segreto: diari 1932–1938* (Milan: Rizzoli, 2009)
Ramperti, Marco. *15 mesi al fresco* (Milan: Ceschina, 1960)
Sarfatti, Margherita. *My Fault: Mussolini as I Knew Him*, ed. by Brian Sullivan (New York: Enigma Books, 2014)
Sibbons, Mike. *From the Archives: An Eclectic Mix of Stories from the History of REME* (Oxford: Osprey, 2016)
Soleri, Marcello. *Memorie* (Ravenna: Edizioni Moderne, 2013; first published 1949)
Spender, Stephen. *European Witness* (London: Hamish Hamilton, 1946)
Theodoli, Alberto. *A cavallo di due secoli* (Rome: la Navicella, 1950)
Valiani, Leo. *Tutte le strade conducono a Roma* (Bologna: Il Mulino, 1995)
Wilson, Edmund. *Europe Without Baedeker* (London: Rupert Hart-Davis, 1967)

Period texts

Arendt, Hannah. *The Origins of Totalitarianism* (New York: Schocken, 1948)
B., D. 'Hitler o l'anticristo in noi stessi', *La Prealpina*, 21 October 1947
Bedel, Maurice. *Fascsime an VII* (Paris: Gallimard, 1929)
Beltramelli, Antonio. *L'uomo nuovo* (Milan: Mondadori, 1923)
Béraud, Henri. *Ce que j'ai vu a Rome* (Paris: Editions de France, 1929)
Berneri, Camillo. *Mussolini: psicologia di un dittatore* (Milan: Edizioni Azione comune, 1966)
Bontempelli, Massimo. *Dignità dell'uomo (1943–1946)* (Milan: Bompiani, 1946)
Bottai, Giuseppe. 'Il regime per l'arte' in *Politica Fascista delle arti* (Rome: Signorelli, 1940)
Brancati, Vitaliano. *I fascisti invecchiano* (Milan: Longanesi, 1950)
Calipso, *Vita segreta di Mussolini* (Rome: unidentified publisher, 1944)
Cassius, *The Trial of Mussolini* (London: Gollancz, 1943)
Caudana, Mino. *Il figlio del fabbro* (Rome: C.E.N., undated but elsewhere indicated as 1964)
Caudana, Mino. *Processo a Mussolini* (Rome: C.E.N., 1964)
Ciarlantini, Franco. *Mussolini immaginario* (Milan: Sonzogno, 1933)
Constant. *Memorie del cameriere di Napoleone* (Milan: Rizzoli, 1941)

Croce, Benedetto. 'L'Anticristo che è in noi' in *La fine della civiltà, l'Anticristo che è in noi*, ed. by Ilario Bertoletti (Brescia: Morcelliana, 2022; essay first published 1946)
Damiano, Andrea. *Rosso e grigio* (Milan: Muggiani, 1947)
D'Andrea, Ugo. *Mussolini motore del secolo* (Milan: Hoepli, 1939)
Delcroix, Carlo. *Un uomo e un popolo* (Florence: Vallecchi, 1928)
Gadda, Carlo Emilio. *Eros e Priapo* (Milan: Adelphi, 2016; first published 1967)
Gravelli, Asvero. *Mussolini aneddotico* (Rome: Latinità, 1951)
Guerri, Giordano Bruno (ed.). *Rapporto al Duce: le interrogazioni delle organizzazioni provinciali del 1942* (Milan: Bompiani, 2020)
Kracauer, Siegfried. *From Caligari to Hitler: A Psychological History of the German Film* (Princeton: Princeton University Press, 1947)
Lami, Guido. *La psiche tedesca: osservazioni sulle psicogenesi del totalitarismo* (Brescia: Morcelliana, 1948)
Longanesi, Leo. *Il destino à cambiato cavallo* (Milan: Ronda, 1951)
Ludwig, Emil. *Colloqui con Mussolini* (Milan: Mondadori, 2000; first published 1932)
Malaparte, Curzio. 'Deux chapeaux de paille d'Italie' appendix to *Ces sacrés Toscans* (Paris: Les belles lettres, 2014; first published 1948)
Malaparte, Curzio. *La pelle* (Milan: Adelphi, 2010; first published 1949)
Montanelli, Indro. *Il buonuomo Mussolini* (Milan: Edizioni Riunite, 1947)
Mussolini, Benito. *Storia di un anno: il tempo del bastone e della carota* (Rome: Libero, 2004; first published 1944)
Mussolini, Benito. *Pensieri pontini e sardi* (Bologna: Libreria Piani 2022; first published 1943)
Mussolini, Benito. *Opera Omnia*, 36 vols. (Firenze: La Fenice, 1951)
Notorius. *Processo a Benito Mussolini* (Milan: Paneuropa, 1959)
Packard, Reynolds and Eleanor. *Balcony Empire: Fascist Italy at War* (New York: Oxford University Press, 1942)
Palazzeschi, Aldo. *Tre imperi... mancati: cronaca 1922–1945* (Milan: Mondadori, 2016; first published 1945)
Pavolini, Paolo. *Il processo Mussolini* (Milan: Beleguese edizioni, 2008; first published 1975)
Picard, Max. *Hitler in Our Selves* (Chicago: Henry Regnery, 1947)
Querel, Vittore. *Il paese di Benito* (Rome: Corso editore, 1954)
Salvatorelli, Luigi. *Leggenda e realtà di Napoleone* (Rome: De Silva, 1944), p.119
Sarfatti, Margherita. *The Life of Benito Mussolini* (London: Thornton Butterworth, 1925)
Satta, Salvatore. *De Profundis* (Milan: Adelphi, 1980; first published 1945)
Somma, Luigi. *Mussolini morto e vivo* (Rome: Vito Bianco, 1960)

Fiction

Albinati, Edoardo. *La scuola cattolica* (Milan: Rizzoli, 2016)
Antonucci, Stefano, Daniele Fabbri and Mario Perrotta. *Quando c'era lui* (Brecsia: Schockdom, 2017)
Baily, Virginia. *The Fourth Shore* (London: Little Brown, 2019)
Brancati, Vitaliano. *I fascisti invecchiano* (Milan: Longanesi, 1950)
Brizzi, Enrico. *L'inattesa piega degli eventi* (Milan: Baldini Castoldi Dalai, 2008)
Brizzi, Enrico. *La nostra guerra* (Milan: Baldini Castoldi Dalai, 2009)
Eco, Umberto. *La misteriosa fiamma della regina Loana* (Milan: Bompiani, 2004)
Farneti, Marco. *Occidente* (Milan: Editrice Nord, 2001)
Farneti, Marco. *Attacco all'Occidente* (Milan: Editrice Nord, 2002)
Farneti, Marco. *Nuovo impero dell'Occidente* (Milan: Editrice Nord, 2006)

Ginzburg, Natalia. *Vita immaginaria* (Milan: Mondadori, 1974)
Melandri, Francesca. *Sangue giusto* (Milan: Rizzoli, 2017)
Meneghello, Luigi. *Bau-sète!* (Milan: Bompiani, 1996), p.40
Mengiste, Maaza. *The Shadow King* (Edinburgh: Canongate, 2019)
Mongai, Bruno. *'Il fascio sulle stelle' di Benito Mussolini* (Turin: Robin, 2005)
Pennacchi, Antonio. *Canale Mussolini* (Milan: Mondadori, 2010)
Pennacchi, Antonio. *Canale Mussolini—Parte seconda* (Milan: Mondadori, 2015)
Ramperti, Marco. *Benito I imperatore* (Rome: Editrice Scirè, 1950)
Scurati, Antonio. *M—Il figlio del secolo* (Milan: Bompiani, 2018)
Scurati, Antonio. *M—l'uomo della provvidenza* (Milan: Bompiani, 2020)
Scurati, Antonio. *M—Gli ultimi giorni d'Europa* (Milan: Bompiani, 2022)
Scurati, Antionio. *M—L'ora del destino* (Milan: Bompiani, 2024)
Scurati, Antionio. *M— La fine e il principio* (Milan: Bompiani, 2025)
Steiner, George. *The Portage to San Cristobel of A.H.* (London: Faber and Faber, 1981)
Stocco, Giampietro. *Nero italiano* (Genoa: Frilli, 2003)

SECONDARY SOURCES

Acquarelli, Luca. *Il fascismo e l'immagine dell'impero: retoriche e culture visuali* (Rome: Donzelli, 2022)
Adorno, Theodor W. *Guilt and Defense: On the Legacies of National Socialism in Postwar Germany* (Cambridge, Mass.: Harvard University Press, 2010)
Albanese, Giulia and Lucia Ceci (eds). *I luoghi del fascismo: memoria, politica, rimozione* (Rome: Viella, 2022)
Antola Swan, Alessandra. *Photographing Mussolini: The Making of a Political Icon* (Basingstoke: Palgrave Macmillan, 2020)
Apor, Balazs. *The Invisible Shining: The Cult of Matyas Rakosi in Stalinist Hungary, 1945–1956* (Budapest: CEU Press, 2017)
Aquilanti, Paolo. *Il caso Bontempelli* (Palermo: Sellerio, 2020)
Aramini, Donatello. 'Renzo De Felice e la recente storiografia italiana', *Studi Storici*, 55:1, 2014, 335–48
Armiero, Marco. 'Making Italians out of rocks: Mussolini's shadows on Italian mountains', *Modern Italy*, 19:3, 2014, 261–74
Armillas-Tiseyra, Magali. *The Dictator Novel: Writers and Politics in the Global South* (Evanston, Ill.: Northwestern University Press, 2019)
Arthurs, Joshua. 'Settling accounts: retribution, emotion and memory during the fall of Mussolini', *Journal of Modern Italian Studies*, 20:5, 2016, 617–39
Arthurs, Joshua. 'Vivere il fascismo: politica e vita quotidiana durante il regime' in Giulia Albanese (ed.), *Il fascismo italiano: storia e interpretazioni* (Rome: Carocci, 2021), pp.237–53
Aymard, Orianne. *When a Goddess Dies: Worshipping Ma Anandamayi after Her Death* (Oxford: Oxford University Press, 2014)
Bach, Steven. *Leni: The Life and Work of Leni Riefenstahl* (London: Abacus, 2008)
Baldassini, Cristina. *L'ombra di Mussolini: l'Italia moderata e la memoria del fascismo (1945–1960)* (Soveria Mannelli: Rubbettino, 2008)
Baldasso, Franco. *Against Redemption: Democracy, Memory and Literature in Post-Fascist Italy* (New York: Fordham University Press, 2022)
Baldissara, Luca. *Italia 1943: la guerra continua* (Bologna: Il Mulino, 2023)
Baldoli, Claudia. *Italian Fascism 1914–1945: Themes and Interpretations* (Cham: Palgrave Macmillan, 2023)

Banti, Alberto Mario. *Sublime madre nostra: la nazione italiana dal Risorgimnto al fascismo* (Rome: Laterza, 2011)

Baratieri, Daniela. *Memories and Silences Haunted by Fascism: Italian Colonialism MCMXXX–MCMLX* (Bern: Peter Lang, 2010)

Baratieri, Daniela. 'Sanity from a lunatic asylum: Ida Dalser's Threat to Mussolini's image' in Gundle, Duggan and Pieri (eds), *The Cult of the Duce*.

Barbu, Zevedei. *Democracy and Dictatorship: Their Psychology and Patterns of Life* (New York: Routledge & Kegan Paul, 1956)

Barisone, Silvia, Matteo Foxchessati and Gianni Franzone (eds). *La Collezione Wolfson di Genova* (Milan: Skira, 2005)

Barthes, Roland. *Mythologies* (London: Paladin, 1972)

Bartolini, Flaminia. 'Fascism on display: the afterlife of material legacies of the dictatorship', *EX NOVO Journal of Archaeology*, 5, December 2020, 19–37

Bartolini, Francesco, Roberto Giulianelli and Amoreno Martellini (eds). *Fascismo e spazi urbani nelle Marche* (Ancona: affinità elettive, 2024)

Bartolini, Guido. *The Italian Literature of the Axis War: Memories of Self-Absolution and the Quest for Responsibility* (Basingstoke: Palgrave Macmillan, 2021)

Baudrillard, Jean. 'Symbolic Exchange and Death' in Baudrillard, *Selected Writings*, ed. by Mark Poster (Stanford: Stanford University Press, 1988)

Battini, Michele. *The Missing Italian Nuremberg: Cultural Amnesia and Postwar Politics* (New York: Palgrave Macmillan, 2007)

Bellassai, Sandro. 'The masculine mystique: antimodernism and virility in Fascist Italy', *Journal of Modern Italian Studies*, 10:3, 2005, 314–35

Bellassai, Sandro. 'L'autunno del patriarca: insicurezze maschili nel secondo dopoguerra' in Penny Morris, Francesco Ricatti and Mark Seymour (eds), *Politica ed emozioni nella storia d'Italia: dal 1848 ad oggi* (Rome: Viella, 2012)

Ben-Ghiat, Ruth. 'Unmaking the fascist man: masculinity, film and the transition from dictatorship', *Journal of Modern Italian Studies*, 10:3, 2005, 335–65

Ben-Ghiat, Ruth. 'Why are so many Fascist monuments still standing in Italy?', *The New Yorker*, 5 October 2017

Ben-Ghiat, Ruth. *Strongmen: Mussolini to the Present* (New York: Norton, 2020)

Berizzi, Paolo. *Bande nere: come vivono, chi sono, chi protegge i nuovi nazifascisti* (Milan: Bompiani, 2009)

Bernstein, David. 'Bedrock' in Stefan Schutt, Sam Roberts and Leanne White (eds), *Advertising and Public Memory: Social, Cultural and Historical Perspectives on Ghost Signs* (New York and London: Routledge, 2017)

Bertelli, Sergio. *The King's Body: Sacred Rituals of Power in Medieval and Early Modern Europe* (Philadelphia: Pennsylvania University Press, 2001)

Bertoldi, Silvio. *Piazzale Loreto* (Milan: Rizzoli, 2001)

Bianchi, Caterina. 'Il nudo eroico del fascismo', in Sergio Bertelli and Cristiano Grottanelli (eds), *Gli occhi di Alessandro: potere sovrano e sacralità del corpo da Alessandro Magno a Ceausescu* (Florence: Ponte alle Grazie, 1990), pp.166–7

Bingham, Dennis. *Whose Lives Are They Anyway? The Biopic as Contemporary Film Genre* (New Brunswick: Rutgers University Press, 2010)

Biondi, Dino. *La fabbrica del duce* (Bologna: Cappelli, 1973)

Bloom, Michelle E. *Waxworks: A Cultural Obsession* (Minneapolis: University of Minnesota Press, 2003)

Bobbio, Norberto. 'Le colpe rimosse di noi italiani', *La Stampa*, 6 December 1988, p.1. Also contained in Pirani, *Il fascino del nazismo*

Boldrick, Stacy and Richard Clay. *Iconoclasm: Contested Objects, Contested Terms* (London: Routledge, 2007)

Borneman, John (ed.). *Death of the Father: An Anthropology of the End of Political Authority* (New York and Oxford: Berghahn, 2004)

Borrini, Anna. 'Firmato M: la propaganda murale' in Adolfo Mignemi (ed.), *Immagine coordinate per un impero: Etiopia 1935–36* (Turin: Gruppo Editoriale Forma, 1984)

Bosca, Giovanni. *La propaganda murale del regime fascista: una memoria storica del XX secolo* (Mondovi: ArabAFenice, 2010)

Bosworth, R.J.B. *Mussolini's Italy: Life Under the Fascist Dictatorship, 1915–1945* (London: Allen Lane, 2005)

Bosworth, R.J.B. 'Dictators strong or weak? The model of Benito Mussolini' in Bosworth (ed.), *The Oxford Handbook of Fascism* (Oxford: Oxford University Press, 2010)

Bosworth, R.J.B. *Mussolini* (London: Arnold, 2002 and, second edition, 2010)

Bosworth, R.J.B. *Mussolini* (London: Bloomsbury, new edition, 2014)

Bosworth, R.J.B. *Mussolini and the Eclipse of Italian Fascism: From Dictatorship to Populism* (New Haven and London: Yale University Press, 2021)

Boym, Svetlana. *The Future of Nostalgia* (New York: Basic Books, 2001)

Bracco, Bracco. 'I segni littori di Milano: costruzione, distruzione e rinascita del volto di una città' in Albanese and Ceci, *I luoghi del fascismo*

Broder, David. *Mussolini's Grandchildren: Fascism in Contemporary Italy* (London: Pluto Press, 2023)

Brunetta, Gian Piero. 'Mise-en page dei cinegiornali e mise-en-scène mussoliniana' in Riccardo Redi (ed.), *Cinema Italiano sotto il fascismo* (Venice: Marsilio, 1979)

Bull, Andy. *Strange Angels* (London: Black Swan, 1995)

Buonanno, Milly. *Italian TV Drama and Beyond: Stories from the Soil/Stories from the Sea* (Bristol: Intellect, 2012)

Burdett, Charles. 'Transnational time: reading post-war representations of the Italian presence in East Africa', *Italian Studies*, 73:3, 2018, 274–88, p.280

Burdett, Charles. 'Secrets and lies: Francesca Melandri's *Sangue giusto* (2017) and the uncovered memory of Italian East Africa', *Forum for Modern Language Studies*, 56:1, 2019, 49–65

Burke, Peter. *The Fabrication of Louis XIV* (New Haven and London: Yale University Press, 1992)

Burke, Peter. 'Freud and cultural history', *Psychoanalysis and History*, 9:1, 2007, 5–15

Cacace, Paolo. *Come muore un regime; il fascismo verso il 25 luglio* (Bologna: Il Mulino, 2021)

Caesar, Michael. 'Writing and the real world: Italian narrative in the period of reconstruction' in Nicholas Hewitt (ed.), *The Culture of Reconstruction: European Literature, Thought and Film, 1945–50* (Basingstoke: Macmillan, 1989)

Calvino, Italo. 'I ritratti del Duce', in *Saggi (1945–1985)*, edited by Mario Barenghi (Milan: Mondadori, 2022)

Campi, Alessandro. *Mussolini* (Bologna: Il Mulino, 2001)

Campus, Donatella. 'Women in politics' in Erik Jones and Gianfranco Pasquino (eds), *The Oxford Handbook of Italian Politics* (Oxford: Oxford University Press, 2015)

Canali, Mauro. *La scoperta dell'Italia: il fascismo raccontato dai corrispondenti americani* (Venice: Marsilio, 2017)

Cannistraro, Philip and Brian Sullivan, *Il Duce's Other Woman* (New York: Morrow, 1993)

Cantrell, Tom and Mary Luckhurst (eds), *Playing for Real: Actors on Playing Real People* (Basingstoke: Palgrave Macmillan, 2010)

Cardillo, Massimo. *Il duce in moviola* (Bari: Dedalo, 1983)

Carlson, Marvin. *The Haunted Stage: The Theatre as Memory Machine* (Ann Arbor: University of Michigan Press, 2001)

Castoldi, Massimo. *Piazzale Loreto: Milano, l'eccidio e il 'compromesso'* (Rome: Donzelli, 2020)
Caudana, Mino. *1922* (Milan: Edizioni del Borghese, 1972)
Caudana, Mino. *I fucilati di Verona* (Rome: C.E.N., 1973)
Cavalli, Luciano. 'Considerations on charisma and the cult of charismatic leadership', *Modern Italy* 3:2, 1998, 159–71
Cesaraccio, Aldo, Antonello Mattone and Giuseppe Melis Bassu (eds), *Mussolini in Sardegna* (Cagliari, Gia editrice, 1983)
Chabod, Federico. *Italia contemporanea (1918–1948)* (Turin: Einaudi, 1961)
Champfleury. *L'homme aux figures de cire* (Paris: Gallimard 2004; first published 1885)
Cigognetti, Luisa and Pierre Sorlin. 'History on television: the problem of sources' in Erin Bell and Ann Gray (eds), *Televising History: Mediating the Past in Postwar Europe* (Basingstoke: Palgrave Macmillan 2010), p.31
Colarizi, Simona. *L'opinione degli italiani sotto il regime, 1929–1943* (Rome: Laterza, 1991)
Colarizi, Simona. *La seconda guerra mondiale e la Repubblica* (Milan: TEA, 1996)
Colarizi, Simona. 'Fascism-qualunquism-neofascism: the rise of neo-fascism in Italy in the first postwar period, until the foundation of the neo-fascist political party' in Stein Larsen (ed.), *Modern Europe after Fascism, 1943–1980s* (New York: Columbia University Press, 1998)
Colombo, Elisabetta, Anna Modena and Giovanni Scirocco. *Il nostro silenzio avrà una voce: Piazzale Loreto: fatti e memoria* (Bologna: Il Mulino, 2021)
Conti, Davide. *L'anima nera della Repubblica: storia del MSI* (Rome: Laterza, 2013)
Conti, Davide. *Gli uomini di Mussolini: prefetti, questori e criminali di guerra dal fascismo alla repubblica italiana* (Turin: Einaudi, 2017)
Contini, Giovanni. 'Novelists, historians and the memory of the Italian Resistance' in John Foot and Stephen Gundle (eds), *Paul Ginsborg and the Historiography of Modern Italy* (London: Palgrave Macmillan, 2024)
Cooke, Philip. 'Recent work on Nazi massacres in Italy during the Second World War', *Modern Italy*, 5:2, 2000, 211–18
Cooke, Philip. *The Legacy of the Italian Resistance* (New York: Palgrave Macmillan, 2011)
Corner, Paul. *Mussolini in Myth and Memory* (Oxford: Oxford University Press, 2022)
Crainz, Guido. 'The representation of fascism and the resistance in the documentaries of Italian state television' in Richard Bosworth and Patrizia Dogliani (eds), *Italian Fascism: History, Memory and Representation* (Basingstoke: Palgrave Macmillan, 1999)
Custen, George. Bio/Pics: How Hollywood Constructed Public History (New Brunswick: Rutgers University Press, 1992)
D'Attorre, Pier Paolo (ed.). *Nemici per la pelle: sogno americano e mito sovirto nell'Italia contemporanea* (Milan: Franco Angeli, 1991)
Davis, Melton S. *Who Defends Rome? The Forty-Five Days, July 25–September 8, 1943* (London: George Allen & Unwin, 1972)
Deaglio, Enrico. *Besame mucho* (Milan: Feltrinelli, 1995)
De Felice, Renzo. *Mussolini il fascista*. Tome 1: *La conquista del potere 1921–1925* (Turin: Einaudi, 1966)
De Felice, Renzo. *Mussolini il duce.* Tome I: *Gli anni del consenso 1929–1936* (Turin: Einaudi, 1974)
De Felice, Renzo. *Le interpretazioni di fascismo* (Bari: Laterza, 1969)
De Felice, Renzo. *Mussolini il fascista. L'organizzazione dello Stato fascista* (Turin: Einaudi, 1969)
De Felice, Renzo. *Intervista sul fascismo*, ed. by Michael Ledeen (Bari: Laterza, 1975)
De Felice, Renzo. *Mussolini l'alleato 1940–1945.* Tome 1: *L'Italia in guerra 1940–1943.* Tome 2: *crisi e agonia del regime* (Turin: Einaudi, 1990)
De Felice, Renzo. *Rosso e nero*, ed. by Pasquale Chessa (Milan: Baldini & Castoldi, 1995)
De Felice, Renzo. *Mussolini l'alleato 1940–1945. La guerra civile 1943–1945* (Turin: Einaudi, 1996)

De Felice, Renzo and Luigi Goglia (eds). *Mussolini: il mito* (Rome-Bari: Laterza 1983)

De Grazia, Victoria. *Storia delle donne nel regime fascista*, new edition (Venice: Marsilio, 2023)

Del Boca, Angelo. *The Ethiopian War, 1935–1941* (Chicago: University of Chicago, 1966)

Del Boca, Angelo. 'Impero' in Mario Isnenghi (ed.), *I luoghi della memoria: simboli e miti dell'Italia unita* (Rome: Laterza, 1996)

De Luna, Giovanni. 'Revisionismo e resistenza' in Angelo Del Bocca (ed.), *La storia negata: il revisionismo e il suo uso politico* (Vicenza: Neri Pozza, 2009)

De Turris, Gianfranco (ed.). *Fantafascismo! Storie dell'Italia ucronica* (Rome: Settimo Sigillo, 2005)

Di Bella, Maria Pia. 'From future to past: a Duce's trajectory' in John Borneman (ed.), *Death of the Father: An Anthropology of the End of Political Authority* (Oxford: Berghahn, 2003)

Di Genova, Giorgio (ed.). *'L'uomo di provvidenza': iconografia del duce, 1923–1945* (Bologna: Edizioni Bora, 1997)

Diggins, John P. *Mussolini and Fascism: The View from America* (Princeton: Princeton University Press, 1972)

Dikotter, Frank. *How To Be a Dictator: The Cult of Personality in the Twentieth Century* (London: Bloomsbury 2019)

Di Nolfo, Ennio. *Le paure e le speranze degli italiani (1943–1953)* (Milan: Mondadori, 1986)

Domenico, Roy Palmer. *Italian Fascists on Trial 1943–1948* (Chapel Hill, N.C.: University of North Carolina Press, 1992)

Dondi, Mirco. 'Piazzale Loreto' in Mario Isnenghi (ed.), *I luoghi della memoria: simboli e miti dell'Italia unita* (Rome: Laterza, 1996)

Dondi, Mirco. 'The fascist mentality after fascism' in R.J.B. Bosworth and Patrizia Dogliani (eds), *Italian Fascism: History, Memory and Representation* (Basingstoke: Palgrave Macmillan, 1999)

Dubowitz, Dan, Patrick Duerdon and Penny Lewis. *Fascismo abbandonato: The Children's Colonie of Mussolini's Italy* (Stockport: Dewi Lewis, 2009)

Duggan, Christopher. *Fascist Voices: An Intimate History of Mussolini's Italy* (London: Bodley Head, 2012)

Duggan, Christopher. 'Coming to terms with Italy's war', *History Today*, December 2013

Duggan, Christopher. 'The internalisation of the cult of the Duce; the evidence of diaries and letters' in Gundle, Duggan and Pieri (eds), *The Cult of the Duce*

Dyer, Richard. *White* (London: Routledge, second edition 2017)

Ebbrecht, Tobias. '(Re)constructing Biographies: German television Docudrama and the Historical Biography', in Bell and Gray (eds), *Televising History*

Edwards, P.G. 'The Foreign Office and Fascism 1924–1929', *Journal of Contemporary History*, 5:2, 1970, 53–61

Elder, Angela Esco. *Love and Duty: Confederate Widows and the Emotional Politics of Loss* (Chapel Hill, N.C.: University of North Carolina Press, 2022)

Elliott, Anthony. *The Mourning of John Lennon* (Berkeley: University of California Press, 1999)

Ellwood, David E. *Italy 1943–1945* (Leicester: Leicester University Press, 1985)

Elsaessar, Thomas. 'Our Hitler: a film by Hans-Jürgen Syberberg' in Karolin Machtans and Martin Ruehl (eds), *Hitler—Films from Germany: History, Cinema and Politics since 1945* Basingstoke: Palgrave Macmillan 2012)

Elsner, John and Roger Cardinal (eds). *The Cultures of Collecting* (London: Reaktion, 1994)

Falasca-Zamponi, Simonetta. 'Ordinary anti-Fascism: Italy and the fall of Fascism, 1943–1945', *Journal of Modern Italian Studies*, 24:1, 2019, 171–89.

Falasca-Zamponi, Simonetta. *Fascism, the War, and Structures of Feeling in Italy, 1943–1945: Tales in Chiaroscuro* (Oxford: Oxford University Press, 2023)

Faldini, Franca and Goffredo Fofi (eds), *L'avventurosa storia del cinema italiano: raccontato dai suoi protagonisti (1960–1969)* (Milan: Feltrinelli, 1981)

Felski, Rita. *The Gender of Modernity* (Cambridge, Mass.: Harvard University Press, 1995)

Fermi, Laura. *Mussolini* (Chicago: Chicago University Press, 1961)

Fiaccarini, Anna et al. (eds). *The Great Dictator: Il grande dittatore di Charlie Chaplin* (Bologna: Cineteca di Bologna, 2002)

Filippi, Francesco. *Mussolini ha fatto anche cose buone: le idiozie che continiano a circolare sul fascismo* (Turin: Bollati Boringhieri, 2019)

Finaldi, Giuseppe. 'Mussolini and the Italian Empire, 1936–1941' in Gundle, Duggan and Pieri (eds), *The Cult of the Duce.*

Finchelstein, Federico. 'The Fascist canon: Renzo De Felice and the writing of history', *Forum italicum*, 40:1, 2006, 85–102

Fleischer, Joachim. 'Political life and super-ego regression', *Psychological Review*, 36:4, 1949, 416–28

Focardi, Filippo. *La guerra della memoria: la Resistenza nel dibattito politico italiano dal 1945 a oggi* (Rome: Laterza, 2005)

Focardi, *Il cattivo tedesco e il bravo italiano: la rimozione delle colpe della seconda guerra mondiale* (Rome: Laterza, 2016). English edition: *The Bad German and the Good Italian: Removing the Guilt of the Second World War* (Manchester: Manchester University Press, 2023)

Focardi, Filippo. *Nel cantiere della memoria: Fascismo, Resistenza, Shoah, Foibe* (Rome: Viella 2020)

Fofi, Goffredo. *Alberto Sordi, l'Italia in bianco e nero* (Milan: Mondadori, 2004)

Fogu, Claudio. '*Italiani brava gente*: the Legacy of Fascist Historical Culture on Italian Politics of Memory' in Richard Lebow and others (eds), *The Politics of Memory in Postwar Europe* (Durham, N.C.: Duke University Press, 2006)

Foley, Michael. *Political Leadership: Themes, Contexts and Critiques* (Oxford: Oxford University Press, 2013)

Foot, John. *Calcio! A History of Italian Football* (London: Fourth Estate, 2006)

Foot, John. *Blood and Power: The Rise and Fall of Italian Fascism* (London: Bloomsbury, 2022)

Forgacs, David. 'Italian massacres in occupied Ethiopia', *Modern Italy*, 21:3, 2016, 305–12

Forgacs, David and Stephen Gundle. *Mass Culture and Italian Society from Fascism to the Cold War* (Bloomington: Indiana University Press, 2007)

Forlenza, Rosario. *On the Edge of Democracy: Italy, 1943–1948* (Oxford: Oxford University Press, 2020)

Forter, Greg. 'Against melancholia: contemporary mourning theory, Fitzgerald's *The Great Gatsby*, and the politics of unfinished grief', *differences*, 14:2, 2003, 134–70

Forth, Christopher. *Masculinity in the Modern West: Gender, Civilisation and the Body* (Basingstoke: Palgrave Macmillan, 2008)

Fraddosio, Maria. 'The Fallen Hero: The Myth of Mussolini and the Fascist Women in the Italian Social Republic (1943–5)', *Journal of Contemporary History*, 31:1, 1996, 99–124

Franzinelli, Mimmo. *Il prigioniero di Salò: Mussolini e la tragedia italiana del 1943–45* (Milan: Mondadori, 2012)

Franzinelli, Mimmo. *Il fascismo è finito il 25 aprile 1945* (Rome: Laterza, 2022)

Freud, Sigmund. *The Ego and the Id* (London: Hogarth Press, 1950)

Freud, Sigmund. *Group Psychology and the Analysis of the Ego* New York: Norton 1989)

Freud, Sigmund. *On Murder, Mourning and Melancholia* (London: Penguin 2005)

Filippi, Francesco. *Noi però gli abbiamo fatto le strade: le colonie italiane tra bugie, razzisimi e amnesia* (Turin: Bollati Boringhieri, 2021), pp.170–3

Gaborik, Patricia. 'Brancati's Gigantic Mussolinis', *Laboratoire italien*, 30, 2023, pages unnumbered

Gabrielli, Patrizia. *Il tempio della virilità: l'antifascismo, il genere, la storia* (Milan: Franco Angeli, 2008)

Gabrielli, Patrizia. *Il 1946, le donne, la repubblica* (Rome: Donzelli, 2009)

Galasso, Giuseppe. *Croce e lo spirito del suo tempo* (Rome: Laterza, 2002)

Gallerano, Nicola. 'Critica e crisi del paradigma antifascista', *Problemi del socialismo*, 7, 1986, 106–33, pp.119–20

Gambetti, Fidia. *1919–1945: inchiesta sul fascismo* (Manziana Roma: Vecchiarelli, 1991)

Gambetti, Fidia. *Gli anni che scottano: il primo lungo viaggio dentro il fascismo* (Milan: Mursia, 1995)

Gaudenzi, Bianca. *Fascismi in vetrina: pubblicità e modelli di consumo nel Ventennio e nel Terzo Reich* (Rome: Viella, 2023)

Germinaro, Francesco. *L'altra memoria: l'estrema destra, Salò e la Resistenza* (Turin: Bollati Boringieri, 1999)

Gentile, Emilio. 'Fascism in Italian historiography: in search of an individual historical identity', *Journal of Contemporary History*, 21:2, 1986, p.183

Gentile, Emilio. *Il culto del littorio: la sacralizzazione della politica nell'Italia fascista* (Rome: Laterza, 1993)

Gentile, Emilio. 'Renzo De Felice: a tribute', *Journal of Contemporary History*, 32:2, 1997, 139–51

Gentile, Emilio. 'Mussolini's charisma', *Modern Italy*, 3:2, 1998, 219–35

Gentile, Emilio. *Fascismo: storia e interpretazione* (Rome: Laterza, 2002)

Gentile, Emilio. *Renzo De Felice: lo storico e il personaggio* (Rome: Laterza, 2003)

Gentile, Emilio. *Fascismo di pietra* (Rome: Laterza, 2007)

Gentile, Emilio. *In Italia ai tempi di Mussolini: viaggio in compagnia di osservatori stranieri* (Milan: Mondadori, 2014)

Gentile, Emilio. *La via italiana al totalitarismo: il partito e lo Stato nel regime fascista* (Rome: Carocci, 2018)

Gentile, Emilio. *Chi è fascista* (Rome: Laterza, 2019)

Gentile, Emilio. *Caporali tanti, uomini pochissimi: la storia secondo Totò* (Rome: Laterza, 2020)

Gerbi, Sandro and Raffaele Liucci. *Indro Montanelli: una biografia (1909–2001)* (Milan: Hoepli, 2014)

Germinaro, Francesco. *L'altra memoria: l'estrema destra, Sal e la Resistenza* (Turin: Bollati Boringhieri, 1999)

Gilroy, Paul. *After Empire: Melancholia or Convivial Culture?* (London: Routledge, 2004)

Ginsborg, Paul. *A History of Contemporary Italy: society and politics, 1943–1988* (London: Penguin, 1990)

Ginsborg, Paul. *Family Politics: Domestic Life, Devastation and Survival, 1900–1950* (New Haven and London: Yale University Press, 2014)

Girolami, Patrizia. 'Il carro di Tespi: Teatro e fascismo' in Mario Biondi and Alessandra Borsotti (eds), *Cultura e fascismo: letteratura, arti e spettacolo di un Ventennio* (Florence: Ponte alle Grazie, 1996)

Goeschel, Christian. *Mussolini and Hitler: The Forging of the Fascist Alliance* (New Haven and London: Yale University Press, 2020)

Grassi, Ludovica and Clelia De Vita, 2016. 'Nostalgia between mourning and melancholia', *L'Autre*, 17:3, 2016, 321–9

Guerri, Giordano Bruno. *Rapporto al Duce: l'agonia di una nazione nei colloqui tra Mussolini e i federali nel 1942* (Milan: Bompiani, 2020)

Gundle, Stephen. 'The death (and rebirth) of the hero: charisma and personality cults', *Modern Italy*, 3:2, 1998, 173–89

Gundle, Stephen. *Between Hollywood and Moscow: the Italians Communists and the Challenge of Mass Culture, 1943–91* (Duram, N.C.: Duke University Press, 2000)

Gundle, Stephen. 'The "civic religion" of the Resistance in postwar Italy', *Modern Italy*, 5:2, 2000, 113–32

Gundle, Stephen. 'Adriano Celentano and the origins of rock and roll in Italy', *Journal of Modern Italian Studies*, 11:3, 2006, 367–86

Gundle, Stephen. 'Un Martini per il Duce: l'immaginario del consumismo in Italia negli anni Venti e Trenta' in Anna Villari (ed.), *L'arte della pubblicità: il manifesto italiano e le vanguardie 1920–1940* (Milan: Silvana editoriale, 2008), pp.46–69

Gundle, Stephen. 'Mass Culture and the Cult of Personality' in Gundle, Duggan and Pieri (eds), *The Cult of the Duce*

Gundle, Stephen. 'Mussolini's appearances in the regions' in Gundle, Duggan and Pieri (eds), *The Cult of the Duce*, pp.110–28

Gundle, Stephen. 'The aftermath of the Mussolini cult: history, nostalgia and popular culture' in Gundle, Duggan and Pieri (eds), *The Cult of the Duce.*

Gundle, Stephen. *Mussolini's Dream Factory: Film Stardom in Fascist Italy* (New York and Oxford: Berghahn, 2013), pp.244–58

Gundle, Stephen. 'The Question of Italian National Character and the Limits of Commedia all'italiana: Alberto Sordi, Federico Fellini, and Carlo Lizzani' in Frank Burke (ed.), *Italian Cinema: A Companion* (Oxford: Wiley Blackwell, 2017)

Gundle, Stephen. 'Laughter Under Fascism: Humour and Ridicule in Italy, 1922–43', *History Workshop Journal*, 79:1, 2015, 215–32

Gundle, Stephen. 'From Mussolini to Berlusconi: masculinity and political leadership in postwar Italy' in Christopher Fletcher and others (eds), *The Palgrave Handbook of Masculinity and Political Culture in Europe* (London; Palgrave, 2018)

Gundle, Stephen. *Fame amid the Ruins: Italian Film Stardom in the Age of Neorealism* (New York and Oxford: Berghahn, 2019)

Gundle, Stephen. 'La mascolinità del leader politico nell'Italia del dopoguerra: le forme nuove di un dominio tradizionale' in Patrizia Gabrielli (ed.), *Elette e eletti: rappresentanza e rappresentazioni di genere nell'Italia repubblicana* (Soveria Mannelli: Rubbettino, 2020)

Gundle, Stephen. 'Mussolini between hero-worship and demystification: exemplary anecdotes, *Petite Histoire* and the problem of humanization', *Comparative Studies in Society and History*, 64:1, 2022, 122–49

Gundle, Stephen. 'Remembering Berlinguer: mourning, nostalgia and the left' in John Foot and Stephen Gundle (eds), *Paul Ginsborg and the Historiography of Modern Italy* (London: Palgrave Macmillan, 2024)

Gundle, Stephen, Christopher Duggan and Giuliana Pieri (eds), *The Cult of the Duce: Mussolini and the Italians* (Manchester: Manchester University Press, 2013)

Gundle, Stephen, Christopher Duggan and Giuliana Pieri. 'Special issue: the cult of Mussolini in twentieth-century Italy—Introduction', *Modern Italy*, 18:2, 2013, pp.111–15

Harrison, Martin. *Brian Clarke* (London: Quartet, 1981)

Hauffner, Sebastian. *The Meaning of Hitler* (London: Phoenix, 2011; first published 1978)

Hazareesingh, Sudhir. *The Legend of Napoleon* (London: Granta, 2004)

Herf, Jeffrey. *Divided Memory: The Nazi Past in the Two Germanys* (Cambridge, Mass.: Harvard University Press, 1997)

Heywood, Paolo. 'Ordinary exemplars: cultivating "the everyday" in the birthplace of Fascism', *Comparative Studies in Society and History*, 64, 2022, 91–121

Heywood, Paolo. 'Out of the ordinary: everyday life and the "carnival of Mussolini"', *American Anthropologist*, 125:3, 2022, 493–504

Hodes, Martha. *Mourning Lincoln* (New Haven and London: Yale University Press, 2015)

Holliday, Ruth and Tracey Potts. *Kitsch! Cultural Politics and Taste* (Manchester: Manchester University Press, 2012)

Hughes, Michael. *The Anarchy of Nazi Memorabilia: From Things of Tyranny to Troubled Treasure* (London: Routledge, 2022)

Hughes, Robert. *Rome* (London: Weidenfeld and Nicolson, 2011)

Humphrey, Caroline. 'Exemplars and rules: aspects of the discourse of moralities in Mongolia', The Ethnography of Morality, 1997, 25–49

Huyssen, Andreas. *Present Pasts: Urban Palimpsests and the Politics of Memory* (Stanford: Stanford University Press, 2003)

Imbriani, Angelo Michele. *Gli italiani e il duce: il mito e l'imagine di Mussolini negli ultimi anni del fascismo (1938–1943)* (Naples: Liguori 1992)

Impert, Laura and Margaret Rubin. 2011. 'The mother at the glen: the relationship between mourning and nostalgia', *Psychoanalytic Dialogues*, 21, 2011, 691–706

Innocenti, Valentina (ed.). *Carlo Lizzani: l'ultimo spettatore* (Rome: Datanews, 2012)

Isnenghi, Mario. 'Aspetti del rituale di massa fascista: stampa e dintorni' in Riccardo Redi (ed.), *Cinema italiano sotto il fascismo* (Venice: Marsilio, 1979), pp.52–3

Isnenghi, Mario. *L'Italia in piazza: i luoghi della vita pubblica dal 1848 ai nostri giorni* (Milan: Mondadori, 1994)

Isnenghi, Mario. 'La piazza' in Isnenghi (ed.), *I luoghi della memoria: strutture ed eventi dell'Italia unita* (Rome: Laterza, 1997)

Isnenghi, Mario. *Storia d'Italia: i fatti e le percezioni dal Risorgimento alla società dello spettacolo* (Rome: Laterza, 2011)

Jarausch, K.H. *After Hitler: Recivilizing Germans, 1945–1995* (Oxford: Oxford University Press, 2006)

Jaspers, Karl. *The Question of German Guilt* (New York: Fordham University Press, 2000; first published 1946)

Johnson, Jeffrey and Anne McClanan (eds), *Negating the Image: Case Studies in Iconoclasm* (London: Routledge, 2005)

Judt, Tony. *Postwar: A History of Europe Since 1945* (London: Vintage, 2010)

Kantorowicz, Ernst. *The King's Two Bodies: A Study in Mediaeval Political Theology* (Princeton: Princeton University Press, 1957)

Karlsen, Patrick. 'I totalitarismi del Novecento nei volumi e negli opuscoli della biblioteca di Benedetto Croce' in Renzo Ragghianti and Alessandro Savorelli (eds), *Biblioteche filosofiche private: strumenti e prospettive di ricerca* (Pisa: Edizioni della Normale, 2014)

Kershaw, Ian. *Hitler 1889–1936 Hubris* (London: Penguin, 1998)

Kezich, Tullio and Alessandra Levantesi. *Dino: De Laurentiis, la vita e i film* (Milan: Feltrinelli, 2001)

Krawcyzyk-Zywko, Lucyna. 'On waxworks considered as one of the hyperreal arts: exhibiting Jack the Ripper and his victims', *Humanities*, 7:2, 2018

Labanca, Nicola. 'Constructing Mussolini's New Man in Africa? Italian Memories of the Fascist War in Ethiopia', *Italian Studies*, 61:2, 2006, 225–32

La Capra, Dominick. *Representing the Holocaust: History, Theory, Trauma* (Ithaca, N.Y.: Cornell University Press, 1994)

Laing, R.D. *The Divided Self: An Existential Study in Sanity and Madness* (London: Penguin, 1960)

Lanaro, Silvio. *Storia dell'Italia repubblicana* (Venice: Marsilio, 1992)

La Rovere, Luca. *Storia dei Guf: organizzazione, politica e miti della gioventu' universitaria fascista 1919–1943* (Turin: Bollati Boringhieri, 2003), p.326

La Rovere, Luca. *L'eredità del fascismo: gli intellettuali, i giovani e la transizione al postfascismo, 1943–1948* (Turin: Bollati Boringhieri 2008)

La Rovere, Luca. 'The "examination of conscience" of the nation: the lost debate about the "collective guilt" in Italy, 1943–5', *Totalitarian Movements and Political Religions*, 9:2–3, 2008, 187–202

Le Bon, Gustave. *The Crowd* (New Brunswick: Transaction, 1995; first published 1895)

Léger, Nicholas. 'Un roman démocratique: M. L'enfant du siècle d'Antonio Scurati', *Esprit*, 7, 2021, 57–62

Levis Sullam, Simon. *I fantasmi del fascismo: Le metamorfosi degli intellettuali italiani nel dopoguerra* (Milan: Feltrinelli, 2021)

Lichtner, Giacomo. *Fascism in Italian Cinema Since 1945: The Politics and Aesthetics of Memory* (Basingstoke: Palgrave Macmillan, 2013)

Lipman-Blumen, Jean. *The Allure of Toxic Leaders* (New York: Oxford University Press, 2006)

Liucci, Raffaele. *L'Italia borghese di Leo Longanesi: giornalismo, politica e costume negli anni '50* (Venice: Marsilio, 2002)

Lo Biundo, Ester. *London Calling Italy: BBC Broadcasts During the Second World War* (Manchester: Manchester University Press, 2022)

Logan, Oliver. 'Pius XII: romanità, prophecy and charisma', *Modern Italy*, 3:2, 1998, 237–47

Lucaroni, Sara. *Sempre lui: perché Mussolini non muore mai* (Milan: Pienogiorno, 2022)

Luzzatto, Sergio. *Il corpo del duce* (Turin: Einaudi, 1997)

Lynn, Steven Jay and others. 'Disassociation and disassociative disorders reconsidered: beyond sociocognitive and trauma models toward a transtheoretical framework', *Annual Review of Clinical Psychology*, 18, 2022, 259–89

MacDonald, Sharon. *Difficult Heritage: Negotiating the Nazi Past in Nuremberg and Beyond* (London: Routledge, 2008)

Machtans, Karolin and Martin A, Reuhl (eds), *Hitler—Films from Germany: History, Cinema and Politics Since 1945* (Basingstoke: Palgrave Macmillan, 2012)

Mack Smith, Denis. 'A monument for the Duce', *TLS*, 31 October 1975, p.1278

Mack Smith, Denis. *Mussolini's Roman Empire* (London: Weidenfeld and Nicolson, 1976)

Mack Smith, Denis. *Mussolini* (London: Weidenfeld and Nicolson, 1981)

Mack Smith, Denis. 'Mussolini: reservations about Renzo De Felice's biography', *Modern Italy*, 5:2, 2000, 193–210

Magnanini, Giannetto. *Il regime badogliano a Reggio Emilia: 25 luglio–Settembre 1943* (Rome: Teti, 1999)

Malvano, Laura. *Fascismo e politica dell'immagine* (Turin: Bollati Boringhieri, 1988)

Malvestio, Marco. 'Cronache del *fantafascismo*: l'ucronia in Italia e il revisionismo storico', *The Italianist*, 38:1, 2018, 89–107

Mammone, Andrea. 'Gli orfani del duce: i fascisti dal 1943 al 1946', *Italia contemporanea*, 239:24(2), 2005, 249–74

Mancosu, Gianmarco. *Vedere l'impero: l'istituto Luce e il colonialismo fascista* (Milan: Mimesis, 2022)

Mancosu, Gianmarco. 'Rituals of colonial memory: crafting imperial nostalgia in republican Italy', *Journal of Contemporary History*, 59:4, 2024, 660–85

Manea, Norman. *Clown: il dittatore e l'artista* (Milan: Il Saggiatore, 1995)

Marcello, Flavia. *After the Fall: The Legacy of Fascism in Rome's Architectural and Urban History* (London: Bloomsbury, 2024)

Marsili, Marzia. 'De Gasperi and Togliatti: political leadership and personality cults in post-war Italy', *Modern Italy*, 3:2, 1998, 249–61

Martellini, Amoreno and Barbara Montesi. *Il Novecento in provincia: storia di Jesi tra memorie e oblii 1900–1970* (Milan: Franco Angeli, 2020)
Martinelli, Franco. *Mussolini ai raggi X* (Milan: De Vecchi, 1964)
Martini, Andrea. *Fascismo immaginario: riscrivere il passato a destra* (Rome: Laterza, 2024)
Matthews, Herbert. *The Education of a Correspondent* (New York: Harcourt, Brace & Co., 1946)
Mazierska, Eva. *European Cinema and Intertextuality: History, Memory and Politics* (Basingstoke: Palgrave Macmillan, 2011)
Mazzantini, Carlo. *In Search of A Glorious Death* (London: Carcanet, 1992; first published Milan 1988)
Milza, Pierre. *Mussolini* (Rome: Carocci, 2000; first published Paris, 1999)
Milza, Pierre. *Les derniers jours de Mussolini* (Paris: Pluriel, 2010)
Mitscherlich, Alexander and Margarete. *The Inability to Mourn: Principles of Collective Behaviour* (New York: Grove Press 1975)
Moline, Karen. *Bob Hoskins: An Unlikely Hero* (London: Sphere, 1988)
Monelli, Paolo. *Roma 1943* (Turin: Einaudi, 2012; first published 1963)
Montanelli, Indro and Marcello Staglieno, *Leo Longanesi* (Milan: Longanesi, 1984)
Montesi, Barbara. 'Potrebbe essere storia, ma è vero? Sui problemi di studiare il fascismo in rete', *Storia e problemi contemporanei*, 20: 44, 2007, 101–26
Montesi, Barbara. *Un 'anarchica monarchica': vita di Maria Rygier (1885–1953)* (Naples: Edizioni Scientifiche Italiane, 2013)
Morelli, Giovanni. *Vitaliano Brancati tra fascismo e gallismo* (Bari: Lacaita, 1989)
Moretti, Marco. *Renato Bertelli (1900–1974)* (Florence: Masso delle Fate, 2007)
Morgan, Philip. *The Fall of Mussolini* (Oxford: Oxford University Press, 2007)
Morin, Edgar. *The Stars* (New York: Grove Press, 1960)
Moro, Renato. *Il mito dell'Italia cattolica: nazione, religione e cattolicesimo negli anni del fascismo* (Rome: Studium, 2021)
Moscovici, Serge. *The Age of the Crowd* (Cambridge: Cambridge University Press, 1983)
Mueller, Jan-Werner. *Another Country: German Intellectuals, Unification and National Identity* (New Haven: Yale University Press, 2000)
Mueller, Roswitha. 'Hans-Jürgen Syberberg's Hitler an Interview—Montage', *Discourse*, 2, 1980, 60–82
Musatti, Cesare. 'Super-io individuale e super-io collettivo' (1961) in Musatti, *Libertà e servitù dello spirito: diario culturale di uno psicanalista (1945–1971)* (Turin: Boringhieri, 1971)
Neiman, Susan. *Learning from the Germans: Confronting Race and the Memory of Evil* (London: Penguin, 2019)
Nicoloso, Pino. *Mussolini architetto:propaganda e paesaggio urbano nell'Italia fascista* (Turin: Einaudi, 2008)
Olick, Jeffrey K. *In the House of the Hangman: The Agonies of German Defeat, 1943–1949* (Chicago: University of Chicago Press, 2005)
Olick, Jeffrey K. *The Politics of Regret: On Collective Memory and Historical Responsibility* (New York: Routledge, 2007)
Olick, Jeffrey K. *The Sins of the Fathers: Germany, History, Method* (Chicago: University of Chicago Press, 2016)
Olick, Jeffrey K. 'In the ashes of disgrace: guilt versus shame revisited' in Efrat Ben Ze'ev, Ruth Ginio and Jay Winter (eds), *Shadows of War: A Social History of Silence in the Twentieth Century* (Cambridge: Cambridge University Press, 2020)
Oliva, Gianni. *La resa dei conti* (Milan: Mondadori, 1998)
Onofri, Nazario Sauro. 'Il mio 25 luglio 1943 (con il seguito del 8 settembre)' in Quaderni della Resistenza oggi, *Vol. 1* 1943: Cade il fascismo, 2003, 69–81

Orwell, S. and I. Angus (eds), *Collected Essays, Journalism and Letters of George Orwell*, Vol. 2, *My Country Right or Left 1940–1943* (London; Secker and Warburg, 1968), p.324

Painter, Borden. 'Renzo De Felice and the historiography of Italian Fascism', *The American Historical Review*, 95:2, 1990, 391–405

Panico, Marco. 'Repetition, recognition, remediation, or Benito Mussolini *after* Benito Mussolini', *Ocula*, 21:22, 2020, 62–78

Pappas, Sara. 'The lessons of Champfleury', *Nineteenth-Century French Studies*, 42:1–2, 2013, 51–73

Passerini, Luisa. *Mussolini immaginario: storia di una biografia, 1915–1939* (Rome: Laterza, 1991)

Passerini, Luisa. 'Mussolini' in Mario Isnenghi (ed.), *I luoghi della memoria: personaggi e date dell'Italia unita* (Rome: Laterza, 2010)

Patriarca, Silvana. *Italian Vices: Nation and Character from the Risorgimento to the Republic* (Cambridge: Cambridge University Press, 2010)

Pavolini, Paolo. *Il processo Mussolini* (Milan; Betelguese, 2008; first published 1975)

Pavone, Claudio. *Una guerra civile: saggio storico sulla moralità nella Resistenza* (Turin: Bollati Boringhieri, 1991)

Pennacchi, Antonio. *Fascio e martello: viaggio per le città del duce* (Rome: Laterza, 2010)

Petacco, Arrigo. *Mussolini ritrovato: storia di una collezione proibita* (Bologna: Minerva edizioni, 2009)

Pieri, Giuliana. 'The destiny of the art and artefacts' in Gundle, Duggan and Pieri (eds), *The Cult of the Duce*.

Pilat, Stephanie. 'Occupying history: film, fascism, and architecture in the work of Kevin Van Braak and Rossella Biscotti', in Where Do You Stand: 99th ACSA Annual Meeting Proceedings, Washington, DC, ACSA, 2011, 344–9

Pooley, Eugene. 'Mussolini and the city of Rome' in Gundle, Duggan and Pieri (eds), *The Cult of the Duce*.

Radius, Emilio. *Personaggi del secolo* (Milan: Palazzi, 1970)

Raulff, Ulrich. *Farewell to the Horse: The Final Century of Our Relationship* (London: Penguin, 2017), p.368

Reich, Jacqueline. *The Maciste Films of Italian Silent Cinema* (Bloomington: Indiana University Press, 2015)

Ridolfi, Maurizio. *Storia politica dell'Italia repubblicana* (Milan: Bruno Mondadori, 2010)

Rivista romana (ed.). *Mussolini* (Rome: Centro editoriale nazionale, 1958)

Rizzo, Sergio and Alessandro Campi, *L'ombra lunga del fascismo: perché l'italia ancora ferma a Mussolini* (Milan: Solferino, 2022)

Roach, Joseph. *It* (Ann Arbor; University of Michigan Press, 2007)

Roberts, Sam and Geraldine Marshall. 'What is a ghost sign?' in Stefan Schutt, Sam Roberts and Leanne White (eds), *Advertising and Public Memory: Social, Cultural and Historical Perspectives on Ghost Signs* (New York and London: Routledge, 2017)

Roghi, Vanessa. 'Mussolini and postwar Italian television' in Gundle, Duggan and Pieri (eds), *The Cult of Duce.*

Rosenfeld, Gavriel D. *Munich and Memory: Architecture, Monuments and the Legacy of the Third Reich* (Berkeley: University of California Press, 2000)

Rosenfeld, Gavriel D. *Hi Hitler! How the Nazi Past Is Being Normalized in Contemporary Culture* (Cambridge: Cambridge University Press, 2014)

Salvati, Mariuccia. *Passaggi: italiani dal fascismo alla Repubblica* (Rome: Carocci, 2016)

Santner, Eric. *Stranded Objects: Mourning, Memory and Film Iin Postwar Germany* (Ithaca, N.Y.: Cornell University Press, 1990)

Saporiti, Piero. *Empty Balcony* (London: Gollancz, 1947)

Schivelbusch, Wolfgang. *The Culture of Defeat: On National Trauma, Mourning and Recovery* (London: Granta Books, 2001)

Schnapp, Jeffrey T. 'Mob porn' in Schnapp and M. Tiews (eds), *Crowds* (Stanford: Stanford University Press, 2006)

Schnepel, Burkhard. *The King's Three Bodies: Essays on Kingship and Ritual* (London: Routledge, 2022)

Schwarz, Guri. *Tu mi devi seppellir: riti funebri e culto nazionale alle origini della Repubblica* (Turin: UTET, 2010)

Scott, Joan W. 'The incommensurability of psychoanalysis and history', *History and Theory*, 51, 2012, 63–83

Scurati, Antonio. *Fascismo e populismo: Mussolini oggi* (Milan: Bompiani, 2023)

Seesslen, Georg. 'Blood and glamour' in Mary Rhiel and Ingeborg Majer O'Sickey (eds), *Riefenstahl screened: an anthology of new criticism* (New York: Continuum, 2008)

Segala, Ariberto. *I muri del duce* (Lavis: Arca edizioni 2000), p.14

Serenelli, Sofia. '"It was like something you have at home and which becomes so familiar that you don't even pay attention to it": memories of Mussolini and Fascism in Predappio, 1922–2010', *Modern Italy*, 18:2, 2013, 157–75

Serres, Michel. *Statues* (London: Bloomsbury, 2015; first published 1987), p.48

Serres, Michel with Bruno Latour. *Conversations on Science, Culture and Time* (Ann Arbor: University of Michigan Press, 1995)

Setta, Sandro. *L'uomo qualunque, 1944–1948* (Rome: Laterza, 2005)

Sheward, David. *Rage and Glory: The Volatile Life and Career of George C. Scott* (New York: Applause, 2008)

Sibbons, Mike. *From the Archives: An Eclectic Mix of Stories from the History of REME* (Oxford: Osprey, 2016)

Sieglohr, Ulrike (ed.). *Heroines Without Heroes: Reconstructing Female and National Identities in European Cinema, 1945–51* (London: Bloomsbury, 2016)

Somigli, Luca. 'From a place in the sun to the heart of darkness: contemporary crime fiction and Italy's colonial past', *Italian Studies*, 73:4, 2018, 413–31

Sontag, Susan. *Under the Sign of Saturn* (London: Writers and Readers, 1980)

Spackman, Barbara. *Fascist Virilities: Rhetoric, Ideology and Social Fantasy in Italy* (Minneapolis: University of Minnesota Press, 1996)

Spinosa, Antonio. *Edda: una tragedia italiana* (Milan: Mondadori, 1995)

Stäheli, Urs. 'Seducing the crowd: the leader in crowd psychology', *New German Critique*, 114, 2011, 63–77

Stefani, Giulietta. *Colonia per maschi: italiani in Africa Orientale—un storia di genere* (Verona: Ombre corte, 2007)

Stellavato, Ornella. 'I giovani romani e la Repubblica sociale' in IRSIFAR, *Roma tra fascismo e liberazione* (Milan: Franco Angeli, 2006), 49–66

Storchi, Simona. 'Margherita Sarfatti and the invention of the Duce' in Gundle, Duggan and Pieri (eds), *The Cult of the Duce.*

Storchi, Simona. 'Mussolini as monument: the equestrian statue of the Duce at the Littoriale Stadium in Bologna' in Gundle, Duggan and Pieri (eds), *The Cult of the Duce.*

Storchi, Simona. 'The ex-Casa del Fascio in Predappio and the question of the "difficult heritage" of Fascism in contemporary Italy', *Modern Italy*, 24:2, 2019, 139–57

Storchi, Simona. *Massimo Bontempelli e la cultura italiana fra le due guerre: l'intellettuale, il fascismo, la modernità* (Milan: Mimesis, 2024)

Stratigakos, Despinga. *Hitler at Home* (New Haven and London: Yale University Press, 2015)

Sturani, Enrico. 'Analysing Mussolini postcards', *Modern Italy*, 18:2, 2013, 141–56

Stylianou, Elena and Theopisti Stylianou-Lambert (eds), *Museums and Photography: Displaying Death* (London: Routledge, 2017)

Sullam, Simon Levis. *I fantasmi del fascismo: le metamorfosi degli intellettuali italiani nel dopoguerra* (Milan: Feltrinelli, 2021)

Susmel, Duilio. *Nenni e Mussolini: mezzo secolo di fronte* (Milan: Rizzoli, 1969)

Syberberg, Hans-Jürgen, Beatriz Schiller and Rod Ott. 'Our Hitler as visual politics', *Performing Arts Journal*, 4:3, 1980, 50–8

Tagliani, Giacomo. *Biografie della nazione: vita, storia, politica nel biopic Italiano* (Soveria Mannelli: Rubbettino, 2019)

Tranfaglia, Nicola. *Labirinto italiano: il fascismo,l'antifascismo, gli storici* (Florence: La Nuova Italia, 1989)

Tranfaglia, Nicola. *Un passato scomodo: fascismo e postfascismo* (Rome: Laterza, 1999)

Tymkiw, Michael. 'Floor mosaics, *Romanità*, and spectatorship: the Foro Mussolini's Piazzale dell'Impero', *The Art Bulletin*, 101:2, 2019, 109–32

Ullrich, Volker. *Hitler: Downfall 1939–1945* (London: The Bodley Head, 2020)

Vacca, Alberto. *Duce truce: Insulti, barzellette, caricature: l'opposizione popolare al fascismo nei rapporti segreti dei prefetti (1930–1945)* (Rome: Castelvecchi, 2011)

Venè, Gian Franco. *Coprifuoco: vita quotidiana degli italiani nella guerra civile 1943–1945* (Milan; Mondadori, 1989)

Ventrone, Angelo. 'Forme e strumenti della propaganda di massa nella nascita e nel consolidamento della Repubblica (1946–1958)' in Maurizio Ridolfi (ed.), *Propaganda e comunicazione politica: storia e trasformazioni nell'eta' contemporanea* (Milan: Bruno Mondadori, 2004)

Versari, Maria Elena. 'Fascist Spoils: Gifts to Mussolini', *Burlington Magazine*, no. 157, June 2015, pp.407–13

Versari, Maria Elena. 'Tra iconoclastia e oblio: guerra e requisizioni alla Rocca delle Caminate', in Maria Giuseppina Di Monte, Giuliana Pieri and Simona Storchi (eds), *Visualizzare la guerra: l'iconografia del conflitto e l'Italia* (Milan: Mimesis, 2016)

Veyrat-Masson, Isabelle. 'Staging Historical Leaders on French Television: The Example of Napoleon Bonaparte' in Bell and Gray, *Televising History*, pp.95–106

Vidotto, Vittorio. 'I luoghi del fascismo a Roma' *Dimensioni e problemi della ricerca storica*, 2, 2005, 39–51

Vittoria, Albertina. *Togliatti e gli intellettuali: la politica culturale dei comunisti italiani (1944–1964)* (Rome: Carocci, 2014)

Volpi, Serena I. '"I wanted to become an Abyssinian": rewriting Indro Montanelli's memories of colonial Africa in Francesca Melandri's *Sangue giusto* (2017)', *Journal of Postcolonial Writing*, 58:5, 2022, 654–68

Ward, David. *Antifascisms: Cultural Politics in Italy 1943–46* (Madison, N.J.: Farleigh Dickinson University Press, 1996)

Warnaby, Gary, and Dominic Medway. 'Ghost fascias: retail corporate identity revenants in urban space' in Stefan Schutt, Sam Roberts and Leanne White (eds), *Advertising and Public Memory: Social, Cultural and Historical Perspectives on Ghost Signs* (New York and London: Routledge, 2017)

White, Leanne, Stefan Schutt and Sam Roberts. 'Uncovering ghost signs and their meanings' in Stefan Schutt, Sam Roberts and Leanne White (eds), *Advertising and Public Memory: Social, Cultural and Historical Perspectives on Ghost Signs* (New York and London: Routledge, 2017)

Wingenter, Anne. '"Mothers of the fallen" between symbolic and experienced political participation' in Karen Lauwers, Sami Suodenjoki and Marnix Beyen (eds), *Subaltern Political Subjectivities and Practices in the Nineteenth and Twentieth Centuries* (London: Routledge, 2023)

Wintrobe, Ronald. 'The tin pot and the totalitarian: an economic theory of dictatorship', *American Political Science Review*, 84:3, 2014, 849–72

York, Peter. *Dictators' Homes* (London: Atlantic Books, 2005)

Zapponi, Nicola. *Il fascismo nella caricatura* (Rome and Bari: Laterza, 1981)

Zunino, Pier Giorgio (ed.). *Scritti politici di Alcide De Gasperi* (Milan: Feltrinelli, 1979)

Zunino, Pier Giorgio. *Interpretazione e memoria del fascismo: gli anni del regime* (Rome: Laterza, 2000)

Zunino, Piero Giorgio. *La Repubblica e il suo passato* (Bologna: Il Mulino, 2003)

Index

Note: Figures are indicated by an italic "*f*", following the page number.

For the benefit of digital users, indexed terms that span two pages (e.g., 52–53) may, on occasion, appear on only one of those pages.

Adenauer, Konrad 79
Adorno, Theodor 79, 203, 217–18
Akkad, Moutstapha 200–1
Allies (in World War II) xii, 2–4, 43, 48–9, 52–3, 54*f*, 55–6, 60, 63–5, 109, 112–13, 145, 147–8, 159, 178, 194–5, 230–3
Almirante, Giorgio 178–9
Amendola, Giovanni 114–15
ANPI (former partisans' association) 132–3
Ansaldo, Giovanni 102–3, 115
Arendt, Hannah 103
armistice, Italian of 1943 43, 55, 58–9, 117–18, 194–5
Arpinati, Leandro 128–9
Artieri, Giovanni 178
Auschwitz 147–8
Avanzini, Carlo 148–9

Badoglio, Pietro 33–4, 39, 42, 53–4, 58–9, 178, 196
Baily, Virginia 233–4
Balbo, Italo xi
Bargellini, Guido 163
Bastaianini, Giuseppe 45–6
Bedel, Maurice 49
Bellini, Aroldo 138–9
Bellocchio, Marco 207
Béraud, Henri 49, 176–7
Berlusconi, Silvio 13–14, 107–8, 204
Berneri, Camillo 26–7, 104
Bertelli, Renato 157–8, 161–2, 167–8
Bertini, Francesca 218–19
Bertolucci, Bernardo 203–4
Biscotti, Rossella 164–8
Blasetti, Alessandro 176–7
Bobbio, Norberto 74–5
Boccardini, Luciano v–ix, xi*f*, 168–70
Bonomi, Ivanoe 194
Bontempelli, Massimo 71–2, 77
Bottai, Giuseppe 37–8, 128–9, 156–7, 175
Braak, Kevin van 164–5
Brancati, Vitaliano 104, 129–30
Brasseur, Claude 207–8
Brizzi, Enrico 228–9

Cadorna, Raffaele 58–9
Calamandrei, Piero 34, 177
Calvino, Italo 19, 27, 202–3
Canevari, Silvio 145
Cardinale, Claudia 204
Casa Pound 183–4
Catholic Church 21–2, 25, 29–31, 75–6, 78, 85, 87–8, 94, 98–9, 173–4
Caudana, Mino 114–19, 121–2, 231–2
Celentano, Adriano 95
Cervi, Alcide 95
Champfleury (Jules Fleury-Husson) 216
Christian Democratic Party (DC) 13–14, 78, 87, 98–9, 102–3, 231–3, 243
Churchill, Winston 48–9, 111–12, 207–8
Ciano, Edda (daughter of Mussolini, wife of Galeazzo) 81, 85–6, 147, 205, 209–10
Ciano, Galeazzo 48, 81, 85–6, 114, 147, 167–8, 177, 199–200, 202–3
Committee of National Liberation (CLN) 57, 59–60, 109, 195
Cragg, Tony 167–8
Craxi, Bettino 107–8, 143
Crispi, Francesco 21
Croce, Benedetto 22–3, 71–2, 74–5, 171, 188–9, 194, 196

Damiani, Damiano viii–ix
Damiano, Andrea 73–4, 76, 177
D'Annunzio, Gabriele 21, 218–19
Da Verona, Guido 104
Dazzi, Arturo 146–7
Deaglio, Enrico 179

De Bono, Emilio 165–6
De Felice, Renzo xii, 19–20, 106, 141–2, 187–98, 187*f*, 220–1, 232–3, 235–7, 240–1
De Gasperi, Alcide 78–9, 98–9, 101–3, 102*f*
dictators in literature 227

empire, Italian in Africa x–xi, 19–20, 29, 35, 37–8, 79–80, 97, 99–101, 114, 119, 130–2, 142–5, 160–1, 196–7, 200–1, 226–7, 233–4, 236–7, 240–1, 243–4
EUR (Rome district) ix–x, 139, 143–7, 165

Fascism
  material legacies of 127–8, 132–4, 138–40, 151–3, 156–65, 158*f*
  and land reclamation 226–7, 229–33
  and masculinity 96–108, 224
  and Nazism xii–xiii, 1–2, 156–7, 175, 188–9, 197–8, 216–18, 240–4
  and social conformism 22–5, 27–9, 73–6
  as German virus 71–3
  in literature 226–39
  see also Hitler, Adolf; Mussolini, Benito
Fascist architecture 128, 156–7
Fascist land art 182–4
Fascist Party (PNF) x, 19–20, 25, 61, 117, 219–20
Fascist propaganda 26, 54–5, 63–5, 157, 167–8, 171–84, 232–3
Fascist revolution, Exhibition of 26, 237
Fascist wall writings 26, 158*f*, 166*f*, 169*f*, 171–82
Fascist youth organisations (ONB, GIL) 32–3, 138–9, 157, 173, 176
Fellini, Federico 203–4
Flaiano, Ennio 79–80, 227
Foot, Michael (Cassius) 110–12, 115–16, 121–2, 168–70
Frassineti, Giorgio 152*f*, 153
Freud, Sigmund 20–1, 40, 211
Fröbel, Friedrich 159

Gadda, Carlo Emilio 22–3, 50–2, 60, 103–4
Galeazzi, Ernesto 173–4
Garibaldi, Giuseppe 10–11, 21–2, 103–4, 129, 188, 202, 204
Gaslini, Gerolamo 135
Germany, in post-World War II period xii–xiv, 1–5, 70–1, 78–9, 222–3, 227–9, 240–4
Giannini, Guglielmo 100–1
Gibbons, John 176–7
Ginzburg, Natalia 203–4
Giurati, Giovanni 27, 38, 177–8, 205–6
Gobetti, Paolo 23–4
Goebbels, Josef 48
Gori, Giorgio 136–40
Gramsci, Antonio 23–4
Grandi, Dino 199–200
Gravelli, Asvero 104
Gray, Ezio Maria 93–4
Graziani, Rodolfo xi, 200–1, 230–1, 233–4, 236–8
Graziosi, Giuseppe 128–9, 133–4, 139–40
Griselli, Italo 139
Gualino, Renato 135–6
Guareschi, Giovannino 101–2
guilt and the Germans xiii–xiv, 1–6, 70–4, 79, 121–3, 242–4
guilt and the Italians xii, 5–6, 71–8, 243–4

Heartfield, John 130–1
Hitler, Adolf xii–xiii, 1–2, 4–5, 50, 63, 70–3, 114, 117, 160–1, 201–2, 214–18, 227–8, 241–4; *see also* Mussolini, Benito, and Hitler
Holocaust, the 2–3, 147–8, 197–8, 238–41, 243–4
Hoskins, Bob 204–8

Italian Communist Party (PCI) 13–14, 98–102, 190, 195
Italian national character 1–2, 23–4, 49–50, 75–6, 84
Italian Resistance 48, 53–4, 57–9, 76, 79–80, 85, 87, 99–100, 159, 190, 193–6, 199–200, 206–7
Italian Socialist Party (PSI) 59–60, 101–2, 107–8, 192
Italian Social Movement (MSI) xi, 91–2, 133–4, 178–9, 190–1, 226–8, 232–3
Italian Social Republic (RSI) v–vi, xvi, 43–4, 48–9, 61–2, 73–4, 76, 79, 109, 119, 154–5, 178, 190–1, 194–6, 215, 230–1, 238–9

James, Challinor 56–7
Jenninger, Philipp 244
Jotti, Nilde 98–9

Kracauer, Siegfried 218

land art, Fascist *see* Fascist land art
Lauro, Achille 100–1
Le Bon, Gustave 2–3
Lenin, Vladimir 20–1, 218
Lennon, John 9–10
Lincoln, Abraham 7–9, 201
Lizzani, Carlo 199–201, 204–6
Longanesi, Leo xv, 50–2, 103–6, 113, 176

Maccari, Mino 50–2
Maciste (Bartolomeo Pagano) 218–19
Mack Smith, Denis 187–8, 187*f*, 192–4, 196–7, 200–1, 235–6
Malaparte, Curzio 23–4, 53–4, 101–3
Maltoni, Rosa (mother of Mussolini) 81, 149
Mao Tse Tung 214–15
Mapplethorpe, Robert 167–8
Marinelli, Luca 208–9
Matteotti, Giacomo 22, 58, 113, 196–7
Matthews Herbert xiii, 54–5, 69–70
Mauri, Fabio 165–7, 166*f*
Mazzantini, Carlo 47–8, 61–2, 79
Mazzini, Giuseppe 93–4
Mazzotti, Antal 60
Melandri, Francesca 233–4
Meloni, Giorgia 107–8
Meneghello, Luigi 60
Michelini, Arturo 90
Mitscherlich, Alexander and Margerete 3–6, 63, 70–1, 76, 93, 122–3, 197, 217–18, 242–4
Montanelli, Indro xv, 61, 105–6, 113, 115, 191, 233–4
Morandi, Rodolfo 195
Moravia, Alberto 79–80, 203–4, 227
Moretti, Luigi 144–5
Morosini, Domenico 153
MSI *see* Italian Social Movement
Mukhtar, Omar 200–1
Musatti, Cesare 6–7, 24–5, 76
Mussolini, Alessandra (daughter of Romano) 153
Mussolini Alessandro (father of Benito) 81
Mussolini, Annamaria (daughter of Benito) 81–3
Mussolini, Arnaldo (brother of Benito) 81, 173
Mussolini, Benito actors playing 207–9
anecdotes about 103–5, 114–15, 237–8
'bodies' of v, 11–12, 56–7, 59–61, 86, 107–8, 168–70
charisma of 20–1, 224
cult of personality of viii–x, xiii, xv–xvi, 2–3, 7, 19–31, 28*f*, 40–1, 45–8, 53, 54*f*, 70, 73–4, 197–8, 218–19, 224–5, 229–33, 239
death of 57–8, 61–3, 115–16, 209–10
discrediting of 39, 42, 50–2, 51*f*, 54–5, 63–5, 100–1, 102*f*
domestication of xvi, 63–5, 82–92, 96–7, 104–5, 154, 206–7, 243
funeral of 94
image of xv, 26–7, 39, 54–5, 96–7, 107–8, 156–70, 212, 214*f*, 219–21, 223*f*, 224
imaginary trials of 109–23
overthrow of 8, 32–4, 38–42, 90, 150, 162–3, 230–1, 242
political decline of 10–11, 35–42
possible trial of 58–9, 109–10
statues of 53, 127–40, 131*f*, 132*f*, 134*f*, 137*f*
waxworks of 165–7, 213–15, 214*f*
and art v–vii, 219–20
and Hitler xiii, 1–2, 7, 43–5, 48–50, 63–5, 69–73, 77–8, 83–4, 119, 143–4, 148–9, 151–4, 202, 218–19, 221, 230–1
and horse imagery 103–4, 127–34, 131*f*, 132*f*, 136–40, 137*f*, 234
and Italian national psyche xi–xii, 3, 19–20, 24, 73–4, 84, 162–3, 231–3
and memory viii–ix, xvi, 240–1
and mourning viii–ix, xvi, 7–10, 63–5, 87–90, 93–4, 224–5, 242–4
and posterity vi–vii, xvi
and youth 32–3, 40–1, 44–5, 84–5, 173
as media icon xiii–xv, 10, 26–7, 49–50, 63–5, 202, 205–6, 218–22
as new type of leader 2, 20–2, 106–8
as object of debate vii–viii, 13–14, 71, 77–8, 227–8, 235–6, 239
as part of the Italian national community 83–5, 229–33, 239
as sexual predator 96–7, 105–7
as toxic leader 103
in literature 226–39
Mussolini, Bruno (son of Benito) 81–3, 85–6, 205–6
Mussolini, Edda (daughter of Benito) *see* Ciano, Edda

Mussolini, Rachele (wife of Benito) 81–3, 86–93, 89*f*, 92*f*, 95, 115, 147, 149–54, 157–8, 160–1
Mussolini, Romano (son of Benito) 52–3, 81, 90–1, 92*f*, 153
Mussolini, Vittorio (son of Benito) 81, 85, 89*f*, 205–6
Mussolini family x, 33–4, 81–95, 153–4
Mussolini forum (Foro Musolini, now Foro italico) ix–x, 143–5

Napoleon (Napoleon Bonaparte) vii, 57–8, 92–3, 103–6, 111, 159–60, 199–202, 206, 217–18, 227, 229
National Alliance xi, 133–4, 179
Navarra, Quinto 104–7, 114–15, 202–3, 237–8
Nazism 1–2, 24–5, 35, 156–7, 216–23, 241–2, 244
Nenni, Pietro 58, 115–16
Nuremberg trials xiii, 2–3, 112–13, 118, 243–4

Obama, Barack 214–15

Packard, Reynolds and Eleanor 141–2
Pagano, Giuseppe 137–8
Palazzeschi, Aldo 60, 73–4
Palazzo Venezia v–vi, x, 38, 41, 44–5, 52–3, 105, 141–3, 165–6, 205, 211, 214–15, 229–30
Parri, Ferruccio 59, 115–16
Pasolini, Pier Paolo 165–6
Pavolini, Alessandro 201
Pavolini, Paolo 118–22, 194
Pennacchi, Antonio 226, 229–36, 239
Petacci, Claretta v–vii, 42, 56–7, 61, 86, 105, 119, 154–5, 201, 204, 237–8
Piacentini, Marcello 137–8
Piazzale Loreto v, viii–ix, xiv–xv, 56–65, 69–70, 83–4, 87–8, 109, 119, 154–5, 168–70, 210–11, 220–1, 231, 238–9, 242
Picard. Max 83–4
Pius XII, Pope 98–9
Pizzoni, Alfredo 195
Poletti, Charles, Col. 168–70
Popolizio, Massimo 211
Praz, Mario 40
Predappio x, 52, 90–2, 94, 100–1, 115, 147, 149–54, 152*f*, 159–61, 183

Ramperti, Marco 227–9
Rauti, Pino 183
Renzi, Matteo 143
Resistance *see* Italian Resistance
Ricci, Renato 138–9
Riefenstahl, Leni 217–18, 221
Rocca delle Caminate 90, 149–53, 157–8, 158*f*, 160–1
Romualdi, Pino 90
RSI *see* Italian Social Republic
Rygier, Maria 99

Scott, George C. 207–8, 210–11
Scurati, Antonio 208–9, 235–9
Salvini, Matteo 107–8
Saporiti, Pietro 142–3
Sarfatti, Margherita 22, 91–2, 129, 157, 237–8
Satta, Savatore 76
Scola, Ettore 203–4
Scorza, Carlo 39, 165–6
Segre, Liliana 238–9
Selassie, Haile 100–1, 234
Serandrei, Mario 178
Severini, Gino 144–5
Sforza, Carlo 115–16
Solaro, Giuseppe 61
Sordi, Alberto 202–3
Squitieri, Pasquale 204
Stalin, Joseph 73, 98–9, 218
Steiger, Rod 199–201, 200*f*, 207–8
Starace, Achille 176
Susmel, Duilio 163
Syberberg, Hans-Jürgen 216–18

Tarde, Gabriel 20–1
Tato (Guglielmo Sansoni) 160–1
Teodorani, Vanni 93–4
Togliatti, Palmiro 74–5, 85, 98–101, 102*f*, 115–16, 143, 173–4
Totò (Antonio De Curtis) 202–3
Treves, Paolo 75–6
Trump, Donald 214–15
Turati, Augusto 237–8

Umberto di Savoia, Prince 81
Uomo qualunque (UQ political movement) 76–7, 79, 100–1

Valadier, Giuseppe 147
Valiani, Leo 191–2

Villa Carpena (Predappio) 90–1, 149, 153–4, 157–8, 160–1
Villa Mussolini (Riccione) 153
Villa Torlonia (Rome) x, 33–4, 86–7, 147–8, 154, 205, 211
Vittorio Emanuele III 32–3, 165, 236–7

wall writings, Fascist *see* Fascist wall writings
Wildt, Adolfo 157–8
Wilson, Edmund 178
Winterburn, Thom 168–70, 169*f*
Wolfson, Mitchell, Jr 167–8
women in the political sphere 95, 98–100, 107–8
World War I 20–3, 97–8, 141–2
World War II 1–2, 35, 37–8, 52, 112–13, 150, 177, 192–4, 226–7, 229
Wright, Joe 208–9, 235–6

Zancanaro, Tono 50–2, 51*f*, 162–3
Zavoli, Sergio 192
Zevi, Luca 147–8